T0390134

Creative Economy

This book series covers research on creative economies based on humanity and spirituality to enhance the competitiveness, sustainability, peace, and fairness of international society. We define a creative economy as a socio-economic system that promotes those creative activities with a high market value and leads to the improvement of society's overall well-being.

As the global economy has developed, we have seen severe competition and polarization in income distribution. With this drastic change in the economic system, creativity with a high market value has come to be considered the main source of competiveness. But in addition to the improvement of competitiveness, we are required to work toward fairness in society.

In the process of developing a mature market, consumers come to understand that what they require most essentially is humanity and spirituality. This cannot be given or bought, but requires sharing with others across cultures and learning and developing further from their richness. Long-term sustainability of a company in this new age also requires building the same values of humanity and spirituality within its own internal organizational culture and practices.

Through this series, we intend to propose various policy recommendations that contribute to the prosperity of international society and improve the well-being of mankind by clarifying the concrete actions that are needed.

More information about this series at https://link.springer.com/bookseries/13627

Stephen Hill · Tadashi Yagi · Stomu Yamash'ta
Editors

The Kyoto Post-COVID Manifesto For Global Economics

Confronting Our Shattered Society

 Springer

Editors
Stephen Hill
University of Wollongong
Wollongong, NSW, Australia

Tadashi Yagi
Faculty of Economics
Doshisha University
Kyoto, Japan

Stomu Yamash'ta
Sound Core Co., Ltd.
Kyoto, Japan

ISSN 2364-9186   ISSN 2364-9445 (electronic)
Creative Economy
ISBN 978-981-16-8565-1   ISBN 978-981-16-8566-8 (eBook)
https://doi.org/10.1007/978-981-16-8566-8

This Springer imprint is published by the registered company Springer Nature Singapore Pte Ltd.
The registered company address is: 152 Beach Road, #21-01/04 Gateway East, Singapore 189721, Singapore

Source: Stephen Hill

Preface

Our Original Objective

This book, *The Kyoto Post-COVID Manifesto for Global Economics* ("KM-PC") is a sequel to our 2018 book, "The Kyoto Manifesto for Global Economics" (KM-I, 2018). Our present book takes us further in seeking to reverse the steadily increasing subservience of our humanity to the demands of an enormously powerful global economic regime based on the principle of self-interest and the monetary assessment of value. World society has become enormously unequal and fragmented as a result, as has our ability to respond to critical events been diminished—in particular, since the mid-twentieth Century. Meanwhile, our planet is fast being depleted of the resources needed to maintain a stable human society. At stake is the very survival beyond the twenty-first Century of the world which sustains us and our humanity.

The fundamental tenet of this book is that our power to 'heal' our currently 'fractured' society lies in the depth of our humanity—that is, in our shared human spirit, or spirituality. What is sacred or of imperishable supreme value is *what we can be* as a human race—*empowered* fulfilled individuals, living in harmony, deeply *sharing* and *caring* for each other across our separate cultural and lifeworlds. Thus, the norms in our economic relations do not have to be those of separative self-interest, the ever watchful distrust in 'the deal' and immediate economic advantage for ME. Instead, we can build the economic frame for our society on *mindfulness, mutual human benefit* and *mutual trust*. On our humanity!

In KM-I we explored starting points for transformation, asserting human values and building 'harmony' across difference.

> We observed the need to widen our concept of knowledge to *trans disciplinarity*, (beyond 'multi disciplinarity' or across scientific and scholastic cultural disciplines alone), ie: to extend knowledge and understanding across different 'domains' or 'territories'—such as 'objective', 'subjective', spiritual, cultural, eastern philosophy, western science, economic, political—each with their own internal validity criteria. The knowledge needs to relate to 'the whole person' in relation to their 'whole environment'.
>
> The principle we used to bring alignment across difference is a term drawn from music, '*polyphony*', bringing two or more separate themes (domains) together into an overall

harmony. The 'harmony' test of validity lies in support for human values of sharing and care rather than self-interest—to be applied to *everything*, every institution, community action, government policy, personal life .... economic relations and organisation.

In planning what was, at that stage, to be basically a *sequel* to KM-I we built on this platform to develop a cohesive strategy for change.

This platform *links* the power of the mind with the power *to* mind, and to transform through collective (mindful) action.

All action and criteria for success are to be based on core humanity values. Examples include individual action, community development, urban design, business, organisation design and practices, government policy, international relations ...

What we are seeking to change is not just the 'surface' instruments of specific policy ... or 'words' in the societal 'script', but the underlying frameworks, the 'grammar'—which normally remains hidden behind daily life and actions but shapes all that we do and express. The 'grammar' of current global economic expression. We argue that to do this requires assertion of *core* humanity-inspired and supportive values in *everything*. This constitutes a profound change in our global culture—away from the dynamic of individual self-interest based on market values—and towards a dynamic of mutual support based on humanitarian values.

We outlined our *vision* in our 'Summary Draft Concept' circulated on Thursday 20th June 2019 amongst us, the authors, shortly after our last Kyoto Manifesto Symposium at Doshisha University, Kyoto, on Wednesday 12th June 2019.

We planned to meet in Kyoto in early June 2020 to finalise and then publish the book.

But

Suddenly!

As 2019 Closed

The Tiniest of Entities

A Virus which either crossed the Species Barrier

From a Bat to a Human in a Chinese Wet Market,

Or, perhaps escaped inadequately hygienic laboratory equipment,

Has thrown whatever Stabilities there were in our Current World

into Total Chaos

COVID caught our plans for this book, KM-PC by surprise. Indeed, the current world is so different that, in mid-March 2020, we postponed immediate publication of KM-PC for a year so that we could take this totally new COVID-influenced world and its consequences into account. To publish before this would have been rather like creating a perhaps beautifully carved piece of driftwood and tossing it in front of a massive turbulent Tsunami."

This Book, "The Kyoto Post-COVID Manifesto for Global Economics— Confronting Our Shattered Society" is the product. The Principles of our prior commitment to the "cohesive strategy for change" we were developing from our earlier book remained. Now, however, we needed to apply these within the suddenly different world society that the COVID Pandemic delivered.

The reader will see how the principles of humanistic-based economics are even more necessary now, but also how the opportunities for this new economics, and a positively different society, are influenced by the trauma of COVID-19.

Wollongong, Australia   Stephen Hill
Kyoto, Japan   Tadashi Yagi
Kyoto, Japan   Stomu Yamash'ta

Reference

KM-I (2018) Yamash'ta, Stomu, Tadashi Yagi and Stephen Hill (Eds), "The Kyoto Manifesto for Global Economics—The Platform of Community, Humanity, and Spirituality", Springer.

Introduction

Moving on from The Kyoto Manifesto for Global Economics Past the COVID-19 Pandemic

Stephen Hill, Tadashi Yagi and Stomu Yamash'ta

COVID-19: The Need to Re-think

As we observed in the Preface, the principles of developing and applying a humanistic-based economics remains the platform for this Book. But COVID-10 radically challenged the society we were dealing with.

The COVID-19 virus crept up on us, at first as a relatively minor problem the Chinese Government needed to deal with in Wuhan, the original place where infection started, but then it broke out.

Immensely contagious, the virus's impact has spread with geometric explosion across the whole world, borne by the very "machines of the global economy's success", cruise ships and airliners travelling across the globe, and a lifestyle where very large international crowds could gather for shared belief or leisure—from pilgrimages and religious ceremonies to football matches, rock concerts and surf carnivals—now, collectively referred to as 'superspreading events'.

Almost all international consumer transport stopped. Increasingly across the whole world *total* attention was paid to survival from a contagion that is invisible, all encompassing, and continuously mutating to ever more contagious and seriously debilitating strains—where enforced 'lock-downs', social distancing, protective masks and antiseptic protection now rule daily life at severe disadvantage to economic activity, whilst unemployment skyrocketed within an infected world.

As at the start of October 2021, over 235 million people have caught the virus worldwide and over 4.8 million have died. The United States, India and Brazil have been the worst hit in death rates with 37% of the world's overall deaths from them. (Worldometer, 2021)

The rich are exposed as much as the poor. Even Heads of Government have not been spared such as for the UK, USA, Brazil, Honduras, Armenia, Belarus, Guatamala and Burundi, as well as the Prime Minister of Russia, whilst Royalty such as Prince Charles of Great Britain and Prince Albert of Monaco are also included (Saraiva et al., 2020). So, the Pandemic infection rates are not, as in many diseases, a product of poverty, more of coordinated response—effective governance. Meanwhile, there has been massive disruption to global economic activity, social life and international connectedness.

Currently, as on October 2021, a range of anti-COVID vaccines have been developed with unheard of speed and are being used—with 'brand' partly dependent on level of national income and access, and also, politics. Four main vaccines with well tested efficacy—AstraZeneka, Pfeizer, Johnson & Johnson (Janssen), and Moderna—are surrounded by a dozen others, with a strong push (but less accredited testing) from China (Sinopharm) and Russia (Sputnik V). At this point, nineteen months since the COVID-19 Virus was declared a World Pandemic by the World Health Organization, just over 34% of the world population has been fully vaccinated and 6.3 billion doses of vaccine have been administered globally. (Our World in Data, 2021) Staggering numbers. But, bear in mind, inequality continues to rule. As of mid-September 2021, just 3% of people in low income countries have been vaccinated with at least one dose, compared with 60% in high income countries. In some countries, the situation is much worse: 0.09% of people in the Congo have been vaccinated and 1.15% in Papua New Guinea (United Nations, 2021). Many low income countries are unlikely to gain access to broad scale vaccination until at least 2023–2024. The world is a long way from anything like herd immunity which may well require 70–80% vaccination rates, almost certainly, COVID-19 will continue to mutate, so, as with the Flu, COVID vaccinations may need to be updated every year.

Suddenly, for 2020 and 2021, *everything* is different. The world, as we knew it, simply … *stopped*! And no-one saw it coming.

COVID-19 and Drafting The Kyoto Post-COVID Manifesto for Global Economics

COVID-19 has radically shaken up world society and the global economy. It leaves behind what could be decades of impact—from unemployment to struggling with massive debt. But the basic message we had already targeted for KM-PC remains. In fact, it is even more relevant for a secure and sustainable future. We need more than ever to focus on a future ruled by our humanity rather than self-interest. We must avoid the trap of falling back into the practices that cause division and even worse levels of inequality. COVID-19 has opened up the visibility of cracks in our society that may actually help us see what to do to reshape that society. Meanwhile the 'shock' to world society, whilst causing disaster, shakes things around so much that it also opens up new opportunities to actually do this reshaping in a potentially receptive environment.

In KM-PC, we explore how such essential reshaping can occur, to create a new world order where the principle of self-interest in economic relations and action *is* replaced by humanistic values, concern for a sustainable future, and society *connected* into its economy rather than ruled by self-centred alienating values.

In our Part I of KM-PC, *The Human Design of a Sustainable Future*, we trawl the resources of our shared humanity's experience and ideas to take on this *essential* reshaping task.

Chapter 1, *Confronting Our Shattered World*, authored by Stephen Hill on behalf of our whole 'Kyoto Post-COVID Manifesto' team, develops our original pre-COVID argument which highlights how deeply self and self-interest is destroying the very foundations of our shared humanity, enframed as our social world is by the assumptions and dynamics of current global economics. This analysis is just to remind—the most basic trap which humanity has fallen into globally by allowing the self to rule over our human sharing and care. In Chap. 2 Stephen Hill applies the 'escape' thesis we shared in KM-I, that is, to replace the self with humanitarian values in economic assumptions, and strengthens this argument by exploring the organising principle of 'the Circle of Wholeness', behind which the concepts of 'polyphony' and '*trans-disciplinarity*' used in KM-I are re-introduced to spread the arms of information and understanding across multiple domains—of objective, subjective and cultural knowledge, gathered towards *harmony* not conflict.

Moving on and led by Tadashi Yagi, we now explore real-world evidence in Chap. 3 (Yagi and Yamash'ta) of how *the circle* of wider social and community focussed business practice, such as is in Japan, strengthens the morality of business at the same time as it connects business with the society and its wider needs. The essential concepts of our Book are developed further. 'Polyphony', in particular, is focussed on in its ability to empower *pro-social behaviour*, that is, drawing difference together into an overall *human* synthesis rather than conflict. The analysis extends to real-life experience, in particular, within a historic Japanese business context where trust and wider human welfare dominate immediate self-interest and contractual control of deviance.

But then we confront COVID-19, the virus which suddenly, without warning, turned world society on its head as the 2020s unfolded. In Chap. 4 Stephen Hill explores the impact of COVID-19 on opportunities for implementing our projected strategy for change. An immediate opportunity arises from the increasingly rapid development of computer-based communications and changed home/office arrangements. These changes have already encouraged some leading organisations to revisit the human relations values which underscore productive employment. More importantly, the *experience* of COVID-19 and of some government responses *opens up extraordinary new opportunities* for establishing a future society and economy based on mutual care, in particular, through implementation of a Universal Basic Income (UBI)—not as relief' from hardship and poverty, but as the *platform* for the Economy of the Future! If only we, and our politicians and decision-makers, seek opportunity out of crisis—with new thinking—rather than fall back into remodelling the past. It is essential though that UBI is not only considered seriously, but *not* left as a standalone strategy. As Stephen Hill goes on to demonstrate in Chap. 5, even for the very poor, UBI *can* be a platform for lifting people out of extreme poverty and offering real hope for their future. Focus *must* be right down at local village levels, however, capitalising on indigenous and community strengths which are there though perhaps not realised. And, as with Hill's prior general conclusions of Chap. 4, action to introduce UBI *must* be set into a wider context, an environment which offers building the creativity and innovativeness of the people *at the local level* and thus catalysing new enterprise.

Chapters 6 and 7 by Tadashi Yagi, and Toshiaki Maruyama, respectively, then deepen the readers' understanding of the two key concepts of KM-PC already introduced. These are, first, the economic sustainability conditions, even with COVID-19 induced hardship, which allow a Universal Basic Income to work; and, second, the depth—in wider human activity and creativity—which demonstrates just how powerful the concept of polyphony is in pro-social behaviour, bringing people and their shared worlds together in harmony rather than conflict—where *difference* is a strength, not a weakness. The analytic power of polyphony as a concept is revealed by going back to its roots in human musical expression, where even themes drawn from very different cultures, musical forms and timing, *can* be brought into new more powerful harmony than when played or experienced separately.

As a reminder of why the argument of this Book is so important, so timely NOW, we reinforce here that our goal is to help to reshape the current self-focussed 'free market' global economy system because it is intrinsically in opposition to the development and vitality of human *community*, and it is only our humanity and our *shared* enterprise and care which *can* create a future we will survive!

In Part II, we then move on to explore two key *Dimensions of Transformation* we seek.

The First, *Managing System Complexity*, recognises the increasingly complex system world which now surrounds us, and our ability to act individually or collectively … and seems—even quite realistically—to be somehow beyond our ability to change. This is a world of algorithms, massive computer power back-up and external control. So, in our present Book, through Len Fisher's expertise, we explore systems and systems theory to seek an entry point for putting into practice the sorts of *human* transformations that our shared Kyoto Manifesto is calling for.

And what do we find? At every decision-making node in the systems the operating assumption and modus operandi is *self-interest!* In Chap. 8 Len Fisher explores the systems themselves, demonstrating that such networks can develop emergent behaviours that are more than the sum of their parts, and indeed can be in conflict with the interests of individual members. In Chap. 9, Len Fisher observes that to avoid this contradiction, we need to work together to transform the network as a whole—so that cooperation replaces competition; the interests of the collective take precedence over the interests of self—building *trust;* governance promotes awareness and cooperation; and the overall system is open to transformation emanating from 'below',—what Fisher calls the "earthworm" solution.

To highlight our Second Dimension, *Applying the Wholeness of Our Humanity*, we then explore our humanity more deeply. So often, the person is assumed to be an 'entity', judged largely by their actions and conscious presence. However, as Masatoshi and Tomoko Murase demonstrate in Chaps. 10–12, 'living nature' of the person is itself a circle—of more outwardly directed 'self' and more inwardly directed 'non-self'. Wider social transformation depends on bridging these two sides of our humanness, and after building the argument in Chaps. 10 and 11, the authors offer a practical case study in Chap. 12 of what this means in the practice of nursing care. This case can be extended generally to wider society and principles of making transformation work.

To complete this Part II exploration of the deeper reaches of the humanity we can depend upon to create a positive future, we draw—in Chap. 13 (Qi) on the wisdom preserved in millennial time—the traditionally acquired philosophical, cultural and educational wisdom of the Chinese Taiji Movement—brought to us by Master Xing Qi Lin, Founder of the Tianzhen Cultural Training School, and Practitioner. The benefit to the reader of this Chapter is to show a clear demonstration of a holistic culture based on harmony which has not just been brought into being over the last few years, or even a couple of hundred years, but has stood the test of *thousands* of years. An enormously important reminder of what matters when we seek to propose serious transformation of our society now. Master Qi, very highly respected in China, came to Kyoto from China—specifically to share time and knowledge with our Kyoto Manifesto team when we were developing the current Book in June 2019.

Finally, and most importantly, our self-focussed, divisive, global economic dynamic has left the world society now at the edge of an enormously dangerous precipice. Slowly, too slowly, the light of global attention has focussed on the fact that we have been living a lie—that we could treat our planet as a limitless resource for extracting our life-supporting resources and throw away the waste we created in the meantime.

In Part III of the Kyoto Post-COVID Manifesto for Global Economics, we move more directly into economics—to explore the newly emerging 'Circular Economy Movement' which re-conceives production design to eliminate waste—a Movement which is of such importance that we devote the whole of Part III in our Book to its presentation and potential.

Within the overall frame of this part, *Achieving Sustainable Life—The Circular Economy Movement*, we present Chaps. 14 (Ladeja Godina Kosir), 15 (Einer Kleppe Holthe), 16 (Janez Potocnik), 17 (Petra Kuenkel & Elisabeth Kuhn) and 18 (Alexander Laszlo et al). This group of authors lead us to see how from initial inspiration and action in Europe and European Business, the basic concept of the Circular Economy is now spreading worldwide as a *New Narrative* of production. The 'old' *linear* narrative follows a 'take → make → dispose' design, where waste consists of the inconvenient leftovers that must somehow be dumped. The 'new' narrative of the Circular Economy (and "Circular Triangle") looks at production design from a higher vantage point and sees waste as an equally important part of production—right from the start, so seeks to design *everything* to be circled back and used in the overall production cycle, thus eliminating waste perhaps entirely. Whilst the Circular Economy Philosophy and Design is intended to ensure profit, not loss, its essence is the practical application of design to human care and cooperation *for our shared sustainable future*, the core dynamics of the Kyoto Post-COVID Manifesto.

Our message is not one of doom and gloom—although that is the dire warning if we sit on our hands and do nothing or wait for 'someone else' to look after us. As we observed earlier, even the enormous impact right now of the COVID-19 Pandemic, *can* be enough of a stimulus, having thrown everything up in the air, to provide potential *opportunity* for a future characterised by sustainable human care and community rather than distortive iniquitous self-interest.

In our Final **Conclusions** Part IV in the Kyoto Post-COVID Manifesto (Chaps. 19 and 20), *From Our Shattered World to a New Economics*, Stephen Hill along with Tadashi Yagi and Stomu Yamash'ta in their Chap. 19, "Our Shattered World—Where Did Humanity Go?", remind the reader of the scale of the global problems revealed throughout the Book and needing to be addressed *right now*—Global Warming, Ecological Destruction, Unelected Centralization of Control, and rampaging Global Inequality—*all* of which, as shown, are directly attributable to the underlying self-focussed dynamic of current Global Economics.

In Chap. 20, "Discovering Our Humanity—Economics of the Future", the authors draw out the essential principles of what our humanity is—from prior Chapters in the Book, and then apply these principles—bedded into practices informed by caring, sharing and trust—to building a New Economics for the Future. Practice of the newly emerging 'Circular Economy' and 'Circular Triangle' Movements are included within strategy which essentially is *local* and community empowering, yet strategically global via the 'Global Localism' Principle presented. Already, even within mainstream economics 'green shoots' of support for such a strategy are emerging. The conclusions then fold longer-term response to the COVID Pandemic into a parallel social design for the future.

The New Economics is firmly anchored within "The Circle of Wholeness" rather then "The Circle of Self-Interested Cronies".

Indeed, to see this humanity-based vision in terms of a metaphor drawn from music, as is our central organising concept for this Book, 'polyphony', we can potentially look forward to a 'Baroque' future. Baroque music emerged in the seventeenth century out of the cultural 'revolution' of the Renaissance period, like now with COVID and Climate Change 'throwing everything into the air'. As with the Baroque music of Johann Sebastian Bach and Antonio Lucio Vivaldi of the late seventeenth century, our 'humanity-based future' can come down with expansion of harmonic relations and the 'tonality' of deeper human caring in the society we can look forward to.

References

Our World in Data, 2021. COVID-19 Data Explorer, "Coronavirus (COVID-19) Vaccinations. https://ourworldindata.org>COVID-vaccinations (1st October: updated every 9 hours)

Saraiva, Augusta, Allison Meakem, Chloe Hadavas (2020), "When the Coronavirus Reaches the Top", *Foreign Policy*, October 2, 4.50pm : *foreignpolicy.com*

Worldometer (2021), COVID-19 Coronavirus Pandemic, 3rd October: https://www.worldometers.info/coronavirus/

Contents

Editors and Contributors

About the Editors

Stephen Hill (AM, FRSN, FTSE, FWIF, Ph.D.) is an Emeritus Professor, University of Wollongong, Australia and a prominent Australian scientist and diplomat. He has degrees and has written extensively in multiple disciplines. Originally a research chemist (Sydney University and Unilever), he also was awarded Australia's first Business Administration Ph.D. (Melbourne University) and after academic positions in Chicago, Sussex and Sydney, was appointed as Foundation Professor of Sociology at the University of Wollongong at age 30. He has lived and worked in the US, Europe and Asia, been policy consultant to most relevant International Agencies and several Asian countries, and founded three research centres including a Centre of Excellence of the Australian Research Council. From 1995 to 2006, he was Asia-Pacific Regional Director for Science for the UN Agency UNESCO, and Representative (Ambassador), based in Indonesia. He was responsible for major UN science, education, media freedom, culture, world heritage and peace initiatives and reforms in the region, as well as being commissioned by the Director-General to reform and decentralise the UN Agency globally. Now retired, an Emeritus Professor of the University of Wollongong, he has been awarded several State Awards including Member, Order of Australia, and continues to write, speak publicly, and be involved in community empowerment and human rights initiatives.

Tadashi Yagi is a Professor of the Faculty of Economics at Doshisha University. He holds a Ph.D. in Economics, awarded by Nagoya University in 1996. His research areas are wide-ranging, including public economics, human resources management, income distribution, welfare economics and cultural economics. He has written many papers in refereed academic journals and chapters in edited volumes. The important papers are "Economic Growth and the Riskiness of Investment in Firm-Specific Skills" (with Taichi Maki and Koichi Yotsuya) European Economic Review (2005), "Income Redistribution through the Tax System:A Simulation Analysis of Tax Reform" (with Toshiaki Tachibanaki) Review of Income and Wealth (1998),

"Public Investment and Interregional Output–Income Inequalities" (with Nobuhiro Okuno) Regional Science and Urban Economics (1990). Recent works include "Moral, Trust and Happiness-Why does trust improves happiness?-" Journal of Organizational Psychology (2017), "Happiness and Self-Determination—An Empirical Study in Japan" (with Kazuo Nishimura) Review of Behavioral Economics (2019).

Stomu Yamash'ta is the creator of modern percussion's music. He was born in Kyoto, and studied music at Kyoto Horikawa Senior High School of Music, The Juilliard School, Interlochen Arts Academy, and Berklee College of Music, and has also lectured in music. His innovation and acrobatic drumming style earned him many accolades. In the 1960s, he performed with Seiji Ozawa music by Toru Takemitsu, and Hans Werner Henze amongst others and became a great master of percussion at a young age. At the turn of the 1970s, he formed the rock supergroup 'GO', which made an incredible impact in the world by taking its lead in fusion/music going beyond the different genres of music. In the 1980s, he began pursuing Buddhism music at Toji Temple in Kyoto and established a new style of music. From his encounter with a stone instrument 'sanukite', which has a wide range far more than any other instruments, he is currently the art director of 'On Zen Ceremony' which is a ceremony incorporating Shinto, Zen and world of spiritual music.

Contributors

Stefan Blachfellner Bertalanffy Center for the Study of Systems Science (BCSSS), Vienna, Austria

Len Fisher School of Physics, University of Bristol, Bristol, UK

Ladeja Godina Košir Circular Change & ECESP, Institute for Circular Economy, Ljubljana, Slovenia

Stephen Hill Faculty of Arts, Social Sciences and Humanities, University of Wollongong, Wollongong, NSW, Australia

Einar Kleppe Holthe Natural State As, Oslo, Norway

Karin Huber-Heim Bertalanffy Cener for the Studies of Systems Science/ Academic Programme Director, University of Applied Sciences BFI, Vienna, Austria

Petra Kuenkel Collective Leadership Institute, Potsdam, Germany

Elisabeth Kühn Collective Leadership Institute, Potsdam, Germany

Alexander Laszlo Bertalanffy Center for the Study of Systems Science (BCSSS), Laszlo Institute of New Paradigm Research (LINPR), Vienna, Austria

Toshiaki Maruyama RINRI Institute of Ethics, Tokyo, Japan

Masatoshi Murase Yukawa Institute for Theoretical Physics (YITP), Kyoto University, Kyoto, Japan;
International Research Unit of Advanced Future Studies (IRU-AFS), Kyoto University (2015–2020), Kyoto, Japan;
International Research Unit of Integrated Complex System Science (IRU-ICSS), Kyoto University, Kyoto, Japan;
2021 Project of Challenges of Advanced Future Studies, Kokoro Research Center, Kyoto University, Kyoto, Japan

Tomoko Murase Japanese Red Cross Toyota College of Nursing, Toyota, Japan;
2021 Project of Challenges of Advanced Future Studies, Kokoro Research Center, Kyoto University, Kyoto, Japan

Janez Potočnik UNEP International Resource panel, Paris, France

Qi-Lin Xing Tianzhen Traditional Culture Training School, Tianjin, China

Tadashi Yagi Faculty of Economics, Doshisha University, Kamigyo, Kyoto, Japan

Stomu Yamash'ta Artist, Kyoto, Japan

Part I
The Human Design of a Sustainable Future

Chapter 1
Confronting Our Shattered Society

Stephen Hill

Abstract This opening chapter builds on the analysis of contemporary economics and society previously published by Springer in this book's 2018 predecessor, 'The Kyoto Manifesto for Global Economics—The Platform of Community, Humanity and Spirituality".

The chapter reveals how deeply self-interest and greed-based enterprise—as the underlying dynamics of global economics—penetrates contemporary society, and has impacted on our planet today. Most significant concerns are centralization of control in very few hands, massive inequality, and physical destruction through, for example, Climate Change and Species Destruction, of the ecosystem which sustains life. Escape to a meaningful, viable future, requires us to *see* behind the curtain of what has become 'normality' to the underlying 'grammar' that shapes it, and change society at this deeper level, not just protest and deal only with surface outcroppings. Even, for example, were we to learn to moderate Climate Change, if we don't transform the underlying economic system dynamic and values which produce it, we will soon be back where we started.

1.1 The Strain and Morality of Inequality

As we wrote in our earlier Kyoto Manifesto:

> "Mainstream neo-classical economists, in general, and unquestioning participants in the economic system, do not seem to realize how close they are to the abyss - partying on in the excitement of stock market gambling, powering global influence for separate economic advantage, living the profits-supported 'good life' ... whilst the luxury bus in which they travel together is carrying them, and us, towards an un-crossable precipice—absolute limits to growth-based economic enterprise. (KM-I, 2018, p. 4)

S. Hill (✉)
Faculty of Arts, Social Sciences and Humanities, University of Wollongong, Northfields Ave, Wollongong, NSW 2522, Australia
e-mail: sthill@uow.edu.au

© Springer Nature Singapore Pte Ltd. 2022
S. Hill et al. (eds.), *The Kyoto Post-COVID Manifesto For Global Economics*, Creative Economy, https://doi.org/10.1007/978-981-16-8566-8_1

1.1.1 Rule of the Self and Inequality

Unfortunately, this self-interest and growth-based enterprise is still calling the shots, not only in its progressively destructive impact on our planet but also in its effect on our society and its ability to respond.

Humans are *social* animals. However the progressive impact of so-called 'free market economics' has driven us into self-absorbed individualism, a guaranteed killer of our very essence, our 'shared' human world.

We need to trawl more deeply through this present 'shattered' world to see where the green shoots of humanity-based change can come from. What is needed is not just stopping major pollution and other global threats, but reshaping the society that has been produced by the self-focused free market growth based economy, for that society is surely in peril just as much as is our physical planet.

World society is dominated by increasing inequality—at an iniquitous level. Oxfam International concluded in 2017 that *eight* men control as much wealth as 50 percent of the rest of the world (Oxfam 2017), and the situation is getting worse. Since 1980 the top one percent of the world's richest individuals captured *twice as much growth benefit* as the bottom 50 percent (Alvaredo et al., 2017). The level of increase in percentage inequality is particularly severe in the United States, supposedly the richest country in the world. To demonstrate:

> The "Gini Index", a coefficient developed originally by Italian statistician Corrado Gini in 1912, measures wealth distribution across a population, with zero representing total equality and 1 representing total inequality - where all wealth is concentrated in a single household. As the Washington Post reported in September 2019 – *before the added impact of COVID-19,* "The indicator for the United States has been rising steadily for several decades. When the Census Bureau began studying income inequality in 1967, the Gini index was 0.397. In 2018, it climbed to 0.485". By comparison, no European nation had a score greater than 0.38 in 2018 (Telford, 2019), a situation which has continued through the COVID-19 Pandemic to remain much the same into 2021, although with European nations in general achieving greater equality – placing the United States distortion of income distribution towards the wealthy in the same ballpark as Argentina, Iran and the Congo! (World Population Review, 2021)

The wealthy stand ready to grasp at any and all opportunity. The present COVID-19 Pandemic has been a financial godsend, a source of added wealth for the already rich.

> A prime exemplar is Hedge Fund Billionaire Bill Ackman. In March 2020, he predicted a Financial Apocalypse to a wide general audience on CNBC Television, "Hell is Coming!" "There will be Depression". He advocated "Shut-Down of the Global Economy."
>
> One week later his firm, Pershing Squire Capital Management, announced that they had netted *$2.6 BILLION* on a $27 million investment they had made on 'credit bets' which paid off if certain bundles of loans declined in value. Guess why! Ackman's public 'advice' to sell was a promotion for him to bet on the outcome.
>
> Others were buying vast stocks of needed goods for the Pandemic, drugs, protective clothing and masks and inflating prices. In one case, an Australian investor noticed the emerging impact of the Wuhan Virus in late 2019, purchased a very large stake in the company Alpha Pro Tech which manufactured the top-of-the-range N95 surgical masks, knocking share

prices up by a factor of six, and producing a 2,000% profit for him …. whilst millions were now starting to become seriously ill, were dying, losing their jobs, income …. houses, future ….! (Paumgarten, 2020)

As OXFAM International reports from a survey of data from 295 economists in 79 countries, by early 2021 the wealth of the ten richest men in the world increased by a *half trillion dollars* since the Pandemic began, more than enough to pay for a vaccine for all and prevent anyone on Earth from falling into poverty because of the virus. (Oxfam, 2021). Separately, an Oxfam Briefing Paper late in 2020 reports that thirty two of the world's largest companies stand to see their profits jump by $109 billion *more* in 2020 compared to 2019, whilst 400 million jobs have been lost globally and up to a half-billion people will be newly pushed into poverty by the time the Pandemic is over. (Gneiting et al., 2020). Jeff Bezos, owner of Amazon, is a good example. As the richest man on earth, with personal worth $179 billion, his wealth increased during the Pandemic by $92 billion in only five months—from 18th March to 20th August 2020. (Dolan et al., 2020).

Even these figures are just the beginning of observation of society-divided: as Oxfam concludes, "Big business and the super-rich are fueling the inequality crisis by dodging taxes, driving down wages and using their power to influence politics" (Oxfam 2017).

And the inequity digs deeper still. In the US economy, the way the stock market now works allows a very small number of corporate owners to control the majority of the overall market for their own direct advantage.

Since the Financial Crisis of 2008, because of lower fees for much the same outcome, there has been a major shift from investment in actively managed *mutual funds* (or "active" funds) where investment companies or individuals are seeking to 'pick stocks to beat the market', to *index funds* which replicate established stock indices, such as the S&P 500 (which measures the performance of the 500 largest capital companies – reporting the risks and returns, a benchmark of the overall market).

Whereas the 'active' funds are fragmented, consisting of hundreds of different asset managers, large and small, the 'index' fund is now massively concentrated – dominated by just *three* giant American Asset Managers, "BlackRock", "Vanguard", and "State Street", popularly known as "The Big Three". Together, they control nearly $(US)11 trillion in assets under management. That's more than all sovereign wealth funds combined and over three times the global hedge fund industry. As a group, they are the largest shareholder in 40% of *all* publicly listed firms in the United States, 90% of America's largest companies – as listed on the S&P500 Index, and exercise coordinated power over corporate decisions – usually in favour of management and against the smaller share holders (Fichtner et al., 2019).

It is then particularly significant that the dominant force within the S&P Index Fund is social media, and their dominance is very recent – doubling in impact over the last 5 years. Apple, the leader, controlling 6.93% of the Index Fund, along with Microsoft, Amazon, Facebook and Google, together controlled 22.22% of total Index capitalization at the start of 2021. (Closed End Fund Tracker, 2021)

And, where are the super-rich (including Jeff Bezos, Founder of Amazon) while the world struggles and four million people die? Launching personal tourist rockets into space.

It was a contest between the three most wealthy men in the world – Richard Branson, Jeff Bezos and Elon Musk. Branson won. On Sunday 11th July 2021 his Virgin Galactica rocket-powered space plane successfully completed a mission into space, including four minutes of weightlessness and fabulous views of the Earth, the first in a space tourist business which will cost $250,000 per ticket for future travellers. Jeff Bezos just missed. His 'Blue Origin' flight is scheduled for nine days later – with one highly prized passenger paying $28 million for a seat. Elon Musk was there waiting for Branson to land, having already paid his $10,000 deposit FOR a quarter million dollar seat on a future flight. However, his goal is much grander – building a private space industry with his company Space X' to "make humans an interplanetary species".

Former United States Labor Secretary, Robert Reich, tweeted on Thursday 8th July – before the flight:

> "Is anyone else alarmed that billionaires are having their own private space race while record-breaking heatwaves are sparking a 'fire-breathing dragon of clouds' and cooking sea creatures to death in their shells?"

(Reimann, 2021)

But do remember. This is not just super-wealthy play. Making money remains the subtext.

> Branson's space-travel company, Virgin Galactica, is a huge favorite amongst retail investors. Its share value *doubled* to $11.8 billion by the Friday before Richard Branson's flight. (Cameron, 2021)

Even at the very birth of a capitalist 'free market' system, Adam Smith, the first person to see its dynamic, was concerned that greed could take it over. Smith projected the ingenuity of the emerging economic system in 1776 in his 'Wealth of Nations', an "invisible hand harmonised resource allocation through trade by *selfish* economic agents". Self-interest would produce harmony! (Smith, 1999) But Smith could see— at the very birth of the system, that 'self-interest' could pose a serious problem. Before he wrote The Wealth of Nations, Adam Smith had written another book, "The Theory of Moral Sentiments", in which he emphasized the need for 'empathy' or 'sympathy' and 'suppressing selfish behavior' if a 'peaceful state of the market' was to be attained. He continued to pay attention to this 'Moral Sentiment' concern and continued to revise the book from its initial publication in 1757 right up until his death (Smith, 2018).

What Smith could not see was how eventually the market became, as Mark Carney, former Governor of the Bank of England, observed, "the *organizing framework*", not only for economics, but also increasingly for broader human relations with its reach extending well into civic and family life" (Carney, 2020a). A key result is that those following free market rules for self-interest may not even see how badly they may affect others. As Carney goes on to show, "When bankers become disconnected from their ultimate clients in the real economy, they have no direct view of their impact. Before this crisis (the 2008 implosion of the world banking system), traders began to see the numbers on their screen as a game to be won, ignoring the consequences of their actions for hundreds of millions of mortgage holders and company borrowers." (Carney, 2020b).

Adam Smith was indeed right to be cautious about the morality of the so-called 'free market'.

Now, nearly two-and-a-half centuries of industrialization later, the 'free' market has turned into its opposite. There is now no such thing as a *free* market. Instead, wider society confronts a system of wealth accumulation which is controlled by and massively skewed toward a thin minority of the *most* wealthy and powerful. Its moral dynamic is to make the system even *more* beneficial for the very very few. Meanwhile the 'system' hides from them the potentially catastrophic impact of their self-interest on wider society. So, they don't have to feel guilty.

How much more evidence do we need that whilst we continue to accept the current control over world society by our current global economic system, our society is increasingly unequal, an anathema to our humanity.

1.1.2 Our 'Shattered Society'—Increasing Social Fragmentation and Separation—Loss of Community and Truth With Digitization

A direct product of such inequality and division within contemporary society is increasing *social fragmentation*. It is here that there is profit to be made, and a mechanism shored into place to insure against the 'collective rise of the poor'.

The 'grammar' or 'frame' of underlying assumptions that structures *how* we live is deeply embedded in the *'self'-centered dynamic* of the global economic system— promoting increasing separation and fragmentation, as this is good for business.[1]

> *The structure of modern living,* in, for example, suburban developments, is more designed for automobile access, separation and anonymity, not community – requiring us to somehow *show* the world we matter through physical objects and symbols – an expensive car, a larger more modern house, boutique clothes.
>
> > Meanwhile, neighbors may be at war over the back fence for some minor intrusion on their lives, or remain anonymous (where an elderly lady, alone, may die and nobody notices until three weeks later when the smell of decay becomes overwhelming).
>
> *Success* – is also largely measured in financial and life-style terms - *but at the expense of others* …. where at the 'top of the heap' a tiny minority hide their absolutely vast wealth behind tall fences and protective security, flying off to their own personal island resort to rest … while children in Ethiopia die because their family is caught in the lowest 20% of income earners and cannot afford the $2 required to access an anti-measles injection. If one of the unvaccinated Ethiopian children from families across a broad range of income levels is then hospitalized for measles infection the inpatient cost of between $60 to $80 will push at least 7% of them below the local poverty threshold of $1.25 per day. (Memire et al., 2021)
>
> > WE are complicit in the 'system' which allows this to happen, generally not too concerned perhaps, until suddenly WE are at the wrong end of the 'deal'.
>
> *Contemporary Communication* is increasingly driven by social media, and social media is driven by profit for the owners - of Google, Amazon, Facebook, and so on – leaving us in a fantasy world commanded by 'viral' explosions of interest rather than reality. And remember, as shown earlier, social media has dominant control over the entire stock market so is not just an add-on to economic life, but basic. Facebook, for example, espouses the value of 'connecting people'. However, this is incidental to the business's main purpose. Facebook trawls intimate exchanged detail of peoples' lives in order to sell the intelligence, providing unprecedentedly accurate targeting of potential customers to commercial advertisers, (Mackay, 2018).

The product is social-media-overload where truth is increasingly a product of the millions of 'hits' the original assertion registers when it goes viral – though remaining untested for truth in the first place. We tend to believe it in particular if it supports our pre-existing views and attitudes.

Meanwhile, our inter-subjective world-within-reach - where we actually *create* meaning with our shared humanity - is overwhelmed by, for example, the number of face-book 'friends' we can point to – even though we may not know them, and an apparent teenage girl is in fact a 40-year old pedophile. The number of friends is largely a statistical assurance of one's worth, not a sharing and caring community.

Social media foster cocoons of self-absorbed individualism (Mackay, 2018, p15). People pay dominant attention in both stories and tweets to what they already agree with, and because, for the sake of one's own personal social profile and sense of worth, it is common practice to pass on one's own tweet input as quickly as possible, often reinforcing what others have already stated but not tested for validity. The result is viral explosion of apparent interest (Zarrella, 2009). Truth has been lost at the very beginning, but the fact that millions now agree with your own views makes the story 'true'. Self-validation, truth validation, are ruled by a fragmented reality.

The sheer scale of social media interaction is mind-blowing.

> The first tweet was sent on March 21, 2006 by Jack Dorsey, the creator of Twitter. It took just three years, until the end of May 2009, to reach the billionth tweet. Today, it takes *less than two days* for one billion tweets to be sent.[2]

> Every second, on average, around 6,000 tweets are transmitted on Twitter, which corresponds to over 350,000 tweets sent per minute, 500 million tweets per day and around 200 billion tweets per year (Whitney, 2020).

> Ex-President Trump alone sent 200 tweets on Friday 5th June 2020, breaking his prior tweeting record during his impeachment trial, this time, surrounded by nation-wide protests against the death of George Floyd (Perrett, 2020)

Here lies the power to seduce truth in the interests of capital or political power – the apparent validity of 'false facts'. Indeed, this power was shown in high relief with ex-President Trump on 6th January 2021 when he and thousands of others were using tweets and other forms of social media to foment insurrection - invasion of the Washington Capitol in an attempt to prevent Congress counting the Presidential election votes and ratifying the Presidency of the winner, Jo Biden. After a six month detailed investigation the New York Times estimated that *one million mentions* promoting a call to arms had appeared on social media concerning the plan to storm the Capitol, including maps of the layout, which lawmakers to target first, and what to bring. The whole event was based on a lie promoted by then-President Trump, against all evidence even ratified in Court, but promoted in particular via social media where no truth test was applied. (Khavin et al., 2021)

Two days later, on 8th January, 2021, Twitter announced the *permanent suspension* of Donald Trump's Twitter Account "due to the risk of further incitement of violence". Powerful stuff against a President still in office! (BBC News, 2021a)

Walter Fisher gave us a clue to the dynamic back in the early 1980s. He observed that human communication fundamentally involves the exchange of stories "by which we comprehend the world beyond the accuracy of the statements that compose them" (Fisher, 1984).

> This need to be included in a social story then provides the power and sustainability of the public lie. It is woven into the story, and provides an internal consistency ("narrative coherence", Fisher, 1984), which gives the recipient a place in the stories from which they were otherwise left out. It also locates within the story

values and ideas that the story teller has already decided to believe in, and which are reinforced when literally *millions* of others agree.

People accept stories even when they contain factual errors because the stories resonate with their own experiences and provide them with an active role in the narrative (Bencherki & Basque, 2018).

When the story is told 'anonymously', it does not need to be tested in subjective discourse since its popularity communicates its validity.

This is '*ghost*' communication. It has not built human community and communication, but instead encourages self-absorbed individualism, with the ghost that has often been conjured up by Corporations making them billions of dollars.

1.1.3 Social Fragmentation: The 'Compasses' of Care and Truth are Missing

A major consequence of such social fragmentation is the loss of a sense of community—the basis for social meaning, cohesion and comfort. There is no longer a 'compass' one can trust for care. Society's collective ability to *act* suffers in particular against new and serious threats, whilst the individual's ability to *cope* is at risk.

A particularly sad outcome is the continuously *increasing* rate of suicide amongst the young, to the point it is the fourth leading cause of death world-wide among 15 to 29 year olds: the World Health Organization estimated that in 2019 over 160,000 people between 15 and 29 years old killed themselves, and alarmingly from earlier (2016) data, a high number would have been younger than 14 years old (10,000 in 2016). Again it is the poor who suffer most. *Most* adolescents who died from suicide (88%) were from low and middle income countries – where 90% of all of the world's adolescents live. (WHO, 2016, 2021)

Another emerging problem, as observed earlier, is the development of a Post-Truth World. The source of truth for the general public is increasingly the *popularity* of knowledge positions on the internet or in the media. The more an untrue statement is repeated, the more it comes to be believed.

We must escape the distortions of this Post-Truth World if we are to assert our shared humanity over divisive self-interested economics. Instead, we must focus on legitimate new knowledge applied to the lifeworld of peoples' experience.

This 'new knowledge' cannot come from the fragmentary distortions of social media where truth is a product of popularity rather than test. It does not, however, lie solely within the realm of 'objective' scientific 'truth'. Such truth is an anchor point in testing the objective validity of experienced 'facts', but this is a very partial representation of the validity in personal experience of our subjective understanding of ourselves and others, or for that matter, of what our humanity means across cultures and life experience.

We must instead bring together different *domains*, or territories, of knowledge – objective, subjective, physical, cultural, spiritual, and other outcomes of human experience – to inform action strategies. For this strategy to be most effective, we need to identify *validity* criteria that work *across* knowledge domains. Our guidance lies in the metaphor of 'polyphony' – bringing different themes of knowledge from across the different domains together into a shared harmony – ultimately measured against our *humanity*.

1.1.4 The Commodification of Love

To carry forward towards the power of our humanity to transform the future, I need to dwell a little further on 'love'. Within the dynamics of social media 'love' and 'mutual care', basic human needs, are subsumed into their surrogate—the drive to be 'seen' and to 'exploit' social media so we can feel we show others our 'worth' by how many others notice us. Day by day, tweet by billion tweet, the 'surrogate' rules, and the essence of what love represents is either sidelined ... or destroyed ... or *replaced* by the self-centered need *to have* applause. *Love* itself has been turned by global economic capital interest into a *commodity*—deeply penetrating our daily life meanings and aspirations.

To be useful to the interests of economic capital, the commodity of love needs to be marketed. Some examples are surrogates such as lipstick or Botox to make you more attractive, or holidays in a Tourist Package Paradise to bring you and partner together. Even paid consultation to deal with problems between you and partner. Or, of course, sex on line. A *deal*—where you pay money for love! Or, more accurately, for 'having' love or its surrogate.

Commercial 'Life-Products' are therefore designed to make us feel perpetually young and, ultimately to *hide* us from the fear of death. We become embalmed in eternal youth products, face and body lift supports to defeat the unfortunate reality of gravity, lifestyle attractions to distract us, even to fundamentally transform the very *essence* of our humanity, empathy and love—into their opposite. Love moves from "giving' into "having", "empathy" becomes a "deal" rather than a "gift" (Hill, 2020).

> Having is passive. Having is opposite to giving. Love in modern times is therefore often confused, as Erich Fromm (Fromm, 1962) points out, with the (passive) object status the person has, and beams out as signals for the rest of the world to notice – a mixture of popularity and sex appeal. To find love is, in most people's eyes, the quest to *be* loved, to be the object that others find attractive.

> Following the wider dynamics of the commodity-exchange system, finding a love-object and being loved follow the same pattern as do the commodity and labor markets. Two persons fall in love when they feel that they have found the best object available on the market, considering the limitations of their own exchange value. (Hill, 1988, p 215)

At a global economic exchange level, the dynamic is about the power of the self-interested *deal*—with very strong self-interest, indeed locked-in contractual arrangements to ensure—*payback!* In the marketplace, the power of the 'gift'—love—is either not admitted into negotiations unless as a 'sweetener' for later advantage, or seen as irrelevant or stupid.

But *love* is central to future transformation as it expresses the essence of the *shared* power of our humanity and connectedness which is currently lost, or at most, entirely secondary, in global economics. Sharing, care, mindfulness, community! Love is about *giving*—the power of the *gift*! It is about mutual benefit without planning pay-back.

Love lies at the heart of transformation in asserting the values of our humanity.

1.1.5 Self and Greed-Oriented Exploitation of Our Physical Environment: Finally Recognized

The current global economic paradigm has led to the erosion, the inequity, the fragmentation of our society and our humanity. The most basic values of what it means to be human have been marginalized. The power to respond to crisis and the need for change requires that mutual care and love be returned to center stage.

We also have to realize however, that our horizon for action, indeed our very survival, is darkened not only by a divided society, but by an increasingly fragile physical world that we are now threatening to destroy. Both are consequences of the continuing dynamic of greed within global self-centered economics. At least some world leaders are waking up to the problem. Pope Francis, for example, made a "passionate call in his address to the United Nations as far back as September 2015 to choose environmental justice over a boundless thirst for power and material prosperity":

> "Any harm done to the environment, therefore, is harm done to humanity", he added, "a selfish and boundless thirst for power and material prosperity leads both to the misuse of available natural resources and to the exclusion of the weak and the disadvantaged." (Bagley, 2015)

But there is so much more we *must* do, and fast.

Within KM-I, we identified the broad-based destruction increasingly being delivered by our global economic system on our planet,[3] an issue addressed further in this current book a little later by Ladeja Kosir and colleagues when discussing the principles of a "Circular Economy."

We have reached a serious *tipping point.*

To add immediate and stark reminders:

> On 6th May 2019, the United Nations Sustainable Development Goals Program announced the results of their Global Assessment of Biodiversity, endorsed by the Intergovernmental Science, Policy Platform on Biodiversity and Ecosystem Services (IPBES) at its 7th Session Plenary, 29th April to 4th May 2019.
>
> > The results are startling. *One million species are currently threatened with extinction;* 75 percent of the world's terrestrial environment and 66 percent of our marine environment altered to date by human actions; 40 percent of amphibian species threatened with extinction; 75 percent of global food crops that depend on animal pollination threatened – the annual value of which, with pollinator loss, is between $235 billion and $577 billion (UN, 2019).
>
> Then, in October 2020, the United Nations reported a "staggering rise" in climate emergencies in the last 20 years.
>
> > There were 7,348 reported climate disaster events worldwide resulting in 1.23 million people dying, compared to the previous 20 year period (1980 to 1999) when 4,212 disasters from natural hazards were reported and 1.19 million deaths - with an increase of 82% in world-wide cost – to $2.97 trillion. The data showed that poorer nations experienced death rates more than four times higher than rich nations (UN, 2020).

We are reaching the tipping point for our planet, but those who control the industrial economies of the world don't seem to care. Certainly, they don't care *enough.*

Mami Mizutori, Chief of the United Nations Disaster Reduction Agency and Special
Representative of the Secretary-General for Disaster Risk Reduction, observes,

"Currently, the world is on course for a temperature increase of 3.2 degrees Celsius or more,
unless industrializing nations can deliver reductions in greenhouse gas emissions of at least
7.2 percent annually over the next 10 years in order to achieve the 1.5 degree target agreed
in Paris." (in 2015) (UN, 2020).

As demonstrated in the analyses of KM-I, a direct product of contemporary Global
Economics is that our contemporary Historic Age is now broadly referred to as 'The
Anthropocene", i.e.,: where humankind is now *affecting* and *changing* the earth's
geology and ecosystems.[4]

1.2 Waking up!

IPBES Chair, Sir Robert Watson, reflecting on the UN's (2019) biodiversity survey
results *pleads* that 'transformative change' is urgently required at every level from
local to global, i.e.,: "fundamental system-wide reorganization across technological,
economic and social factors, including paradigms, goals and values" (UN Sustainable
Development Goals, 2019).

As with world endorsement of this alarming UN Report, world attention *is* finally
starting to shift—towards recognition of the clear interaction between the shape of
society and its impact on our physical environment—and the need to do something
about it.

Building a Sustainable World Society for our future now requires central attention within economic action to sustainability rather than immediate profit—a core
objective of the United Nations in its prioritization of "Sustainable Development
Goals" from 2016 to 2030—which specifically link preserving the planet directly
with inclusive and sustainable economic growth and removal of inequality:

"Sustainable development recognizes that eradicating poverty in all its forms and dimensions,
combatting inequality within and among countries, preserving the planet, creating sustained,
inclusive and sustainable economic growth and fostering social inclusion are linked to each
other and are interdependent." (UN, 2016)

Furthermore, the strategic business action principles recently developing within the
sustainability model of "The Circular Economy", in particular within the European Union, demonstrate attention now being paid amongst the responsible business
community to elimination of waste. What is different to previous recycling strategies
is that the Movement is capitalizing on waste in productive action—creating a full
'circle' of production. Ladeja Godina Kosir, our colleague in this book, has cham-
pioned this Movement so I shall leave this discussion for Ladeja, as she moves on
to 'The Circular Triangle'—of Economy, Culture and Change in Chap. 14.[5] Again,
the dimensions are not only physical but also social and cultural.

Additionally, world attention has re-focused on national criteria by which human
welfare is judged, specifically, in the assertion of a "Happiness Index" and "Social

Values Surveys" rather than long-standing economic criteria alone such as Gross National Product (GNP) and Gross Domestic Product (GDP). Inspired by the tiny Himalayan country of Bhutan, the United Nations has, since 2012, published annual surveys of 'happiness' levels across 156 countries of the world.[6] The 'World Happiness Report 2018', produced *before* the COVID-19 Pandemic, was published on 'The International Day of Happiness', 20th March, focusing on six elements: freedom, generosity, healthy life-expectancy, GDP per capita, social support and absence of corruption. (Helliwell et al., 2018).

> Nordic countries, Switzerland and the Netherlands claimed the top ratings. New Zealand was next. Indeed, Jacinda Arden, New Zealand Prime Minister, announced in May 2019 the world's first 'well-being budget' which provides for projects to tackle climate change, digital transformation, social exclusion, poor health, housing and domestic violence (Tamkin, 2019).

> The OECD has also moved its attention away from narrowly constrained economic indicators to a broader field of wellbeing indicators. These include sustainable and social progress, household income, inequalities, economic and subjective well-being, including 'trust' and 'social capital' (Stiglitz et al, 2018). Yann Algan concludes, "People seem to have more satisfying lives when they live in an environment of trust and trustworthiness, and when they are more trusting and trustworthy themselves, *even controlling for income.* (italics mine)" (Algan, 2018, p. 287). Co-author in KM-II, Tadashi Yagi, has demonstrated the same thing from detailed comparative research, that *happiness* is directly related to level of *trust* people can have in others *regardless of income level* (Yagi, 2019; KM-I, 1988, p. 230) - fundamentally a product of their positive social relations with others. Lara Aknin and colleagues add, from their own research, "people seem most likely to derive happiness from 'giving' experiences that provide a sense of free choice, opportunities for social connection, and a chance to see how the help has made a difference" (Aknin et al, 2019).

It is then instructive to follow these same values, 'trust' and 'caring for others' through the impact of the COVID-19 Pandemic through 2020 and beyond 2021. Economically, except for the super-rich as I demonstrated earlier, times were hard. Global GDP is estimated to have shrunk by roughly 5%, the largest economic crisis in a generation. Job vacancies in many countries were approximately 20% below normal levels.

Not surprisingly, unemployment and not being able to work were associated with a 12% decline in life satisfaction and a 9% increase in 'negative affect'. BUT *trust* and *the ability to count on others* came through as major supports to life evaluations—especially in the face of crises such as the rise in mental illness due to loss of social connectedness—even digital, and increase in uncertainty. Trust in governance and institutions was critical—seen particularly in response to and success of government anti-COVID strategies. Most basically, where there was trust and care, there was *resilience* in the face of economic and social hardship.

So, we see indicators that the world is waking up, and realizing that not only is attention to physical sustainability of our planet imperative but that, in parallel, attention needs to be paid to the *human* side of what development means … *happiness* is most essentially dependent on trust and caring for others, not a life measured just by economic yardsticks like GDP. Indeed, when the Happiness Index explored what were called "Well-Being Adjusted Life Years" or "WELLBY", the community valued a year of additional life as equal to \$750,000. (Helliwell et al., 2021).

These are good starting points. They represent a change in 'world view' about what matters for the people, not just in individual economic or social policies.

Action for change just at this policy-instrument level alone however is not enough—rather like re-arranging the deck chairs as the 'Titanic' creation of our global economy sails through dangerous waters. Whilst self-interest still remains at the core of economic relations, the 'system' is very likely to find a way of absorbing and marginalizing serious interventions, so they remain side-plays to continuing destruction of our planet and our human survivability. Meanwhile those who are already wealthy will get richer and the world will continue to descend into increasing division and inequality. Instead, we must attack the source of contemporary inequality, social fragmentation and impact on planetary processes at the core *…by asserting our humanity!*

We proposed starting points for transformation in KM-1.

First, I quote our basic message about our humanity.

> "What is sacred or of imperishable supreme value is *what we can be* as a human race – *empowered*, fulfilled individuals, in harmony, deeply *sharing and caring* for each other across our separate cultural and life worlds – understanding the fundamental *depth and equality of our shared lives.*" (KM-1, p. 6)

Second, following is our KM-I view about making change happen now.

> "The solution lies, not in theory but in return to the strength that resides in our humanity and its universal quest beyond the everyday world—though expressed in many forms and doctrines - to our ultimate source of meaning, commitment and strength—our collective spirituality." (KM-I, p. 4)

Now, in the present Book we move on to explore this transformation further, first by clarifying what it is we *can't* yet see clearly, and then by identifying how we can go about bringing what is hidden and controlling into the light.

1.3 Power of the Grammar of Life—The Silent Puppet Master of Culture

To place the challenge of fundamental change in values into the metaphor of language or song, we are not just changing the words, or the individual notes, but penetrating more deeply into the underlying 'grammar' or 'arrangement', the assumed *framework* of meaning within which thinking and action is cast. We tend not to think about it, but act within, for this is our *culture,* or "The way we do things around here."

> The 'grammar' of current global economics is a *frame,* predicated on *self-interest* and the *power of the 'deal'* to achieve it, where, "price", for example, equals "value".
>
> Counter to this, the 'grammar' of a humanity-focused system of productive exchange relations is one of *sharing, care,* and the *power of the 'gift,* where *"value" equals "mutual human benefit"*, and *"mutual trust" is the "norm"*.

1.3.1 The Silence of Repression

I observed in my Presentation to our Kyoto-5 Symposium in 2018,[7] "Listening to Humanity Beyond Economic Life", that the current global economic 'frame' remains silent about our humanity as this is lost in the noise of self-interest and inequality. This loss may be seen as a *silence of repression*. We may not even notice this oppression as it is part of our 'taken-for-granted' world order, the grammar behind daily life.

At the time I am writing, I am confronted by two terrible reminders of total *self-interest* from the leading economy of the world through its leader for the last few years up to this year, 2021, Ex-President Donald Trump. In both cases the consequences for the rest of the world are potentially catastrophic.

(1) Ex-President Donald Trump announced to the Annual Convention of the US National Rifle Association (NRA) on Friday 26th April 2019 that he was withdrawing the United States from the United Nations Arms Trade Treaty, the "ATT", signed by the US under President Obama in 2013 (though not formally 'ratified' due mainly to NRA opposition). This Treaty regulates the multibillion dollar global arms trade. With the US included at the time along with near 100 other countries, ATT was brought into effect in late 2014, regulating conventional weapons including small arms, battle tanks, combat aircraft and warships.

> Donald Trump's action has to undermine international efforts to reduce human suffering caused by irresponsible and illegal arms trade.
>
> Welcomed with standing applause by the National Rifle Association audience, President Trump *signed his withdrawal letter to Congress in front of the crowd* stating,
>
> > "Under my administration, we will never surrender American Sovereignty to anyone." (Smith, 2019).
>
> He then threw his signature pen into the audience in a show of dramatic theatre.
>
> An applauded demonstration of arrogant self-interest for the sake of global economic advantage, the result of this act is potentially enormous suffering of humanity as a whole. This is the silence of repression which lies within the 'grammar' of current global economics.

(2) On Wednesday 4th November 2020, the United States officially withdrew from the group of 195 nations which signed (and 189 which formally adopted) the pledge to address climate change. Ex-President Trump had announced US withdrawal three years earlier, claiming the World Agreement was "job-killing" and would "punish the American people while enriching foreign polluters" (Friedman, 2020). Earlier, Donald Trump withdrew United States membership and funds from the World Health Organization as well – leaving the organization critically short of funds to support low income countries just as the COVID-19 Pandemic was taking off.

> On his first day in Office on 20th January 2021, incoming President Joe Biden re-signed the Paris Climate Change Agreement (in place by March 2021), and rejoined

WHO (Kirby, 2021). Damage was already done to the United States leadership credibility because it showed that major world leadership policy could, as Stewart M. Patrick of the U.S Council on Foreign Relations observed, "turn on a dime when administrations change" (Maizland, 2021).

Donald Trump's withdrawal from shared responsibility for the planet for the sake of national selfishness demonstrates not only foolish diplomacy but more deeply, and in keeping with the theme of the current Chapter, that those with the highest benefit from economic wealth are likely also to have the highest level of self-interest to preserve it rather than *share* with our wider humanity even when the consequence is danger to the planet we *all* depend on. This lesson is demonstrated no more clearly and poignantly than in the unprecedented temperatures across Western United States and South Western Canada (up to 50 degrees Celsius in South West Canada, and an astonishing 54.4 degrees Celsius in Death Valley, California) and subsequent uncontrollable bushfires *right now* at the time of writing, June to July, 2021. Hundreds of sudden deaths were recorded, many of them suspected of being heat-related. Climate researchers concluded that this level of heat was "virtually impossible without climate change" (BBC 2021b).

Again, this is the silence of repression which lies within the 'grammar' of self-interest of current global economics. And, as demonstrated in the 2020 Presidential Election, nearly *half* of all American voters support this self-interest and silence.

1.3.2 The Silence that Hides

Most insidious about the 'grammar' of global economics is that it remains *silent* as we *live it*. This 'grammar' sets the goals for our own lives and those of our children—in our daily actions, and in what we are likely to pay attention to and aspire to. The continuing cacophony of globalization structures what seems possible.

For example, as I have pointed out earlier, we *live* a 'grammar' of daily life that we have inherited from an urban design which prioritizes motor cars, privacy, and signals of self-prestige, so local inter-subjective community is largely a phenomenon of the past. Noise, which confronts us continuously in ever-present advertising and television images increasingly now targets *you* specifically as an individual, thus isolating you further from real community. Through the ubiquitous power of social media, the knowledge by which we live and act is increasingly based on the acquired noise in our heads and consciousness. Whilst social media's underlying 'grammar' remains silently in the background but increasingly embeds our subjective world, we cannot hear the *wholeness* of the other.

Do remember what I showed earlier. Social media now dominates even the grammar of economic life so is destined to become ever more powerful, persuasive and intrusive—for the sake of profit for the wealthy.

We do not notice. What is lost is in the silence to interrogation of this, the new normal.

And our wider humanity is impoverished,

1.3.2.1 Confronting and Working with the Hidden Grammar of Culture

I have used the term, 'grammar' to highlight that behind our daily actions and beliefs there is an underlying 'framework' or 'narrative' of the world around us which sets the patterns of daily action and inter-action. I have pointed to the emerging surrogate communication which has now captured the world—social media. The final element in our human relationship to these forces is *meaning*.

At a deeper level we are talking not just about a capital-inspired framework for our individual values and actions, but about our 'culture'—for this is the organising *meaning system* of our lives and those around us, product of our social relations from birth onwards. 'Culture' adds the potential depth of our very *being* to the 'grammar' or 'frameworks' for specific beliefs and actions.

As anthropologist Clifford Gertz points out about culture:

> "The drive to make sense out of experience, to give it form and order, is evidently as real as the more familiar biological needs: the organism cannot live in a world it is unable to understand." (Gertz, 1968, p. 314)[8]

Our human structures of meaning are deeply buried in the progressively sedimented layers of consciousness that are formed during our early socialization, and within our immediate subjectively mediated world of experience.[9] Worlds and Symbols beyond our subjective life remain unpacked, but somehow made sense of within our 'world within reach'. Culture is our underlying 'grammar' for life expression …. NOW, surrounding and nurturing us. As its simplest definition, culture is 'the way we do things around here'. Meanings that are not opened up, just *lived*. We only really notice it when we confront a very different cultural world to which we must respond.

> A fish, swimming in the ocean, has no idea of what water is and how important it is to its life, until it suddenly finds itself stranded on dry land as the tide goes out. The ocean is its whole world, not needing to be questioned or responded to (Hill, 1988, p. 90).

"This 'design for living', as Clyde Kluckhohn calls it, is fashioned collectively. It is constituted 'organically' over time, and passed on to new generations according to what has been proven to 'work'. A culture's 'design for living' is fashioned out of peoples' need to orient their own individual actions—at every moment of conscious-ness – in terms of both the social world they inhabit, and the meanings this social world attributes to action that allows the collectivity, and the individual, to survive." (Kluckhohn, 1951; Hill, 1988, p. 91).

But as the phenomenologists tell us, we construct meaning through *action within our 'world within reach'*,[10] in subjective relations with others, in socially producing together, in direct sharing …. in our *local* world. *Our culture is not produced elsewhere.*

Here lies the enormously dangerous force of social media overload and fragmen-tation under the rule of global economics.

> These forces appear as *'replacement' for the subjective 'world within reach'* where culture and meaning is constituted. But they present a ghost. A shadow of human meaning construc-tion – leaving our society increasingly weak in our understanding and assertion of meaning

and knowledge … a fundamental flaw in what our society is becoming and our ability to *act* to assert a sustainable and humanity-focused future.

Furthermore, what is presented to our consciousness from the world outside our direct subjective learning has the form of an *'ideal type'*, i.e.,: *received 'passively'*, its meaning remaining unpacked.

> It (the ideal type) therefore has the power to 'command', rather than foster responsive communication. We must fit this 'ideal type' into our own way of understanding, but cannot open it to see what its underlying meanings are and were at source. These external symbols simply become fitted in, invisibly, and as 'command', into the development of the person's understanding of meaning and their own culture, into their socialization 'grammar' which forms the meaning framework for living our adult life–like a cyst or even a tumor, not noticed or seemingly irrelevant within our living social body, the impact of which grows unseen (Hill, 2018, p. 302).[11]

There is a significant consequence in increasing our dependency on the status quo of the Global Economic World enframing us. Thomas Luckman and Peter Berger observe that when experience of the world is largely *outside* direct inter-subjective mirroring, the person must depend increasingly on more concrete objectivations—in which ideal–typical constructions of received cultural meanings are housed—objects like cars, houses, consumer appliances—therefore *locate* the person, their meaning system and status both to others and oneself within the sea of anonymity they confront (Luckman & Berger, 1971, p. 103; Hill, 1988, p. 96). In the age since Berger and Luckman wrote—in the 1970s—these physical objectifications are increasingly played out in social media 'objectifications' of our apparent worth—*number* of 'likes' for our social media expressed opinion, *number* of 'friends' we can point to on Facebook, and emojis which *appear* to represent a cut-down expression of love, but, in reality are about 'having', not 'giving, in other words, the very opposite of love.

Thus, we are deeply buried in the culture of global economics, but with meanings constituted elsewhere and 'fed' to us, rather than created within our intersubjective world, they form a kind of fence around our understandings. One which we must break through. The culture of meanings we can access and *live* as our own is forged within our inter-subjective relations, not in preening ourselves in the rear view mirror of our new car or computer screen. Wider social empowerment starts in the same place, within our 'local' world. For it is here that *humanity's* strength resides.

> "Power to *do* only exists in power *to define*."
> (Hill, 1988, p. 104)

Escape to a meaningful, indeed viable, future, requires us to reach into the depths of our subjectivity which appear silent, to confront and deal with the basic *grammar* of *our* world, not just take protest action against individual expressions of the outer consequences of this deeper greed-focused divisive culture.

It is here that we reach towards grasping, and embracing "The Circle of Wholeness", the subject of Chap. 2.

End Notes

1. I introduced this 'rule of the self' in KM-I (2018), eg: pp. 312–313. For analysis of the conditions which gave rise to consumer society around the start of the 20th Century, see Stephen Hill (1988) (1989).

2. See "#numbers", Twitter Official Blog, March 14, 2011. Current tweet estimates are delivered by Worldometers' RTS algorithm, which processes data elaborated through statistical analysis after being collected from a range of sources (Worldometers 2020).

3. See particularly, Stephen Hill, 'The Survivability of Humanity Within the Current Global Economic Paradigm', Chap. 2, pp. 13–34; and, Ryuichi Fukuhara, 'Human and Nature Revisited: the Industrial Revolution, Modern Economics and the Anthropocene", Chap. 3, p. 35, (KM-I, 2018).

4. The concept of 'The Anthropocene', though conceived and discussed for some time, was presented formally to the scientific community at the International Geological Congress in South Africa on 29th August 2016. Though not formally ratified at the time, the idea now enjoys broad acceptance both within scientific communities and broader society. See Carrington (2016).

5. Ladeja Kosir presented these concepts at Doshisha University, Kyoto, on 25th October 2018 at a Doshisha University Seminar supporting preparation of this current book, 'The Circular Triangle: Circular Economy, Circular Culture, Circular Change–Society as a Driving Force of Change'.

6. The United Nations General Assembly stimulated the new perspective on welfare to take off in Resolution 65/309, July 2011, 'Happiness: Towards a Holistic Definition of Development', which called on Member States to measure happiness and include it into public policy. This initiative was then followed by the first UN High Level Meeting, 'Wellbeing and Happiness: Defining a New Economic Paradigm', chaired by the United Nations Secretary General, Ban Ki-moon, and Prime Minister of Bhutan, Jigme Thinley. See, UN General Assembly (2011), and UN High Level Meeting (2012).

7. The current two Kyoto Manifesto books have been presaged by a series of International Symposia hosted by Doshisha University in Kyoto where we explored the ideas and trawled the world for the most appropriate authors. These Symposia began in 2014, and we refer to them as "Kyoto-1" (2014), "Kyoto-2" (2015) … to Kyoto-6 (2019).

8. I had the privilege to meet and share a speaking platform with Clifford Geertz in Jogjakarta, Indonesia, when we were both speaking about the importance of cultural heritage. He was the master–of understanding Indonesia's range of traditional cultures. One of his previous papers on tribal rituals became the tribal community's 'manual' when their previous rituals had been forgotten. They used Geertz's publication to reconstitute their traditional ceremonies.

9. See Hill (1979, 1995), focusing on primary and secondary socialization in the formation of personal identify as a scientist. The theory of this work was based on a prior major empirical study of 1,300 Australian scientists conducted under

commission from the Australian Academy of Science. See Hill et al. (1974a, b).

10. I personally had the chance to share in research and the exploration of phenomenological views of the self and the socialization of consciousness with Thomas Luckman, both in Wollongong where he spent a 6 month visit in my Sociology Department in 1977, then in Constanz, Germany in 1979, where I worked with him on my own sabbatical leave, including living with him in his apartment just over the border in Switzerland. I had the privilege of walking across the border between Switzerland and Germany each morning, debating ideas about phenomenology. Needless to say, I learnt a great deal. See Schutz and Luckman (1974); Hill (1979, 1988, pp. 92–97, 1995).

11. As Alfred Schutz comments, "the anonymity of a typification is inversely proportional to its fullness of content … the fullness of content of the individualized social type conforms to the relative immediacy of the experiences from which it is constituted" (Schutz and Luckman, 1974, pp 80–1). See also Luckman (1977), p. 10, and for development of the idea, Stephen Hill (1988), pp. 95–96.

References

#numbers. (2011). Twitter Official Blog, 14 March: https://blog.twitter.com › en_us › 2011 › numbers

Aknin, L. B., Whillams, A. V., Norton, M. I., & Dunn, E. D. (2019). *Happiness and prosocial behavior: an evaluation of the evidence*, Chapter 4 in Helliwell et al. (2018).

Algan, Y. (2018). *Trust and social capital*, Chapter 6, in Stiglitz et al (p. 287) (2018).

Alvaredo, F., Chanel, L., Piketty, T., Saez, E., & Zucman, G. (2017). *World Inequality Report*. UN-DESA Meeting, 12 September, World Inequality Lab. Working Paper 23119. http://www.nber.org/papers/w23119

BBC News. (2021a). Twitter 'permanently suspends' Trump's account, 09 January: https://www.bbc.com › world-us-canada-55597840

BBC News. (2021b). US heatwave: Wildfires rage in western states as temperatures soar, 12 July: https://www.bbc.com › world-us-canada-57794263

Bencherki, N., & Basque, J. (2018). Why so many Americans continue to believe in Donald Trump, *Conversation*, 07 August: https://theconversation.com › why-so-many-americans-...

Cameron, D. (2021). Richard Branson's Virgin Galactica spaceflight: What you need to know. *The Wall Street Journal*, 11 July: https://www.wsj.com›articles›richard-bransons-virgin.

Carney, M. (2020a). How we get what we value, lecture 1, From moral to market sentiments, *Reith Lectures 2020*, TX: 02.12.2020 at 9am, BBC Radio 4, 15.24 minutes: https://www.bbc.co.uk › ...

Carney, M. (2020b). How we get what we value, lecture 2, From credit crisis to resilience, *Reith Lectures 2020*, TX: 09.12.2020 at 9am, BBC Radio 4, p2: https://www.bbc.co.uk › ... › Features

Carrington, D. (2016). The Anthropocene epoch: Scientists declare dawn of human influenced age. *The Guardian*, 29 August: https://www.theguardian.com › 2016 › aug › 29 › decl...

Closed End Fund Tracker. (2021). S&P 500 Concentration Risk Could Define 2021, *Seeking Apple*, 02 January: https://seekingapple.com›article›4396955-and-p-500.

Dolan, K. A. (2018). Forbes 400 2018: A new number one and a record breaking year for America's Richest people, *Forbes*, 03 September. https://www.forbes.com/sites/kerryadolan/2018/10/03.

Dolan, K. A., Peterson-Withorn, C., & Wang, J., (Eds) (2020). *The definitive ranking of the Wealthiest Americans in 2020 – The Forbes 400*. https://www.forbes.com-forbes-400

Fichtner, J., Heemskerk, E., & Garcia-Bernardo, J. (2019). BlackRock, Vanguard and State Street Own Corporate America, *Ponderwall,* 29 September: https://ponderwall.com › index.php › 2019/09/29 › van...

Fisher, W. R. (1984). Narration as a human communication paradigm: the case of public moral argument. *Communications Monographs, 51* (1): https://www.tandfonline.com › ... › Volume 51, Issue 1

Friedman, L. (2020). U.S. Quits Paris climate agreement: questions and answers, *New York Times,* 04 November: https://www.nytimes.com › 2020/11/04 › paris-climate-ag...

Fromm, E. (1962). *The art of loving.* Unwin Books.

Geertz, C. (1968). Ethos, World view and the analysis of sacred symbol. In A. Dantes (Ed), *Every man his way.* Prentice Hall.

Gneiting, U., Lusiani, N., & Tamir, I. (2020). Power, profits and the pandemic: From corporate extraction for the few to an economy that works for all, *Oxfam Briefing Paper,* September: https://www.oxfam.org › research › power-profits-and-...

Helliwell, J., Layard, R., Sachs, J., & De Neve, E. (Eds.) (2021). UN World Happiness Report 2021. New York: UN Sustainable Development Solutions Network: https://worldhappiness.report>2021.

Hill, S. (1988–1989). *The tragedy of technology – Human liberation versus domination in the late twentieth century.* Pluto Press.

Hill, S., Fensham, P., & Howden, I. (1974a). *The making of professional scientists.* Australian Academy of Science, Monograph No. 7.

Hill, S., Fensham, P., & Howden, I. (1974b). *The future education of scientists.* Australian Academy of Science, Monograph No. 8.

Hill, S. (1979). In search of self: the social construction of meaning in scientific knowledge through the formation of identity as scientist. In Pusey, M. R. & Young, R. E. (Eds.), *Control and knowledge: The mediation of power in institutional and educational settings* (pp. 124–182). ANU Press.

Hill, S. (1995). The formation of identity as scientist. *Science Studies, 8* (1), 53–72—Republished and updated from original 1979 article by invitation and with review editorial by John Ziman.

Hill, S. (2018). *Sacred silence—The stillness of listening to humanity',* Chapter 17 in KM-1: Yamash'ta, Yagi & Hill (Eds).

Hill, S. (2020). Living for life, *Podcast,* Nan Tien Humanistic Buddhism Centre, Soundcloud Series, 28 June: soundcloud.com>nti-hbc.

Helliwell, J., Layard, R., & Sachs, J. (Eds). (2018). UN World Happiness Report 2018. UN Sustainable Development Solutions Network: https://worldhappiness.report>2018.

Khavin, A., Willis, H., Hill, E., Reneau, N., Jordan, D., Engelbrecht, C., Triebert, C., Cooper, S., Browne, M., & Botti, D. (2021). Day of rage: An in-depth look at how a mob stormed the capitol, *The New York Times,* July 1: https://www.nytimes.com › us-capitol-riots-investigations

Kirby, J. (2021). President Biden's international restoration project has begun. *Vox,* 20 January: https://www.vox.com

Kluckhohn, C. (1951). The concept of culture. In Lerner, D. & Lasswell, H. D. (Eds), *The policy sciences.* Stanford University Press.

KM-I. (2018). Yamash'ta, S., Yagi, T., & Hill, S. (Eds), *The Kyoto manifesto for global economics – the platform of community, humanity and spirituality.* Springer.

Luckmann, T. (1977). Personal identity as an evolutionary and historical problem', Constanz, Germany, August 1977 (mimeo) (p. 10) (quoted in Hill, 1988 (p. 104).

Luckman, T., & Berger, P. (1971). Social mobility and personal identity. *Humanitas, 7*(1), 103.

Mackay, H. (2007). *Advance Australia … where?* Australia: Hachett (used in radio interviews when promoting the Advance Australia book: personal communication.)

Mackay, H. (2018). *Australia reimagined – towards a more compassionate, less anxious society* (p. 117). Macmillan.

Maizland, L. (2021). Biden's first foreign policy move: re-entering international agreements, Council on Foreign Relations, January 21: https://www.cfr.org>in-brief>bidens-first-foreign-policy.

Memire, S. T., Nigus, M., & Verguet, S. (2021). Cost-effectiveness and equitable access to vaccines in Ethiopia: an overview and evidence synthesis of the published literature. *Journal of Global Health Reports, 5,* https://doi.org/10.29392/001c.19354

O'Neil, L. (2019). Lies, damned lies and Donald Trump: the pick of the President's untruths, *The Guardian,* Tuesday 30 April: https://www.theguardian.com › us-news › 2019 › apr

Oxfam International. (2017). An economy for the 99 percent, (16 January). https://www.oxfam.org/en/research/economy-99/. See also Oxfam International Press Release, January, 2017. Just 8 men own same wealth as half the world. https://www.oxfamorg/en/pressroom/pressrelease/2017-01-16/just-8-men-own-s

Oxfam International (2021). The inequality virus, 25th January: https://www.oxfam.org>research>inequaliry-virus.

Paumgarten, N. (2020). The price of the coronavirus pandemic, *The New Yorker,* 'The Coronavirus Crisis', 20 April: https://www.newyorker.com › Magazine › Economy

Perrett, C. (2020). Trump broke his all-time tweeting record amid nationwide protests, sending more tweets in a single day than he did during his impeachment trial', *INSIDER, 07* June, 1.24am: *Factbase: https://www.insider.com › Politics › News*

Reimann, N. (2021). Leaving a planet in crisis: Here's why many say the billionaires space race is a terrible idea, *Forbes,* 12 July: https://www.forbes.com › nicholasreimann › 2021/07/12

Schutz, A., Luckmann, T. (Trans. Zaner., R. M. & Engelhardt (Jr) T. H. (1974). *The structures of the life-world.* Heinemann.

Smith, A. (1999). Wealth of nations: (Originally published, 1776), Penguin Books (Book 4, Chapter 2, para 9 in original).

Smith, A. (2018). *"Theory of moral sentiments" (Originally published, 1759).* Eastford.

Smith, D. (2019). Trump withdraws from UN arms treaty as NRA crowd cheers in delight, *The Guardian,* Saturday 27 April: https://www.theguardian.com › us-news › 2019 › apr

Stiglitz, J. E., Fitoussi, J.-P., & Durand, M. (Eds.). (2018). *For good measure – advancing research on well-being metrics beyond GDP.* OECD Publishing.

Tamkin, E. (2019). New Zealand is one of the world's happiest countries. That also makes it resilient. *The Washington Post,* 21 March: https://www.washingtonpost.com › world › 2019/03/20

Telford, T. (2019). Income inequality in America is the highest it's been since Census Bureau started tracking it, data shows, *Washington Post, 27 September: https://www.washingtonpost. com › business › 2019/09/26*

UN General Assembly. (2011). Happiness: Towards a holistic definition of development, Resolution 65/309, New York: https://digitallibrary.un.org › record

UN High Level Meeting. (2012). Welbeing and happiness: defining a new economic paradigm. In *Sustainable development knowledge platform,* Bhutan: http://dev.magerodesign.com › asialeds › resource › defin...

UN. (2016). Transforming our world: The 2030 Agenda for Sustainable Development" (A/RES/70/1, para 13: https://www.un.org › desa › docs › A_RES_70_1_E PDF

UN. (2019). Sustainable Development Goals. UN Report: Nature's Dangerous Decline 'Unprecedented'; Special Extinction Rates 'Accelerating', Intergovernmental Science, Policy Platform on Biodiversity and Ecosystem Services (IPBES)", 7th Series Plenary, 29th April to 4th May: Announcement, Paris: 06 May: https://www.un.org › blog › 2019/05 › nature-decline-un...

UN. (2020). "Staggering" rise in climate emergencies in last 20 years, new disaster research shows. *UN News,* Climate Change, 12 October:/en/news/topic/climate-change: https://news.un.org › story › 2020/10

Whitney, M. (2020). 40 Twitter statistics marketers need to know in 2020, *The Wordstream Blog,* 14 April: wordstream.com: https://www.wordstream.com › Blog

WHO. (2016). Suicide Data-World Health Organization, Geneva: World Health Organization: https://www.who.int/mental_health/prevention/suicide/suicideprevent/en

WHO. (2021). Suicide Worldwide in 2019–Global Health Estimates, Geneva: World Health Organization, 16 June: https://www.who.int>data>global-health-estimates.

World Population Review. (2021). 07 February: https://worldpopulationreview.com>country-rankings.

Worldometers. (2020). Internet live stats-trends and more: www.worldometers.info-sms>ss=twitter.

Yagi, T. (2017). Moral, trust and happiness–Why does trust improve happiness?, *Journal of Organizational Psychology*, 17.

Zarrella, T. (2009). 5 steps to going viral on Twitter, 27th January: https://www.copyblogger.com/go-viral-on-twitter/

Chapter 2
Embracing the Circle of Wholeness

Stephen Hill

Abstract Counter to the destructive *'self'*-based impact on our humanity and thence our planet demonstrated in Chap. 1, this Chapter introduces the power of our *Humanity* as a force of transformation—demonstrating the full existential power as social human persons that lies in what is described as "The Circle of Wholeness." The dynamic of this Circle is formed from full sharing and care for others, along with guidance from *trans-disciplinary* understanding of the interacting *domains* of objective, subjective and cultural knowledge of the *whole person*, connecting, as in a circle, into overall *harmony*. Caring and knowledge are held into relationship by the Circle's central human focal point, *integrity* and *trust*.

The Chapter demonstrates *how* we can embrace the wholeness of this Circle in daily life and create change—from within shared *community*—where meaning and human connection are formed. Whilst the 'tyranny' of unexamined economic and compliant government life may, in general, enclose us as if in a thick blanket of blinded acquiescence, a tiny 'fault' in the whole can break open the system and lead to radical transformation—based in Humanity's underlying power within 'The Circle of Wholeness'.

2.1 Entry Points

The 'Circle of Wholeness' represents the full power of our existential being as social human persons—inclusivity of our full sharing and care for others, of guidance from the many domains of human knowledge connecting in overall harmony, with caring and knowledge held into relationship by the 'circle's' central point, integrity and trust.

S. Hill (✉)
Faculty of Arts, Social Sciences and Humanities, University of Wollongong, Northfields Ave, Wollongong, NSW 2522, Australia
e-mail: sthill@uow.edu.au

© Springer Nature Singapore Pte Ltd. 2022
S. Hill et al. (eds.), *The Kyoto Post-COVID Manifesto For Global Economics*, Creative Economy, https://doi.org/10.1007/978-981-16-8566-8_2

To 'embrace and assert' the Circle of Wholeness for a Harmonious Humanity-based World Order therefore requires us to do three things.

First, we must *listen* to the silence otherwise occluded by the noise of the self in economic globalization.

Second, we need then to drill down to the most basic values of our humanity – mutual care, mindfulness, compassion, and, truth.

Third, having found these values, we must act within their rule in *every action*, starting *in my street*, that is, 'my immediate inter-subjective community or organization – with a clear litmus test', i.e.: "does my action strengthen or weaken my own and wider 'community' and values of sharing and mutual care?"

Embracing the Circle of Wholeness also requires paying new attention to the knowledge base we live by – which needs to be one of truth across all worlds – subjective, objective, cultural, spiritual ... across all Domains of Knowledge surrounding and guiding our life actions. Here, the music-based metaphor of 'polyphony' provides cohesion – drawing the different Domain 'themes' into a 'harmonic whole'.

At the center of the Circle is our humanity's truth - action, not for a deal but as a gift anchored in honesty and integrity – the basis of trust.

Only in this way can we release ourselves from the 'grammar' of daily life and exploitation of others which is endemic in the current system of global economic command. This 'grammar', set deeply within the self-centered economic relations *frame* for our social world, surrounds us without our knowing because its reach is so complete—like a fish in water which does not know what air is, until suddenly stranded on the shore, i.e.,: for us, unexpectedly confronting a world which was always there but not noticed. We tend to not penetrate beneath our 'world within reach' to see the 'self-interest' assumptions of economic relations which hold our current social world in place.

However, as with the dialectic process, the contradiction, or antithesis to what feels like our whole (self-interest generated) world lies within the world itself—within its 'thesis'. Greed and self-interest do indeed produce enormous benefits for the few but at the same time, poverty and/or tyranny for many, along with the potential to destroy the very planet on which we all must depend. Eventually this *cyst of oppression* must burst as the disadvantaged start to claim equity for themselves, and as those within the clutches of the self-interest world start to wake up to the dangers of their unrecognized complicity and begin to take restorative action.

Within the context of deeply entrenched oppressive practice by economic interests or the State, the 'antithesis, or, its expression in a 'cyst of oppression' can be burst even by an individual or specific event …….. if the time is right. And the implications can spread much more widely back into changing the basic tyranny of the overall system itself.

First an example of basic change in environmental awareness and legislation:

Rachel Carson's book, 'Silent Spring', a damning indictment of DDT, published in 1962, originated from a visit by Carson to her friend, Olga Huckins' private conservation sanctuary where she confronted the massive poisoning potential of DDT, at that time the most publicized synthetic chemical in the world. Carson was so disturbed she went exploring and discovered the ubiquitous and incredibly toxic impact of DDT and related pesticides even at a distance through groundwater and species transfers. The result of her research and publication, against enormous opposition of the chemical industry, brought the issue of pesticides center stage and into public consciousness. From there, her insight underscored the subsequent nationwide ban on DDT for agricultural use and development of the US Government Environment Protection Agency, and the far reaching wider global ecological movement from the late 1960s onwards. Her opening quote from Albert Schweizer was timeless,

> "Man has lost the capacity to foresee and forestall. He will end by destroying the earth."[1]

Second, an example of basic social change against repression:

On 25th May 2020, unarmed 46 year old African American, George Floyd, was killed by Police Officer Derek Chauvin kneeling on his neck in a choke hold for eight minutes and 46 seconds, even against Floyd's cries that he could not breathe, and pleas from the surrounding crowd. Chauvin's two police colleagues were sitting on Floyd's legs and body pinning him to the ground. And they stayed there. Floyd had been arrested after a Convenience Store employee phoned 911 to report Floyd had bought cigarettes with a counterfeit $20 note.

The murder was videoed and went viral on social media. The incident stimulated what may have been the 'Largest Movement' in US history across the United States and extended around the World – "The Black Lives Matter" Movement (Buchanan et al, 2020). In the United States alone protest numbers were estimated at between 15 and 26 million people. Between 22nd May and 22nd August 2020, there were 10,600 Black Lives Matter Protest Events in the U.S (Ross, 2015; ACLED, 2020).

The Black Lives Matter Movement, a localized, community and social media based movement had actually been born 17 months earlier when Alicia Garza and two other black women, Patrise Cullors and Opal Tometi, reacted to a very similar event, the shooting death of young African American Trayvon Martin, in particular, as was usually the case, the police officer involved, George Zimmerman, was fully acquitted (Day, 2015). Already, the 'cyst' of oppression was deeply planted within American law enforcement. In 2014 to 2015, for example, African American men were three to four times more likely to be killed by police than White Men, and one third of these African Americans had no weapon whatsoever. Invariably the responsible police officers escaped without punishment (Ross, 2015)

Film of the George Floyd event went viral on social media and 'its time was right' for the cyst of oppression to burst. Police budgets which had largely gone untouched for decades before – while education, youth, housing, and public amenities budgets had been invariably cut, were suddenly exposed. Immediately, the US Congressional House Committee on the Judiciary introduced the 'Justice in Policing Act of 2020 (Congress, 2020). During the second half of 2020 local policy makers in Philadelphia, Baltimore, Washington DC, San Francisco and other American cities supported moves to defund police, and Council Members in Minneapolis – where Floyd had been killed, were talking about disbanding the embattled Police Department entirely. In some cases, proposed 'defunding' actions were merely sleight of hand to appear to be defunding but in fact moving more civil-related departments to other agencies. However, the general move was instead towards funding violence preventative community initiatives guided by social workers, counsellors, and the communities themselves (Levin, 2020)

---

[1] See Carson (1962), 'The Silent Spring', Houghton Mifflin–reprinted as Crest Book Reprint, Fawcett Publications, Greenwich, Connecticut: library–united diversity.coop: rachel carson–United Diversity Library. Also, Cristobal S. Berry-Caban (2011), 'DDT and Silent Spring: Fifty years after', JMVH Review Article, 19 (4).

In both these examples, the 'tyranny' of the 'system' was well in place for at least decades, but allowed to continue. Change happened through individuals who 'seized the moment' to expose and work against the repression ... capturing the first green shoots of a developing wider consciousness. The result in both cases was a significant assertion of the inner 'antithesis' of the established system, quietly bubbling away until that moment.

In other words, the self-interest based assumptions and tyranny of economic and complicit government life may indeed completely enclose us as if in a thick blanket of perhaps unintended complicity. But this system cannot be perfectly obscure and what may seem a 'tiny fault' in the whole *can* lead to radical transformation.

Leonard Cohen therefore offers a useful lesson in his song "Anthem" from his 1992 Album, "The Future":

> "Ring the bells that still can ring
>
> Forget your perfect offering
>
> There is a crack, a crack in everything
>
> That's how the light gets in."

We come back to the basic thesis of this book, "The Kyoto Post-COVID Manifesto for Global Economics" (KM-PC). The entry point for *spreading* the Circle of Wholeness as a *new grammar* of our wider future society is standing right in front of us—in the 'crack' within global economics which, though ideologically papered over as thickly as possible to pretend otherwise—exposes the inequity, the fragmentation, the fundamental self-centeredness of what serves as our global social order! This 'crack' exposes a life-threatening precipice just beneath—including, and most dramatically, in the very real danger that we could destroy the very planet on which we all depend. We need to learn to *see* the 'crack' or key weak points in the 'system' and start by exposing them and gathering those around us to 'look inside'.

Our quest is then to build what I call 'global localism',[2] capturing the power of the local where meaning is constituted, our immediate and subjective relationships and culture, and exploding our connectedness at this human level across the global human world. This was what worked in the two Case Examples I presented earlier, with the second case—of George Floyd's murder, then exploding across social media, a means of connecting socially that did not exist at the time of Rachel Carson.

---

[2] Originally, I used the phrase 'New Localism' to describe the dynamic we had observed from a comprehensive research program we conducted across all areas of science and its organization from within the national Australian Research Centre of Excellence, the Centre for Research Policy, at the University of Wollongong which I founded and directed in the early 1990s. A particular focus was on contemporary scientific knowledge construction and communication. See Hill and Turpin (1994, 1995). The parallel idea of 'global localism' as a basic concept for social change is developed in Hill (2010, pp. 272–278). It was based in particular on a subsequent decade of UNESCO programs we ran through the UNESCO Office, Jakarta: experience is reported in UNESCO Annual Reports of the Jakarta Office, 1995 to 2005. I spoke about the global localism dynamic with Sacred Bridge, in Jakarta in 2012. See Stephen Hill, 'Harnessing the Power of Culture for Sustainable Development and Community Empowerment', Address to Sacred Bridge, Jakarta, 03 March, 2012 (available from the author).

Action therefore 'starts in our street', or in our own local community or organisation, but we then build this intersubjective power into an increasingly wide force for change by networking and learning from each other.

Meanwhile, ALL action in this change agenda is guided by basic humanistic values ... ALL action whether it be in strengthening a community which cares, or developing new 'mindful' business, or targeting politically-mediated change for business, community strengthening and daily life.

This is expression of the Circle of Wholeness ... consciously building *culture and meaning,* and targeting holistic community-centred action ... *HARMONY RATHER THAN COMPETITION.*

I will explore what we need to include in our quest for change in terms of mental and social skills as well as the structure of the knowledge we must end up with.

2.1.1 Creativity and the Circle of Wholeness

What we are planning as a Harmonious Humanity-based World Order rather than Global Economics-based Order requires *creativity* at every step—looking at things from side-field or from a totally different perspective—breaking out of the established pattern, *giving the world something it did not know it missed.* In the present case, 'seeing' what we take for granted through the eyes of humanistic values.

Promotion of creativity needs to be built *into* our Circle of Wholeness design as we need to work out mechanisms and processes to make the transition from a self-interest based economy thence society to one which is human centred. We then need to grow new conceptual and organizational tools for a quite different world.

2.1.2 Time to Think and Redefine the Question

Most essentially this 'creativity perspective' probably means designing for non-design, for approaching problems from completely unexpected perspectives, and ... 'free time', even 'dream time' where the mind is free to wander. The 'classic example' in science innovation is the story of how August Kekule, German Chemist, claimed in his book in 1865 then at an 1890s conference on 'Benzene' that he had a dream in Belgium during the winter of 1861–1862, when he came up with the revolutionary concept of the shape of the *benzene ring*, basic to organic chemistry:

> "I was sitting writing on my textbook, but the work did not progress; my thoughts were elsewhere. I turned my chair to the fire and dozed. Again the atoms were gamboling before my eyes. This time the smaller groups kept modestly in the background. My mental eye, rendered more acute by the repeated visions of the kind, could now distinguish larger structures of manifold conformation; long rows sometimes more closely fitted together all twining and twisting in snake-like motion. But look! What was that? One of the snakes had seized hold of its own tail, and the form whirled mockingly before my eyes. As if by a flash of lightning

I awoke; and this time also I spent the rest of the night in working out the consequences of the hypothesis. Let us *learn* to *dream*, gentlemen, and then perhaps we shall learn the *truth* . But let us beware of publishing our dreams before they have been put to the proof by the *waking understanding*."[3]

I watched a 'TED' Talk recently by ex-Disney Executive, Duncan Wardle. He asked his audience to tell him of situations where they had had creative ideas. They talked of 'the bath', 'wandering along a forest track', 'swimming' ... but, as he then pointed out, *no one had mentioned having creative ideas at work!* Often the excuse is "I don't have time to think." He then pointed to the critical importance of 'playfulness' and 'reframing the challenge', for example, when Disney was replacing Receptionists, they reformed the challenge ... as "Director of First Impressions" (Wardle, 2018).

Dream.... Play!

Albert Einstein indicated in 1922 in Kyoto at a Physics Conference that he used images to solve his problems and found words later (Pais, 1982). As Max Wertheimer reports Einstein in 1959, he "never thought in logical symbols or mathematical equations, but in images, feelings, and even musical architectures" (Wertheimer 1959, pp. 213–228).

Confront the 'normal way of explaining' from as totally different a perspective as you can.

When I was completing my Ph.D. at the University of Melbourne in the mid-1960s, a story emerged, perhaps apocryphal, perhaps not, of a physics student who had been failed in his exam because, when asked 'How do you measure the height of a building with a barometer', he replied, 'Take it to the roof, drop it on a string and measure the distance on the string."

He protested and was told that his answer did not embody enough physics.

The student responded that such an answer was not a problem though it had not been specified in the question. He was given the opportunity to re-sit that part of the exam.

After 15 minutes he had not written anything and his invigilator enquired somewhat sarcastically, "Can't you think of anything now?"

The student replied,

> "No problem, but there are so many answers I was not sure which one to write down."
>
> "For example, the answer you are probably looking for is to test barometric pressure at the ground floor and roof and compare."
>
> "However, you could also swing the barometer on a string around your head and calculate the height from the difference in centrifugal force; you could *drop* the

---

[3] Account of Kekule's famous dream of the benzene structure, as quoted in A Life of Magic Chemistry: Autobiographical Reflections of a Nobel Prize Winner by Olah (2001, p. 154). There has been some debate about whether Kekulé really did have this dream or invented it as a way of claiming precedence for the benzene structure when others had already suggested very similar ideas. See, for example, Browne (1988); Wotiz and Rudofsky (1982), Bonnan (1993), and Olah (2001), pp. 154–155. What is clear though, including from the later example of Einstein is that creative inspiration can often arrive when pragmatic consciousness is switched off, in dreams, attention to symbols and so on.

barometer over the roof balcony, measure the time it took to hit the ground and using the gravity/acceleration constant, calculate the height."

He then suggested several other alternatives, like treating the width of the barometer as a unit and measuring how many barometer lengths it took up the staircase to go from bottom to top.

The student then concluded,

"The best answer of all is to take the barometer down to the basement. Then, you knock on the caretaker's door, and say, "I have here this lovely barometer. I will give it to you if you tell me the height of the building."

What the example shows is that many solutions may exist to the same problem but we tend to get trapped in what already exists, potentially a particular problem in science where established ways of thinking in a specialized area have come to form the 'norm', indeed a 'paradigm' for solving all problems.

Re-examine what we take for granted.

As an additional creativity note, we should also pay attention to what may be glaringly obvious, standing in front of us, but so 'normal' by our established way of seeing things that we don't notice it.

A good example is represented in the discovery of penicillin by Alexander Fleming in 1928 when experimenting with the influenza virus in the Laboratory of the Inoculation Department of St Mary's Hospital in London.

"Often described as a careless lab technician, Fleming returned from a two-week vacation to find that a mold had developed on an accidentally contaminated staphylococcus culture plate. Upon examination of the mold, he noticed that the culture prevented the growth of staphylococci.

Published reports credit Fleming as saying: "One sometimes finds what one is not looking for. When I woke up just after dawn on Sept. 28, 1928, I certainly didn't plan to revolutionize all medicine by discovering the world's first antibiotic, or bacteria killer. But I guess that was exactly what I did" (Kalvait, 2008).

Fleming won a Nobel Prize for poor laboratory discipline … but good observational attention to what he would normally throw into the sink, a dirty laboratory culture plate.

So, if we are to foster a new 'take' on creativity for the future, we need to *encourage* people in all walks of life and employment to 'stop' what they are doing … and have free time to 'think' about it, best of all, activities such as meditation which allow the person to escape the ongoing noise of the 'normal', promotional activities during the day such as 'time-out' with music or gentle exercise, and helping them to see what they take for granted in a new way.

This new take on creativity needs however to be a *central feature* of our Circle of Wholeness and the design of enterprise within it, not an accidental or neglected side-trip.

2.1.3 Promoting Creativity

There are a number of ways in which we can encourage this 'creative' attention.

Edward de Bono, arguably the most famed exponent of lateral or creative thinking, suggests techniques which may be used to enhance thinking about an issue or problem from a quite structured perspective. Most famous is his 'Six Thinking Hats' strategy for either individuals or groups to unpack the dimensions of a difficult problem systematically, consider solutions and monitor the individual thinking moves along the way. The hats are colored Black, Blue, Green, Red, White and Yellow, each hat representing a different or logical and philosophical approach to thinking about a problem and trying to solve it.

> The White Hat is the 'Information Hat' – when wearing the hat the thinker is identifying information needed. The Yellow Hat symbolizes possibility, positivity and optimism, e.g.,: what are the benefits? The Black Hat is the 'devil's advocate hat, considering risks and weaknesses. The Red Hat is the 'Feelings Hat', bringing in emotions and intuition – asking what do we like and dislike. The Green Hat is the 'Creativity Hat', concerned with new ideas, creative possibilities and potentially brainstorming. Finally, the Blue Hat is the 'Management Hat' of all Six Hats thinking processes, starting points, stumbling blocks, checking on what is being learnt.

> The purpose of de Bono's technique is to encourage thinking not only about 'what is', but about 'what can be' - to push thinking in new, unfamiliar directions (de Bono, 2008; Payette & Barnes, 2017).

Indeed, it is possible, indeed desirable, to build 'creativity' into the very structure of the organization and relations between its people.

> I came across an excellent example when completing my Ph.D. in Business Administration (a Social Anthropology program) back in 1966 at the University of Melbourne. As a previous Research Chemist I was reasonably literate in science so studied research management in applied Australian research organizations through *participant observation*–spending time in the laboratories along with the scientists. One of the companies I worked with was Australian Paper Manufacturers, APM, in Melbourne.

>> This company was unusual in that it employed a man in the laboratory who was not a specialist, indeed relatively untrained in science and a recent Yugoslavian immigrant, but who had a good lateral imagination. He was the laboratory's "Question Asker".

>> The paper company had encountered a problem in the folding of cardboard boxes. Consistently, the folding process on the production line caused cracking along the outside edges. The laboratory specialists defined the problem in terms of their own scientific expertise, i.e., the structure of fiber. If the fiber is cracking, they reasoned, then the problem must concern the fiber itself.

>> A team of eight researchers initiated research into the properties of the fiber in the cardboard that the company produced. They spent a large amount of money, discovered "interesting" new properties, and published a number of scientific papers. But after more than nine months they had not solved the problem that existed in the factory. The cardboard boxes continued to crack on the folded edges.

> I then directly overheard a conversation between the 'Question Asker' and the leader of the team dealing with the cardboard cracking problem.

The team leader talked excitedly about the new findings on fiber they were starting to reveal but bemoaned the fact that so far they had not solved the cardboard-cracking problem.

The "asker of good questions" inquired, "But what if you see the problem in a different way? If the cardboard cracks, perhaps it is because the surface area on the outside of the fold is larger than that on the inside, which would put an unequal strain on the material. Why don't you simply fold the cardboard so that the two surfaces have the same surface area?"

Subsequently, by introducing a second wheel in the folding machine, thus creating a bubble of cardboard inside the fold, the problem of cracking was solved. The cost to the company was ten cents." (Hill, 1973, 70)

In my own work managing both the Australian Research Council Centre of Excellence on Research Policy (1991 to 1995) which I established at the University of Wollongong, and then my UNESCO Regional Office in Jakarta, Indonesia (1995 to 2006), I applied a lesson I had learnt from, of all places, the 1960s Sydney-based Applied Research Organic Chemistry Laboratories of Union Carbide. The research facility was directed by a scientist I regarded as one of the few 'geniuses' I have met, Doug Ford. He was so significant to the corporation that they moved their entire organic chemistry research facilities from the U.S to Australia because Doug said he wanted to work in Sydney and refused to head up a Laboratory in the United States where their Central Laboratories were located. When I met him, Doug was supervising one project exploring his theories of death as a product of cellular complexity—and this was in a company focused on mastering the world market in industrial chemicals! Doug's practical experiment was focused on the pupation of flies in the insect maturation process. He tied cotton around the necks of the pupae, thus preventing the pupation hormone to get to the rest of the body. Somewhat unnerving, as the insects continued to grow but not pupate so he had cages of really giant fly-worms staggering around looking distinctly uncomfortable. All to explore Doug's developing theory about organic complexity and death.

In both my own Offices I employed a Librarian. But, as with the Disney re-definition of their Receptionists' role to be 'Managers of First Impressions', and following Doug Ford's example, I turned my Librarians' attention away from just collecting, classifying and stacking books, and towards *exploring*. That is, they learnt what the professionals were doing – and went searching the literatures and websites for research or ideas which the scientists might find interesting, or more importantly, which could bring teams from *across* disciplines together.

The results were magic. Not only in transforming the energy, enthusiasm and interest of the 'Librarian', but, perhaps more importantly, in contributing creative new ideas for the teams and their projects whilst bringing teams across disciplines together around a common problem. What mattered then was providing as much freedom as possible to the professionals–with a lot of team discussion back-up and attention rather than control – all within a clear overall organization 'vision' … applied to *everything*. I gave the teams tremendous freedom to be creative, made sure they had the skills needed, talked with them a lot but not as much to control but to keep an eye on things, make my own *suggestions* (rather than 'instructions'), find how they could usefully connect with others, and then 'back them to the hilt'. The Librarian played a central role in bringing unexpected ideas to the table.

Together we had fun. Together we created some pretty interesting programs that produced very useful applied results.

2.1.4   Knowledge for Our Future: 'Bringing Different "Knowledge Domains" Together in Harmony

'Community' is at the core. So too is a quite new approach to knowledge and the way it is used in dealing with our future—towards 'wholeness'.

Current *specialization* of knowledge, though a potential contributor to under-standing, can only very partially represent our full humanity, platform for the transformation needed now to survive our future.

2.1.5   "Trans Disciplinarity" and "Polyphony"

Two key *new* concepts concerning the knowledge needed for our future have been developed in writing and discussing our previous book, 'The Kyoto Manifesto for Global Economics' (KM-I, 2018). These concepts are 'Trans disciplinarity' and 'Polyphony'.

Trans disciplinarity, as a concept—refers to alignment across different *Domains* (or, 'Territories') of knowledge such as 'scientific', 'objective', 'subjective', 'spiritual' 'cultural', 'economic', and 'political'—each with their own internal validity criteria.

> 'Trans disciplinarity' is not the same as *'Multi disciplinarity'* which seeks synthesis across *Specialized Disciplines* of Scientific, Social Scientific and Humanities focused Knowledge.
>
> The concept of trans disciplinarity was originally implied by Jean Piaget at a Seminar at the University of Nice on 'Interdisciplinarity in Universities' in 1970 in referring to the unity of knowledge *beyond* disciplines. (Nicolescu, 2010). The concept was formalized by Basarab Nicolescu as "The Manifesto of Trans disciplinarity", adopted by the First World Conference on 'Trans disciplinarity' in Portugal in 1994, where the key idea is: "Trans disciplinarity' defines a space for synthesis "across, between and beyond disciplines" (Nicolescu, 2002, pp. 147–152).
>
> Recent ideas have been developing in the literatures in parallel with our own work in our Kyoto Symposia Series since 2014, but whilst others started to talk about it, we were applying it – from 2014 onwards, though not aware or referring to the wider emerging theoretical literature.

Polyphony is our own creation, stimulated by Stomu Yamash'ta's original concept drawn from music, then developed and applied in KM-I, i.e.,: drawing two or more separate Domains of Knowledge, or 'Themes' together into an overall 'Harmony', e.g.,: objective and subjective; systems and culture theories; economics and humanity; spirituality; creativity and sustainable 'circular' economy action, and so on.

In particular, these two concepts now need to be brought into action to confront current global economics and its general assumptions, our task in KM-II. Polyphonic resolution provides the mechanism for bridging different knowledge *domains*.

2.1.6 Application of Trans Disciplinarity and Polyphony Across 'Domains' of Knowledge

Mainstream and honored global economic analysis and thought would appear to play increasingly only *at the edges* of dealing with what our humanity is and how to strengthen it. Mainstream Global Economics—and its Econometric support in particular, does not deal with our identity, our values, being *connected* human beings—rather than separate self-interested decision makers. At core, mainstream global economics does not deal with the development of social community based on 'the power of the *gift*' where immediate return is waived for the sake of wider social benefit rather than assertion of the 'self-interested *deal*'.

Instead, attention may be paid more to 'wrinkles' on economic marketability.

One example: the 2017 Nobel Prize in Economics was awarded to Richard Thaler for 'Nudge Theory', i.e.,: change the wording on a sign, 'nudge' the readers to think a little differently and people will react more directly in relation to the purpose (and purchasing attraction) of the original message. In particular, Thaler advocated 'nudging people through subtle changes in government policy to do things that are in their self-interest' (Chu, 2017). A good reminder to a marketing executive for a new soap, but not a major step forward for humanity as a whole.

At a more general level there is a focus in behavioral economics on the individual rather than the social, yet 'the social' is the very basis of being *human* in the first place. Against this tendency, Stomu Yamash'ta and Tadashi Yagi, our colleagues here, are taking a lead in the context of KM-I to move economics towards 'the social'—exploring implications of the social collective and relationships for 'social capital' more—in particular, reflecting on trust and happiness:

Intuitively, we know that a person cannot be happy if he or she is isolated from society. To live together in a society, trust is indispensable. This is the basis of the relationship between the trust and the happiness (Yamash'ta and Yagi, 2018, p. 227).

However, the closer one approaches the central core of mainstream global economics the more that 'society' and 'humanity' disappear.

Contemporary and expert knowledge in general and in particular, 'scientific' knowledge, is largely located in internally-referring 'silos', separated into specialized discourses—where *much is left unexplored in the spaces in between*.

More importantly, the silos of 'objective' knowledge remain, in general unconnected with the rest of the knowledge which informs and powers everyday life, in particular, the subjective, the spiritual, the 'common sense' by which people live and are likely to respond to a need for change.

Even within *scholastic disciplines*, the 'internal' criteria basic to validity can vary enormously.

Ideally, for econometric equations, the project for evidence is to *simplify, simplify then simplify further* as was expressed to me by Professor Takashi Kamihigashi in a personal conversation at the time of our Kyoto 2017 Symposium.

As I responded to him, in contrast, serious sociological analysis requires seeking to develop a *holistic* understanding as this is what social meaning is about, and this requires dealing with *complexity* not atomizing individual traits out of their wider meaning context.

As I mentioned in Chap. 1, in the late 1970s I worked with Professor Tom Luckman, International Guru of Phenomenology, the Sociology of Consciousness, in both Wollongong (where he came to work with me for 6 months) and Constanz, Germany – his main academic base.

In Constanz, Tom Luckman was running a very well funded three year project with a team of a dozen specialists, e.g.: on linguistics, facial expression, non-verbal posture and presentation, etc. to definitively understand a filmed 10 minute interaction between two people – by breaking the interaction down into its component (atomistic) parts.

His project could not find significance in any of the individual indicators and he learnt from this. Social interaction is *holistic* and as with herbal products which depend on context for their potency, intrinsically *cannot* be explained from its atomistic parts. As it turned out, Tom's meticulous research to prove the 'null' hypothesis, i.e.,: that social interaction *could* be broken down and understood through the separate dimensions of expression, was very valuable. The results reinforced the centrality in social processes of a holistic perspective.

Think, if I may suggest, of why you form a first impression to like or dislike someone you just meet – or decide he or she is for real or a charlatan or a sex maniac after your body.

So, as opposed to econometrics, the project for evidence in exploring *social* phenomena is more to *complexify, complexify then complexify further* – and work out a methodology which can make sense.

One methodology I developed back in the early 1970s was to follow a geological metaphor: sink 'shafts' of deep sociological observation and conclusions of individual cases, then, as with a geologist, determine the direction of the 'lode' of (theoretical) ore by charting each 'shaft' against an overall 'terrain' theory. I did this in exploring 'professionalism' (Hill, 1973).

I also learnt a basic lesson about the difference between physical and social science when I moved from being an Hons I research chemist at Sydney University plus Unilever Research Labs, to (Australia's first) MBA then Business Administration Ph.D–where my research was guided social anthropology–working alongside scientists in commercial labs using participant observation.

I *knew* when I entered this 'sloppy' sociological discipline, that, based on the assumptions of physical science, "I would clean up this unprincipled discipline (this was the mid-1960s) by identifying underlying *laws* of social behavior."

It took me a year to escape the arrogance – as I steadily came to realize that this was an entirely different disciplinary world where the phenomenon I was observing and seeking to explain was … holistic … and complex … and not available to explanation by any kind of universal laws. And certainly not clarified by trying to break observations of social behavior into 'atomistic' bits.

More broadly, knowledge of contemporary life is contained in separate *'Domains'* not just Specializations. Each has its own *internal* criteria for validity—which intrinsically *cannot* be applied across separate Domains, e.g.,: applying subjective experience to objective scientific conclusions (to the *inside* perspective of the specialized scientific 'silo'), or, for that matter, applying objective scientific conclusions to how you actually *feel* within your own subjective world.

For example, if we are exploring inter-subjectivity, passion, trust, empathy, consciousness, conscience … internal states of the person and action, all are *socially* conditioned.

'External' criteria of science are not appropriate, i.e.,: reproducibility, reliability of observation, unpacking of a holistic 'internal' phenomenon into separate 'atomistic' elements – because we would be using validity criteria from a different universe … or Domain.

Instead, we need to explore how 'you and I know', and can 'feel' connected with the emotion and expression experienced at an intersubjective level. This is where the truth of the 'internal' lies. Not on the clip board of an external observer.

2.1.7 Exploring the Space Between Domains of Knowledge

In the presence of several levels of Reality, the space between disciplines and beyond disciplines is full of information. Disciplinary research concerns, at most, one and the same level of Reality. Moreover, in most cases, it only concerns fragments of one level of Reality.

On the contrary, trans disciplinarity concerns the dynamics engendered by the action of several levels of reality at once.

This space between Domains is populated by cross-over lessons, e.g.,: learning from scientific experiments what causes anxiety and then taking alternative subjective action to deal with our own problems, or vice-versa.

More importantly, this space is also populated by knowledge domains we have yet to see—a frequent basis, for example, for *new* vision and paradigm change in science, as I observed earlier about the discovery of penicillin by Alexander Fleming in 1928 where Fleming explored some mold on his dirty equipment rather than washing it down the sink.

In KM-PC we need to confront and find a way of incorporating 'Transdisciplinary Knowledge'—across Knowledge Domains—into our debates and analyses.

Ultimately, *we* must assume the integrity of internally-directed validity criteria of each Domain as we have no authority or adequate 'internal' experience to change these.

So, we leave these internal criteria where they are and focus on shared resolution, in particular, for our present enterprise, in contrasting where each 'domain' comes together with the others in a shared quest to strengthen human community and empowerment and sustainability.

So, we *can* reflect the *knowledge product* of each Domain – according to its relevance and fit against the basic principles of our KM-PC enterprise, ie: community-based "wholeness-oriented social transformation". We use a polyphonic process to explore separate contributions to a shared *theme* of *harmony*.

For example, if we bring together systems theory with culture theory (with *very* different validity criteria), we explore how they mutually interact to change *the social relations of producing together* - in the 'system', the basis (at least in my own sociological understanding and analyses) for developing meaning and cooperation.

Tadashi Yagi has suggested a specific application in Chap. 3, i.e.,: to refer 'the knowledge product' and its impact on developing *creative cities* as parallel action to the development of their *circular economies*. Masatoshi Murase expands the application of 'creativity' to "co-creation beyond destruction" in Chap. 10, a concept which admits the possibility of moving beyond what exists, indeed even destroying it if it gets in the way of creative transformation, but also creating in parallel.

> The link between creative cities and circular economy is a good example of *polyphonic* resolution of *trans disciplinary knowledge across domains.* The concept of a creative city expresses a general world view of the community as a whole, i.e.,: one which is willing to explore and 'see' the new, and put it into practice - even as a pressure from the people on the political and decision-making process, an excellent platform for building a *new* circular economy.

Furthermore, we can learn from indigenous knowledge, honed, as for example in Australia for over 60,000 years. Here, nature and culture are one; past, present and future time are not distinguished from each other. The people were living in harmony with their world—these separate knowledge domains bridged in daily life—for all this time until European settlement came to disturb the balance in the late eighteenth century.[4]

In other words, whilst internal validity criteria might vary, the 'harmony' of polyphony lies in the product, so the'test' lies in the 'product'—in particular, a *human* product of greater empowerment.

2.2 Putting the Circle of Wholeness into Practice—Surviving Our Shattered World: Summary of Our Platform for Change

Our Humanity!

> What is sacred or of imperishable supreme value is *what we can be* as a human race – *empowered*, fulfilled individuals, in harmony, deeply *sharing and caring* for each other across our separate cultural and life worlds – understanding the fundamental *depth and equality of our shared lives.* (KM-1, 2018, p. 6)

We presented compelling evidence and argument in The Kyoto Manifesto (KM-I), platform for this Kyoto Post-COVID Manifesto Sequel (KM-PC), chilling reminder and a serious warning. Our very *humanity* is now subsumed under the command of a massively powerful, socially and physically destructive Global Economics System. Social harmony and empowerment and even our very physical support environment are seriously at risk as a result.

We *have* to find a new way.

As we construct our Kyoto Post-COVID Manifesto, we explore the 'home' of *meaning,* our *cultures,* and our *creativity.* For here lie the starting points in breaching

---

[4] See, for example, the report by Bill Griffiths on the role of archaeologist Isabel Mc Bryde in developing World Heritage recognition in the 1970s for indigenous Australians of 'the significance of whole landscapes, the inseparability of natural and cultural heritage and the intangible values of connections to country. (Griffiths 2018, p. 49).

all cultural difference and moving towards entirely new solutions—in particular to the fragmentation of our society and marginalization of truth now exacerbated by the rapidly expanding (corporate power shaped) 'social media'.

On the surface, the leading phenomenon of the 2000s, social media, offers an extraordinary power to make change happen—through communicating issues rapidly to millions, gathering people together in debate and more importantly, in taking social action, for example, via 'flash crowds' and virus-level publicity of a protest action.

We can indeed capitalize on this power to *introduce ideas* to a wide public.

But, whilst apparently expanding social power, social media is at the same time weakening it. So we must be very cautious.

> For, as I argued earlier, social media *replaces* inter-subjective community, the basis of culture and values formation, and ultimately of strength in one's own identify and security. The Social Media phenomenon has now proven itself to easily mislead down paths of unverified knowledge until 'lies' appear as truth to those who have already made up their minds and are now included along with literally *millions* of others. And personal worth, in particular, for the young, comes to be measured by social media 'popularity' – number of 'hits' on one's 'tweet' or number of 'friends' (perhaps largely anonymous) collected on one's Facebook Network.
>
> Social media is contributing to increased anxiety, stress, uncertainty … 'anomie' as a sociologist would remind us, that is, 'loss of norms to live by, so we *drift*' in insecurity. As but one signal, youth suicides are increasing dramatically at a global level.

These erosive forces to the essence of human 'community' fundamentally weaken our ability to make transformative change happen and stop the human-induced climate change and exhaustion of finite resources and species on which we must depend.

We must remember: we cannot fix our physical world without first fixing our social and community power and relationships, currently set within the frame of Global Economics. To do this is a *holistic* exercise. We must penetrate below the surface!

The frame of Global Economics is experienced, as I also introduced earlier, as a 'grammar' which sets the pattern of social relations, values and everyday life experience, but which we do not notice, in the same way we do not notice the grammar which stands behind and organizes speech and communication. We must penetrate this 'silence' behind the cacophony of global economic self-centered 'noise', recognizing that such a 'grammar' set by the 'system' *becomes* the meanings, the culture, the essence of our being and understanding of ourselves. "The way we do things around here".

Transformative change must therefore target this 'whole'—the basic values and practices which maintain the status-quo of Global Economic action and systems. Our entry point however may well be to look inside and beyond the 'cracks' within the system we confront, and use what we can glimpse of system weak points to draw others into our quest for transformation to more humanistic values.

This is whole-of-humanity exercise though. To 'adjust' just the odd economic or social policy 'levers' without targeting the underlying 'system' allows the underlying grammar to remain relatively untouched though perhaps adjusting at the edges to absorb the new intervention whilst still maintaining the system's basic 'grammar' structure and power.

With 'culture' as reference point, we move *across* cultures to search for lessons in transformation away from a society based on a self-focused greed-based set of values, to a society based on caring, mutual support, integrity and trust, mindfulness and charity—back to the essence of what 'humanity' is.

Much can be learnt from drawing Eastern Philosophies into *harmony* with Western Scientific Knowledge, but now paying new attention to the breadth of knowledge we need to make a difference—for it must not remain in separate 'scientific' or other knowledge silos—each with its own separate validation criteria, but combine across the various 'Domains' or different 'territories' we need—from objective and scientific to subjective and emotional, Eastern to Western, pragmatic to spiritual, intuition to formal .... and so on. Our task is *Harmony. Connection*!

> Stomu Yamash'ta expresses what this means well in relation to music, mutual understanding comes from "hearing the sound of another singer, and choosing an optimal tune for harmony".

Hence, our focus on 'polyphony' as the strategic concept of connection. Polyphonic validity lies less in separate validations within each knowledge 'domain'— though these are contributors—and mainly in the product of polyphonic synthesis, shared resolution, harmony, in strengthening human community, empowerment, and sustainability.

At the center of transformative change is *creativity*. For we must *see* the world from a perspective we had not admitted to our 'taken-for-granted' way of doing things in the past. Creativity has to be built into every action—from individual to institutional.

At a general level this means that a core principle of transformation is providing 'creative space' as part of all activity and 'work'—time to reflect—desirably backed by a creative visual and sound environment or meditative program—and 'planned', not treated as accident, as is so often the case in many current organizations, where people are too busy at work to 'think'.

Additionally, it is important to build 'creativity' *into* the organization as I demonstrated earlier, through 'redefining' jobs, e.g.,: from 'receptionist' to 'manager of first impressions' in the case of Disney, and from 'librarian' to lateral search 'connector' in my own Research and UN Offices; and even employing a person as a lateral thinking 'question asker' as I reported from an applied research lab I spent time in during the 1960s.

But most important of all is the paradigm-changing assertion of a new culture in *every* action and structure—based in the power of the gift rather than the deal, concerned with benefit to all rather than just the profits and careers of the individual organization, that is, the customers, the staff, the wider community ... a circle of responsibility towards "Strategically oriented Pro-Social Behavior" as demonstrated in the range of case studies of long-standing Japanese business presented in Chap. 3 by Tadashi Yagi and Stomu Yamash'ta.

> They present the case of the traditional Japanese Oumi Shounin (merchants), continuing to this day successfully since Mediaeval times based on Buddhist-inspired principles of high

ethical behavior, 'Sanpo-yoshi' or 'Triple Win – sharing profits between sellers, buyers and wider society.

At a wider society level, change needs to be centered where culture, meaning and empowerment are formed—at the local inter-subjective community and organization level. But not left there. I talk of the principle of 'global localism' which I employed when seeking to make environmental change happen from community level under my previous United Nations responsibilities. It works. Build action at the local community level and then, with this case and experience to hand, build linkages and networks to other communities—including sister-community relations, exchange of community leaders, participation in education programs in the original village or community, mentoring, and so on. At a wider level social media may be used to expand interest in the ideas and successes. However, *action is at local community level.*

> Our task is to create and use 'The Circle of Wholeness'.

Ladeja Kosir draws our attention in her Chap. 14, as do other authors in Sect. 3 of this book, to 'The Circular Economy Movement' now emerging in European Union business, in particular, where production is seen as a circle—ALL inputs and products are used. Nothing is wasted—an innovation which, for serious uptake requires governments to rethink their investment incentive policies and science support to identify new recycling ways. Ladeja is now moving us on further, to 'The Circular Triangle' of Circular Economy, Circular Culture and Circular Change.

This is the Circle of Wholeness—but with a fundamental addition—of attention to sustainability—*All Circles are based in the fundamental humanity values of care, mutual benefit, community empowerment and charity*—not of separative self-interest. Applied at every level of action and institution. These are inescapable reference points for *all* government policy—no matter what 'domain' it might refer to. Taxation incentives, for example, could well be applied to *social benefit* rather than profits alone.

The Sioux Oglala Indians of America may offer us an instructive symbolic lead drawn from their past.

> "The Oglala believed the circle to be sacred because the great spirit caused everything in nature to be round except stone. Stone is the instrument of destruction.
>
> The sun and the sky, the earth and the moon are round like a shield, though the sky is deep like a bowl. Everything that breathes is round like the stem of a plant. Since the great spirit has caused everything to be round mankind should look upon the circle as sacred, for it is the symbol of all things in nature except stone. It is also the symbol of the circle that makes the edges of the world and therefore of the four winds that travel there. Consequently, it is also the symbol of the year. The day, the night, and the moon go in a circle above the sky. Therefore the circle is a symbol of these divisions of time and hence the symbol of all time.
>
> For these reasons the Oglala make their tipis circular, their camp-circle circular, and sit in a circle at the ceremonies. If one makes a circle for an ornament and it is not divided in any way, it should be understood as the symbol of the world and of time." (Hill, 1988, p. 100; Geertz 1968, p. 303).

Along with the Oglala, *we* are putting the symbol and meaning of *The Circle* at the center of transformative change strategy.

We are also putting the *power* of this Circle symbol at the center of action.

In the case of the Oglala, it was the other way around.

When Western Civilization invaded – the fragileness of 'whole culture' was exposed to the influence of alternative symbols backed by power to change. 'White Man' introduced *square houses*, symbolizing the encroachment of the invading culture on everyday life. At the same time they symbolized the power of this invasion which was located in the guns and other technologies which supported homestead living at the frontier. Along with emancipation from the power of the circle – as the Oglala were confronted by modern life, came erosion of the wholeness of the Sioux Oglala culture.

In our Kyoto Post-COVID Manifesto we are doing the reverse. Asserting the power of The Circle over the Ideological, Structural and Values *'Square'* of current Global Economic rule.

Our strategic entry points for transformation may well target intrinsic weaknesses within the current Global Economic System—weaknesses, that is, in supporting and empowering community and humanity values. Following the poetic wisdom of Leonard Cohen which I reported earlier, there *are* cracks in the system and we can target them *to bring the light in!*

Let's keep The Circle' as our own 'super-ordinate symbol' in creating our future "Society of Harmony and Co-Creativity".

Our task from KM-PC, is now to develop comprehensive and creative change strategies to bring the Circle of Wholeness into being globally, to bring into being a new social order based on the depth of values of our humanity rather than the demands of the global economy.

Green shoots of world attention and concern are already appearing for us to nurture. They are growing through the 'cracks' in the global economic system which the 2020–2022 Coronavirus Pandemic has exposed so dramatically.

References

ACLED (2020). Demonstrations and political violence in America: New data for summer 2020. In *ACLED,* 3 September. https://acleddata.com/2020/09/03/demonstrations-political-violence-in-america-new-data-for-summer-2020

Berry-Caban, C. S. (2011). DDT and silent spring: Fifty years after. *JMVH Review Article, 19*(4).

Bonnan, S. (1993). 19th-century Chemist Kekulé charged with scientific misconduct. *Chem Eng Archive, 71*(34), 20–21.

De Bono, E. (2008). *Six thinking hats.* Penguin Books.

Browne, M. W. (1988). The Benzene ring: Dream analysis, *The New York Times,* August 16. https://www.nytimes.com/1988/08/16/science/the-benzene-ring-dream-analysis.html

Buchanan, L., Bui, Q., & Patel, J. K. (2020). Black rights matter may be the largest movement in U.S. history, *The New York Times,* 3 July. https://www.nytimes.com›interactive›2020/07/03›us

Carson, R. (1962). 'The Silent Spring', Houghton Mifflin–reprinted as Crest Book Reprint, Fawcett Publications, Greenwich, Connecticut: library–united diversity.coop: Rachel Carson–United Diversity Library

Chu, B. (2017). Father of 'nudge theory' Richard Thaler wins 2017 Nobel prize in economics', *Independent*, Monday 9 October. https://www.independent.co.uk/news/business/news/richard-thaler-nobel-prize-in-economics-winner-2017-behavioural-economics-nudge-theory-a7990291.html

Congress, U.S. (2020). House Committee on the Judiciary, 'Chair Bass, Senators Booker and Harris, and Chair Nadler Introduce the 'Justice in Policing Act of 2020', *Press Release*, 8 June 2020. https://judiciary.house.gov/news/documentsingle.aspx?DocumentID=3005

Day, E. (2015). Black lives matter: The birth of a new civil rights movement. *The Guardian*, Sunday 19 July. https://www.theguardian.com/world/2015/jul/19/blacklivesmatter-birth-civil-rights-movement

Geertz, C. (1968). Ethos, world view and the analysis of sacred symbol. In: A. Dantes, (Ed.), *Every man his way*. Prentice Hall.

Griffiths, B. (2018). *Deep time dreaming – uncovering ancient Australia*. Australia Black Inc.

Hill, S. (1973). Professions: "Mechanical Solidarity and Process or, How I learnt to live with a primitive society". *Australian and New Zealand Journal of Sociology, 9* (3) (October).

Hill, S. (1988–1989). *The tragedy of technology – human liberation versus domination in the late twentieth century*. Pluto Press.

Hill, S. (2010). Ways of Seeing – science and technology within their cultural setting. In Invited Chapter in Jain, A. (Ed.), *Science and the public*, Section: 'Science in society', New Delhi: Sage (Volume in the Series, *Civilization, philosophy, science and culture* (Series Editor: Prof. P. Chatapadhyaya) (pp. 252–280).

Hill, S. (2012). Harnessing the power of culture for sustainable development and community empowerment, Address to *Sacred Bridge*, Jakarta, 03 March (available from the author).

Hill, S., & Turpin, T. (1994). Academic research cultures in collision. *Science as Culture, 4*(20), 327–362.

Hill, S., & Turpin, T. (1995). Cultures in collision: The emergence of a new localism in academic research. In M. Strathern, (Ed.), *The uses of knowledge: global and local relations. The reshaping of anthropology, volume 1 - shifting contexts*, Chapter 7. Routledge.

Hill, E., Tiefenthaler, A., Triebert, C., Jordan, D., Willis, H., & Stein, R. (2020). How George Floyd was killed in police custody, *New York Times*, 31 May (Updated, 5 November). https://www.nytimes.com›george-floyd-arrest-death-video

Kalvait, K. (2008). Penicillin: An accidental discovery changed the course of medicine. In *Endocrine today*.

KM-I (2018): Yamash'ta, S., Yagi, T., & Hill, S. (Eds), *The Kyoto manifesto for global economics – the platform of community, humanity and spirituality*. Springer.

Levin, S. (2020). What does defund the police mean? The rallying cry sweeping the U.S. – explained', *The Guardian*, Saturday, 8 June, 2020. https://www.theguardian.com/us-news/2020/jun/05/defunding-the-police-us-what-does-it-mean

Nicolescu, B. (2002).(Trans: Voss, K. C.) *Manifesto of Transdisciplinarity*. Albany: State University of New York Press, pp147-152..

Nicolescu, B. (2010). Methodology of transdisciplinarity – levels of reality, logic of the included middle and complexity. *Transdiscip J Eng Sci, 1*, 17–32.

Olah, G. A. (2001). *A life of magic chemistry : Autobiographical reflections of a nobel prize winner*. Wiley.

Pais, A. (1982). *Subtle is the lord … the science and the life of Albert Einstein*. Oxford University Press.

Payette, P., & Barnes, B. (2017). Teaching for critical thinking: Edward de Bono's Six thinking hats, March 21, 2017. https://doi.org/10.1002/ntlf.30110

Ross, C. T. (2015). A multi-level bayesian analysis of racial bias in police shootings at the county-level in the United States, 2011–2014. *PLOS ONE, 10*(11), e0141854. https://journals.plos.org/plosone/article?id=10.1371/journal.pone.0141854

UNESCO, Jakarta Annual Reports, 1995 to 2006, Jalan M.H. Thamrin 14, Tromolpos 1213/JKT, Jakarta 10002, Indonesia.

Wardle, D. (2018). The theory of creativity, 'TEDx Talk', *You Tube,* 4th May. https://www.youtube.com›watch

Wertheimer, M. (Ed.), (1959). *Productive thinking* (Enlarged Edn.).Harper and Brothers, New York and London.

Wotiz, J. H., & Rudofsky, S. (1982). Was there a conspiracy when Kekulé's first German benzene-structure paper was frequently listed as published in 1865. *Journal of Chemical Education, 59,* 23.

Yamash'ta, S., & Yagi, T. (2018a). Trust, not competition, as a source of the creative economy. In *Chapter 14 in KM-1.*

Chapter 3
Polyphony as a System for Delivering Co-Creation and the Empowerment of Individuals

Tadashi Yagi and Stomu Yamash'ta

Abstract It is too optimistic to think that our future society will develop prosperously without changing the system of market mechanisms that promote the creativity of each individual. In particular, it is predicted that artificial intelligence will worsen unemployment, increase income inequality, suppress the well-being of people, and endanger the environment and sustainability of our planet. These issues will not be automatically solved by the current market mechanisms under capitalism. In this chapter, we discuss policies to amend the functioning of market mechanisms by introducing a co-creation system that promotes the creative activities of individuals and reduces the ecological burden of our society. We introduce the concept of "polyphony", and propose that it is time to rethink our business models and focus on the future of the global economy and how to replace our current linear "take, make, dispose" model with a new sustainable circular economic model. The essence of polyphony is the creation of new value and harmonization of different people.

Keywords Polyphony · Co-creation · Circular economy · Prosocial socio-economy · SDGs

3.1 Introduction

In a globalized economy, the various negative effects of capitalism on humanity have been escalating, including competition and inequality. Without doubt, market pricing is still an important mechanism that contributes to the efficient allocation of resources in a market, as Adam Smith predicted in his book The Wealth of Nations published in 1776 (Smith, 2007). Smith posited the concept of the "invisible hand" and predicted harmonized resource allocation through trade by selfish economic agents; however, he also stressed the importance of empathy and altruistic behavior of individuals in

T. Yagi (✉)
Faculty of Economics, Doshisha University, Karasuma Higashiiru, Kyoto 602-8580, Japan
e-mail: tyagi@mail.dosihsha.ac.jp

S. Yamash'ta
Tokiwashimodacho 20-511, Kyoto 616-8228, Japan

© Springer Nature Singapore Pte Ltd. 2022
S. Hill et al. (eds.), *The Kyoto Post-COVID Manifesto For Global Economics*,
Creative Economy, https://doi.org/10.1007/978-981-16-8566-8_3

his book The Theory of Moral Sentiments published in 1757 (Smith, 2002). It is noteworthy that he revised the latter book until his death, and the final version was the sixth edition, which shows how much importance he placed on the book.

In The Theory of Moral Sentiments, Smith advocates for the concept of "empathy," which allows people to suppress selfish behavior and attain a peaceful state of the market. It is important to discuss the reason why empathy is needed in an economy where market mechanisms allocate resources efficiently. In economics, many studies have been conducted on the limitations of market mechanisms, and well-known causes of market failure include (1) externalities (external economy/external diseconomy), (2) public goods, (3) information asymmetry, and (4) economies of scale.

Among these causes, information asymmetry is a market failure factor that is closely linked to issues of conscience. Take, for example, the mislabeling of food. To prevent informational asymmetry, various rules have been established to prevent mislabeling. The moral hazard from such information asymmetry results in the loss of efficiency in production and an increase in costs. This example illustrates that the efficiency of the entire market is greatly reduced if companies behave immorally or unethically.

Another example that illustrates the importance of conscious in the economy is the Lehman Brothers crisis that occurred in the United States in 2008. The primary driver of this crisis was immoral behavior in residential mortgage market. By utilizing mortgage-backed securities, the original lender of a home loan could avoid the risk of default. This caused companies to lower lending standards and to make subprime loans without checking borrowers' ability to repay the loan. As long as the housing market was booming, investors could enjoy a high rate of return from risky derivatives and financial instruments based on these mortgage-backed securities. This escalated the immoral behavior of lenders, and elevated risks in the financial market. When the housing market boom ended, the value of those derivatives dropped precipitously, and the financial system faced a serious crisis. At the root of the Lehman shock were greedy capitalist actors who lacked conscience, and it was their unethical economic activity that drove a serious economic incident that disrupted the global economic system.

The Lehman crisis revealed the greedy state of capitalism and its loss of conscience, and many economists had to grapple with serious challenges in the capitalist system. Sedlacek (2011) is an influential book that revealed the limitation of capitalism in which he discussed good and evil in the economy. In his book, Sedracheck introduced statements of the philosopher Bernard Mandeville from the first half of the eighteenth century, which argued that vice is inseparable from a great and powerful society (Mandeville, 1989). According to Mandeville, greed is often the driving force that strengthens selfishness, which causes people to make effort to succeed, which leads to the development of society. Sedracheck admits that there is evil in society and suggests that it is a realistic response in human society to strive to move from evil to good without denying the existence of evil. Nevertheless, he also stresses that the statement of Mandeville was criticized by Adam Smith in terms of economic sustainability and society.

In our view, it is too optimistic to think that our future society will develop prosperously without changing the system of market mechanisms that promote the creativity of each individual. In particular, it is predicted that artificial intelligence will worsen unemployment, increase income inequality, suppress the well-being of people, and endanger the environment and sustainability of our planet. These issues will not be automatically solved by the current market mechanisms under capitalism.

In this chapter, we discuss policies to amend the functioning of market mechanisms by introducing a co-creation system that promotes the creative activities of individuals and reduces the ecological burden of our society. Section 2 discusses the prosocial socioeconomy and clarifies the conditions for prosocial behavior to be consistent with a competitive economy. Section 3 proposes a long-run sustainable ecological socioeconomic system in circular economy. Finally, Sect. 4 discusses the system of co-creation by showing how polyphony is used to enhance creativity.

3.2 Prosocial Socio-economy

3.2.1 Factors that Determine the Characteristics of Prosocial Behavior

The evolution of human behaviors, such as self-protection, mate selection, navigation of status hierarchies, and building of social coalitions, were shaped by adaptive responses to survive in the world. Helping members of your family makes it more likely that your family members will survive. In this sense, prosocial behavior can be viewed through the lens of natural selection (Kaschak and Maner, 2009).

Prosocial behaviors are regarded as a crucial factor in modern society for sustaining a stable modern life. Environmental issues such as global climate change and marine plastic pollution are examples where prosocial behaviors must play a leading role. Implementation of economic incentives, such as environmental taxes and similar strategies, is limited in the real world. Instead, prosocial behaviors are needed to tackle these problems.

As discussed in Böckler et al. (2016), prosocial behaviors are induced by a number of factors, including selfish reasons, reciprocal benefits, and more altruistic reasons. According to their research results, all three factors were found using various assessment methods from different disciplines. Altruistically motivated behavior, for instance, has been observed in the dictator game in behavioral economics (see Fehr and Fischbacher (2003)). In addition, the identified subcomponents of prosocial characteristics were characterized by their different relationships to affective and cognitive dispositions. Higher altruistically motivated behavior is related with less negative affect and better cognition. For example, people tend to withdraw from the suffering of another person—instead of helping—if they have a strong negative affect. Also, altruistic behavior requires skills such as the ability to suppress one's own proponent selfish impulses. These results are consistent with Batson (2011) and

Knoch et al. (2006). Knoch et al. also showed that reciprocal fairness is observed in the ultimatum game, where players often reject their bargaining partner's unfair offers.

In addition to these three factors, Böckler et al. (2016) confirmed social norms as an important factor in prosocial behavior by using second-party and third-party punishment games (see Fehr and Fischbacher (2004) for the details of these games). The concept of social norms is quite complicated and little is known about how they are formed, how they are changed, how they are related with social values, and so on. However, it is known that social norms are important for the evolution of human altruism because they compel selfish members of the society to behave altruistically. Through the social process, the group of members who behave altruistically dominates the group of members who behave in a selfish manner in cases where punishment is available (Bowles et al., 2003). In this sense, social norms are an important factor for cultivating prosocial behavior in a society.

3.2.2   *Optimality of Prosocial Behavior in Business*

Based on the research results on prosocial behavior, we examine the optimality of prosocial behavior in business by analyzing several examples of long-running companies in Japan that place a strong emphasis on prosocial practices. By focusing on the longevity of companies, it is possible to examine the relationship between prosocial behavior and sustainability in business. Admittedly, it is difficult to categorize the types of prosocial behaviors in businesses, but we view it as effective for clarifying the specific character of business policy by our categorizations. In categorizing the cases, we refer to the factors that generate prosocial behavior. The first category is "long-running company driven by altruistically motivated prosocial behavior." The second category is "long-running company driven by norms and philosophically motivated prosocial behavior." The third category is "long-running company driven by strategically motivated prosocial behavior." We examine the optimality of the prosocial behavior in businesses for each category.

3.2.2.1   Category 1: Altruistically Motivated Prosocial Behavior

As a case for this category, we consider the "Oumi shounin" (Oumi merchants). The Oumi merchants originated in Oumi Province, which is now Shiga Prefecture, and expanded their businesses not only in Oumi Province but also in other areas in medieval and modern Japan. Prominent companies that still exist today include (1) Daimaru, Takashimaya, and the Seibu Group in the distribution industry; (2) Itochu, Marubeni, Sumitomo, and Sojitsu in the trade industry; (3) Nisshinbo, Toyobo, and Tore in the textile industry; and (4) Nissei, Takeda Pharmacy[[Pharmaceuticals]], and Sumitomo Bank in other industries (Yasuoka et al., 1992).

These firms are famous for their highly ethical behavior, especially in the 17th to nineteenth centuries. Their principal philosophy is the "Sanpo-yoshi" (triple-win) concept. This concept means that the business should be good for sellers, buyers, and society. According to Yasuoka et al. (1992, p. 197), "Sanpo-yoshi," advocated by Chubei Ito, who established the successful trading company Itochu, is rooted in Buddhist philosophy, in particular the Jyodo-shinsyu school. He argued that business is the work of Buddhist saints, and believed that employees should be treated with the mercy of Amitabha Buddha. As a result, he formed a business philosophy that required the company to share its profits among employees, business partners, and society members. It should be noted that this philosophy is rooted in Buddhist religious belief, which implies that the concept of "no-self" is quite important in this business philosophy.

Another important example is the philosophy of "Sengi-Kouri" (Social obligation first, profit later; see the Daimaru website). This philosophy was established as the principal ideal of the Daimaru business by its founder Hikozaemon Shimomura in 1736, and is cited from a Chinese Confucian Junshi's words that "a business that gives higher priority to social obligation than to profit will be successful." This principal ideal is still effective in designing the business policy of Daimaru.

Based on these philosophies, the companies rooted in the tradition of the Oumi merchants have certain characteristics in their corporate social responsibility (CSR) activities, as described in Kawaguchi (2004). Specifically, these firms aim to do the following:

- Keep business profit and social profit in harmony.
- Share the same ethical values among top management and every employee.
- Respect employees.
- Create and maintain relationships of trust among clients and suppliers.
- Support the local community for its sustainable development.
- Commit to environmental protection and the effective use of nature.

3.2.2.2 Category 2: Norms- and Philosophy-Motivated Prosocial Behavior

An important example of norms- and philosophy-motivated prosocial behavior in business is the "Inamori philosophy" advocated by Kazuo Inamori, a founder of Kyoto Ceramic Corporation. There are some commonalities between this philosophy and "Sekimon Shingaku" (a merchant norm philosophy started from the mid-eighteenth century in Japan). According to Yoshida (2010), in its early stage, Inamori philosophy was defined by the fundamental principle of making the right decisions in life and work, with the right decisions being judged according to righteous behavior as a human. In the next stage of the Inamori philosophy formation process, Inamori philosophy was strongly influenced by Buddhist and Confucian philosophy. Based on these philosophies, Inamori argues that the original meaning of being human is to contribute to society. This example illustrates that businesspeople should make decisions not to fulfill their self-interest, but to achieve the object of being a good human.

Being a norms- and philosophy-based business affects business strategy in several ways in terms of human capital formation and management. These impacts are summarized in the sections below.

(i)   Effects on human capital formation

Inamori influenced employees' way of thinking by constructing a system of philosophy that penetrated deeply into their minds. As the philosophy is adopted, employees come to believe that working diligently cultivates their mind, and leads one to enlightenment in a Buddhist sense. According to the philosophy, working is a means of polishing their soul. The philosophy tells employees that self-love is necessary for leading the company to prosperity, but the idea of co-existence based on universal love is needed as a philosophical foundation. This suggests that there is a strong principle of educating employees, and this strengthens the human relationships among employees that share the same values.

(ii)   Amoeba management

The core strategy of the Inamori management style is "Amoeba management", where the company's business is subdivided into small branches and each branch is required to sustain a self-supporting accounting system. This management style is effective when there are common ideals and goals for the business that are shared by all employees; otherwise, the local optima cannot be consistent with the global optimum, and the direction of the company would not be socially optimal. The success of amoeba management can be attributed to success in human capital management.

3.2.2.3   Category 3: Strategically Motivated Prosocial Behavior

Kyoto businesses are managed with consideration given to the relationship between government (emperor) and business. This required businesspeople to behave strategically, because they would otherwise find it difficult to survive in society. The art production group called the Kano School, which operated in the 16th– to nineteenth centuries, is an example of a typical long-running Kyoto business (see Nakatani, 2013). The important point is that the business was protected by the government through regulations restricting new entrants into the industry for many years. This art group developed innovative techniques in painting such as "Tarashikomi", which expresses vagueness and softness by applying a new layer of paint before the previous layer is dry".

The close relationship with the authorities had various impacts on the status of artists. One important point is that the artists' group was offered important projects for decorating public buildings and religiously important places. For these works, huge amounts of funds were made available using public resources, which enabled the group to produce luxury paintings using precious materials.

On the other hand, the close relationship with the authorities gave the artists a conservative image, and the works were not accepted as innovative, even though the pioneering artists established the original styles. In particular, the Kano school during the Edo period was comprised of several different painter's groups. The top ranking groups consisted of 4 families, and the second ranking group consisted of 15 families. These groups had close relationships with authorities and rulers such as the government, temples, and successful merchants. Those groups were not regarded as innovative artists, but as professional creators or craftsmen. The close relationships with the authorities made the group dependent on these power structures and the groups could not continue when the authorities lost their power or position.

This example clarifies the risks of strategically motivated prosocial behavior. In the case of the Kano school, the dependency on the authorities increased as the return from the relationship increased. This implies that the range of society supporting the Kano school shrank and the target of prosocial behavior narrowed to limited groups, which caused to the erosion of reliable support from most of society.

Another example of strategically motivated prosocial behavior is the corporate behavior associated with the Sustainable Development Goals (SDGs), which were set in 2015. The incentives for working toward the SDGs are primarily the drive for long-run profit and security. The SDGs appeal to various prosocial objectives such as environmental sustainability, solutions for poverty and inequality, and improvement of educational opportunities of all children.

The reason for this is that decision-making in an organization requires the justification in terms of profit maximization, especially when the voice of investors is strong. Participation in SDG activities has some merits for collecting information about global socioeconomic changes through various kinds of events such as conferences or workshops. Such information is valuable in designing long-run corporate strategy. The strategically motivated prosocial behavior, however, easily changes when the merits of the activities to the companies diminish. In this sense, the sustainability of this kind of prosocial behavior is not guaranteed.

In considering the modern Kyoto business, we need to refer to long-running companies in Kyoto, such as famous traditional Japanese cake companies or craftsman companies. According Imamura (2010), the following factors are important for long-running companies:

- Continuous innovation and safeguarding the secrecy of original technology.
- Good long-term relationships with stakeholders such as trading partners
- Maintaining tradition while also introducing various innovations
- Continuous restructuring of the organization in response to environmental changes
- Maintaining core competencies and continuous investment in core competencies
- Systematic human resource development and systematic transfer of corporate ideals
- Stable finances.

These factors are not inconsistent with altruistic behavior or norms-based behavior, but the difference is the strategic focus. The important point is that long-running Kyoto companies behave strategically in response to environmental changes while also maintaining tradition and the companies' ideals that are expressed through their prosocial objectives as members of society.

3.2.2.4   Differences in Business Policies Resulting from the Different Approaches to Prosocial Behavior

Next, we summarize the pros and cons of the three types of prosocial behavior, and propose several policies for better promoting prosocial behavior. We set the following criteria for evaluating the merits of each approach, which include the following:

- Opportunity costs: missed profits
- Trust formation
- Flexibility in responding to environmental changes
- Loyalty of consumers
- Stability of the organization and relationships between employees
- Importance of community

Table 3.1 summarizes the pros and cons of the three types of prosocial behavior. Altruistically motivated and norms and philosophically motivated prosocial behavior have some commonalities. In most cases, behaving as a good person based on shared humanity is consistent with altruistic behavior. In deciding what constitutes altruistic behaviors, some long-run consistent principles are necessary to avoid certain losses from cheating or opportunistic behavior using [[that takes advantage of]] altruistic behavior. Norms and philosophy provide a priority ranking on the various types and occasions of altruistic behavior.

When people in a society believe that a firm's prosocial behavior comes from altruistic motivation or from a norms- and philosophy-based motivation, people have trust in and loyalty to the business. However, the stability of the organization and relationships between employees are dependent on various factors. Altruistically motivated behavior would be sustainable only when a majority of members in the organization recognizes the importance of altruistic behavior, and when profit levels are stably positive. Norms and philosophically motivated prosocial behavior stresses that certain core values are essential for the business to be sustainable in the long

Table 3.1 Summary of pros and cons of three types of prosocial behavior

	Altruistically motivated	Norms and philosophically motivated	Strategically motivated
Opportunity cost: missed profits	Possibly high	Possibly high	Low
Trust formation	Very high	Very high	Low
Flexibility in responding to environmental changes	Low	Low	High
Loyalty of consumers	High	High	Low
Stability of organization and relationships between employees	Conditional	Conditional	Conditional
Importance of community	High	High	Conditional

run, and such an approach works well when the values are shared by employees of the organization. Strategically motivated prosocial behavior can become unstable when decisions on the optimal path differ among the members of the organization. In particular, this instability happens when predictions about future changes in the business environment differ among members.

Concerning the importance of community, altruistically motivated prosocial behavior regards the community as the basis of business and human capital development, as described in the case of Oumi merchants. Norms- and philosophy-based prosocial behavior has a slightly different stance on the community from altruistically motived prosocial behavior in that these firms have a broader range of social relationships that are not restricted by area and space. Strategically motivated prosocial behavior considers the community to be important as long as the community is judged to be important from a long-run perspective.

The discussion in this section suggests that there are difficulties in terms of the long-term sustainability of prosocial behavior. We conjecture that strategically motivated prosocial behavior is the least stable for the following reasons. First, the benefits of prosocial behavior are easily lost as the environment and situation change. Second, it is not easy to share common values among members of an organization unless there are strongly held principles and ideals within the organization. Third, opinions on the optimal strategy may differ among members of strategically motivated organizations.

The lessons from long-running companies suggest that businesses need to invest in human capital development and maintain close relationships with the community. Human capital development may include education on the importance of altruistic behavior based on norms and philosophy. This kind of education is important for companies of all sizes. Even global companies needs to educate employees on the importance of altruistic prosocial behavior within the community in order to improve human relationships and cultivate social trust in the company. In this sense, CSR activities based on community can be regarded as investment in the human capital development of an organization.

Without education on the importance of altruistic prosocial behavior based on norms and philosophy, a company faces various kinds of risks. The most important risk is the erosion of trust from society and stakeholders as a result of inconsistent and short-sighted behavior. A second risk is the difficulty of sharing common values, which leads to disagreements in decision-making about optimal strategy. A third risk is that there are difficulties in developing innovative products and services due to a lack of understanding of society and its needs. These risks are consistent with the arguments by Porter (2006, 2011).

3.3 Management Based on Shared Values: The Conditions for the Compatibility Between Economic Value and Social Value

Globalization impacts global markets, but the livelihood of people is working in the community. There is no mechanism for the development of the global economy that is consistent with the development of community. In the global economy, competitive companies expand their market and increase their production. The production site is, however, different from the location of the headquarters of the companies—workers employed by the global companies often live in places different from where companies and their leaders are located. The global economic system is separated from the community system, and the circulation of economic value from workers does not stay in their communities.

The problems that arise from the separation of value cycles within communities can be summarized as follows. The most important point is the difficulty in mutual cooperation between community members, and the resultant poor human capital development of employees. Competition enhances the efficiency of the economy in many cases, but competition does not guarantee any security for the business or sustainability in the long run. Moreover, competition in the economy is not consistent with the development of the community that forms the basis of people's lives.

However, new business models can arise that enhance the co-creation of social values by local communities and companies (see Fig. 3.1). A business can start by re-defining the well-being and happiness of consumers. The value judgements of consumers have been changing as markets mature and technological innovation proceeds. The value of an experience depends on the degree of happiness and well-being attained from it. It is important that personal happiness and well-being are closely related with self-achievement, security, human relationships, and sympathy, and that these are consistent with social value. In other words, the compatibility of economic and social values must increase as markets mature.

Next, let us look at an example of a new business based on the co-creation of social value by a company and the community. Specifically, we examine the case of Toho Leo Co., which is a "creating shared value" business. This company contributes to the design of communities and cities by greening environments.[1] The important point is that green development proceeds through cultivation of community culture and improvement of the atmosphere of the community area so that people want to stay and gather together. Land values improve as the number of people who visit a place increases. When designing green development projects, Toho Leo Co. redefined the happiness and well-being of people by utilizing leading technologies from various fields. Improving the atmosphere of public spaces leads to an increase in both economic and social value of the commercial area.

The core of the system for circulating value generated by the business stems from improving community value. In the initial stage, various innovators enter into

---

[1] See https://www.toho-leo.co.jp/division/.

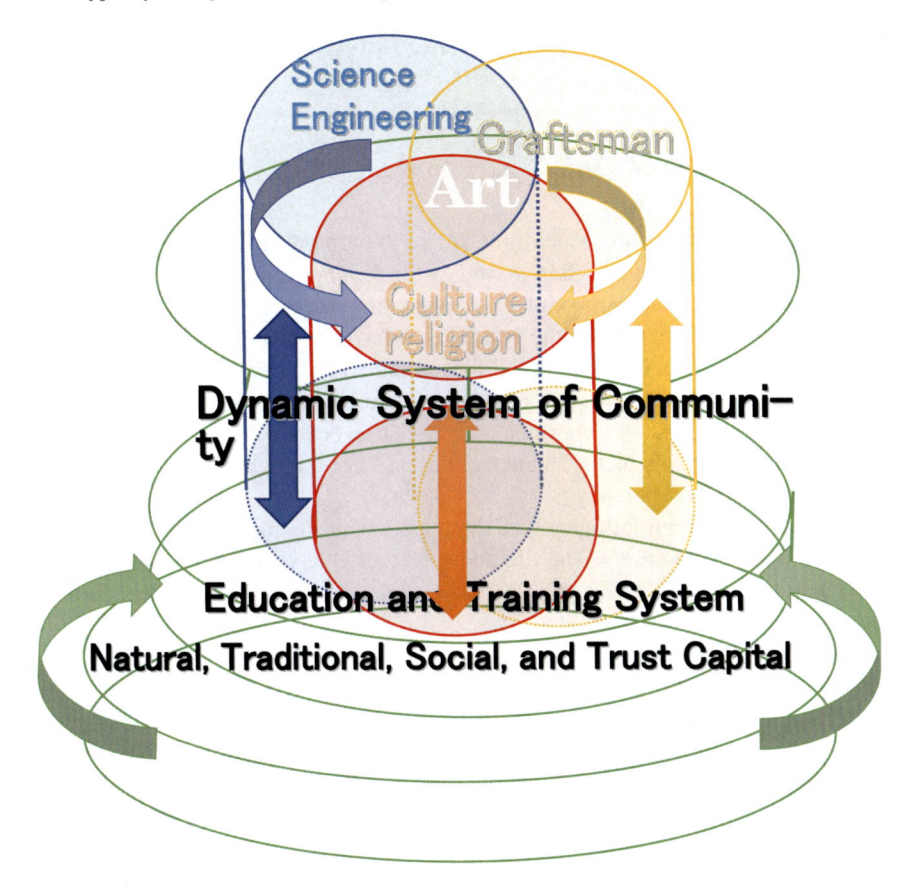

Fig. 3.1 Diagram of a long-term sustainable ecological socioeconomic system

the community, and those people who innovate to create new services and new products with existing community members attract influential people from other areas. Through this inflow of new entrants to the community, the products and services in the area attract a wider range of consumers in the market. As relationships in the community become flatter, a wider range of people gather in the community, and a wider range of consumers are attracted by the area. The example of Toho Leo Co. illustrates this cycle of enhancing the social and economic value of business.

3.4 A System of Co-Creation: How Polyphony is Used to Enhance Creativity

3.4.1 Polyphony and the Arts

Polyphony, the combination of multiple voices in harmony, is an important concept in the arts. This concept is illustrative well by the film *Bohemian Rhapsody* (released in November 2018). The climax of the movie is the performance by Queen at Live Aid in 1985, which expresses the band's zeal (especially Freddie Mercury's) for accepting diversity, including the LGBT community, in a society.

The movie suggests that Freddie Mercury had been struggling with the social pressures affecting sexual minorities and that he expressed his agony through his music. He expressed his sexual characteristics on stage through his music, costumes, appearance, and choreography.

It would be meaningful to analyze the factors contributing to the success of the movie *Bohemian Rhapsody*. The life and music of Queen generated sympathy for different and socially "unacceptable" individuals. The charity concert, Live Aid, created harmony in Wembley Stadium.

One of the special roles of arts is to break through the limitations of "taboos" in a society. Taboos and norms have a quite delicate relationship. Norms are required to stabilize the society. On the other hand, norms reflect the preferences of the majority in a society, and the preferences of minorities is suppressed. There is conflict between norms and taboos. Art makes it possible to transform the preferences of minorities into the creation of new concepts and new social orders, and to harmonize society by reducing conflicts among groups with different preferences and opinions. *Creation of new value and the harmonization of different people is the essence of polyphony.* Queen transformed the conflicts between the majority and minorities into a harmony of people in the world through its performance at Live Aid.

The reason why audiences were impressed by Queen stems from their sympathy for the anguish of the minority. Many people have feelings of isolation for various reasons. Only a small portion always feels like the majority, and most people, in one way or another, feel like they are in the minority at times. That is, people can intrinsically share sympathetic feelings and empathize with members of minority communities, and art helps facilitate this.

From the case of Queen's performance at the Live Aid concert, we can examine the incentive mechanism and pure altruistic behavior in a prosocial activity. Without doubt, altruistic behaviors can be combined with some strategic reasons or selfish interests. In this example, Queen had a good incentive for their prosocial behavior, performing at Live Aid to help victims of the African famine. The organizer of Live Aid, Bob Geldof, aimed to gather artists who could attract a large audience to the concert site.[2] The movie *Bohemian Rhapsody* describes the situation where

---

[2] See https://en.wikipedia.org/wiki/Bob_Geldof and https://en.wikipedia.org/wiki/Live_Aid (accessed in March 2019).

Freddie Mercury expressed his strong incentive for performing in the concert after he heard that top artists such as Paul McCartney and Elton John planned to appear in the concert. In addition, the audience also has strategically motivated prosocial behavior, which is shown by the fact that the amount donated increased as the audience became more impressed by the performance. According to the movie, the donation phone line hardly rang before Queen's performance. However, after the performance, a huge number of calls came in. We can interpret this as the audience behaving according to the gift-exchange motivation, that is, audiences paid money for receiving an exciting experience.

Admitting that the behavior of artists and audiences are based on strategically motived prosocial behavior, we cannot deny the existence of altruistically motived prosocial behavior in Live Aid. The point that should be noted is that these donations were induced by the increased sympathy stimulated by artists' music. This is because the audience, including TV viewers, was not obligated to donate to the concert, and no one thought that the artists would change the quality of their performance according to the amount of donations.

Thus, this raises the question of why the arts stimulate people's sympathy so strongly. Damasio (1994, Chap. 6) provides us with an interpretation from neuroscience. Simply speaking about the messages in his book, emotion is built into the human brain and body structure so that the probability of survival is increased. Altruistic behavior based on sympathy comes from the instinctual propensity for increasing the probability of survival. The human brain reacts to a stimulus by intrinsically filtering it as "good" (reward) or "bad" (punishment), which is referred to as the primary reinforcer. The stimulus generated by the arts is accepted as a strong reward by the audience, with an intrinsic link to social experience, and this social experience is remembered in the brain as a positive stimuli. In sum, it is reasonable that the emotional experience produced by music strongly enhances the prosocial behavior of the audience.

The point to be stressed is that humans are structured so that positive stimuli in social relations promote prosocial behavior. In the case of Queen's performance, Freddie Mercury himself was a member and symbol of a sexual minority. In addition, Fleischman et al. (2015) provide some neuroscientific evidence on the positive relationship between prosocial propensity (i.e., stronger desire for making ties with people) and LGBT status. Thus Freddie Mercury himself had a potentially superior talent for uniting people.

3.4.2 Relationship Between Empowerment and Polyphony

The essence of polyphony is the creation of new value and harmonization of different people. In particular, differences include the differences in preferences between minorities and the majority. Norms in a society often suppress the human rights of minorities and endanger human empowerment. In this section, "empowerment" is defined as giving hopes and dreams to people and encouraging them to stimulate and promote their innate ability.

The important question is how to empower minorities. Banducci et al. (2004) give some evidence on the positive effect of improving representation of minorities on empowering minority groups in the political world. In the case of sexual minorities, activism may support their well-being, as discussed by Hagen et al. (2018), who argue that empowerment may occur via three levels of activism: intrapersonal, interpersonal, and sociopolitical. At the intrapersonal level, individuals may examine and challenge experiences of prejudice, harassment, and invisibility. The interpersonal level of activism connects communities of people who work to achieve social recognition. The sociopolitical level of activism strives to change political institutions, cultural ideologies, and historical understandings.

The concept of polyphony is used to promote empowerment by discovering the hidden ability of minorities to create new values, and leads to a more harmonized society. One example is collaborations in the arts involving persons with disabilities. The term "Art Brut" was coined by painter Jean Dubuffet in 1946, and means "raw art." Art Brut describes the creations of institutionalized patients, prisoners, inmates, and the homeless (O'Flynn et al., 2018). Dubuffet found something authentic in art from these groups that was lacking in the mainstream arts. The important point is the art created by marginalized people has different sensibilities and perceptions of the real world.

The art center "Hana" in Nara prefecture in Japan, which is co-managed by the Tanpopo-No-Ye Foundation, Wataboshi-No-Kai Social Welfare Corporation, and Nara Tanpopo-No-Kai, is a prominent case that illustrates the virtues of the co-creation of art through the collaboration of artists and persons with disabilities.[3] In 1995, this center started the "Able Art Movement" for forming a new relationship between art and society and propelling the movement to culturally empower citizens. The center has been organizing exhibitions and workshops, operating the Able Art Company, running "artification" seminars, and promoting inclusive design.

Wataboshi-No-Kai Social Welfare Corporation aims to support people with disabilities, children, and the elderly. It provides social services that combine art, care, and daily life, and offers day-time activities and job assistance in which "work" is the production of art, counseling and consultation, and livelihood support.

The prominent feature of the art center is the numerous projects it promotes that feature co-creation by artists and persons with disabilities. One example is the collaborative project with the students of Kyoto City University of Arts that started in 2016. The importance of this co-creation is the discovery of the specific senses of persons with disabilities and the improvement of quality through this collaboration. One example is enjoying the sense of touching the art products produced by a blind visual artist. The blind artist has a specific sense of touch, and expresses emotion by designing for this sense.

Another prominent feature of the art center is the development of market channels for distributing art products made by persons with disabilities. For example, the center exhibits art products in various places such as shops or restaurants so that people in the community can enjoy in their daily lives the art produced by these individuals.

---

[3] See http://tanpoponoye.org/english/ (accessed in April 2019).

In addition, the center promotes the art products made by persons with disabilities through various channels including department stores and galleries to showcase the virtues of their art.

The art center "Hana" is an excellent example of polyphonic co-creation, in the sense that the project empowers minorities to utilize their specific abilities, and is able to continue these activities by generating revenues through market mechanisms.

3.4.3 A System that Realizes the Working of Polyphony in the Economy

The basis of polyphony is continuous communication and the exchange of ideas among stakeholders. An example that illustrates how polyphony can work in business is the "Yufuin model" (see Osawa and Yoneda, 2019). Yufuin is a district within the city of Yufu located in Ōita Prefecture, Japan. This town is located in a green valley beneath the spectacular Mount Yufu. Yufuin is a tourist town and there are some outdoor baths called *rotenburo* with a view of the mountain. In developing the town, there were serious conflicts among stakeholders including tourism-related companies, developers, dairy farmers, farmers, environmentalists, and residents. The main concern was the balance between economic development and environmental protection.

To attain a good balance, the stakeholders repeatedly gathered and held discussions, and gradually developed an original system called the "Yufuin model," which is still in use today. The system includes various features. In 1972, the "One Cow Farmer Movement" started (see Izume, 1994). This system is explained as follows: Dairy farmers in Yufuin sell ownership of a cow and then breed the cows for 5 years in place of the owner. When the cows are sold in the market, the invested money is returned to the owners. In addition, the return to the owner includes regional products as interest from the investment, and the owners are invited to special events. The owners enjoyed owning the rights to a cow and were able to spend time in a beautiful landscape. This system arose from difficulties in the dairy farm business due to a shortage of funds and the importance of preserving the landscape for dairy farming.

It is important to note that the "One Cow Farmer Movement" deepened people's understanding of the importance of maintaining the natural environment for regional development, and people came to realize that they could find an original solution through continuous discussions among stakeholders. Each member has a unique experience and opinion, which is knowledge in society that is often hidden away. Through repeated discussions, this hidden knowledge from many members of society can be combined together as explicit knowledge that is used to form a new business model. It should be noted that the discussion is not a negotiation, and that enforcing bargaining power in the discussion could result in the failure to create a new business model.

The most important feature of polyphonic problem solving is extracting hidden knowledge from the members of the society or community, and using this knowledge to find solutions based on creative ideas.

3.4.4 Polyphonic Co-Creation in an Economy with Diversified Consumer Preferences and Its Implications for the Circular Economy

An increase in the degree of diversity of firms in response to an increase in the degree of diversity of consumers' preference not only increases the probability of surviving in the market but also increases the probability of innovation (Tisdell, 2013). The reason why the ratio of companies remaining in the market increases can be explained by the diversified impact of market shocks when the market consists of large number of diversified company types. In other words, the greater the diversity of company types, the greater the ratio of companies that are not damaged by the market shock. Also, with greater diversity, in a market increases since monopoly power decreases. However, in a purely competitive market, profit disappears and R&D investment shrinks. This implies that there exists an optimal degree of diversity that derives the maximum level of innovation in a market.

Increasing diversity in a market leads to diversified strategic cooperation among diversified companies in a market. Because the companies are diversified, the combination of the cooperation in the market is also diversified. A diversified combination may include cooperation between a large strong company and a small weak company, if it is beneficial for both companies. For example, it is possible that a small weak company may have special technology that enhances the value of products produced by the large strong company. In sum, polyphonic co-creation increases the possibility of increasing the social and economic value of companies, not through competition but rather through diversified cooperation.

In a globalized economy, competitive large-scale companies have economies of scale and the market is dominated by a small number of competitive companies. The diversified preferences of consumers are, however, not consistent with the pursuit of economies of scale. In this sense, some possibilities for polyphonic co-creation arise, and this possibility can improve the state of income inequality in the globalized economy.

An example of polyphonic co-creation in apparel industry is the business "Factelier."[4] This company was established to revive the apparel industry in Japan by utilizing the sophisticated skill of Japanese craftspeople. As the globalization of apparel industry proceeded, many Japanese apparel factories faced difficulties due to lower quality and cheaper competition. This worsened the working conditions of Japanese craftspeople in the industry, and their number was decreasing. Mr. Yamada, who established the company, sought an suitable collaborating partner and started the

---

[4] See https://factelier.com (accessed May 2019).

process of polyphonic co-creation. Mr. Yamada offered Japanese factories the opportunity to produce apparel products at the price that they wanted to set. Mr. Yamada then established a business model under which the products are sold at double the price at which the company purchased them from the factories.

In the case of Factelier, the relationship between the apparel maker and the factory is not hierarchical, but even and flat. The company appeals to consumers through the high quality of its products and the stories behind its production process. Factelier regards its customers as enthusiasts and produces special stories on the apparel products and craftspeople. Factelier sends various proposals to factories so that workers can exhibit their creativity, for example, by reflecting the design ideas proposed by the workers in the factory in their products.

Factelier facilitates various avenues for communication between consumers and producers, such as a special event held at some factories for exhibiting the production process to consumers. Through these kinds of experiences, consumers consume not only apparel products but also enjoy the stories behind their production. This business model does not pursue the economies of scale, but rather tries to increase the value of products by coupling them with the value of experience. In other respects, this business model has valuable implications for the circular economy, as this model does not rely on mass production and avoids the problems caused by the disposal of huge amounts of unsold apparel. Creating a culture of consuming high-quality products for long periods of time by paying a reasonable amount of money to workers in a factory is an important and necessary characteristic of the circular economy.

3.5 Concluding Comments

Our current global economy is driven by market mechanisms, and it is quite difficult to change this system to alternative systems. The main difficulty comes from the incentive structure that fosters the development of the economy and promotes various kinds of innovations that are driven by profit-seeking and utility-maximizing behaviors of economic agents. Thus, we need to investigate ways to avoid the greedy, unethical, and strongly selfish behaviors under capitalism without eroding the incentives for each agent to make efforts for future development. The ideal way would be to provide people with some experiences of joy from contributing to other people and society. The experience of joy could be an engine for prosocial behavior, and this kind of emotion could replace the desire for monetary rewards to some extent.

In the long run, this prosocial behavior is necessary for our planet to be sustainable. The depletion of natural resources and climate change should be avoided by pursuing policies based on the circular economy. Key policy options for moving in this direction include carbon taxes or green taxes. However, strong incentives for pursuing the circular economy arise from the business opportunities based on new technologies developed by the co-creation of various economic agents. A sense of prosociality is necessary for these activities to work well in a competitive market economy.

References

Batson, C. D. (2011). *Altruism in humans.* Oxford University Press.

Banducci, S. A., Donovan, T., & Karp, J. A. (2004). Minority representation, empowerment, and participation. *The Journal of Politics, 66*(2), 534–556.

Böckler, A., Tusche, A., & Singer, T. (2016). The structure of human prosociality: Differentiating altruistically motivated, norm motivated, strategically motivated, and self-reported prosocial behavior. *Social Psychological and Personality Science, 7*(6), 530–541.

Bowles, S., Choi, J.-K., & Hopfensitz, A. (2003). The co-evolution of individual behaviours and social institutions. *Journal of Theoretical Biology, 223*, 135–147.

Damasio, A. R. (1994). *Descartes' error: Emotion, reason and the human brain: Putnam.*

Fehr, E., & Fischbacher, U. (2003). The nature of human altruism. *Nature, 425*(6960), 785.

Fehr, E., & Fischbacher, U. (2004). Third-party punishment and social norms. *Evolution and Human Behavior, 25*, 63–87.

Fleischman, D. S., Fessler, D. M. T., & Cholakians, A. E. (2015). Testing the affiliation hypothesis of homoerotic motivation in humans: The effects of progesterone and priming. *Archives of Sexual Behavior, 44*(5), 1395–1404.

Hagen, W. B., Hoover, S. M., & Morrow, S. L. (2018). A grounded theory of sexual minority women and transgender individuals' social justice activism. *Journal of Homosexuality, 65*(7), 833–859.

Imamur, H. (2010). A study on cooperative co-development of company: Hypothetical model on sustainable longevity company (in Japanese). *Innovation Management Study, 6*, 1–17.

Izume, N. (1994). Study on the historical debates on the country scenery of Yufuin (in Japanese). *Journal of Gardening, 57*(5), 97–102.

Kaschak, M. P., & Maner, J. K. (2009). Embodiment, evolution, and social cognition: An integrative framework. *European Journal of Social Psychology, 39*(7), 1236–1244.

Knoch, D., Pascual-Leone, A., Meyer, K., Treyer, V., & Fehr, E. (2006). Diminishing reciprocal fairness by disrupting the right prefrontal cortex. *Science, 314*, 829–832.

Kawaguchi, M. (2004). GSR: Examples of relevant practices of Japanese SMEs. *Corporate Social Responsibility in the Promotion of Social Development: Experiences from Asia and Latin America*: 141.

Mandevill, B. (1989). *The fable of the bees: Or private vices, Publick Benefits* Penguin Classics.

Nakatani, N. (2013). Trading of artistic folding fan: From Japan and China to France (in Japanese). *Bulletin of East-West Study of Kansai University, 46*, 51–71.

O'Flynn, D., Szekir-Papasavva, S., & Trainor, C. (2018). Art, power, and the asylum: Adamson, healing, and the Collection. *The Lancet Psychiatry, 5*(5), 396–399.

Osawa, K., & Seiji, Y. (2019). *Yufuin Model: Innovative tourism strategy by utilizing regional advantages* (in Japanese), Gakugei Publishing Company.

Porter, M. E., & Kramer, M. R. (2006). Strategy and society: The link between competitive advantage and corporate social responsibility. *Harvard Business Review*, 78–92.

Porter, M. E., & Kramer, M. R. (2011). Creating shared value. *Harvard Business Review*, 1–17.

Sedlacek, T. (2011). *Economics of good and evil the quest for economic meaning from Gilgamesh to Wall Street.* Oxford University Press.

Smith, A. (2002). *The theory of moral sentiments.* Cambridge University Press.

Smith, A. (2007). *An inquiry into the nature and causes of the wealth of nations*, edited by S.M. Soares, MetaLibli Digital Library.

Tisdell, C. (2013). *Competition diversity and economic performance: Processes.* Edward Elgar Publishing.

Yoshida, K. (2010). Philosophy of Baigan Ishida and Kazuo Inamori: Modern meaning of Sekimon philosophy and comparative study with Inamori philosophy (in Japanese). *Bulletin of Inamori Academy in Kagoshima University, 2*, 105–150.

Yasuoka, S., Teiichiro, F., & Kenjiro, I. eds. (1992). Legacy of Ohmi Merchants-Reevaluation of its business management- Dobunkan Publishing Company.

Chapter 4
Creating an Economy of Care

Stephen Hill

Abstract With the power of pro-social behavior, community, interdependent co-creation and care now demonstrated, this chapter confronts the unexpected recent impact of the COVID Pandemic, how society *can* best cope, and, more importantly, transform positively in a Post-COVID world. At heart is the Chinese expression, 'Weiji' representing *both* danger and opportunity. Individual nations have responded to the danger with immensely varying degrees of success. The *opportunity* which delivers hope for the future, lies, however, in care. Within this context, the Chapter's argument returns to Economics for the Future and demonstrates the power of Universal Basic Income (UBI)—that potentially offers care and dignity for all. However, two critical qualifiers must be added. The first is the need to see UBI not as a source of 'relief'—from economic and social stress, but as a 'platform' for economic action and resilience. The second is the need, *in parallel,* to build a surrounding pro-social, nutritive, creative and enterprise empowering context for UBI at local community level.

World Society in 2020 experienced a major and unexpected *shock* with the sudden explosion of the COVID-19 Pandemic.

Separation, lockdown, and social distancing *had* to rule and economic enterprise was forced into the shadows—by the sheer mathematics of network expansion. What the 'shock' exposed above all else was the intrinsic weaknesses within the global economic and social system—the *cracks* through which the *light* can now get in—towards developing the "Circle of Wholeness", the path of recovery from our 'shattered world', the main theme of this book.

The power of 'shock' is important as it has been with other times in history. This power is reflected in the Western use of the Chinese word for 'crisis', *Weiji*, which offers both *trouble* and *opportunity* as everything was suddenly thrown into the air[1],[2]

S. Hill (✉)
Arts, Social Sciences and Humanities, University of Wollongong, Northfields Ave, Wollongong, NSW 2522, Australia
e-mail: sthill@uow.edu.au

© Springer Nature Singapore Pte Ltd. 2022
S. Hill et al. (eds.), *The Kyoto Post-COVID Manifesto For Global Economics,*
Creative Economy, https://doi.org/10.1007/978-981-16-8566-8_4

and against a sudden exponentially exploding deadly infection rate spreading across the whole world, the norms of social life had to be suspended.

On the 'trouble' side, the world as we knew it simply *stopped*, leaving behind as at July 2021, the time of drafting this Chapter, over 185 million people who have caught the virus world-wide and over four million who died as a result (Worldometer, 2021)—statistics which will inevitably continue to climb through the rest of 2021 and beyond, even with broader take-up of vaccinations across the world's people, as new more virulent strains of the virus mutate, governments falter in effective action, and whole populations—in low income countries—are left behind.

4.1 Trouble—Trust the Free Market to Fix Things for Us!

Response varied—largely according to the level of trust which government action was able to depend on within their communities, and the ego-centeredness of those in power, in particular, The 2020 President of the United States Donald Trump. Though well advised at the start by health experts, Trump chose to minimize COVID-19's importance, originally classifying it as a *Chinese Hoax*, acting against it by simply preventing Chinese immigration to the U.S., and emphasizing his personal power to make it all go away. He did virtually nothing to actually make COVID-19 go away, more concerned, as the year 2020 and early 2021 have made very clear, in promoting *himself* over all else. The result is that the United States heads the world's country count with nearly just under 35 million confirmed COVID-19 cases of infection leading, already, to well over 600,000 deaths—as at mid-July 2021, an increase by one-third in the six months since the start of the year. These figures constitute, respectively 15.3% of world infections and 18.4% of world deaths—percentages which are now decreasing since the Biden Administration took office. Still, the US population represents only 5% of the world's people (Worldometer, 2021). Meanwhile, in spite of Legislative Efforts in March 2020 to address the problem, many of the poor— who could not afford private medical care, also could not afford even the price of being tested, or confronted bankruptcy when faced with hospital costs for a loved one taken by the COVID pandemic. The prices of testing ranged between $20–$850 per diagnostic test, with a median of $127 (Kurani et al., 2020).

Taiwan, South Korea, Singapore and New Zealand, on the other hand, reacted swiftly and aggressively, with positive results from strong restrictions on human contact and sanitation care. New Zealand, under the leadership of Prime Minister Jacinda Ardern, with the benefit of being an island, closed its borders within three weeks of the first diagnosed case—on 28th February 2020, shut down non-essential business and instituted a total Level 4 Lockdown Strategy one week later where people could only interact with people within their home. New Zealand eliminated the virus by June 2020 (Bremmer, 2020), and even now, 13 months later, has suffered only *twenty six* deaths in total. China, after initial tardiness in response, imposed very strict controls and, from government accounts, all but eliminated the virus where it started, in Wuhan, announcing in late April that all hospital cases in Wuhan had been sent home (ABC, 2020; Worldometer, 2021).

Sweden followed a strategy of proposing *only* voluntary (not compulsory) restrictions in order to maintain economic vitality—no sanctions, no nation-wide lockdowns, no compulsion to wear masks whilst bars and restaurants remained open. Architect of Sweden's strategy, epidemiologist, Anders Tegnell, whilst promoting voluntary self-restraint as policy, still had "herd immunity" as his subtext, projecting in April 2020 that with his measures, herd immunity was not there yet but might be a few weeks away (Hjelmgaard, 2020).

Neither the economic or infection sides of the strategy seem to have worked well however. Although Sweden did suffer less economic decline than the European Union as a whole (8.6% vs. 11.9%), countries which *did* impose compulsory lockdown restrictions, the Czech Republic and Lithuania declined less −8.4% and 5.1% respectively. Meanwhile, Sweden has gone nowhere near establishing herd immunity: requiring 70% of its population to have been infected, Sweden's COVID-19 infection rate has only affected 11% of its population so far, but its death toll has been appalling. Indeed, in December 2020 (Le Page, 2020), the Swedish King, Carl XVI Gustaf, sharply criticized policies which were to blame for a high death toll amongst the elderly, announcing publicly that Sweden's coronavirus strategy had failed. Prime Minister Stefan Lofven agreed. Sweden had suffered more deaths than the rest of the Nordic countries combined (Henley, 2020; BBC News, 2020). As a comparator of polar opposite strategies, compare the death rate of Sweden's voluntary self-restraint strategy (14,606 deaths) with New Zealand's total protection policy (26 deaths) and realize that Sweden is only *twice* as large in population as New Zealand (roughly 20 million vs, 10 million) and Sweden's comparative death rate per million to the alternate New Zealand COVID-19 protection model is over 280 times greater. King Carl XVI Gustaf was absolutely right! (Worldometer, 2021).

The COVID Pandemic therefore confronted the free market head on.

Where open trading, social interaction and consumer behavior were *not* seriously restricted by Lock-Downs, strict Rules of Social Association and Distancing, along with rigorous Anti-Virus Hygiene, the rate of COVID infection and death escalated exponentially. COVID-19 directly confronted the very essence of economic activity—manufacturing, marketing and consumption, travel for business or paid pleasure. Where national or state governments sought to *not* restrict market conditions COVID-19 exploded in infection and death rates.

In the U.S. the White House even refused to take the advice of top business leaders—*representing the market* but arguing that the White House must *override* the market in order to handle the pandemic.

On Saturday 21st March 2020, a small group of Silicon Valley entrepreneurs, business executives and venture capitalists gathered in the White House Situation Room to *offer their help* to the Trump Administration which was confronting a harrowing shortage of lifesaving supplies to battle COVID-19. The business executives had already canvassed and gained support from major industry and manufacturing corporations, where, for example, General Motors was prepared to redirect their automobile manufacture towards making ventilators for intensive hospital care of COVID victims. In order for business to help (outside normal market rules) however, the White House had to invoke the Federal *Defense Production Act* which would have unleashed powerful central government procurement powers in particular to produce adequate 'Protective Personal Equipment' (PPE) such as masks, protective clothing and so on, and in particular, ventilators required for intensive care.

As one attendee observed, out in the marketplace American companies were bidding against each other and radically driving prices up for PPEs, whilst at the same time making access for some almost impossible.

The business delegation to the White House was met by the son-in-law of President Donald Trump, Jared Kushner, for whom Trump had created a special post inside the Federal Emergency Management Agency. Kushner had Trump's approval to speak with full Presidential authority.

Kushner's response to the plea for Federal Government leadership and direction was to immediately dismiss the idea stating that the individual States could do this, but most importantly, arrogantly and unresponsively asserting,

"Free Markets will solve this. That is not the role of government." (Eban, 2020)

Behind Kushner was President Donald Trump's support, and a disaster of self-centred mismanagement. As Ed Yong wrote in September 2020,

"Trump embodied and amplified America's intuition death spiral. Instead of rolling out a detailed, coordinated plan to control the pandemic, he ricocheted from one overhyped cure-all to another, while relying on theatrics like travel bans. He ignored inequities and systematic failures in favor of blaming China, the WHO, governors, Anthony Fauci, and Barack Obama. He widened the false dichotomy between lockdowns and reopening by regularly tweeting in favor of the latter. He and his allies appealed to magical thinking and steered the U.S. straight into the normality trap by frequently lying that the virus would go away, that the pandemic was ending, that new waves weren't happening, and that rising case numbers were solely due to increased testing. They started talking about COVID-19 in the past tense as cases surge in the Midwest." (Yong, 2020)

Market forces ruled and their failure to have any impact on the Pandemic was shrouded from the people of America from the very top of uncaring self-centered governance by a thick curtain of lies.

Donald Trump himself caught COVID-19 largely because he paid attention only to his own self-interest, not protection—and he suffered minor impact assisted by immediate radical medical care, providing a model of total negligence for millions of his followers—in particular when attending Trump's Election Rally Circuit—close together, proudly *not* wearing masks. Many died. Market Economy and Self-Interest ruled. And the United States chalked up the worst death toll in the world.

The world's richest country—so-called democratic and humanity leading model to the rest of all peoples!

Lesson of the Age: Free Markets and Self-Interest Cannot Guarantee
the Public Good In Response to Crises.

As a consequence, the key thing which the COVID-19 Pandemic has exposed is that *there is even MORE reason* for us to argue for and support the need for a Future Global Economics based on the Platform of humanity, community and sharing rather than the fallacious ideology of the 'good' of self-interest—applied in the interests of the privileged across a massively diverse world. This conclusion supporting the fundamental importance of our humanity in times of crisis is firmly reinforced by the demonstrated results of measuring 'The Happiness Index'—reported in Chap. 1— *during* the COVID-19 Pandemic. *Trust* (including in both other people and Government) and the *Ability to Count on Others* were the (measured) bases of *resilience* in the face of economic and social hardship.

4.2 The Shock!

Viewing the 'shock' of the 2020–2021 COVID Pandemic through the 'double-vision' of *Weiji,* world society confronts severe danger but also opportunity—if only one looks.

4.2.1 Danger

On the 'danger' side, global society is suffering not only the horrific infection and death rates of the Pandemic but also the very real specter of a massively bankrupt world struggling back through the scattered bodies of previous enterprise now lost, and in particular the severe social suffering and trauma from the sudden impact of shut-downs and loss of markets on unemployment.

As the Pandemic took hold in early 2020, unemployment initially increased dramatically even across the most developed (OECD) countries—by an unprecedented 2.9% in April 2020 to 8.4%—by 18.4 million people to 55 million in a month—with the main rise in unemployment being in the United States, ie: 86.4% of total. However, after this initial spike the rates for OECD countries started to fall—back to 7.3% in September (OECD, 2020a), primarily as the more advanced countries started to channel relief through employers to their employees (Rothwell, 2020). The more casually employed and less well paid young—in hotels, restaurants and tourism—were however the hardest hit (King, 2020).

Globally, the rich remained far less affected than the poor. Of the $10 billion spent worldwide supporting workers in industry since the Pandemic began 88% was spent by and on advanced countries whilst only 2.2% was spent on the vast populations of the developing and emerging countries (OECD, 2020b). Not only that, even within advanced countries, the rich most commonly benefitted at the expense of the poor in particular, those whose income is derived from service sector employment, the most severely threatened sector. The United States is a criterion example. A Report by the U.S. Joint Committee on Taxation showed that even though emergency unemployment relief of $600 per week to December was offered for the hardest hit workers, 82% of those who stood to benefit most from the relief provisions of the 'Cares' Act, proudly and very publicly signed into force by President Trump on 27th

March, earn at least *$1 million* and only 5% earn less than $200,000 annually. Large companies gain major tax relief which can last for years whilst measures such as lump sum payments and higher jobless benefits targeting the poor are short-term. (Polity et al., 2020).

Emerging change entered the American scene with incoming U.S. President Joe Biden (20th January 2021) towards what PBS News Hour Commentator, David Brooks, described as a strategy of *care for the people* to redress both the COVID and Presidential Administration damage to the country inherited from 2020 (Brooks, 2021). President Biden then signed into law his massive $1.9 *trillion* Stimulus Plan mandating funding from Congress on 12th March 2021. This funding is planned to prioritize COVID vaccination and care with $25 billion, and is intended to provide direct relief to those who are economically in difficulties - including one-off $1,400 grants to individuals earning less than $60,000 pa as well as children and dependents (costing $80 billion overall, plus a $400 per week benefit for the unemployed until September 2021. Importantly though, the Plan targets funding for more community centered needs, education ($163 billion) and $350 billion to strengthen community resilience including small business and local-to-state governance, and families with children (Economic Times, 2021). This change in funding perspective *may* rebalance support more towards the less wealthy, and to building community resilience and interdependency. Government is acting on the Plan: since President Biden's Stimulus Plan was signed on 12th March 2021, and the first checks went out, the U.S. Government has sent out $(US)395 billion in stimulus payments to the needy – to mid-2021 (11th June). (Morris, 2021) What Biden's Stimulus Plan most certainly *does* demonstrate is that we can throw away forever the fantasy that free market forces will resolve major social or connected economic crises. It is the poor who suffered by far the most.

For low income countries the disastrous COVID-stimulated situation is exacerbated for the poor much more than in higher income countries. Their particular employment problem is the sheer size of the informal sector and the fact that those within it are unlikely to benefit even from the 2.2% of global finance directed towards their governments from international development assistance sources.

In Latin America, for example, the informal sector includes one out of every two working people (53.8%). Meanwhile, the vast majority of people living in sub-Saharan Africa (85.8%) and Southern Asia (89.0%) are employed in the informal sector and more than one third of all jobs and incomes in Africa are likely to be lost. (Bonnet et al, 2018; WIEGO, 2018). Even COVID-minimization strategies hurt - as their governments seek to introduce often severe lockdown restrictions in a desperate attempt to restrict the infection rates of COVID-19. With no income, those in the informal sector literally face starvation for themselves and families. And workers in the informal sector have no safety net of unemployment, sickness or other benefits to fall into. As Secretary-General of the United Nations, Antonio Gutteres, observed in July 2020, "More than one billion children are out of school and an *additional* 130 million people could be on the brink of starvation by the end of the year." (Gutteres, 2020).

Not only that, but being at the wrong end of the wealth generated from the global economy—which most certainly does *not* 'trickle down', the poor face absolutely enormous medical risk both of *catching* the virus and *accessing medical support if they do catch* the virus.

Many simply cannot follow WHO recommended practice and avoid close contact with others or follow appropriate antiseptic practice as their only accommodation is likely to be a shared single room house with no running water to wash their hands. Medical facilities, particularly for intensive care are simply not there. Ten African countries, for example, have *no* ventilators at all; across all Africa there are only 20,000 critical care beds, that is, 1.7 per 100,000 people, whilst, according to OECD, the African Health Budget Per Citizen is $12 – compared for example, to the United Kingdom where it is $4,000 per citizen (Goldin, 2020).

What is clear on the 'danger side' is that the negative impact of the COVID-19 Pandemic, following the general dynamic of the global self-interest based economy, primarily affects those already left out, the poor. As argued in Chap. 1, whilst we continue to follow the rule of current self-interest based global economics, inequality will intrinsically continue to grow and further divide world society.

4.2.2 Opportunity in Recovery

Though some world leaders, such as Prime Minister Morrison of Australia, talked up the idea in the early days of the Pandemic of 'Snapping Back' to the Economic System and Dependent Society which preceded the COVID-19 Pandemic (Farr, 2020), the 'opportunity' side of *Weiji* lies in the fact that others with more broad-ranging vision, are instead proposing the possibility of *Renewal*—made possible by the sheer shock to the 'normal' from COVID-19.

Early in the impact of COVID-19, Dame Polly Courtice, Director of the Cambridge Institute for Sustainable Leadership, proposed that "we take this moment to reflect on the need to change and transform society" (Courtice, 2020). Hugh Mackay, in May 2020, honored Australian writer and social commentator, observed further, "This is an opportunity to reflect—perhaps to rethink our values, reset our priorities and reconsider the ways we approach our relationships, our work, our institutions. How should we respond to this heightened sense of our interconnectedness?" (Mackay, 2020). Then, in late September, Prime Minister of Canada, Justin Trudeau, speaking to the United Nations General Assembly, noting that COVID-19 has pushed many countries to the brink, and generated a humanitarian crisis, as well as a greater threat of climate change, "urged countries to use the present moment to *shift course* and work together to achieve a better future for all people" (UN News, 2020).

Meanwhile, others projected positive consequences. Oxford Economists Paul Collier and John Kay observe, for example, in their July 2020 book, "Greed is Dead", "As the world emerges from an unprecedented crisis we have the chance to examine society afresh and build a politics beyond individualism." The recently retired Governor of the Bank of England, Dr Mark Carney, offers additional support, observing, as we do in this Kyoto Post-COVID Manifesto $\approx$ book, that "the market is becoming the organizing framework, not only for economies, but also increasingly for.. "broader human relations with its reach extending well into civic and family life."(Carney, 2020a). Consequently, as Carney continues, increasingly a *market economy* has become a *market society* so to be valued currently an asset or activity (eg: health or education) has to be in the market. In developing our future now, "we need to act as an interdependent community, not as independent individual."(Carney,

2020b)[3] Critically, Maja Gopel of the European Greens pointed out that as we do "bounce forward" towards "sustainable and thus resilient societies which leave no one behind" (rather than "bounce back"), "the more that *trust* will consolidate" (Gopel, 2020). This, as we argue in the present book is the basic fabric of a caring and sharing society.

Applying these projections of *renewal, o*pportunity lies in front of us to *build* "The Circle of Wholeness" which, as this book, "The Kyoto Post-COVID Manifesto for Global Economics" argues, provides the caring, sharing, sustainable society the world needs now to address our 'shattered' world—where the dynamic of connectedness and enterprise is not the *fantasy* of supposed free-market altruism, but the *reality* of mutual trust and care.

4.3 The Way Forward

4.3.1 The Significance of Care

Indeed, as a number of observers noted, particularly in the early stages of the COVID-19 Pandemic, the value of care for others started to emerge—in particular at local community level as a *result* of the Pandemic. Hugh Mackay points out that, intrinsically, we are *social animals*, so enforced social isolation such as has been required as common response to the coronavirus Pandemic is leading to unprecedented introspection and social isolation—loneliness. Working from home reinforces this. But it also has tended to focus attention back on neighborhood—the 'local', on 'our street'—*connecting*, perhaps partly to overcome this loneliness. Mackay observes that a result is that there are many signs of increased *care*, of *compassion*—concern for neighbors, offering assistance to others such as the elderly. Even the fact that people are obeying the lockdown rules, maintaining social distancing, present acts of *care* for others, not just ourselves (Mackay, 2020b).[4]

> A small 'green shoot' for our post-COVID future towards a more caring society.

As Hugh Mackay observes, humans are intrinsically *social animals* yet the overwhelming dominance of economic *self*-interest denies our'mutuality' and has resulted in massive inequality and suffering worldwide.

In spite of protestations which still may perhaps be heard from some recalcitrant 'market fundamentalists' still hanging on to the 'free market' sledge as it slides irrevocably over the precipice of lived experience into a swamp of wrong ideas, *mutuality and community are basic to market vitality.* Collier and Kay emphasize in their book, "Greed is Dead", "markets can function effectively only when embedded in a network of social relations." The authors go on to point out that humans are not self-maximizing individuals, pursuing their conception of happiness, but seek fulfillment which arises largely from their interaction with others—in families, in streets and villages, at work … in *community* (Collier & Kay, 2020).

Japan's culture of business provides good lessons to take into account – with the "Sanpo-Yoshi" or *Triple Win Concept* – where sellers, buyers and society are treated with equal care to maintain harmony, a base for highly ethical behavior. Key elements include (1) sharing the same ethical values among top management and every employee; (2) respecting employees; (3) creating and maintaining relationships of *trust* among clients and suppliers; (4) support for the local community for its sustainable development; and (5) commitment to environmental protection and the responsible use of nature (Yagi et al. Chap. 3 in this Book).

If we can capture this intrinsic human value—of mutuality and care—into our future, the previous self-centered ideology is destroyed at its foundations. Ideally as we build our future society out of the chaos of the COVID-19 Pandemic we can capture 'care' at community level into building a general 'culture of care' world-wide. *And this is good for the economy!* For economic exchange and values are embedded in community where social relations and mutuality will keep fair exchange bedded in. This is an economy built on *trust* rather than the *deal* which is housed in contract words reflecting our *distrust,* requiring us to remain forever vigilant to catch *deviation,* even in detail.

This transformation to a culture of care will not happen from wishful thinking. There has to be a structural strategy in which *care* is comfortably housed.

Look Up! It is right there in front of us.

4.3.2   Leaping Forward

We start by capitalizing on what governments are doing *now*.

So *many* people have very suddenly been precipitated into unemployment as businesses have been closed down to prevent further spread of COVID-19, and also, as COVID-19 accelerated the pre-existing trend towards automation—as some firms sought to 'proof' their organizations against the insecurity of workers suddenly leaving work to handle COVID infection. As a specific example, OECD reported in September 2021 that 26% of Australian firms reported an increase in the take-up of new technology or automation because of the COVID-19 Pandemic (OECD, 2021b). Many more companies faced bankruptcy however. Across the world, governments have been forced to withdraw *massive* amounts of money from federal reserves (or print more money against value to be achieved later) to feed out to businesses unable to operate and previous workers now inescapably unemployed—with no alternate jobs to go to.

In just the first two months after the Pandemic took hold governments around the world announced expenditures of $10 *trillion* for relief, three times more than the response to the 2008–2009 financial crisis, with Germany leading, having devoted 33% of GDP to the task and Saudi Arabia paying 60% of the salaries for private sector companies (Ziyad et al., 2020). The United States brought into law $3 trillion in economic stimuli to June (Polity et al., 2020), the majority, $2.2 trillion, under its 27th March 'CARES' Act (Imbert, 2020). In my own context of Australia, over 10% of GDP was quickly invested in economic stimulus actions of wage subsidies (the 'job keeper' scheme), doubling unemployment benefits (the "job seeker) scheme) and free child care (Bremmer, 2020). Still mainly response to each new round of required Lockdowns as new waves of COVID-19 particularly infectious 'Delta' strains take off, the *idea* of Government provision of a basic income for all is bedded in, though still in relation to specific crises rather than as a general economic platform.

Having started down this path, unimaginable before COVID-19 came along, lets not go backwards, although the money must be spent differently to promote greater equality and concern for humanitarian values.

Instead of 'snapping back' to our pre-existing *self-centered* economic paradigm, we can 'leap forward', or 'bounce forward', continuing the idea of pervasive government support towards a living wage for *all*, a Universal Basic Income (UBI), a realistic current strategy with relatively minor adjustments in taxation rates and other strategies (Philipsen, 2020).[5] Apart from anything else, world society needs to be prepared for the projected impact of computer-based job replacement and therefore potentially crippling unemployment within 15 to 20 years' time. Indeed, right now, according to OECD's surveys, 14% of jobs in OECD countries are likely to be automated and another 32% are at high risk—*short-term* (OECD, 2021a).

The alternative, continuation of an economic *growth* policy within a self-interest focused free market system as priority would be a dangerous fallacy—certainly for its effects on our planet as observed in Chap. 1, but also for the sheer distortion of human enterprise it implies.

Assuming a generally accepted 3% growth rate in the US, as example, doubling output every 23 years or so, the US economy would need to produce 16 times present output within another 100 years, 5,000 times in 300 years (Philipsen, 2020).

Somewhat from left-field, the idea of moving the world economy towards the wide implementation of Universal Basic Income has now been given the authority of Pope Francis of the Roman Catholic Church in his new and timely book, "Let Us Dream".

Very much in line with our own thesis, Pope Francis argues, that by its very nature, crisis presents us with a choice (Francis, 2020, p. 46). We make a grievous error if we try to return to some pre-crisis state: it is a "dead-end street" (Francis, 2020, p. 54). Pope Francis, instead calls for us to abandon the self-defeating isolation of individualism and obsession with profit (Francis, 2020, p. 103 and p108) – where earth's resources are used for the few not for all with minimal overall control.

"For me it's clear", he states. "We must redesign the economy so that it can offer every person access to a dignified existence while protecting and regenerating the natural world." (Francis, 2020, p. 44).

In the course of devoting one third of his book to possible actions to change the world, whilst noting that global leaders are currently debating the rethinking of the economic system and work in a post-Pandemic future, Pope Francis observes that the institution of a universal basic income is one of the avenues for getting out of the crisis caused by the Coronavirus Pandemic: "an unconditional lump-sum payment to all citizens which could be paid through the tax system" (Francis, 2020, pp. 131–132).

4.3.3 Evolution in Understanding the Creation of Value via Universal Basic Income as the PLATFORM for the Economy of the Future

Universal Basic Income does provide a means of pulling the world back towards greater equality and away from the brink of desperate all-pervading suffering.

In our present proposal however the prime *economic* purpose of moving forward to a UBI-led future is *not* just 'Relief' from Distress. Instead we see UBI as a *Platform for a New Economics—where humanistic sharing values and trust form the basis for enterprise decisions,* and spending is generated where the people are, locally at community level where they create the meaning of their lives and culture, where, as demonstrated earlier, mutuality and care are fundamental to the Economy of the Future.

Also, whilst not 'snapping back', we can *look back* for lessons from traditional societies and cross-culturally—for our goal is recapture of the power which can be drawn from our wider *humanity.*[6]

4.3.4 Wider and Longer-Term Economic Context

It is also constructive to 'look back' at the fundamental shift in understanding of what creates *value* in an economy as seen and practiced in the 20th Century compared with today, for this demonstrates very clearly that there has been evolution in ideas and practice, and where it leads us into the future, locates value where the people are, not in the machines or in large faceless corporations or economic theories which, as was taken-for-granted until recently, extract out the inconvenience of including real people from their equations. Instead, the Future puts people—social actors, on the economic stage and at *community* level, and as a core value, their creativity. The Platform for an Economics of the Future to be built at Community Level *beds into* the longer term evolution of the source of economic value.

A community focus now is not just an idea plucked from ideological assertion.

I will take you, the reader, briefly on this Darwinian-Economic voyage.

Around 25 years ago, towards the end of the 20th Century, the world woke up to the fact that value was increasingly being derived from *knowledge* rather than increasingly widespread and heavy industry. Representing this recognition, the *idea* of a knowledge based economy was captured in both OECD and World Bank Reports in 1996 (OECD, 1996; World Bank, 2007). Empirical Results such as for Canada backed up the reality of this transformation (Gere and Mang, 1998). Increasingly, the power of knowledge in economic value and growth was recognized also within the developing world such as in the Middle East and North Africa (Barkhordari et al., 2019).

Meanwhile, the dynamics within a *Knowledge-based* Economy, started to be revealed in an understanding of what lies behind a 'Knowledge' Economy, and that is a *'Creative' Economy*. The increasing role of creativity in economic growth has, not unexpectedly, led to increasing research interest and therefore empirical results on the existence and power of the 'Creative Economy' along with its significance in political agenda (Correla, 2014).

So, creativity hit the highlights. Empirical studies then increasingly observed the power of *creative industries* (UNCTAD, 2004). Daubaraite and Startienne specifically focused on an empirical comparison of the role of creative industries in Lithuania and Latvia, where they demonstrate in both cases that the average total growth in creative industries far exceeds average total growth for the economy as a whole (13.62 vs 3.01%). The authors then conclude:

> As Western nations move away from the production of goods and services and concentrate instead on the production of ideas and knowledge, creative industries have become the subject of research and theoretical development. (Daubaraite and Startienne, 2017)

'Creativity' would not stand still however and the power of individual human actors came to be demonstrated in economic practice as the 'onion' of value within the 21st Century Economy continued to be unpeeled to what lies behind the Creative Economy. What is demonstrated to be driving economic value now is *people and creativity*—not 'systems' or economic theory abstracted from the human actors who make it work: ie: the *relationship* between *human capital* (linked to education), *entrepreneurship* (measured in a variety of ways) and the existence of a *creative class* (associated with worker occupations) (Faggian et al., 2016).

> There has now therefore been a quantum shift in the assumed sources of value in economic enterprise that used to be taken for granted as recently as in the 20th Century.

Particularly, as the digital age came upon us, creativity moved out of institutions and into the hands of *individuals*—straight out of university or perhaps moving on with an invention even before graduating, or just from home and within their personal community, as with Netflix on 29th August 1997 in Scotts Valley, California; Google on 4th September 1998 in Menlo Park, California; and more recently, Facebook on 4th February 2004 in Cambridge, Massachusetts; Twitter on 21st March 2006 in San Francisco, California; and, as demonstrated most dramatically, by Jeff Bezos, the richest man in the world from his creativity in founding and developing Amazon (though temporarily replaced by Elon Musk on 8th January 2021 (Klebnikov, 2021)—also, enormously wealthy from his personal single-minded technical creativity. Bezos brought Amazon to life in his garage on 5th July 1994 in Bellevue, Washington, USA (Hartmans, 2020), and Elon Musk started with inventing and selling a computer game, 'Blaster' to 'Spectravideo' for $500 at age 12, later moving on to California where he and his brother founded a software company, Zip 2 with $28,000 capital (Blystone, 2020). From these examples, note the consistency of California and nearby as the environment for creative enterprise, ie: the significance of *place* and flow of ideas and interaction within *community*.

Indeed, as Potts and colleagues. demonstrate, as you examine the industrial dynamics of new digital media from the perspective of consumer co-creation, you find "that consumer-producer interactions are an increasingly important source of value creation" (Potts et al., 2008).

Economic value, as we progress through the 2100s is circling closer and closer to where the people are …. in community and the personal power of creativity.

So, the economy of recovery, as the economy of the future, is fundamentally built on the 'local', on *communities*, on *people*—not the 'big end of town' assuming a phantom 'trickle-down' effect to those less wealthy, or an abstract self-interest focused economics which inevitably serves the interests of the wealthy far more than the poor.

This focus on 'local' is then particularly reinforced when it is realized that *meaning, creativity and value* are created here[7]—more in the 21st Century, than in the 20th Century, where large scale technology and business were more significant in providing the economic base for creating *value*.

> We have a new focus of value now, that is, the sheer *economic* benefit of focusing at local level, the local and community focused platform for the economics which will get the world economy past the COVID-19 Pandemic and then on to an Economics Platform for the sustainable long term. The *strategy* which follows is then to build the strength and connectedness of community—as an economic strategy. But, meanwhile, we are also *strengthening the basis of our humanity* as sharing social animals. A double benefit.

So, at the end of a brief journey through our economic past, we arrive firmly within the 'local', the community. Not only that, we arrive with *culture* firmly in sight. Daubaraite and Startienne observe, for example, of creativity,

> Creativity, more than labour and capital or even traditional technologies is deeply embedded in every country's cultural context, thus it is not the privilege of rich countries. With effective nurturing, these sources of creativity can open up new opportunities for developing countries to increase their shares of world trade and to 'leap-frog' into new areas of wealth creation. (Daubaraite and Startienne, 2017)

Culture is created, embedded and expressed at the *local* inter-subjective level within every society.

Richard Denniss, Chief Economist of The Australia Institute, demonstrates the power of the 'local', in particular now as we move forward from the impact of the COVID-19 Pandemic, drawing our attention to the organizing principles of what he calls the "3 Ls"—"local, labor, long-term". Here, we finally also return to the critical importance in the Economics of the Future of long-term sustainability including of our planet.

With this framework in mind, Dennis observes however how misdirected Government Stimulus Funding has been in response to the Coronavirus Pandemic in the case of Australia, and by implication, other developed countries as well.

> The focus of government spending needs to be at the local and community level with an emphasis on *long-term sustainability,* not 'the big end of town' as evidence is increasingly clear that focus on investment at local levels is by far the most productive – where jobs have been lost and are most likely to be immediately created with investment, particularly

if focused on labor intensive industry. OECD's September 2021 Report, "Preparing for the Future of Work Across Australia", specifically reinforces this strategy,

> Businesses and governments could work together at the local level to develop practical solutions and help workers transition to the jobs of tomorrow. Co-designed and co-funded training programs as well as on-line learning platforms could play an important role. (OECD, 2021b)

Denniss's position aligns with the OECD strategy to focus on people and building their capacities. He further argues, strategy needs to focus on long-term objectives to be most effective … the "3 L's as he summarizes, "local, labor, long-term" (Denniss, 2020a).

At heart, as Richard Dennis concludes, such a strategy is fundamentally Keynesian (Keynes, 2007), ie: a high level of government spending *is* required when private sector demand is failing – because people are not spending (having lost their source of income), when small businesses are not able to operate at a profit – because the locals cannot afford to use them … The financial support is however *replacing* private sector spending, 'filling the hole' – *where the hole exists*, in order to stimulate the economy … through spending at local levels, ie: from the bottom up.

But, particularly in the case of Australia, as exemplar of wide ranging strategy worldwide, general government spending has focused more on the 'top' end of town (eg: cutting tax rates for the privately owned billion dollar enterprise (which creates virtually no jobs) rather than on direct labor producing enterprise: $90 billion (AUD) to provide a line of credit to privately owned banks but nothing to superannuation funds to help individuals desperately in need of urgent withdrawals; $50 million (AUD) for the media industry, but zero for individual artists; $95 million (AUD) to support Zoos, but zero dollars to Universities where creative enterprise and knowledge for our future are hatched in individual knowledge and vision. Such spending pretends to be Keynesian but fundamentally is not, instead relying on a (yet to be seen) 'trickle down' effect to get to the people who will re-generate the economy by their direct action (Denniss, 2020b).

4.3.5   Building the Environment Around UBI to Turn It into the Platform for the Future Economy

We now come back to the central role of Universal Basic Income—within a funding environment which places priority on building value from within the community. Apart from the potential freedom UBI allows for individual initiative—if managed well—we must be conscious that whilst we may pass by the Coronavirus Pandemic within a few years, we *will* confront what is equivalent to another Pandemic, as mentioned earlier, within the next 15–20 years. Computer-based technological and network systems, artificial intelligence and genetic engineering, *will* have an exponentially powerful impact on employment. Even now, as Yuval Harari tells us, "*We* are what gives networks power: they use our ideas of meaning to determine what will happen to us". The question follows:

What will happen to the welfare state when computers push humans out of the job market and create a massive new 'useless class'. (Harari, 2016; Runciman, 2016)

Universal Basic Income, or UBI, allows us to prepare NOW.

It is very important then to note that introducing UBI even with a focus on community and the local is, of itself, still not enough. *It is critical to build an environment around it* to equip people with an understanding, commitment and competence in enterprise and creativity, as well as to facilitate easily accessible broad ranging access to community support action—which, perhaps could be rewarded by 'social credit' vouchers accountable against UBI funding.

Apart from anything else, in particular at the start, people need to feel it is worthwhile to take initiative and to be connected and contributors, rather than do nothing and perhaps watch mindless TV. They also need to have access to the knowledge and experience to know how they can contribute or even create new enterprise and therefore economic value.

The task of creating an environment at community level into which a UBI initiative could bed in and be successful as *the Platform for the Economy of the Future* is both short-term and long-term—building community strength can start NOW. Developing capacity across the community of enterprise and creativity, basic to creating value, needs to start now right back to early education, but will take time to fully implement.

Building Community Strength:

The first and immediate 'environment-creator' for the wider economic and social impact of UBI, requires *building community strength* as an essential component of the 'Economic Platform' which UBI can provide – through sharing participants' working time with their building community support and linkages. Activities could include, for example, caring for the elderly, providing teaching support for disadvantaged community children.

BUT decision and funding also needs to be *at* community level where locals can see and know what is needed, and not at the distance of central government. For example, government could establish networks of funded and finance-distributing Community Culture Centers which, though accountable, would have the authority to act relatively independently.

Building a Culture of Creativity and Enterprise:

In parallel to immediately strengthening community via UBI, significant funding needs to be dedicated in parallel to building *a culture of creativity* and *enterprise* to *surround* UBI and so establish it as *Platform* for the New Economy of the Future – within a fully supportive context.

It follows that support needs to be provided from pre-school education onwards in order to prepare UBI recipients to seek creative opportunity and develop enterprise based on it – to create *a New Economy for the Future* based on the strength of our humanity, building on the *shared* power and *creative potential* of *community,* the *shared equity of their enterprise and results.* Again, Community Culture Centre Networks can provide direction and local support.

This is not irresponsible lack of care about debt but an absolutely *essential* government support strategy—with monitored tolerance for debt to avoid hyper-inflation—for establishing the societal platform for a *resilient, sustainable and humanity-focused future*—fed by re-organizing government spending priorities.

4.4 Conclusion

The central objective of this book, "The Kyoto Post-COVID Manifesto for Global Economics" is to place our Humanity at the center of the Economics for our Future, to replace the currently prevailing value of self-interest at the core of economic thinking and practice with humanistic values of our mutuality—caring, mindfulness, compassion, sharing and trust. For whatever the economic frame for daily life is it sets the 'grammar' or underlying assumptions of how we relate to each other and *build together*.

Our ideal is, as I outlined in Chap. 2 to move world society to "Embrace the Circle of Wholeness" for a harmonious, humanity-based World Order.

The 'Crack' in our all-encompassing economic 'system' has been flooded with attention as a result of the impact of the Coronavirus Pandemic. But, so too has a serious opportunity, a design for our future—the Universal Basic Income—representing a radical shift from past ways but already partially adopted in remedial action of support and stimulus to get us out of the clutches of the Pandemic, and already 'situated' in the new attention now being paid to the source of value which lies with people, their community, their creativity.

Both the rationale and need for introduction of a Universal Basic Income is increasingly clear, and government stimulus packages are even preparing the way. The UBI should *not* be seen as *relief* from economic difficulty, but as the *platform* for the economy of the future. As argued in this Chapter, this new Platform for the Economy must be *housed* within a supportive environment of strengthening community and building widely distributed creativity and enterprise within this community. Indeed, UBI provides us protection which will be absolutely necessary from the harsh winds of unemployment which, inevitably will blow over world society within the very near future from our enchantment with but obeisance to machines and artificial intelligence.

The Platform for the Future Economy, UBI, therefore offers us the possibility to rebuild world society towards "Embracing the Circle of Wholeness" which can enrich our very humanity and to do this within a community-centered 'Economy of Care'.

Notes

1. Use of the Chinese word *Weiji* to mean 'danger' and 'opportunity' was most famously made by President John F. Kennedy in a Speech on April 12, 1959, and has lasted – in English – to mean this since. In fact, the first brush stroke, *wei* does mean 'danger', but the second brush stroke, *ji*, means 'incipient moment' or 'crucial point' (Nguyen, 2014). Opportunity does, however, associate with Crisis in everyday experience because 'when everything is suddenly disturbed, the rigidities of the past are left open to question and therefore, possible change.

2. I personally was able to capitalize on such a crisis-led 'opportunity' when serving as UNESCO Director and Ambassador in Indonesia in May 1998 when President Soeharto was suddenly forced from power in the face of revolution

on the streets. Freedom of Expression, one of my UN mandated responsibilities, became possible—with change of the law and practical implementation of an investigative reporting radio network across the country when previously the 'Ministry of Information', consisting of 50,000 personnel, totally controlled *all.* media expression. Centralized Education – appropriate to dictatorial control, was questioned in the minds of the people, again allowing us enormous *opportunity* to assist the incoming Government and people of Indonesia to develop decentralized and creative education across the whole country for 42 million children (Hill, 2005, 2017, 2018a, b; 2022).

3. Dr Mark Carney retired from his position as Governor of the Bank of England during 2020 to take up the new positions as UN Secretary General Special Envoy for Climate Finance, and Finance Advisor to UK Prime Minister, Boris Johnson, for the 2021 UN Climate Change Conference in Glasgow. His interdependent societal rather than individual self-centered approach to economics is therefore likely to now have strong influence in world action to deal with climate change.

4. See also Mackay (2020a).

5. I will not discuss alternate economic means here for generating the funding for making a Universal Basic Income realistic. Instead, this is covered in the subsequent Chap. 6 in this book, by Tadashi Yagi, "Sustainability Conditions for Universal Basic Income in the Economic Depression Caused by COVID-19".

6. A quite beautiful example of what we can learn about our shared humanity from a very remote indigenous culture is presented in our earlier book, 'The Kyoto Manifesto for Global Economics'. Within months of the 9/11 terrorist attack on New York, Maasai tribespeople heard about it and a representative group came to the United States Consulate in Kenya and, in a formal ceremony, donated 14 cows, their most prized possession, to the United States 'to help them' at this time of crisis (Hill 2017).

7. See Chap. 2 of the present book.

References

ABC. (2020). Coronavirus update: China says all patients discharged from hospital in Wuhan, Boris Johnson returns to work after recovery. *News*, 27 April.

Barkhordari, S., Fattahi, M., & Aliazimi, N. (2019). 'The impact of knowledge-based economy on growth performance. *Evidence from MENA Countries', Journal of the Knowledge Economy, 10*, 1168–1182.

BBC News. (2020). 'Europe'—Annual Review of the Year with the Royal Family', 17th December.

Blystone, D. (2020). How elon musk became Elon musk: A brief biography. *INVESTOPEDIA, 4* March.

Bonnet, F., Leung, V., & Chalcatana, S. (2018). Women and men in the informal economy: A statistical picture, 3rd Ed.', International Labour Organization (ILO), March, p 23.

Bremmer, I. (2020). The best global responses to COVID-19 Pandemic. *TIME,* 12 June.

Brooks, D. (2021). 'Commentary', *PBS News Hour,* 15 January: *pbs.org/newshour.*

Carney, M. (2020a). 'From Moral to Market Sentiments', *The Reith Lectures 2020: 'How We Get What We Value'*, Lecture 1, *BBC Radio 4*, 2 December, 9am.

Carney, M. (2020b). 'From COVID Crisis to Renaissance', *The Reith Lectures 2020: 'How We Get What We Value'*, Lecture 3, *BBC Radio 4*,16 December, 9am.

Collier, P., & Kay, J. (2020). Greed is dead—politics after individualism. Allen Lane.

Correla, C. M. (2014). Measuring creativity in the EU member states. *Journal of Regional Research, 30*, 7–26.

Courtice, D. P. (2020). *COVID-19 and creating the future we want*. Cambridge Institute for Sustainability Leadership (CISL), 2 April.

Daubaraite, U., & Startienne, G. (2017) 'The role of creative industries in economic development of Lithuania and Latvia, *Research Gate,* 'Country Experiences in Economic Development, Management and Entrepreneurship', November, pp 91–103. https://doi.org/10.1007/978-3-319-46319-3_5.

Denniss, R. (2020a). 'After the Crisis'—Conversation With Jim Chalmers, Shadow Treasurer, Australia. *Australia Institute Webinar*, 29 April.

Denniss, R. (2020b). Weal of Fortune—Rebuilding the economy means government investment, but not all public spending is equal. *The Monthly*, July.

Eban, K. (2020). 'That's Their Problem'—How Jared Kushner Let the Markets Decide America's COVID-19 Fate", *Vanity Fair*, 17 September.

Economic Times. (2021). "What's in Joe Biden's stimulus plan?" 12th March.

Faggian, A., Partridge, M., & Malec, Ed. (2016). Creating an environment for economic growth: creativity, entrepreneurship or human capital. *MPRA, Munich Personal RePec Archive,* MPRA Paper No. 71445, May: https://mpra.ub.uni-muenchen.de/71445.

Farr, M. (2020). Morrison reminds us nothing lasts forever—especially the coronavirus spending spree. *The Guardian* (Australian Edition), 02 Thursday, 17.31 (AEDT).

Francis, P. (2020). 'Let Us Dream—The Path to a Better Future', (with Austen Ivereigh), Simon & Schuster.

Gere, S., & Mang, K. (1998). The Knowledge-based economy: shifts in industrial output. *Canadian Public Policy* 24 (June), 149–184.

Goldin, I. (2020). The Coronavirus is the biggest disaster for developing countries in our lifetime. *The Guardian*, 21 April.

Gopel, M. (2020). A Social-Green Deal with just transition—the European answer to the coronavirus crisis. *Social Europe Series—Beyond Ideology*, 31 March.

Gutteres, A. (2020). Secretary-General's remarks to the Security Council Open Video-Teleconference on the Maintenance of International Peace and Security: Implications of COVID-19 (as delivered). United Nations Secretary-General, 02 July.

Harari, Y. N. (2016). "Homo Deus" A Brief History of Tomorrow', Harvill Secker.

Hartmans, A. (2020). 'Amazon wasn't the original name of Jeff Bezos' company, and 14 other little-known facts about the early days of Amazon', *Business Insider*, 17 July.

Henley, J. (2020). 'King of Sweden blasts country's "failed" coronavirus response', *The Guardian*, Friday 18 December.

Hill, S. (2005). 'Lessons of a Decade', Director's Report, Annual Report, UNESCO Office, Jakarta, pp 6–9: www.unesco.or.id.

Hill, S. (2017). 'Captives for Freedom—Hostages. *Negotiations and the Future of West Papua'*, University of Papua New Guinea Press, 2017, 133–134.

Hill, S. (2018a). '"Sacred Silence"—The Stillness of Listening to Humanity', Chapter 17 in Yamash'ta, Yagi and Hill, 2018, pp. 293–4.

Hill, S. (2018b). '"Community": Platform for Sustainable Change', Chapter 18 in Yamash'ta, Yagi and Hill, p. 311.

Hill, S. (2022). 'Being There', forthcoming, Chapter 5, "Opportunity".

Hjelmgaard, K. (2020). "Tegnell says 'herd immunity' in Sweden might be a few weeks away", *USA Today*, April 28th.

Imbert, F. (2020). 'How the U.S. economic response to the coronavirus pandemic stacks up to the rest of the world', *CNBC*, 28 September.

Keynes, J. M. (2007). 'The General Theory of Employment, Interest and Money', Palgrave Macmillan (originally published 1936).

King, B. (2020). 'Unemployment rate: How many people are out of work. *BBC News,* 26 November.

Klebnikov, S. (2021). 'Elon Musk is Now The Richest Person In The World, Officially Surpassing Jeff Bezos', *Forbes*, Friday 8 January.

Kurani, N., Pollitz, K., Cotliar, D., Shanosky, N., & Cox, C. (2020). 'COVID-19 Test Prices and Payment Policy', *Peterson-KFF Health System Tracker,* 15 July.

Le Page, M. (2020). 'Is Sweden's coronavirus strategy a cautionary tale or a success story', *New Scientist*, Health, 13 August.

Mackay, H. (2020a). 'Building Community in a Crisis', *ABC Podcast*, 'Conversations with Sarah Konovski', 09 April.

Mackay, H. (2020b). 'Bouncing Back or Bouncing Forward—Shaping a post-pandemic society', *Webinar* hosted by the Australian Baha'i Community, Friday 29 May: https//events.humanitix.com/post-pandemic society.

Morris, C. (2021). "Treasury Department sends out another 2.3 million $1,400 stimulus checks", *Fortune*, 11 June: https://fortune.com>2021/06/10>where-is-my-stimulus.

Nguyen, S. (2014). 'In Chinese: Crisis does not mean danger and opportunity', *Workplace Psychology*, August 10.

OECD. (1996). The knowledge-based economy. *Organisation for Economic Cooperation and Development, OECD, Paris, 2*, 1–46.

OECD. (2020a). 'Unemployment Rates, OECD, Paris—Updated', 09 June.

OECD. (2020b). 'Marginal fall in OECD unemployment rate in September 2020 as pace of improvement slows', *Home, Labour Statistics*, 10 November.

OECD. (2021a). The future of work. OECD, Paris: https://www.oecd.org>future-of-work.

OECD. (2021b). Preparing for the future of work across Australia. *OECD Reviews on Local Job Creation, OECD Publishing, Paris*. https://doi.org/10.1787/9e506cad-en

Philipsen, D. (2020). Economics for the people. *AEON Essays*, Thursday 22 October: *aeon.co.*

Polity, J., Fontanella-Khan, J., & Allaj, O. (2020). Why the US pandemic response risks widening the economic divide. *Financial Times*, 18 June.

Potts, J., Hartley, J., Banks, J., Burgess, J., Cobcroft, R., & Stuart Cunningham and Lucy Montgomery. (2008). Consumer co-creation and situated creativity. *Industry and Innovation, 15*(5) Issue: 'Managing Situated Creativity in Cultural Industries'.

Runciman, D. (2016). Homo Deus by Yuval Harari. Review: 'How data will destroy human freedom, *The Guardian*, 24 August.

UNCTAD. (2004). Creative Industries and Development (on line), United Nations Conference on Trade and Development (UNCTAD), available at: http://unctad.org/en/docs/tdxibpd13_en.pdf.

UN News. (2020). Justin Trudeau Speech to the U.N. General Assembly. *U.N. Global Perspectives Human Stories*, 25 September.

WIEGO. (2018). Women in informal employment globalizing & organizing, 'Statistical Picture': wiego.org.

World Bank. (2007). *Building knowledge economies: Advanced strategies for development*. World Bank.

Worldometer. (2021). COVID-19 Coronavirus Pandemic, July 7th: https://www.worldometers.info/coronavirus/.

Yagi, T., Kosir, L. G., & Yamash'ta, S. (2021). Polyphony as a System for delivering co-creation and the empowerment of individuals. Chapter 4 in the present book, KM-PC.

Yong, Ed. (2020). Conceptual Errors in Treating COVID Epidemic: https://www.theatlantic.com/health/archive/2020/09/pandemic-intuition-nightmare-spiral-winter/616204/.

Chapter 5
Universal Care—Including the Excluded

Stephen Hill

Abstract "But, what about the very poor?"—the opening question of the Chapter. They must not be forgotten when building a new Global Economics for the Future. Indeed, given the underlying value of care that is central to this Book's economic philosophy and strategy, we have to be fully inclusive. A Universal Basic Income (UBI) offers real hope, but perhaps appears a 'bridge too far' in poor countries. This is not necessarily so however. Basing argument on empirical experiments and practices *now* in a number of developing countries, this chapter demonstrates the very real applicability of UBI in very poor national situations—adjusted in economic terms to relate, and, as with advanced economies, also delivered within a deliberatively nutritive, skill-development, enterprise supportive and community empowered environment.

But, what about the very poor?

The Circle of 'Wholeness' is not *whole* unless it is fully inclusive—including of those who may be forced to live on just over a dollar a day in a developing country village. Is it possible for a Universal Basic Income (UBI) strategy to lift people permanently out from desperate poverty and even into innovative enterprise?

At first, the possibility of applying a UBI Strategy to Poor and Developing Countries appears a 'bridge too far', its strategy unachievable in a poor country. Remember, a Universal Basic Income has three key openly funded features. A UBI is a *cash transfer* scheme rather than subsidized goods or coupons; *non-conditional,* so not contingent on the recipient satisfying any compliance conditions; and, *universal,* so not targeted to any specific group based on socio-economic or demographic criteria (Ghatak, 2017).

But maybe UBI is *not* 'a bridge too far'. Let's look at the evidence.

S. Hill (✉)
Arts, Social Sciences and Humanities, University of Wollongong, Northfields Ave, Wollongong, NSW 2522, Australia
e-mail: sthill@uow.edu.au

© Springer Nature Singapore Pte Ltd. 2022
S. Hill et al. (eds.), *The Kyoto Post-COVID Manifesto For Global Economics*, Creative Economy, https://doi.org/10.1007/978-981-16-8566-8_5

5.1   From Targeted to Unconditional Financial Transfers

Certainly alleviation of poverty in low income countries by some form of income support is firmly on the world agenda. India, as prime example, has implemented public distribution systems since the 1960s. Containing food and fuel prices whilst ensuring food and fuel access for urban consumers was supported by ration cards and subsidized prices—systems which have been reformed several times since, particularly towards greater coverage of very remote areas with high concentrations of poor households (Coady and Prady, 2018).

More generally, the World Bank estimates that *now*, 552 million people who live in developing countries receive some form of income supporting cash transfer from their governments (Ivaschenko et al., 2018).

Primary interest however over the last few years has been in *targeted* financial support for the poor (Bastagli et al., 2016). *Conditional* cash transfer programs have, as a consequence, spread to 63 countries throughout the world.

An example is Mexico's *Prospera* Program which gives cash transfers to poor households which meet basic maternal, child health and education conditions (Bastagli et al., 2016).

An alternative work-related strategy similar to the Depression-targeted "US Works Progress Administration" in the 1930s, is currently in place in India. Named the "National Rural Employment Guarantee Act" (NREGA), any Indian in a rural area is entitled to cash assistance for 100 days of work at the official minimum wage rate. Currently 180 million people per year are employed through the program, making it one of the largest anti-poverty programs in the world today. This is a universal entitlement with no poverty screening, only the potential barrier of wishing to avoid manual labor in the hot sun (Hanna and Olken, 2018, p. 222).

Implementation of long-term *unconditional* income support has been in place in only one developing country, Iran.

Back in 2011 the Iranian Government introduced a universal cash transfer into the bank accounts of all citizens to offset the withdrawal of food and fuel subsidies. This transfer was equivalent to 29% of median household incomes and cost 6.5% of GDP – possible because of the country's oil revenue.

However, government commitment appears to be flagging. Over the decade since it was established, the real value of this system has fallen by more than half as the government has not increased the value of transfers along with inflation. (Banerjee et al., 2019, p 4). Iran was a special case though. It had access to oil revenue whilst most developing countries do not have this financial privilege. Most important for those exploring the possibility for a broader application of UBI in developing countries, impact of the Iran program has not been adequately assessed (Banerjee et al., 2016).

5.2   The Potential of UBI: Experimental Exploration

So, we are very much at the beginning of thinking about applying UBI, unconditional basic income for everyone, to developing countries.

What is most encouraging now however is that serious experimental testing of the UBI concept is starting to happen, and significant signs of success are emerging through more recent increasingly wide-ranging untargeted income support programs.

> For example, in a trial program in Namibia in the Otjivero-Omitara area from January 2008 to December 2009, unconditional financial transfers were offered to a *category* of people who qualified—under 60 years of age and registered as living there for the previous six months—but they were not means tested. There was no control group but a before-and-after assessment suggested that rates of poverty and child malnutrition fell, while rates of income-generating activity and children's school attendance rose – in spite of significant in-migration (Haarmann et al., 2009).

> Along with UNICEF, the Self-Employed Womens Association (SEWA) in India's State of Madhya Pradesh initiated a successful two year experiment between 2010 and 2011 including 6,000 individuals across nine villages. Against control comparators, improvement was demonstrated in a wide range of indicators – financial inclusion, housing and sanitation, nutrition and diet, health, education, income and assets. In particular, there was an *increase* in labor and work as people were stimulated to improve their general living conditions.... not, as some commentators propose without evidence, an increase in *laziness* (Standing, 2013; Standing, 2016).

> Further support for positive outcomes from unconditional cash support schemes in developing countries is provided by Zambia, where from 2010 to 2013 the government significantly broadened eligibility for its "Social Cash Transfer" Scheme. Means testing was removed and all households with children under age 5 years, orphans, or disabled members, were included. Evaluation showed that the scheme not only reduced immediate poverty but also substantially improved assets and earnings (van Ufford et al., 2016; Banerjee et al., 2018, pp. 22–23).

Each of these UBI test cases remains as encouraging experimental results, not as on-going national programs ...... yet! Overall, they show, for example, that transfers led to an average *reduced* expenditure on *temptation goods*—people not 'blowing their transfers on alcohol and tobacco', suggesting that lack of money may be the cause of substance abuse rather than a constraint on it (Evans and Popova, 2017). There was also no evidence that transfers *discourage* work (Banerjee et al., 2017).

A particularly significant large-scale experimental evaluation of UBI which could tip the balance of interest however is currently being conducted in Kenya.

> The experiment, beginning in 2017, is purposively long term – to remove already demonstrated short-term distortions – and is being conducted by NGO "GiveDirectly." The program gives transfers of 75 cents per day to *all* adults over 18 years within two sectors of its 295 village and 14,474 households population within 295 Kenya's Siaya and Bornet Counties. The study is intentionally comparing one group who receive the income supplement for two years to another receiving the income for twelve years primarily to distinguish between differences in outcome when *anticipation* of continued income transfers is taken into account. Apart from the short and long-term groups, participants in one other were given a lump sum payment of $(US) 500 which is equivalent to the overall amount the short-term two-year group were given overall. The Banerjee-led "GiveDirectly Basic Income Evaluation" team from the US "National Bureau of Economic Research" is maintaining long-term evaluation of the Kenya program (Banerjee et al., 2018; Banerjee et al., 2020).

Then COVID-19 struck in 2020. Early results from the Kenya Experiment are very supportive of the impact of Universal Basic Income transfers.

Initially, prior to COVID-19, the guarantee of some ongoing income no matter how bad things got, led many people to take larger risks in setting up a business than they otherwise would have taken, an encouragement of innovation.

When COVID-19 arrived along with defensive Lockdown Strategies business income plunged, but those who had the additional income did not have to entirely exit the business.

Those who did not start businesses were less likely to be hungry or get sick. They were also less depressed (Piper, 2020) (Banerjee et al., 2020).

What is therefore starting to emerge is evidence that unconditional cash transfers to the poor in developing countries may not be 'a bridge too far' at all, but a serious strategy for lifting people out of the poverty trap and all the damage this causes both to individuals and their communities. Additionally, a UBI-style *unconditional* support program has a number of implementation advantages over targeted strategies—in particular because of the developing country administrative context (Banerjee et., 2018, p16).

Targeting requires competent, uncorrupted officials who can develop and run the programs along with potentially detailed repeated data collection and possibly means testing: apart from anything else, many people change their poverty status each year. A UBI system is far less demanding.

By *not* targeting benefits, corruption and abuse of power to *favor* some for kick-backs is substantially reduced.

In the case of India, an official Government Report on the existing system of food and energy subsidies showed they were typically fraught with inefficiencies and inequities (Government of India, 2017). Numerous studies fill out these government conclusions to include incomplete coverage of the poor, extensive leakage of benefits to the rich as well as having a high potential for fraud and corruption (Khosla, 2018). UBI offers a practical alternative where many of these problems can be more easily avoided.

Broad eligibility builds the political base for sustained UBI redistribution.

5.3   Practical Constraints and Opportunities

Many developing countries are now making ongoing investments into digitized ID and payment systems across their whole population, so implementation and access to a UBI system is increasingly straightforward—even in the majority of developing country economies where up 85% to 89% of workers are in the *informal* economy—casual labor, undocumented firms, small farms, have transient living conditions, so are outside the tax net (Bonnet et al., 2018; WIEGO, 2018; Hannah & Olken, 2018). With UBI, only ID is required along with a way of receiving the money, eg: a bank account. Meanwhile, the oft-heard but negative cry, particularly from the political right, that a UBI will make people lazy, is *not* supported by the evidence. Instead, unconditional cash transfer appears to be a stimulus in developing countries for people to move to a better life-style and to seek enterprise to move up the income hierarchy.

But, lets face it, the most basic problem of introducing *any* poverty alleviation or a Universal Basic Income program in developing countries is the problem of underdevelopment itself—poverty. As the World Bank demonstrates, 1.89 *billion* people of the world live in extreme poverty, with nearly *half* of the population of developing countries living on less than $(US) 1.25 per day. The majority scrabble for income from 'the informal economy', ie: working on the streets with no backup support when times are hard (World Vision, 2020).

Then, foreign Development Assistance is trivial compared with national taxation revenue except in the poorest of poor countries, and there, the overall level of available national income is very very low.

> For countries ranked as 'upper middle-income' by the World Bank, such as Peru, Lebanon and the Dominican Republic, overall tax revenue was approximately 157 times the amount of net official development assistance received in 2010.

> For 'lower middle-income countries such as Indonesia, India and Morocco the aid/tax ratio is 14 times.

> Only in 'low-income' countries such as Afghanistan, Ethiopia and Mozambique did official development assistance exceed tax revenue – by 1.2 times in 2010. But then remember that the gross *national* per-capita income of $(US)1,025 per year for *all* citizens including the more wealthy, is just under $(US) 3 per day. It is difficult to see *any* financial pool from which a UBI could be drawn (Hannah & Olken, 2018; World Bank, 2015).

Nevertheless, as Hannah and Olken observe: "For most developing countries, a substantial universal basic income would need to be financed via domestic taxation, because official development assistance is a small fraction of government budgets." (Hannah & Olken, 2018, p 203). But, the reality is cruel. In most developing countries only a small fraction of the population pays income taxes. In the case of India, only 2.3% of the population file tax returns and 1.0% pay taxes. Therefore as Maitresh Ghatek, Professor of Economics at the London School of Economics, argues, UBI would need to depend substantially on a *range* of tax options—capital gains, goods and services, as well as increase in tax paid by the more wealthy. The programs also would have to be scaled down significantly to the local context (Ghatek, 2017). Remember however, the previously mentioned GiveDirectly Test Program currently being conducted in Kenya where UBI recipients receive just 75 cents per day … and the program is making a significant difference.

Some authors such as Yanis Varoufakis, former Greek Finance Minister, propose whole new international financial protocols, such as with trade, to provide greater equity for poor countries. All trade and all money movements between different monetary jurisdictions (eg: the UK, the Eurozone or the US) would be denominated in a new digital accounting unit which Varoufakis calls "The Kosmos". If the Kosmos value of a country's imports exceeds its exports, or vice-versa, it is charged a levy in proportion to its trade deficit or surplus. A further Kosmos Levy is charged on particularly large speculative money movements. Fruit of the Kosmos Levy would end up in developing country support (Varoufakis, 2020a, b).

Currently, world financial markets are so deeply embedded in national and self-interest that it is difficult to see such altruism setting international trade protocols any time soon, though, for the sake of our wider humanity, we should not give up dreaming and trying.

Even so, and although far more limited than desirable, UBI can be a realistic economic option for developing countries, though perhaps starting with relatively small transfers—financed through proportional or progressive taxation and other supportive goods and services levies. Such a strategy depends primarily on the vision of care a national community has of itself—including in particular its more wealthy members who would need to be prepared to give up a relatively high proportion of their wealth. UBI in developing countries is therefore a fundamentally a national political question. Advanced economies and their development assistance budgets could then add a major stimulus—again based on a wider inclusive national political vision of care for humanity as a whole over just direct self-interest.

So, UBI for developing countries is by no means "a bridge too far". Instead the strategy may provide a fire to light the path towards liberation from poverty towards empowerment of so many who so deeply suffer now.

5.4 UBI Context: Inclusive Grass Roots Innovation

As with my proposal in Chap. 4 for the developed world however, a UBI strategy for developing countries must not stand alone, but in a supportive context—again, of creativity and innovation—at grassroots levels. UBI recipients must have a context of *inclusive innovation options* to *create* their own future, not just receive a little financial relief. As Venni Krishna describes it, "inclusive innovation strives to bridge and connect indigenous with modern science based knowledge to promote equity and inclusiveness". The objective of inclusive innovation is to enhance the public good through helping "poor, marginalized and underprivileged sections of society to improve their livelihoods and enable them to climb up the socio-economic ladder" (Krishna, 2017b, pp. 171–172.

India leads the way. Very much based on Gandhian economic thought and philosophy, the Honey Bee Network (HBN) is an excellent model. A grassroots innovation institution, the Honey Bee Network was founded by Anil Gupta in 1988–89. HBN is inclusive—of innovators, farmers, scholars, academics, policy makers, entrepreneurs and NGOs, and has grown to include links and presence in 75 countries. Three strict principles guide HBN initiatives: (1) assignment of intellectual property rights; (2) acknowledgement of the source of knowledge used; and, (3) any rents generated from commercialization of intellectual property rights (IPR) must be shared with the knowledge holder. Innovation emerges from village practices and creativity, and wider application brings the economic benefits back to the village.

> The fundamental source of HBN's 185,000 ideas, forms of knowledge and innovations from across India is the local indigenous community. Bottom-up, not Top-down. Most important inputs come from two *shodhyatras* or 'research trekking' in different parts of rural India. Led by Anil Gupta, each *yatra* covers a distance of 120 km to 160 kms over 7–9 days – collecting ideas and local innovation *from the villages*. Now, supported by a number of government

and network initiatives, the *yatras* provide an excellent model for building a creative and innovative culture at village level to empower possible UBI initiatives (Krishna, 2017a, pp. 4–5).

As a further strategy for establishing a nutritive context for UBI to have maximum impact in a developing countries context, India, again, offers a leading model, "The Barefoot College of Tilonia". Founded in 1972 by Sanjit Roy, more commonly known as "Bunker" Roy, the beliefs of the College internalize and reflect what the rural, impoverished and marginalized think important. As distinct from literacy, *education* is what one gains from family, tradition, culture, environment and personal experiences. Even (external) technologies are demystified so the local (uneducated) villagers develop the capacity to learn technical information and skills regardless of their formal education qualifications (Barefoot College, 2012; Krishna 2017b, pp 9–12).

Bunker Roy developed a particular focus on women's education. In 2012 he signed an agreement with UNESCO, a "Global Partnership for Girls' and Women's Empowerment", which demonstrates the style of grass-roots empowerment which characterizes The Barefoot College's strategy. This was an international program to produce "Barefoot Engineers" competent to manage village level solar lighting. Many of the participants, all women, were illiterate or semi-literate, often middle-aged and grandmothers. They were trained to install, repair, and maintain solar powered lighting systems. Further, they were to develop "Rural Electronic Workshops" where components and equipment were to be stored, a future learning hub for using new technologies and skills training (UNESCO, 2012).

5.5 Conclusion

To conclude my story of the real possibility of implementing a Universal Basic Income Strategy across the Developing World, I will refer back to my Conclusion for Chap. 4 where I argued the general case. It is the same so I will quote:

The central objective of this book, "The Post-COVID Manifesto for Global Economics" is to place our Humanity at the center of the Economics for our Future, to replace the currently prevailing value of self-interest at the core of economic thinking and practice with humanistic values of our mutuality – caring, mindfulness, compassion, sharing and trust. For whatever the economic frame for daily life is it sets the 'grammar' or underlying assumptions of how we relate to each other and *build together*.

And, as the platform for our project,

Our ideal is, as I outlined in Chapter 2, is to move world society to 'Embrace the Circle of Wholeness' for a harmonious, humanity-based World Order.

Arguably, we don't yet know enough about how best to implement a UBI in an impoverished 'lesser developed countries' (LDC) context, although it will need to depend on a broad national taxation scheme and be seriously scaled down for the local economic environment. Empirical research is starting to show, however, that UBI—even with small funding per person, can be very effective in developing both a better life and stimulus for enterprise (rather than laziness) at grassroots levels. Meanwhile, a UBI strategy of *income for all* is rather less problematic to deliver for LDC bureaucracies—with less mature skill than most advanced nations—compared with (present) targeted programs of poverty relief.

However, as I concluded also in my general Chap. 4 support for a Universal Basic Income, it must *not* be seen in isolation of its context. Exactly as with advanced nations, UBI must be delivered within a nutritive context which creates the environment for even barefoot villagers to create, innovate, and bring to life their own futures. The two particular examples from India that I have described are instructive—the Honey Bee Network—finding and encouraging grass roots innovation, and the Barefoot College which teaches even the illiterate to understand and use technology and innovation. These are but two of many models of poverty relief we can learn from. UBI helps the participants to get there by providing the cushion where they can rest more easily and from which they can see without total attention to immediate survival.

Thus, we see and greet the wider emancipation of our whole humanity, the ultimate goal of creating and reaching out to create "The Circle of Wholeness". Still, none of us should leave this task to others. *We* have to contribute. *We* have to turn world attention and international support around to assist—for we cannot claim to *love* humanity whilst people just up the map are seeking to live on a dollar a day whilst their children starve. As is demonstrated by so many cases these days, such as teenager Greta Thunberg, the Swedish Climate Change Leader, an *individual* can lead the world to a more humane place.

References

Bannerjee, A., Kreindler, G., & Olken, B. (2017). Debunking the stereotype of the lazy welfare recipient: Evidence from cash transfer programs. *The World Bank Research Observer, 32*(2), 155–184.

Banerjee, A., Niehaus, P., & Suri, T. (2019). 'Universal basic income in the developing world', National Bureau of Economic Research, Working Paper 25598. http://www.nber.org/papers/w25 998.ng.

Bannerjee, A. P. N., Suri, T., Faye, M., & Kroeger, A. (2020). The Effects of a Universal Basic Income during the COVID-19 Kenya Pandemic' Working Paper: https://www.povertyactionlab.org>eva luation>effects-universal-basic-income: summarised by Abdul Latif Jameel, Poverty Action Lab, 2020: povertyactionlab.org.

Bastagli, F., Hagen-Zanker, J., Harman, L., Barca, V., Sturge, G., Schmidt, T., & Pellerano, L. (2016). Cash Transfers: what does the evidence say? A rigorous review of program impact and the role of design and implementation features, Technical Report, Overseas Development Institute.

Bonnet, F., Leung, V., & Chalcatana, S. (2018). *Women and men in the informal economy: A statistical picture*, 3rd Edn', International Labor Organization (ILO), March, p. 23.

Coady, D., & Prady, D. (2018). Universal Basic Income in Developing Countries: Issues, Options and Illustrations for India, IMF Working Paper, WP/18/174, July.

Evans, D. K., & Popova, A. (2017). Cash transfers and temptation goods. *Economic Development and Cultural Change, 65*(2), 189–221.

Ghatak, M. (2017). Combatting poverty in developing countries with a universal basic income. *VoxDev*, 17th July.

Government of India. (2017). *Economic Survey 2016–17*, Ministry of Finance.

Hannah, R., & Olken, B. A. (2018). Universal basic incomes versus targeted transfers: Anti-poverty programs in developing countries. *Journal of Economic Perspectives, 32*(4)*, Fall, 201.

Ivaschenko, O., Alas, C. R., Novikova, M., Romero, C., Bowen, T., & Zhu, L. (2018). *The state of social safety nets 2018*. The World Bank. _FNL_w_covers.pdf.

Khosla, S. (2018). India's universal basic income, Bedevilled by the details. Washington Carnegie Endowment for International Peace: http://carnegieendowment.org/files/CEIP_Khosla_Report_FNL_covers.pdf.

Krishna, V. V. (2017a). Inclusive innovation in India: contemporary landscape. *Asian Journal of Innovation and Policy, 6*(1), 001–032.

Krishna, V. V. (2017b). Inclusive innovation in India: Historical roots. *Asian Journal of Innovation and Policy, 6*(2), 170–191.

Piper, K. (2020). How a basic income experiment helped these Kenyans weather the COVID-19 crisis, *Vox*, September.

Standing, G. (2013). Unconditional basic income: Two pilots in Madhya Pradesh. *International Delhi Conference, May 30–31: Downloaded by Griffin Mitchell*, October 2016, published in Silo-Tips.

Standing, G. (2016). *Basic income and how we can make it happen*. Penguin Books.

UNESCO. (2012). India's Barefoot college and UNESCO join forces for Girls' and Women's Empowerment, UNESCO int, UNESCO Press, 27th July.

van Ufford, P. Q., Harland, C., Michelo, S., Tembo, G., Toole, K., & Wood, D. (2016). *The role of impact evaluation in the evolution of Zambia's cash transfer program*, UNICEF.

Varoufakis, Y. (2020a). Another Now: Dispatches from an Alternative Present, Penguin Books.

Varoufakis, Y. (2020b). Capitalism isn't working. Here's an Alternative. *The Guardian*—Economics, September: theguardian.com.

WIEGO. (2018). Women in informal employment globalizing & organizing, 'Statistical Picture': *wiego.org*.

World Vision. (2020). *Global poverty: Facts, FAQs, and how to help*. 16 October: www.worldvision.org.

World Bank. (2015). *World Development Indicators 2015:* https://documents.worldbank.org/en/publication/documents-reports/documentdetail/795941468338533334/world-development-indicators-2015

Chapter 6
Sustainability Conditions for Universal Basic Income in the Economic Recession Caused by COVID-19

Tadashi Yagi

Abstract The coronavirus disease 2019 (COVID-19) pandemic has caused a severe recession in the world economy, which led to an increase in unemployment, and worsened the life of people, especially in the low-income class. In this chapter, we examine the properties of universal basic income policies as a measure for improving the unequal society and providing people with a safety-net in life. In the last part of the chapter, we examine the sustainability conditions of UBI with Seigniorage. Seigniorage refers to government revenue earned by printing money. We insist that UBI policy financed by Seigniorage would be sustainable as long as GDP gap does not bring about inflation. In other word, UBI would work to improve the macroeconomic situation and the life of people in deflationary situation.

6.1 Introduction

The coronavirus disease 2019 (COVID-19) pandemic has caused a severe recession in the world economy. Mandatory or semi-mandatory reductions in human contact for preventing the spread of infection have put a stranglehold on economic activity and transactions, leading to drastically reduced business revenue and many bankruptcies of various kinds of businesses.

The COVID-19 crisis has decimated labor markets around the world. Millions have lost their jobs, and most workers have seen their income or working hours significantly reduced. In today's globalized economy, the negative impacts of the COVID-19 recession have accelerated the spread of this economic crisis to all countries around the world.

Young people, women, and the elderly have been particularly impacted. These groups have been the targets of layoffs, have high and rising unemployment rates, and face the prospect of large reductions in income. Young people have relatively limited networks and less work experience, most women have been employed as irregular

T. Yagi (✉)
Faculty of Economics, Doshisha University, Karasuma Higashiiru, Kamigyo, Kyoto 602-8580, Japan
e-mail: tyagi@mail.doshisha.ac.jp

S. Hill et al. (eds.), *The Kyoto Post-COVID Manifesto For Global Economics*, Creative Economy, https://doi.org/10.1007/978-981-16-8566-8_6

workers, and the elderly are regarded as being less adaptable to developments in IT, suggesting that the economic situations of these groups are especially vulnerable to the adverse effects of the COVID-19 crisis. These were low-income groups even before the pandemic, so we can surmise that the state of income inequality has worsened in the wake of COVID-19.

The important fact is that socially vulnerable people are seriously harmed by the economic recession due to COVID-19. There is limited scope for individual efforts at self-support to improve their economic situation, and government support is inevitable for maintaining people's livelihood. One policy measure proposed by many politicians around the world, such as Mayor Michael Tubbs of Stockton, California, in the United States,[1] is the provision of universal basic income (UBI). In a pilot program in Stockton, $500 was paid to 125 people in the city, and this was reported to be an effective tool for maintaining livelihoods during the COVID-19 crisis.

The idea of providing UBI as a means of support arose amid ongoing debate over the effectiveness of modern monetary theory (MMT). In a depressive economic situation, the only the way of financing UBI would be issuing a government bond purchased from the central bank. This financing method is the way that MMT proposed. Conventional economic theorists, on the other hand, argue that policies based on MMT cause devaluation of government bonds in the international capital market, which in turn leads to currency devaluation in the foreign exchange market, increases the price level of imported goods, and triggers inflation. They fear a downward spiral caused by inflation and a resulting economic crisis.

In Japan, the financial resources for fiscal expansion in response to COVID-19 are mainly underwritten by the central bank through the issuance of Japanese Government Bonds in line with MMT, and there is concern about the impact this will have.

In this chapter, we discuss the appropriateness and effectiveness of UBI policy. We then analyze macro models for deriving the sustainability conditions for introducing UBI based on MMT by using the models in Romer (1996). By using these macro models, the conditions for the sustainability of the provision of UBI can be clarified.

Section 2 discuss the superiority of UBI as a means of supporting vulnerable people in an economy. Section 3 discusses inflation theory and investigates the sustainability conditions of providing UBI with financing by printing money.

6.2 Definition of UBI and Criteria for Evaluating the Effectiveness of UBI

According to Hoynes and Rothstein (2019), the definition of UBI is as follows:

a. It provides a sufficiently generous cash benefit to live on, without other earnings.
b. It does not phase out or phases out only slowly as earnings rise.

---

[1] Forbes Japan, June 30, 2020.

c. It is available to a large proportion of the population, rather than being targeted to a particular subset (e.g., single mothers).

It is possible to oppose various aspects of this definition. First, it is not easy to support the argument that UBI should provide a "sufficiently generous" cash benefit. It seems that financial feasibility and maintaining work incentive should be balanced with the benefits of UBI. This point is quite crucial in evaluating any experiments of introducing UBI into society. Van Parijs and Vanderborght (2017) and Banerjee et al. (2019) have similarly argued to exclude the term "sufficiently generous,"

Second, it is necessary to compare UBI with other transfer programs such as in-work tax-based assistance, child allowances, social security retirement, and negative income tax (NIT) (Friedman, 1962; Mirrlees, 1971). In comparing these with UBI, we need to establish criteria such as work incentive, effectiveness, efficiency, fairness, contingency, or sufficiency.

Third, long-run changes in labor market caused by AI and the wider use of robots as substitutes for human labor should be discussed.

6.2.1 Properties of UBI

a. Work incentive

UBI is thought to reduce the work incentive, especially when a job is difficult, dirty, or dangerous. UBI has an income effect on the leisure-work choice behavior, decreasing work and increasing leisure as long as an increase in work time decreases utility. The negative effect on work time increases as the amount of UBI increases. Thus, the introduction of UBI could possibly cause a labor shortage especially in difficult, unsanitary, and dangerous jobs. In this sense, the amount of UBI would be limited such that the negative effect on labor supply would be minimized.

b. Effectiveness

UBI would be effective for supporting basic life, especially for those below the poverty line. Contrary to income support for households below the poverty line, UBI does require a means test as a requirement for receiving support. Thus, the failure to support poor families whose income levels are low but still above the level required for receiving income support never occurs.

iii. Efficiency

The cost of UBI would be relatively smaller lower the administrative costs associated with checking qualifications are low. On the other hand, the initial cost of paying UBI would be high because the government has to create procedures for paying money to large numbers of households. This cost, however, would be reduced once the systems are established.

iv.   Distributional effect

The degree of the distributional effect of UBI depends largely on the financing method. A lump-sum transfer from the government to all households has the largest impact on inequality in most measures, including Gini-coefficient. Therefore, UBI has the basic effect of reducing inequality. This effect is strengthened by a progressive income taxation system, especially when UBI is financed by an income tax. For high- or upper-middle-income classes, the introduction of UBI will decrease after-tax income, while low- or lower-middle-income classes will see increases in after-tax income with the introduction of UBI. Hoynes and Rothstein (2019) simulated the impact on income inequality of the introduction of UBI and concluded that UBI would have quite substantial distributional and cost effects.

e.   Flexibility to macroeconomic situation

UBI is designed to pay a fixed amount of money to all people in the nation. The amount would be necessarily fixed for the following reasons. First, macroeconomic situation fluctuates, and the inflation rate would not be constant in the future. Second, it is safe to start a UBI scheme with smaller payments. After evaluating the effects of UBI on labor supply behavior, labor market equilibrium, and the inflation rate, it is possible to increase the amount in a piecewise manner.

Flexible payments have a negative effect on the stability of household income and a negative impact on consumption. Unstable income may reduce consumption by more than the reduction in payments because households may reduce consumption to prepare for risk of the further reductions. Thus, payment amounts need to be composed of two parts (a fixed part and a flexible part), and the range of the flexible part should be a set portion of the fixed part.

6.2.2   Comparative Evaluation of UBI

6.2.2.1   NIT Systems

In this section, we compare the properties of UBI with alternative measures such as NIT, social security systems, and the Earned Income Tax Credit (EITC) system.

NIT is a system that reverses the direction of payment of tax for incomes below a certain level. The tax amount starts as a negative amount and increases linearly as income increases. Thus, earners below a certain level receive money. This system was proposed by Milton Friedman in the 1960s (Friedman, 1962).

In an NIT system with a linear income tax, the amount of transfer from the government decreases as earned income increases, and becomes zero at certain income level. Under such a system, after-tax income increases as before-tax income increases. In this sense, the reversal of income ranking of after-tax income and before-tax income never happens. This incentivizes work. Under this system, however, the elderly and those in working generations are treated in the same way, contrary to a social security system. Under a social security system, the amount of benefits is independent of earned income in many countries for the those above a certain age. This implies that the elderly have reduced work incentives because the money received decreases as they work harder.

More importantly, the fairness of this depends on the accuracy of declared income. Improving this accuracy would require higher administrative costs, which this decreases the effectiveness and fairness of the system. As the means test becomes more severe, the number of people who actually need government assistance but cannot receive it may increase, and in this sense, the effectiveness of the system would be decreased.

In addition, it is not easy to determine the optimal tax rates and transfer amounts (i.e., it is difficult to determine the intercept and slope of the linear income tax system) because distributional judgment is independent of the efficiency criteria.

Mirrlees (1971) shows that an optimal tax system improves the efficiency of the work-leisure choice, while Friedman (1962) argues that the overall efficiency of providing a safety net to people could be improved by unifying the social security system and public assistance into the NIT system. In addition, although a linear income tax system with negative income tax exhibits progressive and distributive properties, there is no guarantee that such a system will achieve a strong distributional effect for the reasons mentioned above.

The amount of negative tax and the marginal tax rate in a negative income tax system could be adjusted according to the macroeconomic situation. The important point, however, is that the linear income tax system automatically adjusts transfer and tax revenue according to the economic situation. When the economy booms, tax revenue automatically increases, and transfers from the government to the poor decrease.

6.2.2.2 Social Security Systems

Social security commonly includes pension benefits for the elderly and the disabled. Social security is funded primarily through payroll taxes or contributions by self-employed people. Thus, benefits are mostly restricted to the retired, And in this sense, social security systems do not affect the work incentive.

The main purpose of social security systems is to maintain the living standards of retirees, and therefore such systems do not cover the people of working generations under the poverty line. In this sense, social security systems are not effective for supporting those under the poverty line.

Since social security systems are funded by payroll taxes, such systems are highly efficient and are regarded as fair. The amount of benefits is closely related to the contribution amount. This implies, however, that the distributional effect is limited.

The benefit amount in a social security system is basically determined by the amount of contributions paid during the working period, and thus the benefit amount is not related with the macroeconomic situation. However, the rate of return of the fund invested in capital markets depends on the macroeconomic situation. Social security systems are vulnerable to inflation because the adjustment of the benefit amount to inflation is quite limited in general.

6.2.2.3   EITC

EITC is a refundable tax credit for low- to moderate-income working people, particularly those with children (see Hotz & Scholz, 2003; Eissa & Hoynes, 2006; Nichols & Rothstein, 2016). The amount of EITC benefit depends on income earned and number of children. In the United States, working families with children can receive EITC if their annual incomes are between \$37,870 and \$51,567 as of 2013 (depending on the number of dependent children; see Nichols & Rothstein, 2016).

EITC was introduced to support poor households with children without affecting the work incentive. The benefits are paid to working families whose income levels are below a certain amount. This implies that the benefit is not paid to people who do not work.

The effectiveness of this system for supporting the poor is limited for the unemployed. The administrative costs of running such a system include a system for checking declared income. As with negative income tax, unfairness arises when the declared income is false, and thus the distributional effect is limited. In addition, the flexibility of the system to the macroeconomic situation is low because the number of unemployed earners increases when the economy is in recession. Thus, the number of workers eligible for EITC decreases as the economy is depressed.

6.2.2.4   Superiority of UBI

The superiority of UBI is evident from the six criteria shown in Table 6.1. In particular, support for poor households is quite large. Since UBI is paid to individuals rather than to families, the amount of UBI increases as the number of members in a household

Table 6.1 The summary of comparative evaluation of UBI

	Work incentive	Effectiveness for supporting the poor	Administrative efficiency	Fairness	Distributional effect	Flexibility to macroeconomic situation
UBI	Dependent on the amount	High	High	High	High	Possibly high
NIT	Middle	Middle	Middle	Low	Middle	High
Social security	High	Low	Middle	High	Low	Low
EITC	High	Middle	Middle	Low	Middle	Middle

increases. This is consistent with the idea that the support amount should be dependent on the degree of necessity.

The lump-sum transfer of UBI improves the efficiency of a transfer system because the administrative costs of checking declared income are unnecessary. Considering that the false declaration of income would decrease the fairness of the system, UBI is quite robust for ensuring fairness. UBI is quite effective at redistributing income, especially when UBI is financed through progressive income taxation. Finally, UBI could be designed so that the amount of UBI could be flexibly changed according to the macroeconomic situation.

In sum, we can conclude that UBI is superior among the above-mentioned alternative policy measures. However, there is are issues of financial burden and a negative effect on work incentive. Therefore, we believe that UBI should be introduced starting from a small amount, and then adjusted after evaluation of its performance in a real economy.

6.3   Sustainability Condition for the Provision of UBI

6.3.1   Cost-Push and Demand-Pull Inflation

According to the basics of inflation theory, inflation can be classified into two main types: cost-push inflation and demand-pull inflation.

Cost-push inflation, which is also called supply shock inflation, occurs when the supply curve shifts upward owing to rising costs, such as rising import prices. As shown in Fig. 6.1, cost-push inflation not only causes inflation but also decreases GDP, resulting in stagflation. An increase in the price of imported goods is often caused by a depreciation of the exchange rate, which then increases the burden of repaying foreign currency-denominated debt held by companies.

Demand-pull inflation occurs when the demand curve shifts upward. This upward shift often occurs when aggregate demand increases owing to exogenous factors (e.g., demand associated with major events such as the Olympics). In this case, as shown in Fig. 6.2, GDP increases along with the price increase.

6.3.2   Aggregate Demand and Aggregate Supply Model (AD–AS Model)

We next present a macro model of a closed economy to refine the theories of cost-push inflation and demand-pull inflation in the previous section.

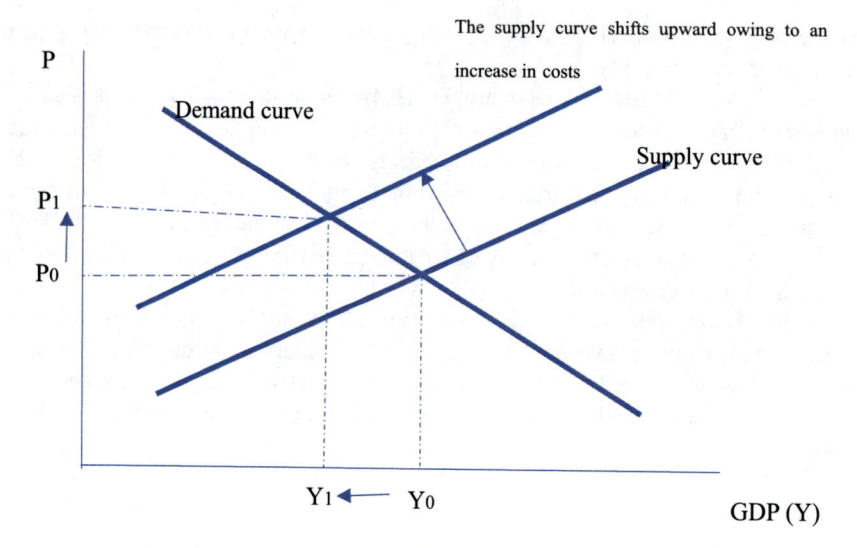

Fig. 6.1 Cost-push inflation

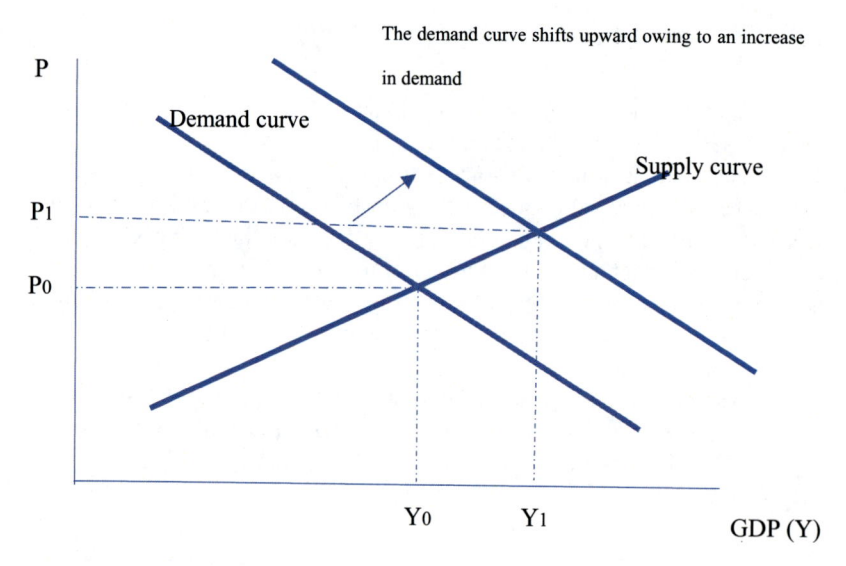

Fig. 6.2 Demand-pull inflation

6.3.2.1 Equilibrium Conditions of the Goods Market

The macro equilibrium conditions for the goods market are described by the following equation.

$$Y = C(Y - T) + I(i - \pi^e) + G$$

$$= E(Y, i - \pi^e, G, T) \qquad (6.1)$$

Here, Y is the gross domestic product, C is the consumption function, T is tax, I is the investment function, G is government spending, i is the nominal interest rate, and π^e is the expected inflation rate. The nominal interest rate i is defined as the value of the real interest rate r plus the expected inflation rate:

$$i \equiv r + \pi^e. \qquad (6.2)$$

This equation is called Fisher's identity. Therefore, the real interest rate r can be obtained by subtracting the expected inflation rate from the nominal interest rate.

Consumption C is a function of disposable income $Y-T$, investment I is a function of real interest rate, and government spending G and tax T are exogenous variables.

Since consumption is a positive function of Y and investment is a negative function of the real interest rate, the IS curve giving the combination of Y and i has a negative slope at the equilibrium of the goods market (see Appendix 6.1).

6.3.2.2 Equilibrium Conditions of the Money Market

Given that the demand for money L is a negative function of the nominal interest rate i (speculative demand for money) and a positive function for the gross domestic product Y (transaction demand for money), the demand for money is given by

$$L = L(i, Y), \quad \frac{\partial L}{\partial i} \leq 0, \quad \frac{\partial L}{\partial Y} \geq 0. \qquad (6.3)$$

The equilibrium condition for the money market with money supply M/P is given by

$$\frac{M}{P} = L(i, Y)$$
$$= L(r + \pi^e, Y). \qquad (6.4)$$

The LM curve giving the combination of Y and i has a positive slope at the equilibrium of the money market (see Appendix 6.2).

6.3.2.3 Aggregate Demand Curve (AD Curve)

As shown in Appendix 6.3, we can derive the aggregate demand curve, which has a negative slope. The aggregate demand curve becomes flatter when the demand for money increases less strongly in response to a decrease in interest rate. Note that as government spending increases, the IS curve shifts to the right, so output increases at the same price and the AD curve shifts to the right.

6.3.2.4   Aggregate Supply Curve (AS Curve)

As is shown in Appendix 6.4, we derive the aggregate supply curve which has a positive slope. However, if the nominal wage and nominal interest rate rises as prices rise, the increase in labor demand and capital will be moderated, and the slope of the supply curve will approach a vertical line.

When productivity in production rises, the aggregate supply curve shifts to the right owing to increases in employment and capital input at the same price, as shown in Fig. 6.3. Therefore, in a process where the productivity of capital and labor increases owing to the development of AI and other such technology, both an increase in production volume and a decrease in the price level may proceed simultaneously.

The effects of increasing government spending to provide special cash payments in response to COVID-19 can be considered as follows. First, as shown in Fig. 6.4, the aggregate demand curve shifts to the left owing to the decline in economic activity as a result of measures to combat COVID-19. This reduces the output level from $Y0$ to $Y1$. Therefore, if fiscal expenditures, such as special cash payments, are increased to restore aggregate demand to the original level, the leftward-shifted aggregate demand curve returns to the original level, and the equilibrium output can recover to the same level as before the COVID-19 crisis.

When the response to COVID-19 spreads technological advances that enhance business productivity, such as telework, the aggregate supply curve shifts to the right reflecting an increase in productivity. In this case, prices will not increase even if government expenditures, such as special cash payments, are increased.

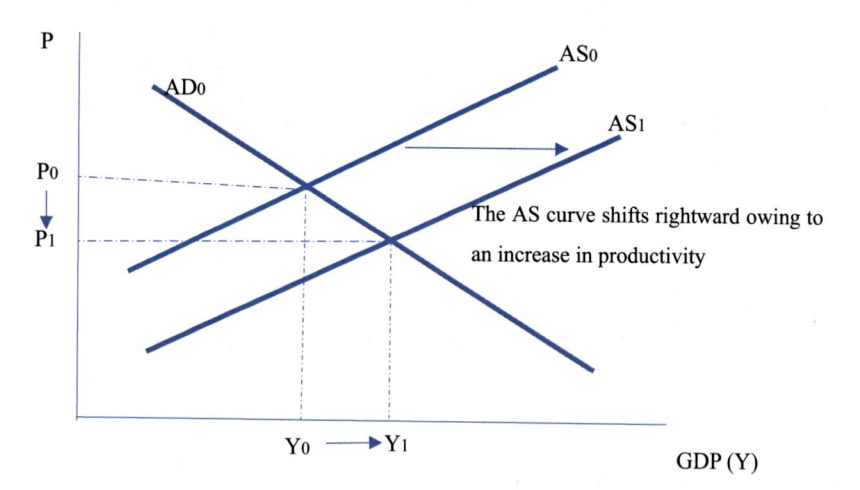

Fig. 6.3   AD-AS curve and the effect of an increase in productivity

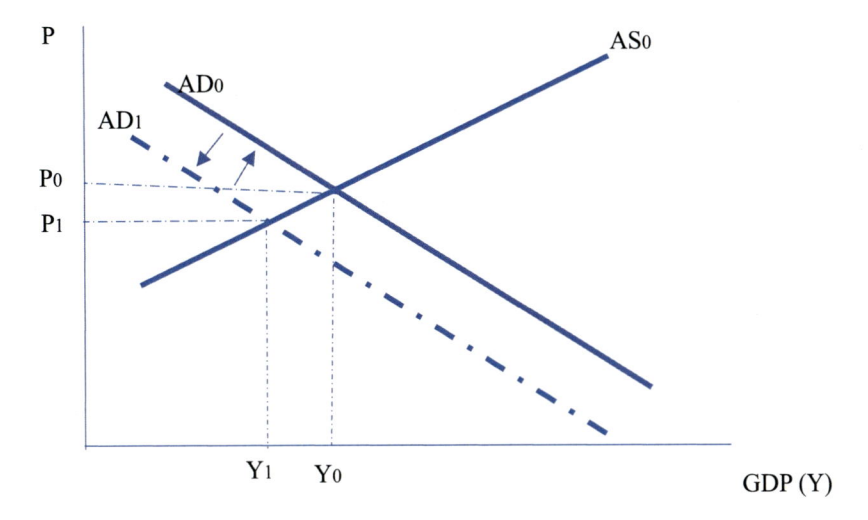

Fig. 6.4 Effect of special cash payments

6.3.3 Seigniorage and Inflation

From Eq. (6.4), we can write

$$P = \frac{M}{L(r + \pi^e, Y)}. \tag{6.5}$$

This means that even in the case where Y is constant, if M rises and the expected inflation rate rises, then prices will rise. However, in the situation in which Y rises, the denominator increases and the price does not necessarily rise. This means that even when the supply of money is increased in response to the economic downturn caused by COVID-19, prices will not increase as long as Y increases in response to the increase in the money supply.

Seigniorage refers to government revenue earned by printing money. This financing method is advocated by MMT. We take M to be high-powered money (currency and reserve deposits issued by the government) because we are interested in government income from money creation. L is the demand for high-powered money.

The real government spending S per unit time that can be covered by seigniorage is equal to the increase in the nominal money balance per unit time divided by the price level.

$$S = \frac{\dot{M}}{P} = \frac{\dot{M}}{M}\frac{M}{P} = g_M\frac{M}{P}, \tag{6.6}$$

where g_M is the growth rate of the money supply. In other words,

$$S = g_M L(r + \pi^e, Y). \tag{6.7}$$

If the expected inflation rate is 0, the government spending covered by seigniorage will be proportional to the rate of increase in the money supply. However, in the situation where the rate of increase in the money supply due to seigniorage equals to the expected inflation rate, we get

$$S = g_M L(r + g_M, Y). \tag{6.8}$$

Assuming that r and Y are constant, we examine the effect of an increase in the growth rate of the money supply by the following calculus:

$$\frac{dS}{dg_M} = L(\bar{r} + g_M, \bar{Y}) + g_M \frac{dL(\bar{r} + g_M, \bar{Y})}{dg_M}. \tag{6.9}$$

Since the demand for money is a negative function of the nominal interest rate, we get

$$\frac{dL(\bar{r} + g_M, \bar{Y})}{dg_M} \leq 0. \tag{6.10}$$

Thus, real government expenditures decrease as g_M increases.

When the inflation rate increases as the growth rate of the money supply increases, this can be interpreted to mean that the special cash payments in response to COVID-19 are partially covered by the inflation tax, and this means that people's real standard of living will not increase as much as the nominal value increases. If the effect of the first term on the right-hand side is smaller than the effect of the second term on the right-hand side, an increase in the money supply may cause a decline in real living standards owing to inflation.

6.3.4 Mandel-Fleming Model

In this section, the closed economic model in Sect. 2 is extended to an open economic model. Here, the nominal exchange rate, which is the price obtained by converting one unit of the foreign currency into the home currency, is represented by ε. The nominal exchange rate for the yen against the dollar is the yen price per dollar. An increase in ε means a decrease in international currency value, such as that of the yen. When the price level in a foreign country is expressed as P^*, the real exchange rate is $\varepsilon P^*/P$. When the real exchange rate rises, foreign materials will become more expensive than domestic goods, imports IM will decrease, exports EX will increase, and the trade balance will improve. Current balance, which consists mainly of trade balance, is given by

$$CB = EX(\varepsilon P^*/P) - IM(\varepsilon P^*/P, Y).\qquad(6.11)$$

Therefore, Eq. (6.1) can be rewritten as

$$Y = E(Y, i - \pi^e, G, T, \varepsilon P^*/P).\qquad(6.12)$$

Since depreciation of the real exchange rate improves the trade balance, E is a positive function of $\varepsilon P^*/P$.

Next, we consider the capital balance. If the real interest rate level of the home country is high internationally, the rate of return on financial assets in the home country is relatively high, and the inflow of funds to the home country increases. Denoting the foreign real interest rate by $i^* - \pi^{e*}$, the capital balance KB is given by

$$KB = KB((i - \pi^e) - (i^* - \pi^{e*})).\qquad(6.13)$$

Under the floating exchange rate system, governments basically do not intervene in the market. Thus, the balance of payments (BOP) is given by

$$CB + KB = EX(\varepsilon P^*/P) - IM(\varepsilon P^*/P, Y) + KB((i - \pi^e) - (i^* - \pi^{e*})) = 0.\qquad(6.14)$$

The real exchange rate is determined so that Eq. (6.14) holds.

Figure 6.5 shows the *BOP* curve on the IS-LM plane, and it is shown that the slope of BOP is downward as is shown in Appendix 6.5.

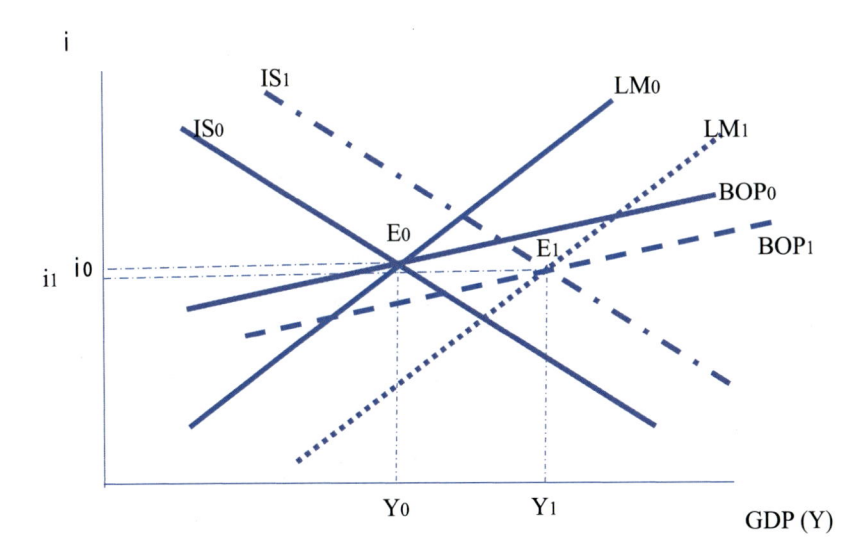

Fig. 6.5 Effects of special cash payments in the Mandel-Fleming model

Now, we consider the case where an increase in government spending is covered by seigniorage. Since the money supply and government spending increase simultaneously, both the *IS* curve and the *LM* curve shift to the right. Therefore, the initial equilibrium (Y0, $i0$) moves to the new equilibrium (Y1, $i1$). At the equilibrium point E1, the interest rate is below the rate that puts BOP in equilibrium and capital outflow occurs. Thus, the real exchange rate depreciates. Since the real exchange rate is $\varepsilon P^*/P$, the nominal exchange rate will depreciate unless the relative price level changes.

When the price level in the home country increases and that in the foreign country is constant, the real exchange rate depreciates even when the nominal exchange rate is constant. When the real exchange rate changes, the BOP line shifts rightward and the new equilibrium will balance the goods market, the money market, and the balance of payments.

In the Mandel-Fleming model, if only fiscal policy is implemented, the increase in interest rate will cause appreciation of the real exchange rate and restore equilibrium of the balance of payments. However, if the supply of high-powered money increases at the same time, the interest rate may decline, output may increase, and the real exchange rate may depreciate. This point is noteworthy.

In the global response to COVID-19, similar fiscal expansions are taking place worldwide, so relative prices and nominal exchange rates have not changed significantly. For this reason, import prices will not increase.

6.4   Sustainability Conditions of UBI with Seigniorage

From the above analysis, the sustainability conditions of UBI with Seigniorage are summarized as follows.

a.   If the aggregate supply curve shifts to the right owing to increased productivity, inflation can be controlled and the expansion of government spending covered by seigniorage will enable economic recovery. If the slope of the aggregate supply curve is nearly flat, the effect of increasing government spending on prices will be small.

b.   If the factors that cause international capital movement are weak, such as when international relative price levels have not changed, fluctuations in exchange rates will be small and inflation due to rising prices of imported goods is unlikely to occur.

c.   In the case where similar economic policies are adopted internationally, the collapse of government bond prices is unlikely to occur as long as the long-term relative credibility of government bonds in the international capital market does not change.

d.   If there is supply capacity but demand falls owing to a shock, expansionary fiscal policy can increase output without causing inflation.

Appendix 6.1: Derivation of IS curve

Totally differentiating Eq. (6.1), we derive the *IS* curve as follows.

$$dY = \frac{\partial E}{\partial Y} dY + \frac{\partial E}{\partial (i - \pi^e)} di$$

$$\therefore \ (1 - \frac{\partial E}{\partial Y}) dY = \frac{\partial E}{\partial (i - \pi^e)} di$$

$$\frac{dY}{di} \Big|_{IS} = \frac{\frac{\partial E}{\partial (i - \pi^e)}}{(1 - \frac{\partial E}{\partial Y})}$$

Appendix 6.2: Derivation of LM curve

Totally differentiating Eq. (6.4), we derive

$$0 = \frac{\partial L}{\partial i} di + \frac{\partial L}{\partial Y} dY$$

thus

$$\frac{di}{dY} \Big|_{LM} = -\frac{L_Y}{L_i}.$$

Because $\frac{\partial L}{\partial i} \leq 0$, $\frac{\partial L}{\partial Y} \geq 0$, the *LM* curve giving the combination of Y and i has a positive slope at the equilibrium of the money market.

Appendix 6.3: The derivation of AD curve

By differentiating Eq. (6.1), we get

$$\frac{dY}{dP} \Big|_{AD} = E_Y \frac{dY}{dP} \Big|_{AD} + E_{i-\pi^e} \frac{di}{dP} \Big|_{AD}. \tag{6.15}$$

By differentiating Eq. (6.4) with respect to P, we get

$$-\frac{M}{P^2} = L_i \frac{di}{dP} \Big|_{AD} + L_Y \frac{dY}{dP} \Big|_{AD}. \tag{6.16}$$

From these two equations, we can derive

$$\frac{dY}{dP}\Big|_{AD} = \frac{-M/P^2}{[(1 - E_Y)L_i/E_{i-\pi^e}] + L_Y}. \tag{6.17}$$

Because $L_i \leq 0$, $L_Y \geq 0$, and $E_{i-\pi^e} \leq 0$, the right-hand side of Eq. (6.17), which is interpreted as the aggregate demand curve, has a negative slope. To describe the aggregate demand curve in the Y-P plane, we write

$$\frac{dP}{dY}\Big|_{AD} = \frac{[(1 - E_Y)L_i/E_{i-\pi^e}] + L_Y}{-M/P^2}. \tag{6.18}$$

Appendix 6.4: Derivation of AS curve

The production function is given by

$$Y = AF(K, L). \tag{6.19}$$

Here, A represents the technology level, K is capital, and L is labor. Denoting the nominal wage by W, the optimality conditions for profit maximization are given by

$$\Pi = PAF(K, L) - iK - WL$$
$$\frac{\partial \Pi}{\partial K} = PA\frac{\partial F}{\partial K} - i = 0$$
$$\frac{\partial \Pi}{\partial L} = PA\frac{\partial F}{\partial L} - W = 0.$$

Therefore, we derive

$$F_K = \frac{i}{PA}, \quad F_L = \frac{W}{PA}. \tag{6.20}$$

If the nominal wage is fixed and does not change even when prices rise, the demand for labor will increase and employment will increase as prices rise because the marginal productivity of labor diminishes as labor increases. Therefore, the aggregate supply curve has a positive slope.

Appendix 6.5: The slope of BOP curve

From Eq. (6.14), we derive

$$-\frac{\partial IM}{\partial Y}dY + \frac{\partial KB}{\partial i}di = 0$$

$$\frac{di}{dY}\Big|_{BOP} = \frac{I M_Y}{K B_i} \geq 0.$$

Thus, the *BOP* curve has a positive slope.

References

Banerjee, A. V., Niehaus, P., & Suri, T. (2019). Universal basic income in the developing world. *Annual Review Economics, 11*, 961–985.

Eissa, N., & Hoynes, H. (2006). Behavioral responses to taxes: Lessons from the EITC and labor supply. In J. Poterba (Ed.), *Tax Policy and the Economy* (Vol. 20, pp. 73–110). MIT Press.

Friedman, M. (1962). *Capitalism and freedom.* University Chicago Press.

Hotz, V. J., & Scholz, J. K. (2003). The Earned Income Tax Credit. In R. Moffitt (Ed.), *Means-Tested Transfer Programs in the United States* (pp. 141–197). Univ. Chicago Press.

Hoynes, H., & Rothstein, J. (2019). Universal basic income in the United States and advanced countries. *Annual Review of Economics, 11*, 929–958.

Mirrlees, J. (1971). An exploration in the theory of optimum income taxation. *Review of Economic Studies, 38*(2), 175–208.

Nichols, A., & Rothstein, J. (2016). The Earned Income Tax Credit. In R. Moffitt (Ed.), *Economics of Means-Tested Programs in the United States* (Vol. 1, pp. 137–218). Univ. Chicago Press.

Romer, D. (1996). *Advanced macroeconomics.* Mc-Graw-Hill Companies, Inc.

Van Parijs, P., & Vanderborght, Y. (2017). *Basic income: A radical proposal for a free society and a sane economy.* Harvard Univ. Press.

Chapter 7
Towards the Reconstruction of the Cosmos: In Consideration of a Polyphonic Way of Life

Toshiaki Maruyama

Abstract Our world today is one of increasing confusion, overrun with an ominous and widespread nihilism even as it needs a vision for the near future, while Japan itself suffers from stagnation: In this chapter, we discuss the way to overcome this situation by applying the concept of "polyphony." Then we argue the necessity of reconstructing the cosmos. As the world is increasingly becoming a mere aggregation of fragmented and inorganic individuals, I think there is a need to reconsider the ways of thinking surrounding the correspondence between the microcosmos and the macrocosmos. The world of animism as discussed herein offers fertile ground, as does Eastern philosophy that is rooted in "nothingness" and "non-being" that could ably guide us on such a path. In this chapter, I would like to present a model as well as practical daily tasks that we could use towards the reconstruction of the cosmos, all using polyphony as a keyword.

7.1 Introduction

Stomu Yamash'ta, one of the editors of this publication, is a renowned musician, the only performer in the world who plays on instruments made from ancient stones called sanukite. In his article that appeared in the volume preceding this current publication, *The Kyoto Manifesto for Global Economics*, Yamash'ta wrote about "the essence of 'polyphony' as taught to [him] by the dialogue with [his] stones" in the conclusion, to wit:

> 'Polyphony' is the essence of the ecological scheme, namely the word that represents the world of multiple sound tracks generated by activities in nature. Scientifically, this continuously circulates. In other words, we call it Kanzeon, bodhisattva of mercy and salvation. In Nirvana, sutras teach that mountains, rivers, grass, trees, and all things have the Buddha nature in them.

Translated by Voltaire Cang, Specialist Researcher, RINRI Institute of Ethics, Tokyo.

T. Maruyama (✉)
RINRI Institute of Ethics, Tokyo, Japan
e-mail: toshiaki-maruyama@rinri-jpn.or.jp

© Springer Nature Singapore Pte Ltd. 2022
S. Hill et al. (eds.), *The Kyoto Post-COVID Manifesto For Global Economics*,
Creative Economy, https://doi.org/10.1007/978-981-16-8566-8_7

In the 21st century, digital technology occupies most of our daily lives. The same thing is true in the musical world. That is to say, we hear through virtual sound technology, which actually only imitates real sound. However, the most important factor is the polyphony, which essentially circulates in nature and requires music with impromptu inspiration and innovation to coexist in harmony.

When digital sound, with its virtual reality covers the earth, it implies that the natural world itself will disappear. It is crucial to rethink what it means to live as a human being with nature. For this reason, I want to suggest understanding polyphony in a new way to know better the world of analog.[1]

Yamash'ta and I have enjoyed a close friendship for more than seven years now, and I firmly believe in his statement about polyphony. I am not a musician; I have been working for a long time as the chairman of a private social education organization that was founded more than 70 years ago, as I also conduct research in my main area of specialization in East Asian ethical philosophy.

Our world today is one of increasing confusion, overrun with an ominous and widespread nihilism even as it needs a vision for the near future, while Japan itself suffers from stagnation: How can we overcome this situation? I have seriously grappled with these problems and issues through my work, and I have since realized that a great hint for their solution lies in the concept of "polyphony."

In this article, I would like first to describe an unusual personal experience, from which I will discuss our current crises and then the need for humanity to reconstruct the cosmos in light of our situation. Polyphony will be a major keyword in the discussion that follows.

7.2 Consolidation with Flowing Magma: A Personal Experience

On 12 October 2015, my organization marked the 70th year of the founding of its education movement with an anniversary celebration at the 5000-seat Tokyo International Forum, a convention center in Japan's capital. Our celebration consisted of two main events: a public lecture by a specialist in the field for the first half of the program, followed by a musical performance produced and participated in by Stomu Yamash'ta for the second. These two seemingly unrelated events were linked, as in a basso continuo, through the theme of Jōmon. Jōmon was the earth's oldest and longest civilization that existed for more than 10,000 years in the Japanese archipelago and became the very root of Japanese civilization. As will be explained in more detail below, it was during the Jōmon period when an astonishingly abundant way of life and culture were formed as they were also based on the Jōmon spirit of harmonious coexistence between nature and human beings.

Yamash'ta was born in Kyoto. At 17, he left Japan for the United States where he launched his career as a classical percussionist performer while he also delved into the study of various music genres. He eventually established the experimental theater company, Red Buddha Theatre, which achieved fame especially in the US and Europe. Mr. Yamashita, however, would abruptly retire from the commercial music industry. After returning to Japan in 1980, he began his research on religious music. It was during a period of seclusion and spiritual training in a Buddhist temple that he made his fateful discovery of sanukite, the natural stones through which he created a completely new field of music.

Sanukite stones are bronzite andesites with glass-like properties that were formed on Earth 13.5 million years ago. Along with obsidian, our ancestors used sanukite to produce tools during the Stone Age. For his instruments, Yamash'ta uses pieces of sanukite that have slits cut into them. When these stones are struck, their sound can reverberate for more than two minutes on a very wide range of vibrating frequencies, from very low to very high. The highest frequencies transcend 50,000 Hz and are undetectable to the human ear; they are said to be able to stimulate our brains and promote concentration.

During our anniversary event, Yamash'ta's performance began with sanukite sounds echoing across the hall which were amplified by speakers. As my organization's representative, I first read a message onstage, after which I climbed and sat on a two-meter wooden platform that was set at the center of the stage. I was on this platform for about 30 min, and during the whole time, I felt my body being transported to another dimension in space. The swirling waves of sanukite sounds that arose from under me challenged all my five senses with a tremendous intensity. As I closed my eyes, I envisioned red and black colors glowing and emitting light, like a giant flow of magma gushing out from inside the Earth.

I was enveloped in the swirl of sanukite sounds that were also merging with the magma, and I felt my consciousness being transformed. My emotions were at an extreme state of exhilaration. Even after the performance ended and I had stepped down from the platform, my feet did not seem to touch the ground, and the eerie sensation in my consciousness continued for almost a week. Even today, I can still vividly recall my mental and emotional intensity at the time.

After that experience, which remains difficult to describe in words, I wished strongly for an opportunity to have the sounds of sanukite played around the foot of Mount Fuji. That wish materialized three years later in October 2018, when my organization held a small event named the "1st Fuji Polyphonic Forum." With Japan's symbolic and sacred Mount Fuji right in front of us, we expressed our debt of gratitude for Mother Nature's blessings through a sanukite performance. The following section describes the aims of this event, as announced.

Mount Fuji symbolizes Japan. Since ancient times, its majestic and dignified appearance has inspired reverence among the people as *kami*, a "mountain deity." Underlying this reverence and at the very roots of the spiritual culture around the sacred Fuji is the fact of its singularity, a word which may be rendered in Kanji characters as "不二", also pronounced as *fuji*. This very singularity therefore renders the truth, goodness, and beauty that constitute the primary values of Mount Fuji as irreplaceable.

All people, all things, and all events take form and are made manifest through the power (forces) and energy (faculties) of cosmic phenomena, each finding its place in this world that brims with the grace of Life. In this world, the "individual" does not exist, for everything is bound to everything else by a common "fate," each sustaining life while resonating with one another. As human beings, we exist due to the wondrous graces of natural phenomena, of which we are also part.

At this moment in time when the first twenty years of the 21st century are coming to an end, humankind continues to build an artificial society through digital systems, which are now regarded as the paragons of science and technology. In these circumstances, we are brought face to face with a most significant issue: the meaning of our existence. That is, we are now frequently prompted to ask ourselves, "What is the human being?" Human history has been the history of our evolution from microorganisms to fish, then to reptiles, mammals, and to primates. What comes in the future then, beyond our current evolution?

The Fuji Polyphonic Forum was established with these themes and issues in mind.

The main purpose of the Forum is to enable participants to use their senses, that of hearing in particular, and make steps toward achieving true coexistence and harmony as is meant by "polyphony." It is in the finetuning of our five senses and the drawing out of the hidden potential in our inner lives that we can go beyond the current analog-digital duality that defines contemporary life.

We will inquire into the essence of art that is built on "sound" and "vibration," basing our inquiry on fundamental and historically tested truths that underlie the relationship between humans and sound. This inquiry will not result in our subjugation nor control of the natural world, but will instead lead to a reassessment of the order that regulates the coexistence of all life on earth. It will ultimately lead us to a deeper understanding of life and the capacity to listen to and discern from its wisdom. This will be a search for "nostalgic memory."

In the field of music, the word *polyphony* originally refers to a musical form produced from a combination of different individual melodies, in contrast to *monophony* which refers to only one melody constituting its form. In recent years, we incessantly hear about the need to respect diversity among living things and cultures. However, polyphony goes beyond diversity, since it refers to diverse elements retaining their individual and unique characteristics as they also co-exist with one another and maintain their harmony as a whole. It is this polyphony that is exquisitely realized in the singular music genre created by Yamash'ta.

Without going into much detail, I will just mention that during the event at the foot of Mount Fuji, the participants became witnesses to a miraculous change in weather. Rain that started falling the previous night turned into a downpour that continued throughout the whole morning, but just before the dedication ceremony that was the Forum's climactic event, the skies suddenly cleared, and the snow-capped peak of the sacred Mount Fuji came into full view, very clear and shining brilliantly.

The third Forum was held on 25 October 2020, a date which falls on the ninth day of the ninth month in the old calendar, and said to be the day when life energy is at its strongest throughout the year. We were blessed with a clear, cloudless day on our stage at the foothills surrounding Mount Fuji. Although clouds appeared in the afternoon and covered the mountain, when the offering ritual began at 3 PM, Mount Fuji emerged amidst the clouds, as if to show its pleasure, and continued to hide and reemerge throughout the event.

Needless to say, no one predicted that the third Forum would be held at a time when the whole world would be in the middle of an outbreak of the novel coronavirus that surfaced in Wuhan, China. By March 2020, it was already as if the whole world was in isolation, and people's movements and close contact were strictly regulated even in Japan. With no end in sight for the crisis, all kinds of events were postponed or cancelled altogether, such as the Tokyo Olympics that were set at a later date, as well as Stomu Yamash'ta's annual event at Daitokuji Temple in Kyoto, *ON ZEN Hōyō*, which is a joint Shinto and Buddhist gathering to pray for world peace and security, that had to be cancelled.

In view of the circumstances, we completely reorganized the third Forum into one in which Yamash'ta would invite priests and representatives from Daitokuji Temple and Imamiya Shrine in Kyoto to perform as they would in their annual event, through their words (recitation) and music (traditional Japanese musical instruments). It is significant that we were able to hold the Forum in the middle of the pandemic, as it was also held to offer prayers for the quelling of the infectious disease. The following section is taken from the message of offering given by the author during the third Forum, which he wishes to record for posterity.

Words of Offering

To the *kami* that reside in the sacred mountain of Fuji and are the source of life in all things in the universe, and to whom one is in fear of speaking, I offer these words with all awe and reverence.

Today we gather with feelings of deep gratitude for the blessings from the symbol of Japan that is Mount Fuji, and with hopes for mitigation of the many calamities and dangers that beset us, as we hold the festive ritual gathering of "The Third Fuji Polyphonic Forum."

The imperial reign has shifted from Heisei to Reiwa, but in the first year of this new era, an unforeseen and most fearful calamity befell humankind. It would soon spread worldwide and proceed to freeze transportation and other networks that are the driving forces of civilization, and cause great confusion.

If we look into the distant past of our nation, in the eleventh year of the long Jōkan era during the Heian period, which is the year 869 in the western calendar, a great earthquake and tsunami struck the northern region of Mutsunokuni. The scale of the disaster was similar to that of the 3.11 Great East Japan Earthquake on 11 March 2011.

In addition, an outbreak of dysentery, malignant influenza, and other infectious diseases also spread first in Kyoto and later to other areas. In the year 864, five years before the disaster in the northeastern region, Mount Fuji had erupted violently and completely transformed its surrounding landscape. Many Asama shrines were constructed thereafter, to seek the protection and pacification of *kami*.

More than one thousand years have passed since these events. However, with the recent great earthquake and the current outbreak of infectious disease, it is understandable that people are apprehensive about a corresponding large-scale eruption that could happen on Mount Fuji. As we contemplate the dangers from this potential event and relate it to the calamities that beset us today, we can but only realize the great transformation that human civilization is undergoing in the present era.

The world today has fallen into chaos and faces an uncertain future. However, even if we may not be able to know or predict the future, we are still enabled with a clear sense of the direction to which we are heading.

One of the key words that will guide us toward this direction is the musical term of polyphony, which we seek to express to the utmost through today's festive ritual gathering.

All things and phenomena on Earth are mutually dependent and form one grand ecosystem while they continue to repeat the life cycle. In the natural world, different parts emit their own diverse sounds as they also retain their individuality and uniqueness within their coexistence and maintain the harmony of the whole. Such is polyphony.

Underlying all this is the dimension where everything is joined together as one. The oneness of this and all other worlds, the all-in-one complete unity – this is the true way of the entire cosmos.

Let us then pause to hunker down and retrieve that which is important to us, but which we have forgotten and lost. These same words I have already said here during our two previous ritual occasions. This year, however, humankind has been forced, needfully, to isolate from one another and shut the world out, indeed, to hunker down.

Our society today is a society of excess. The flow of people, things, information – nothing ever stands still any more. If we stay too long in such an environment, our spirit becomes exhausted and corrupted. If, however, we make ourselves do the opposite, if we pause our movements and quiet down, a divine, noble, and luminous spirit will emerge from within us. The corona panic has truly served to remind us of that we have forgotten.

If we bend down, we will see a different landscape. That is why if we crouch low to look up to the mountain of Fuji, it appears even more majestic and sacred, and imposing in its presence.

In this year's ritual celebration, we are fatefully joined by representatives from Buddhist and Shinto organizations in Kyoto who are all gathered here at the bosom of sacred Mount Fuji. It is a contemporary enactment of the syncretism of Shinto and Buddhism of the past, and it brings us great joy.

Let us place ourselves completely inside the world of the sounds of the sanukite, which opens the path to a new era of mutual coexistence and great harmony that is polyphony. As we bring back our memories of the "nostalgic future" and gather here as one family, let us offer our gratitude to sacred Mount Fuji from the bottom of our hearts and pray for the peace of Japan and the world.

7.3 Stagnation in the Contemporary World: The Sweep of Nihilism

In today's world, there are too many events that occur at dizzying speeds all at the same time, the consequence of rapidly developing information technology (IT). Human society is now buried in digitized virtual spaces and virtual sounds. Nobody knows what exactly is happening in the world, and making forecasts even for the near future is difficult. Peter Drucker (1909–2005), who has been lauded as today's "modern prophet," proclaimed in one of his last works, *Managing in the Next Society*, that "If there is one thing that can be forecast with confidence, it is that the future will turn out in unexpected ways."[2] We are incapable of drawing a clear vision and plan for the future, overcome as we are with anxiety in our hearts while the world falls into stagnation and chaos. Humankind has never had this kind of experience before.

However, it is not only the rapid development of IT that is causing the world's stagnation and chaos. Another major cause is the destruction of previously universal modern values. The situation that we are in today is similar to that in Europe one hundred years ago. At the beginning of the twentieth century, Europe's pursuit of modern society's ideals of freedom, equality, democracy, and prosperity had succeeded to a certain extent, although its imperialism led to a scramble for colonies that eventually resulted in an unprecedented world war. When the First World War ended in 1918, Oswald Spengler's *The Decline of the West* had just been published and became a bestseller. It was from this era onwards that people in Europe lost confidence in themselves, resulting in the rapid spread of nihilism soon after.

Within the situation, people subsequently turned to the works of Friedrich Wilhelm Nietzsche (1844–1900), who had died earlier relatively unknown to his peers and the public. Until this period, supernatural concepts– e.g., "theory of Ideas," "pure eidos," "God"—that formed people's values were at the foundation of European culture and thought. Nietzsche, however, proclaimed this way of thinking as futile ("God is dead"), and that morals, justice, or democratic principles that people held dear were fraudulent and hypocritical. Through Nietzsche's ideas, nihilism thus spread throughout European society and resulted in even more confusion.

Nihilism is the rejection of those things that we hold to be valuable. When we lose things of value to us, our social relationships become weak, morality is destroyed, and apathy comes to prevail. Under these conditions, according to Nietzsche, our "will to power" is activated and society becomes a place of ceaseless struggle. Although the nihilism that emerged in Europe 100 years ago was to be obscured by the Second World War and by the subsequent East–West Cold War, it has come back with a renewed vigor in recent years and is spreading throughout the world.

As pointed out early on by Kyoto University professor emeritus Keishi Saeki, the "imperialism" in the past has become the "global economic war" in the present, as yesterday's "mass society" is now the "postmodern society" of today. We can thus say that the present global economy, which first emerged in the 1990s, coupled with our postmodern cultural condition together form the face of nihilism. Indeed, both the global economy and postmodern society conform to the monistic and one-dimensional idea that we need but only to secure profit and fame in life while we abandon the "legitimate ideals in human values" that enable the coexistence of diverse and independent individuals.

As a nation engulfed in the current global economic war, Japan is not exempted from crises, although its situation changed when it was hit by the only giant natural disaster to ever hit a developed country, that is, the Great East Japan Earthquake of March 2011. Until then, there had been growing concern that Japan had become a "disconnected society," but the overwhelming calamity blew those concerns away. In the disaster's aftermath, victims upheld public order despite their having to deal with their own distress, acting selflessly while also reviving the bonds of family; all of Japan then was bound together in love. However, with the passage of time, the utopia that developed from the emergency situation (described by Rebecca Solnit as a "paradise built in hell"[3]) crumbled and nihilism reared its head once more in daily life.

Can we overcome this critical problem of nihilism now spreading in the world? What must be done so that we truly can?

7.4 Losing the Cosmos

As mentioned earlier, it was the rejection of values based on modern principles that lay at the heart of the nihilism that spread in Europe one hundred years ago. It must be emphasized in turn that it is precisely the loss of the cosmos that is behind the universalization of these modern principles.

In ancient Greek, the term *cosmos* signified the order in the universe, which was regarded as a complete system that possessed an order like that found among constellations. Beauty was a natural manifestation within this order. Philosophies ranging from the "primitive" to the cognitive and rational have attempted to explain humankind's relationship to the natural world (that is, the Earth and our environment), as studies in religion and cultural anthropology have shown. Indeed, since ancient times many different cultures of the world have attempted to determine the corresponding relationship between people (including community and family units)—that is, the microcosmos—and the natural world—the macrocosmos.

In the case of Europe, people carried out their lives within the corresponding relationship that had formed between the dual cosmoses. People then had lived in awe of and in harmony with the macrocosmos of the outside world, which provided abundant blessings as it also possessed a terrifying power. This consciousness about the universe would change, however, when Christianity reached the lower classes of society and a worldview based on Christian doctrine spread in the eleventh and twelfth centuries. In Christian teaching, the macrocosmos was God, and this one God embodied the universe. Under Christianity, thus, the cosmos became of one dimension, and the dual cosmos structure of the world that had prevailed in people's minds until then collapsed.

Medieval European history scholar Kinya Abe (1935–2006) pointed to one fascinating aspect about "sounds" in the cosmos within the context of medieval European society. Abe infers that:

> In medieval cities, sounds were differentiated in terms of whether they were everyday or banal microcosmic sounds on the one hand or mystic macrocosmic sounds of the natural world on the other. In this period, the Christian church had begun to target even the world of sound, which it wanted to consolidate into a single dimension as they did with the cosmos. One way was through their failed attempt to have the Gregorian chant sung in a single voice. Instead, singers supplemented the single voice with more voices and sounds, further enriching the chant. In the process, they invented polyphony.

> I think that polyphony was the consequence of efforts to consolidate the two cosmoses into one dimension, albeit one that resulted from the desire to maintain a certain level of harmony while incorporating the mysterious sounds of the great cosmos.[4]

As for the anthropologist Keiji Iwata (1922–2013), he was much inspired by the later writings of Alexander von Humboldt (1769–1859) in the five-volume *Cosmos* that he set out to establish the study of anthropology with Southeast Asia as the main field of study. In his work, Iwata discovered that all religions were founded on "animist knowledge" from which they built their animistic cosmologies. The term *animism* here does not refer to the concept as defined by earlier anthropologists, who previously identified "primitive" religious consciousness among ancient peoples and "barbarians" in the eras before the establishment of so-called higher-order forms of religion. Instead, it refers to animism that considers the world of nature as it is and is without a God as Creator. However, numerous and diverse *kami* (i.e., spirits) coexist within this universe. And while everything in it is a manifestation of one *kami*, each thing also has *kami* dwelling within it. This is precisely the description of a polyphonic universe.

One distinctive feature in the animism as described by Iwata is the concept of *kami* existing in the manner of "two (or many) as one and one as two," and not as individual atoms of *kami* dwelling in each object in the universe. This grand cosmic diagram of life is like that found in Buddhist mandalas, wherein no permanent and immutable world exists. There is only a cosmos consisting of a dynamic world where *kami* are interwoven together, "two as one." Thus, given that the Earth is one cosmos onto itself, it can no longer be considered as the vehicle named "Spaceship Earth," for the Earth and myself (yourself) are the embodiment of the same *kami* and, in a hidden dimension, we are one and the same being.[5]

However, the one-dimensionality of Christianity along with the modernization that has been propped up by science, which are in turn underpinned by rationalism and positivism, brought about the loss of the cosmos as conceived under animism. This loss has also meant the loss of one's own reality and identity, which therefore links easily to the problem of nihilism.

Having lost the cosmos and being overcome with a nihilism that rejects universal values, human society can only exist in a state that is the exact opposite to that of the cosmos, which is chaos. Chaos originally meant the absence of order before order existed; it was initially powerless and was not in conflict with the cosmos. Over time, however, the destructive and negative forces of chaos came to attack the cosmos from within and from the outside. This type of chaos was named the "anti-cosmos" by Toshihiko Izutsu (1914–1993), the world-renowned scholar of linguistic philosophy and Islamic philosophy. Izutsu pointed out that the confrontation between the cosmos and the anti-cosmos has long been a dominant presence in the historical development of Western thought all the way to the present. He wrote:

> From the time of Nietzsche, who embodied the spirit of the tragic Greek god Dionysus, the anti-cosmos tendencies of Western thought gained strength rapidly, progressing through an existentialist phase before arriving at the postmodern philosophy that we have now. The avant-garde front of philosophy in Europe today, represented by Jacques Derrida's "destruction" philosophy and Gilles Deleuze's "rhizome" theory, are clearly anti-cosmos.[6]

Astonishingly, Izutsu argued that major Eastern schools of thought have traditionally taken the position of the anti-cosmos. It was Eastern philosophy that shook the structure of order to its foundations, as in its situating of the origin of existence in "nothingness" (空) like in Buddhism, or in "non-being" (無) as in Taoist thought. In such contexts, the reality that we perceive in the world of experience is nothing but a dream or a temporary image of a vision. However, "nothingness" and "non-being" do not result in an anarchistic destruction of existence; instead, because the starting point is fundamentally undifferentiated and unrestricted, order is formed in the diverse universe of "being" (有). The significance of this paradoxical philosophy on contemporary thought, which is already on the verge of destruction, was indicated by Izutsu as follows:

> Many people have begun to search for a new cultural paradigm for this new era, to replace the one-dimensional totalism in human culture that has been dominant until now, and which will offer a contemporary vision for a multi-ethnic, multi-cultural coexistence in which the importance of a multi-dimensional cultural relativism is emphasized. Towards this end, many keenly feel the need for closer exchanges and viable dialectics between Eastern and Western philosophical traditions. Considering the current cultural condition of the world, there is an important role to be played by the philosophy of "non-being" in Eastern thought, which can potentially help in establishing a "flexible cosmos" that had been internally dismantled.[7]

7.5 Reconstructing the Cosmos

In order to overcome the confusion of our times, there is a need to reconstruct the cosmos, that is, to create a new cosmology. As the world is increasingly becoming a mere aggregation of fragmented and inorganic individuals, I think there is a need to reconsider the ways of thinking surrounding the correspondence between the microcosmos and the macrocosmos. The world of animism as discussed herein offers fertile ground, as does Eastern philosophy that is rooted in "nothingness" and "non-being" that could ably guide us on such a path. Below, I would like to present a model as well as practical daily tasks that we could use towards the reconstruction of the cosmos, all using polyphony as a keyword.

For my model, I would like to use the Jōmon civilization, considered the base of Japanese civilization itself. Some years ago, global politics scholar Samuel Phillips Huntington (1927–2008) clearly emphasized that Japan was the only nation where a "single state" constituted a "single civilization."[8] This can be attributed with certainty to Japan's geography and climate. The Japanese archipelago stretches over a wide area from north to south and is blessed with diverse and beautiful natural features that are unique in the world. However, Japan is also a volcanic archipelago where natural disasters such as earthquakes and volcanic eruptions occur frequently.

Massive climate change occurred on Earth 20,000 years ago, after which a new civilization emerged in the Japanese archipelago more than 15,000 years ago. People began to settle in the archipelago, pursuing a way of life in which they coexisted with nature; they became known for producing earthenware vessels with distinctive rope patterns—Jōmon literally means "rope pattern" —and decorations on the rims. Their unique way of life continued for about 10,000 years until the arrival of the next era, the

Yayoi. The famed French cultural anthropologist Claude Levi-Strauss (1908–2009) once wrote:

> In any event, I have often wondered whether, despite the upheavals introduced by Yayoi culture, something of what could be called the "Jōmon" spirit" does not persist in contemporary Japan. Perhaps we should attribute to it an invariant trait of the Japanese aesthetic…[9]

What, then, have the Japanese today inherited and retained from the roots of their civilization, the Jōmon? I have reached the following four conclusions:

The first is *a heart of reverence for the origins of life and deep gratitude for life's blessings*. Jōmon people found *kami* and spirits in all things in the universe (i.e., animism) and expressed their love and attachment to people and things even after these disappeared from the face of the Earth.

The second is *a pure and selfless spirit of prayer*. Around 15,000 clay *dogū* (earthenware dolls) have been excavated from many Jōmon sites, most of them female figures that were found to have been destroyed on purpose. It is believed that they were deliberately damaged as a form of prayer for a prolific family, for safe childbirth, or for the rebirth of a child who died prematurely.

The third is *a deepened and unique aesthetic sense combined with skilled craft techniques*. Jōmon peoples' rich modes of expression and their aesthetic spirit are expressed in the different forms and rich decorative variety of Jōmon earthenware. Communities of skilled and professional lacquerware technicians also existed, and they lived in different regions, settling in with other communities. These craft technicians possessed highly skilled techniques that allowed them, for example, to bore holes in jadestones that were as hard as diamonds.

The fourth is *a balanced mind equally maintaining both gentle and tough dispositions*. The natural environment of the Japanese archipelago was an abundant fount of blessings as it was also a fearful source of disastrous calamities. As they lived in such an environment, Jōmon people came to develop a spirit that sought harmony with nature while exhibiting a tough attitude towards it at the same time. This disposition later translated into the ability to master both pen and sword as is valued in Japanese culture, as well as the development of the bushido spirit.

These characteristics of Jōmon civilization can form the model for the creation of a polyphonic community. Japan, with its roots in Jōmon civilization, possesses a polyphonic national character, one where its original Shinto spiritual culture has coexisted harmoniously with Buddhism as well as Taoism that had come from foreign shores, the mingling of which has not caused interreligious conflict within the islands.

With regard to practices for restructuring the cosmos, I would like to propose two everyday tasks, as follows.

First, we must live our lives with an even stronger consciousness about our planet, with both feet firmly planted on the ground.

In the second half of the twentieth century, the space race between the United States and the former Soviet Union enabled humankind to become more cognizant of the Earth and to regard it as our mother planet. We have been deeply moved by visual images of the Earth from this time, which appear as a beautiful, brilliant, and quietly moving blue object within jet-black space. Indeed, people today have become more conscious of the Earth as one life and a cosmos onto itself, which is a way of thinking that did not exist in the past. The Earth has also come to be called "Gaia," in reference to the name given to the Mother Earth goddess in Greek mythology.

Looking back on humankind's past journey, we can see that humans were one with the Earth before the beginning of agriculture, in the time when they lived as hunter-gatherers. Agriculture, however, gave birth to civilizations that exploited the Earth. Industrialized societies that arose later then focused their goals on developing industries for the future while depending on underground energy sources, thus turning into civilizations that gradually depleted the Earth. Furthermore, today's information industry society (i.e., the IT era), which grew from even more developed technical revolution, has made us into a civilization that is completely detached from the Earth.

We are already in the midst of a "hyper-IT" civilization. Young people today grow up in an internet environment from the time of their earliest recollections, and they are able to operate all kinds of machines at will. They are, however, also drowning in their world of virtual spaces and sounds, with a rapidly increasing number of youths now suffering from "gaming disorder." Along with innumerable potential victims who exhibit symptoms of the disease, there is already a fast-increasing and -spreading number of people all over the world who live restless and ungrounded lives.

It may be redundant to say that human beings live their lives on the surface of the Earth as do other living beings. We may be able to roam the skies or even fly out into space, but the basic place where we carry out our lives is on the Earth. We need to deepen our consciousness about this planet through education and other human activities, while we consider the Earth not merely as a vehicle for humans but instead as the "life form of Gaia" on which all living and non-living things co-exist. We must consider the "security of the Earth" as the highest good and develop the common sense to make such security as the ultimate goal of humankind.[10]

The root cause of the confusion and crises today is ultimately human egoism, that is, our selfish way of life. We need to break away from this egoism which undermines the harmony of our human community while we promote peaceful cooperation to strengthen and increase joy among humankind and live with respect towards all other beings that exist with us on this Earth. This kind of behavior will enable us to have our feet firmly planted on the ground and lead to the reconstruction of the cosmos, with polyphony as our guide.

Finally, I would like to stress the importance of a most everyday form of exercise, that of the act of listening.

As mentioned earlier, Stomu Yamash'ta has also been producing a ceremony called *ON ZEN Hōyō*, a Buddhist Zen memorial service for sound that is held at the Daitokuji temple in Kyoto every year in June. Buddhism and Shinto come together in this "offering ceremony for sound," fusing "sound" (*on*) with "Zen." Regarding the term *on* or sound, Yamash'ta says:

> "On" means "Otodama (soundspirit)". The mysterious energy of sound leads us to a world harmonized with universe, nature, man, and stone. Zen teaches Nothingness. Nothingness

means ultimate truth, virtue and beauty. It is said that all living things, all beings, and all reality are of the truth, virtue, beauty and blessing coming out of Nothingness.[11]

During the *ON ZEN Hōyō* held in 2018, a four-person Gregorian chant choir had come to participate from France. Yamash'ta told me later that during rehearsals, the choir encountered a dilemma and said that it was unable to sing in the space that was provided. Their reason was that they always sang in churches that were built of stone, where sound reverberated loudly. In these spaces, each choir member would sing by layering each individual part over the other voices that were heard echoing around them. (In other words, they were engaged in the practice of polyphony.) The problem with temples in Japan, however, is their wooden construction which makes it difficult for sounds to reverberate, thus causing challenges for the layering of voices. The choir's problem was eventually solved, however, using microphones and speakers.

What I found most intriguing from this account was the fact that polyphony could only be achieved by carefully listening to the sound (i.e., voice) of the other. If one insists on emphasizing one's part alone, the harmony of the whole would not be achieved.

On reflection, how much do we really listen to other peoples' voices or words in our daily lives? The act of listening is the concrete practice of accepting others. And when we acknowledge the happiness or sadness of others as if these were our own, or understand their thoughts from their standpoint, we are putting ourselves in a position that is the exact opposite of self-assertion, which is difficult to actually practice. The capacity to listen is a skill that we gain in the process of our growth as human beings and which we learn through our parents and the people around us who also serve as our models. Today, however, the numbers of such models are diminishing, and more and more people are unable to develop the capacity to listen.

As in psychotherapeutic counseling where the act of listening is basic to its practice, we can only open up and communicate with our hearts as long as the other person acknowledges us and approaches us with empathy. This kind of reciprocal heart-to-heart communication in daily life is one way to reconstruct the cosmos on the basis of polyphony, our keyword; it may be a banal practice, but it is nonetheless indispensable.

7.6   Conclusion

The correspondence between the macrocosmos and the microcosmos had heretofore been basic in human thought. With the advent of theocracy in Western society, however, the ancient idea of a world composed of many diverse *kami* disappeared as we entered the modern era. By placing value on rationalism, modern society has reached the stage where the two cosmoses that were previously seen intuitively and symbolically as an interlocking, inseparable whole have been completely cut off from one another.

However, even if the corresponding and sympathetic relationship between the dual cosmoses is no longer found in regular daily life, it does not mean that it has disappeared: It is but only dormant. When human beings as the microcosmos transform into the way they should through their daily experience, the wholeness of the dual cosmos can be restored. As described in the introduction to this article, my experience of merging with flowing magma while enveloped in the sounds of the sanukite offers an insight into what is possible. Eastern philosophy incorporates many kinds of physical and spiritual practices that are all called "training," which are actually practices for enabling the self to realize a higher form beyond that of the normal self, if not to actualize the completeness of the self. These practices deserve our attention in our goal towards achieving the reconstruction of the cosmos.

I see the chaos and the many crises that characterize our contemporary world as phenomena that needed to arise for the sake of creating a new human civilization. Without the transformation of humankind and the evolution of our inner lives, it will be impossible to create this new civilization.

In Chinese culture, *chaos* is often rendered as 混沌 [*hundun*], a concept that originally indicated a certain ideal situation. In the classical Chinese text *Zhuangzi*, the following anecdote precisely describes chaos as follows:

> The emperor of the southern sea was called Swoosh 儵. The emperor of the northern sea was called Oblivion 忽. The emperor of the middle was called Chaos 渾沌. Swoosh and Oblivion would sometimes meet in the territory of Chaos, who always attended to them quite well. They decided to repay Chaos for his virtue. "All men have seven holes in them, by means of which they see, hear, eat, and breathe," they said. "But this one alone has one. Let's drill him some."

> So each day they drilled another hole. After seven days, Chaos was dead.[12]

The cosmos refers to a universe possessed of an order of its own, not one dictated by human beings. Order is latent even in places that appear to be in disorder. If indeed the actual cosmos indicated order within disorder, it would not stand in confrontation with chaos. I believe that it is not at all impossible to reclaim this cosmos back into our lives today.

Notes

1. Stomu Yamash'ta, "Listen to the Stone: Searching for Spiritual Harmony in Polyphonic Coexistence." In Stomu Yamash'ta, Tadashi Yagi & Stephen Hill (eds.), *The Kyoto Manifesto for Global Economics: The Platform of Continuity, Humanity, and Spirituality* (Singapore: Springer, 2018), 131–139, p. 139.

2. Peter Drucker, *Managing in the Next Society* (NY: St. Martin's Press, 2002), p. 296.

3. Rebecca Solnit, *A Paradise Built in Hell: The Extraordinary Communities That Arise in Disaster* (NY: Penguin, 2009).

4. Kinya Abe, *Jibun no naka ni rekishi wo yomu* [Studying history from inside myself] (Tokyo: Chikuma Shobo, 1988), p. 207.

5.   Keiji Iwata, *Kosumosu no shisō* [Philosophy of the cosmos] (Tokyo: NHK Books, 1978). See also Keiji Iwata, *Sōmoku chūgyo no jinruigaku* [Anthropology of plants, insects, and fish] (Tokyo: Kodansha, 1991).

6.   Toshihiko Izutsu, *Kosumosu to anchikosumosu* [Cosmos and anti-cosmos] (Tokyo: Iwanami Shoten, 1989), p. 193.

7.   Ibid, p. 196.

8.   Mentioned during a lecture in Tokyo in December 1998. See Samuel Huntington, *Bunmei no shōtotsu to 21 seiki no Nihon* [Clash of Civilizations and 21st Century Japan] (trans. Chikara Suzuki) (Tokyo: Shueisha, 2000).

9.   Claude Levi-Strauss, *The Other Face of the Moon* (trans. Jane Marie Todd) (Cambridge, MA: Belknap Press, 2013), p. 20.

10. One of the pillar programs in my social education organization is the Earth RINRI movement – RINRI of, by, and for the people of the Earth. For space reasons, this practice cannot be discussed here. For details, see Toshiaki Maruyama, *Understanding RINRI: Guide to Practice and Principles* (trans. Voltaire Cang) (Tokyo: Shinsei Shoboh, 2013).

11. Yamash'ta, "Listen to the Stone," p. 137.

12. Brook Ziporyn, *Zhuangzi: The Essential Writings with Selections from Traditional Commentaries* (Indianapolis: Hackett Publishing, 2009), p. 52.

Part II
Dimensions
of Transformation—Complexity
and Wholeness

Chapter 8
Achieving Transformation in Our Highly Interconnected World I: Systems Thinking and Network Thinking

Len Fisher

Abstract The central thesis of the *Manifesto* is that we can transform our societies from their present unhealthy focus on economic self-interest, to a condition where cooperation, mutual support and sustainability are the norm, through the application of humanistic values, as exemplified by many Buddhist principles. In this and the next Chapter I examine how such change might be achieved in practice. In the present Chap. 1 consider our increasingly interconnected socio-economicecological world as a whole, and show how it may be seen as a giant complex adaptive network (a CAN). It is a network because its individual members (such as people, plants, animals, institutions, rocks and oceans) are connected with each other, and interact either directly or indirectly. It is adaptive because the interactions are dynamic, driving change and being changed themselves in turn and over time. Finally, it is complex because the direction and nature of overall change is often both unpredictable and uncontrollable.

8.1 Summary

The central thesis of the *Manifesto* is that we can transform our societies from their present unhealthy focus on economic self-interest, to a condition where cooperation, mutual support and sustainability are the norm, through the application of humanistic values, as exemplified by many Buddhist principles. In this and the next Chap. 1 examine how such change might be achieved in practice.

In the present Chapter I consider our increasingly interconnected socio-economicecological world as a whole, and show how it may be seen as a giant *complex adaptive network* (a *CAN*). It is a *network* because its individual members (such as people, plants, animals, institutions, rocks and oceans) are connected with each other, and interact either directly or indirectly. It is *adaptive* because the interactions are dynamic, driving change and being changed themselves in turn and over

L. Fisher (✉)
School of Physics, University of Bristol, Tyndall Ave, Bristol BS8 1TL, UK
e-mail: Len.Fisher@bristol.ac.uk

© Springer Nature Singapore Pte Ltd. 2022
S. Hill et al. (eds.), *The Kyoto Post-COVID Manifesto For Global Economics*,
Creative Economy, https://doi.org/10.1007/978-981-16-8566-8_8

time. Finally, it is *complex* because the direction and nature of overall change is often both unpredictable and uncontrollable.

The science of complexity is a relatively recent development, but already it has revealed several significant features of CANs:

- They are liable to sudden, dramatic and often unpredictable system-wide change, as witness the collapse of marriages, societies and civilizations, or the growth of communications networks, social movements and the industrial revolution
- The change may be initiated by external (*exogenous*) or internal (*endogenous*) forces. In either case, change may be rapidly amplified, so that a small event in one part of the network (the collapse of a financial institution, or an infected bat in a Chinese market) can produce profound effects in other parts (collapse of the global financial system, or a global pandemic)
- Such change is often preceded by warning signs, although these are seldom heeded in time
- The structure and arrangement of the links within a CAN play a vital role in determining its evolution and long-term stability

In the following Chapter I focus on the individual, and ask how we can use our role as members of a complex socio-economic-ecological network to help guide social transformation. In a technical sense we are *nodes* in that network, joined to other nodes by *links*, which may be social interactions, practical actions (such as choosing which energy sources or materials to use) or simple physical proximity. In all cases, we can use those links to influence/affect whatever we are linked to.

By planning these interactions in a coordinated way, we can initiate change which, under suitable circumstances, may propagate throughout the network. This is the basis of both evolution and revolution. Here I examine how humanistic values in particular offer an opportunity to use our links within our socio-economic-ecological CAN to help guide it in directions that are both socially fair and economically and environmentally sustainable.

It is not an easy task, and the modern science of game theory has shown that just a few individuals pursuing their own self-interest can disrupt efforts at cooperation. This is one of the biggest problems facing the world today, and not to be minimized. I argue that our best chance of overcoming this major barrier lies in the adoption, application and spread of humanistic principles (for example, with the minimum wage and the circular economy), initially in restricted areas, and use case studies and theoretical examples to show how our new understanding of network science may be used to help atalyse and amplify the spread of these approaches.

8.2   The Need for Change

Many international organizations have identified the pursuit of economic and social self-interest as a primary threat to a sustainable and equitable future. The Intergovernmental Science-Policy Platform on Biodiversity and Ecosystem Services (IPBES) has identified it with regard to the preservation of biodiversity (IPBES, 2019). The Intergovernmental Panel on Climate Change has identified it as a major driver global warming (IPCC, 2016). The EAT-Lancet Commission on healthy diets has identified it as a threat to sustainable food supplies (Willett et al., 2019). In a report on these and other global issues, including wealth disparity and the many refugee crises, the World Economic Forum declares that "the current economic model is unsustainable" (WEF, 2017). The United Nations has even initiated a programme to develop "a new economic paradigm—one that has as its goal human happiness and the well being of all life on earth …" (United Nations, 2012). The possible paths to that future have been outlined by a number of authors (e.g. Harangozo et al., 2018 One problem in gaining support for such a programme is that the pursuit of economic self-interest has brought benefits and raised the standard of living for many people (Stephen Hill, this volume). The bargain, however, has been a Faustian one. Damage to the natural world (Díaz et al., 2019) and to our social structures (Diffenbaugh & Burke, 2019; Pope Francis, 2020) has now reached the stage where competition increasingly needs to be replaced by cooperation, and where the world's natural resources can no longer be regarded as "externalities" freely available to whoever wishes to plunder them (Beeks & Ziko, 2018). "The 'Devil'" says Hill "has delivered," but 'the 'Devil' claims the benefits *back* after a limited period of time" and "*We have reached this time limit.*"

8.3   Interconnection

We have reached the time limit because the world is increasingly behaving as an interconnected whole, with actions and events ever more impacting on each other, sometimes in unexpected ways. The COVID-19 pandemic has brought this aspect of the modern world to political and public attention (Collins et al., 2020). The disease has affected not just health, but livelihoods, travel, mental health and education in a vicious interconnected network of cause and effect, with present effects becoming future causes in a complex endless loop (EASAC, 2020).

Such complexity can sometimes bring us back unexpectedly to our starting point. "Deforestation in Brazil" for example "due to soybean production provides food for people and livestock in China. Food trade between Brazil and China also contributes to changes in the global food market, which affects other areas around the world, including the Caribbean and Africa, that also engage in trade with China and Brazil. Dust particles from the Sahara Desert in Africa—aggravated by agricultural practices—travel via the air to the Caribbean, where they contribute to the decline in coral reefs and soil fertility and increase asthma rates. These in turn affect China and Brazil, which have both invested heavily in Caribbean tourism, infrastructure, and transportation. Nutrient-rich dust from Africa also reaches Brazil, where it improves forest productivity." (Liu et al., 2017).

Other examples include the link between human diet and environmental sustainability described in the EAT-Lancet Commission report *Food, Planet, Health* (Willett et al., 2019), the bankruptcy of the Californian PG&E utility, which has been strongly linked to climate change (MacWilliams et al., 2019), and increased global economic inequality between countries. "[F] or most poor countries," say climate scientists Noah Diffenbaugh and Marshall Burke (2019), "there is >90% likelihood that per capita GDP is lower today than if global warming had not occurred".

To tackle such problems, we need to consider the world system as an interconnected network (Sayama et al., 2013). To do so requires *systems thinking*, which "looks at relationships (rather than unrelated objects), connectedness, process (rather than structure), the whole (rather than just its parts), the patterns (rather than the contents) of a system, and context. [It] also requires several shifts in perception, which lead in turn to different ways to teach, and different ways to organize society." (Ackoff, 2008).

At first sight, systems thinking would appear to suggest that global trends towards increasing interconnectedness and diversity are good things. This was the received wisdom in ecological theory up until 1972: larger and more diverse systems were held to be more stable, since there were more pathways for adaptation to change. This doctrine was effectively destroyed by the Australian physicist Bob May in 1972 when he proved mathematically that randomly connected ecological networks should be *LESS* stable than their smaller counterparts. It was a staggering blow, especially since larger and more diverse networks are often more stable in practice. The secret turned out to lie in the word "random". Networks that are truly random do collapse more easily than their smaller counterparts. Those that survive are those where the connections are far from random (May called them "the winnowed products of evolution"). This may happen either by chance or design.

But this does not mean that we can reach a stable equilibrium. The world's interconnected social, economic and ecological networks constitute an *open system* (Postrel, 1998) where fresh influences and fresh connections are constantly arising in a dynamic interplay where the past is no guarantee of the future and the present is in a constant state of flux. May's "winnowed products" offer temporary periods of apparent stability, but the mathematics shows that these cannot be relied upon in the long term. That mathematics has been reinforced by complexity scientist Geoffrey West, who has looked at the way that different metrics scale with size in our complex socio-economic-ecological world (West, 2017). Some aspects scale "sub-linearly"— in other words, they show economies of scale. Among these are transport networks and the supply of different utilities (gas, water, electricity) in cities—the bigger the city, the more efficient the network.

Other aspects, though, scale "super-linearly", displaying runaway growth with increasing network size and eventually leading to the collapse of the network in which they are embedded. In this category are many social and economic metrics, such as average wage, crime rate and the occurrence of infectious diseases. Technological innovation, such as the development of a vaccine, can resolve some of the issues, but it turns out that innovation itself scales super-linearly, so that discovery must happen at a faster and faster rate as each problem arises, until it can no longer keep up and social collapse ensues.

So where do we stand? At first sight prospects for the future look grim, for three reasons:

(1) *System-wide collapse or other dramatic change can be "near-impossible to predict, model and estimate"*

Take the 2008 financial crisis, where a primary cause for collapse was the tight, uncontrolled interconnections between the banks and other financial institutions (Haldane & May, 2011). As Bank of England chief economist Andy Haldane later pointed out (Haldane, 2017), "the radical uncertainty in such complex webs generates emergent behaviour which can be near-impossible to predict, model and estimate." This is a general problem with the complex networks in which we are embedded, and where we a trapped in a web of causalities where "The actual stability properties and the net effects along causal chains depend critically on the relative strength of the different mechanisms involved." (Scheffer & van Nes, 2018).

Climate change provides an example, with many interacting physical drivers contributing to the change (Zscheischler et al., 2018), and human activity further complicating the picture in this and many other cases (Vorogushyn et al., 2018).

(2) *Small effects, whether external (exogenous) or internal (endogenous) can have profound consequences*

We need look no further for examples than the birth of the Buddha, the assassination of Archduke Ferdinand, or the purchase of an infected bat in a Chinese market—all small events in themselves, but which had world-wide ramifications. Those ramifications spread through connections that could not have been, or were not, foreseen, and in which in some cases did not even exist when the original event took place. A recent example is the recognition of nuclear fission in 1939 by the German scientists Lise Meitner and Otto Frisch. This underpinned the invention of the atomic bomb, but this consequence (which emerged through interactions in the network of scientists) was certainly not foreseen by the German scientists; otherwise, they would surely not have published their discovery in the English journal *Nature* (Meitner & Frisch, 1939), at a time when Germany was clearly preparing for war with England.

(3) *Super-linear scaling of social metrics means that cycles of growth and collapse in societies, economies and ecosystems are likely to occur with increasing frequency as the system grows bigger and more complex*

The overall picture is one of great uncertainty in a world where our minds simply cannot grasp, let alone predict or control, what is going on in this complex, interdependent world.

8.4 Hope

Nevertheless, there is hope. We need to embrace uncertainty, but this does not mean resigning ourselves to fate. Instead, we must learn to live with uncertainty, and even to use it.

We need two major tools to help us carve out a trail towards a sustainable future in the face of increasing uncertainty. Cooperation is one such tool. Understanding and respect for the way in which the networks to which we belong actually function is the other.

One aspect of real-life networks that offers some hope is that many of them are constrained by the pressures of information transmission. These pressures select for specific structural features—features that allow us to make effective decisions (Lynn et al., 2019). According to these authors "efficient communication arises in networks that are simultaneously heterogeneous, with high-degree hubs, and clustered, with tightly-connected modules—the two defining features of hierarchical organization." But efficiency is not enough. To fulfil our human needs and the needs of all who share our socio-economic-ecological network, our behaviour as members of that network also requires a moral, ethical dimension. The Scottish economist Adam Smith, often seen as the godfather of the doctrine of individual self-interest and the market economy, was one of the first to recognize this (Bonar, 1926; Smith, 1759). The message has sadly been lost in many Western economies over the past century or so (Klein, 2007), but is now being spelled out by a number of leading economists (Bowles, 2016; Carney, 2020), social philosophers (Bodanis, 2020) and others. It is not just a matter of ethical behaviour, fairness and consideration for our fellows; it is a matter of practical necessity (Bodanis, 2020). Cooperative behaviour, mutual support and trust are essential tools in guiding our interconnected world through the many perils that now confront it.

The history of the COVID-19 pandemic offers an example. A detailed analysis of successful government responses (Anttiroiko, 2021) demonstrates a distinct difference between "Asian cases reflect proactivity and diligence, while Western responses are reactive and more often than not slightly delayed."

This difference, according to Bavel et al. (2020), arises because "Western European and North American cultures … endorse individualism …, whereas most other cultures share a stronger commitment to collectives such as country, tribe and family and are considered interdependent. While medical policies are different across societies, some differences in the response to the pandemic may be better described as cultural, and many of those have a linkage to the dimension of independence vs interdependence."

In other words, social cooperation and mutual support have been much more effective tools in response to the pandemic than has the pursuit of individual selfinterest, however rational.

The pandemic provides a particularly clear example because just one major action has been needed, which is to cut links and rearrange the network to minimize transmission of the disease. A similar strategy for stabilizing the global financial network was suggested by May and his colleagues in the wonderful "Ecology for Bankers" (2008), published just a few months before the collapse of Lehman Brothers. If economists had acted on it, instead of thinking that they knew better, the global financial crisis that followed may have been less severe.

The idea of influencing the network as a whole (not necessarily just by cutting links) is a strategy that will often be needed in dealing with global threats and the maintenance of stability and sustainability. Here I consider the general principles, before going on in the next chapter to consider the changes in behaviour that will be necessary to implement those principles.

8.5 Changing the Network

Network science is still a young disciple, but already some general principles are emerging when it comes to effective actions for change. Three of these are of particular importance:

- Warning signs
- Sensitive intervention points
- Changing network structure and behaviour.

8.6 Warning Signs

A feature of all complex adaptive systems is their liability to sudden, system-wide, sometimes catastrophic change (technically called a *critical transition* (Scheffer, 2009)). There may be a definable cause (at least in retrospect), but often there is none. Repeat, *none*. It is a behaviour of the system *as a whole*.

This is a point that is extraordinarily difficult to get across to economists, politicians, policy-makers and the general public. It has strong mathematical foundations in René Thom's catastrophe theory.

Thom (1989) identified seven types of catastrophe that could occur within a complex system. The one that concerns us most is also the simplest—the *fold* catastrophe.

Here it is (Fig. 8.1).

It looks simple, but conceals a wealth of information, some of which is revealed in this diagram by the Dutch mathematical ecologist Marten Scheffer (Fig. 8.2).

In particular (see right hand side of diagram), the closer that the system gets to a point of catastrophic change, the less the perturbation required to push it over the edge. The practical implication is that we need to find ways to steer the system away from these points before it gets too close.

Scheffer used Thom's theory to show that there existed of set of warning signs for imminent systemic critical transitions (Scheffer et al., 2001, 2009). They include the more frequent occurrence of extreme events, increasingly violent and rapid swings between extreme events, and a decreased ability to recover from small perturbations. Unfortunately, the significance of these signs often only becomes apparent when it is too late to act, and they need to be supplemented by other considerations if they are to be useful. Climate change provides an obvious example, where the effects

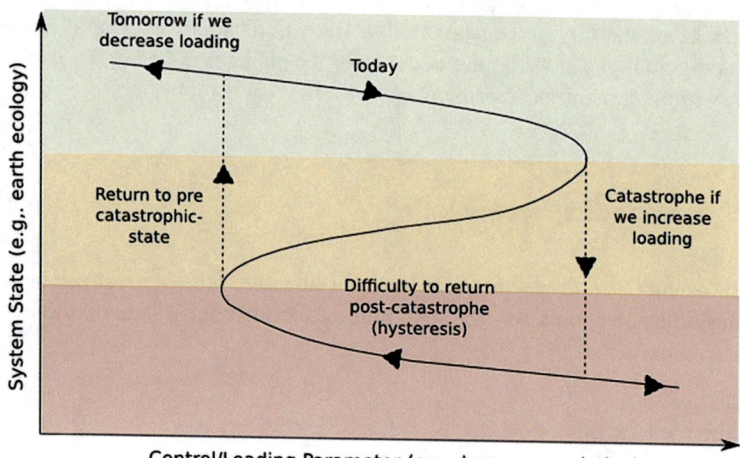

Fig. 8.1 Fold catastrophe

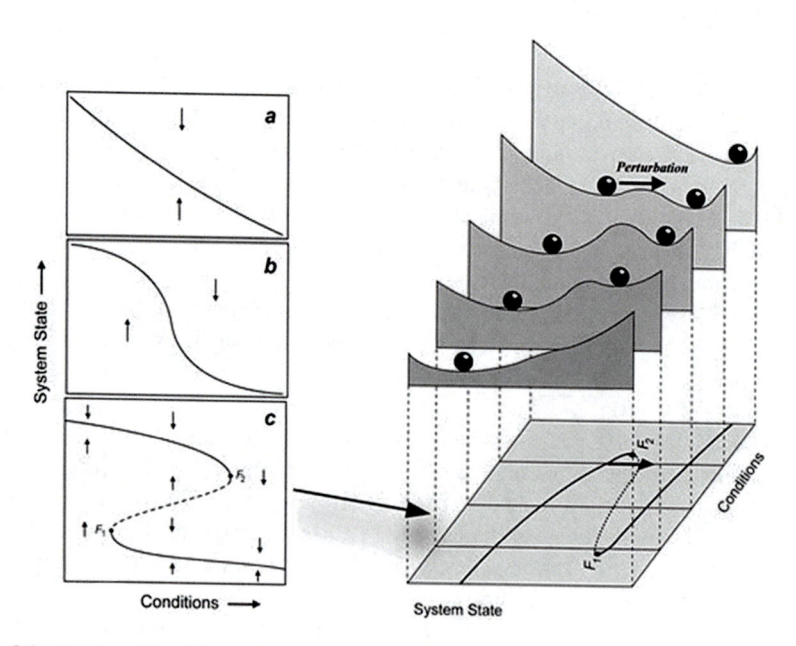

Fig. 8.2 Origins of the fold catastrophe (Scheffer et al., 2009)

of increasing greenhouse gas emissions are both well understood and well documented. What is missing here is not understanding or knowledge, but the *will* to
act—something that will be considered in the next chapter.

8.7   Sensitive Intervention Points

Even with the will, the timing may need to be right. This is where the concept of sensitive intervention points can be useful.

Sensitive intervention points, or SIPs, are points in the evolution of a system where the system is ripe for change, and the opportunity is there to be grasped (Farmer et al., 2019).

"There are two types of SIPs" according to Doyne Farmer and his co-authors. "The first involves a kick to the current state of the system, moving it onto a new trajectory without any change in the underlying system dynamics. If the new trajectory diverges rapidly from the old trajectory, then a small kick at the right point can trigger a large change. A small kick can be effective when the system is chaotic or when it is near a critical point. Subsidizing renewable energy sources to lower their costs provides an example of a kick [to move a system away from dependence on fossil fuels as a source of energy]."

"The second type of SIP involves a shift in the underlying system dynamics, where the rules of the system itself change and trajectories alter substantially. A shift can be effective even without a kick. In the socioeconomic-political sphere, a shift may entail a change in key concepts and institutions. For example, the shift from the rigid Kyoto regime to the more flexible (if still imperfect) Paris structure has altered the rules of the game, enabling new forms of cooperation."

The *Manifesto* is mainly concerned with type 2 SIPs, which require "a critical threshold of the total population, but above the threshold it grows rapidly and becomes prevalent." In other words, relatively small groups can make a big difference to cultural values and attitudes so long as their actions are focused and timely. Examples of how this may be applied in the context of the *Manifesto* are offered in the next chapter.

8.8   Changing the Network Structure and Behaviour

The pattern and nature of the interconnections governs how susceptible the network is to internal and external influences, and just where it sits on the fold curve in Fig. 8.1.

<u>Patterns</u>

Let us take the patterns first. Network scientists have identified many (Perera et al., 2017), but four are particularly important when it comes to understanding interactions, influences and stability within social networks (Vespignani, 2018). These are:

- *Random* networks (Fig. 8.3a), where connections are established at random between different members. This may occur at a large conference or other gathering, for example, where people who do not know each other simply begin talking in pairs or in larger groups.

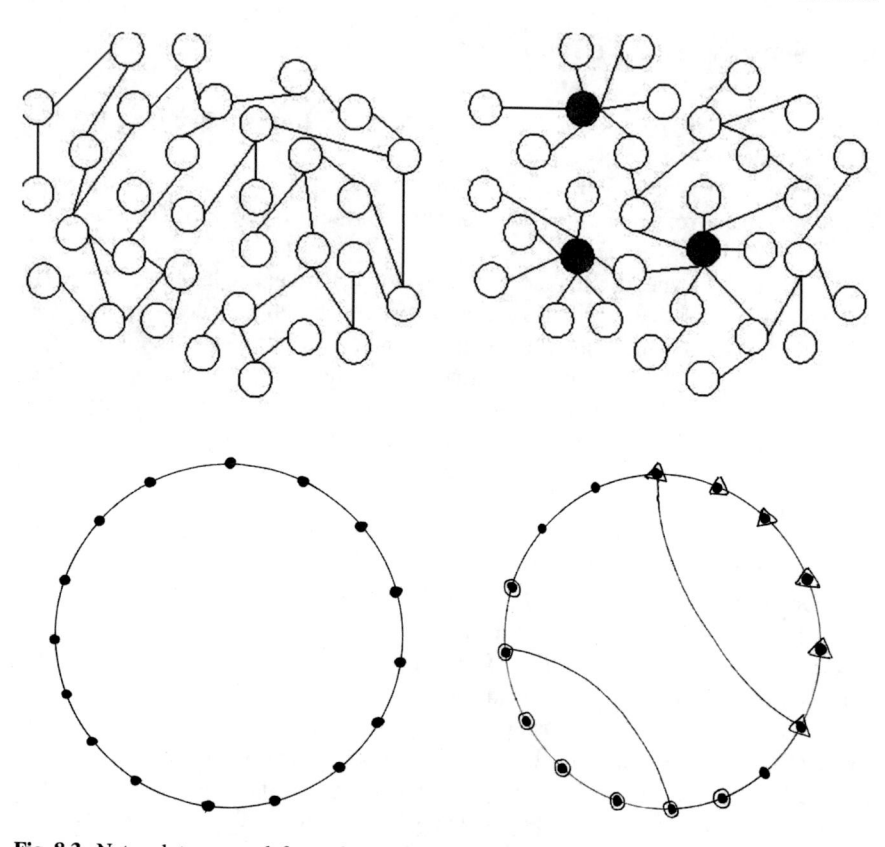

Fig. 8.3 Network types top left: random; top right: scale free; bottom left: regular; bottom right: small-world

- *Scale-free* networks (Fig. 8.3b)—a term that unfortunately has little intuitive meaning to non-mathematicians. These are networks where number of links possessed by different members follows a power law (Inset, Fig. 8.3c), so that just a few members (called *hubs*) have many more links than most. I prefer to call these *preferential attachment networks*, after a major mechanism that has been proposed for their formation, where members with many links tend to attract yet more links (an example is the distribution of followers across the World Wide Web). This was dubbed by the sociologist Robert Merton (1968) as the *Matthew effect*, after the biblical quote "For to every one who has will more be given, and he will have abundance; but from him who has not, even what he has will be taken away" (Holy Bible, Revised Standard Version, Matthew *25:29*).
- *Regular* networks (Fig. 8.3c), where each member (technically called a *node*) has the same number of connections (technically called *links*) with other members. This could occur in a large open-plan office, for example, where the desks are laid out in a square array, so that the occupant of each desk (except for those at the boundary) has direct links only with his or her four nearest neighbors.

- *Small-world* networks (Fig. 8.3d) are those where most members are not in direct contact with each other, but can be reached in a relatively small number of steps. This arises primarily when the members are grouped into *clusters* (e.g. communities), with the clusters being joined by a few long-range links. Much of the world is organized in this way, including social influence networks (Gandica et al., 2018) and many cultural networks (Huang et al., 2005).

Note that a regular network can be converted into a small-world network just by the addition of a couple of long-range links, as happened during the COVID-19 pandemic when just a few symptomless victims travelled by air to distant places.

Addition of long-range links has two primary effects:

- The network becomes broken up into communities (clusters). In the example shown, each member of the regular network (left) has links with just two others, and can reach another two with a second step. It can, however, take as many as eight steps to reach the most distant members of the network. With the addition of the two long-range links (right), the network is broken into two communities (open circles and diamonds), in each of which any community member can reach *all* of the other community members in no more than three steps. The rapid transmission of COVID-19 within small local communities (e.g. workers in meat factories (Elliott, 2020) provides a sad, but salutary example.
- Concomitantly, the average number of steps to get from any member (node) to another is also reduced (in fact, the number of steps scales with the logarithm of the number of nodes, and so increases relatively slowly as the size of the network grows).

It is intuitively obvious that different network patterns may require different strategies for change. To give one example, it is very difficult to induce change in a regular network, since the number of links connecting two distant members can be very large, and a message may be diluted and altered in the manner of "Chinese whispers" as it is passed along from member to member (Lyytimäki et al., 2014).

It is much easier to transmit social and cultural influences in a small-world network. Many real-life human social networks take this form (Conti et al., 2012), which brings widely separated members into closer (albeit still indirect) contact. The structure is also suited to maintaining contact within affinity groups and promoting the interests and programmes of those groups (Conti et al., 2012).

This has obvious implications for the implementation of the *Kyoto Manifesto* programme. The changes that are required are of two types:

- *Social change*: change in the relationships between individuals; especially, change from competition to cooperation, mediated through trust, mindfulness, caring, sharing and altruism
- *Cultural change*: Change in the meaning of those relationships and overall social context. Some important points (to be considered in more detail in the following chapter):

o   Awareness of ourselves as being an integral part of the system, rather than
    treating parts of the system as "externalities"
o   Appreciation that different domains of knowledge (e.g. "objective" "subjec-
    tive" "cultural" "religious") are judged by their own internal criteria, but are to
    be validated in the overall context by how they contribute to the strengthening
    and integration of humanity and of humanity's place in the greater scheme of
    things o Use of diversity as a binding force rather than a disruptive force.

Just how these changes are to be achieved in the network context is the subject of
the next chapter. *The known behaviour of complex adaptive networks means that
the role of individual "game-changers" is often paramount* (Avelino et al., 2017).
The process is often two-way: networking may be used to guide and promote the
changes, but the changes may also be used to help develop the network(s).

•

The elucidation of small-world network properties by the Australian-American
combination of Duncan Watts and Steve Strogatz in (1998) caused a revolution in network science and its practical applications that continued to this day.
Before that time, mathematicians had concentrated their attention on random
networks (Erdös & Rényi, 1959), which are sufficient to account for the famous
"six degrees of separation" (the idea that almost everyone in the world is
connected to everyone else through a chain of, at most, six mutual acquaintances) (Vespignani, 2018), but which are too simplistic by far when it comes to
the cliquishness and clustering that characterizes many human social networks.
    The 'small-world' picture allowed scientists to analyze the behavior of
such realworld networks, which have high "clustering coefficients" and short
average path lengths between members.
    Also pivotal was the 1999 paper by Albert-László Barabási and Réka Albert
in which they described preferential attachment ("scale-free") networks. These
differ from small-world networks in that focus on heterogeneous connectedness
rather than clustered connectedness. Between them, the two sorts of network
account for the behavior of the majority of real-world networks, although the
preferential attachment process (with its implication that just a few highly
connected members could exert undue influence) has proved to be much less
common than was first thought (Broido & Clauset, 2019).

Further thoughts on patterns

Before moving on to the nature of links and their influence, I add a few more
comments on some relevant properties of network patterns.

In particular, networks can be vulnerable to internal or external attack in different
ways. Preferential attachment networks, for example, can collapse completely if just
a few (or sometimes even one) of their highly connected members is removed or

damaged, as has happened with national power grids (Simpson-Porce et al., 2016) and as could happen as a prelude to a sixth mass extinction (Brannen, 2017). Because of their structure, small-world networks are not vulnerable in the same way.

But social networks in the real world can simultaneously take on "small-world" and "scale-free" properties (Krivitsky et al., 2009), with short-cut ties (a "small-world" characteristic) and increasing connectivity of some members (a "scale-free" characteristic) often changing simultaneously. This seems odd, since the two types of network are quite different in character. "Small-world models are in fact not scalefree at all, but randomly derived from rewired lattice rings with no central nodes. Conversely, a central rationale for the formation of scale-free networks is the notion of preferential attachment or accumulative advantage, i.e., popular nodes get even more popular, but this rationale bears no resemblance to local clustering." (Aarstad et al., 2013).

As it turns out, small-world networks often evolve *through* a relatively scale-free stage. To quote Aarstad et al. "At an early stage in a relatively dispersed network, we can observe a simultaneous positive change in a network's small-world property *and* scale-free distribution [my emphasis LRF]. This implies that networks that are in a shaping of a small-world structure can also be vulnerable for targeted attacks in a similar way as scale-free networks are. Later on, when a further decrease in average path-length is associated with a decrease in scale-free distribution, the network's increasing small-world structure will be more robust against targeted attacks (due to high-degree nodes' less critical and vulnerable role in bridging nodes and local clusters)."

There are many real-life examples of small-world networks, possibly including the human brain (Hilgetag & Goulas, 2016). There is some subtle thinking and intricate mathematics behind the construction of such networks (e.g. Barmpoutis & Murray, 2010), but there are also some basic principles that are particularly relevant to the development and evolution of small-world networks.

In particular, small-world properties can emerge or be driven through *dual phase evolution*, where connections are added during a "global" phase and then reinforced (or removed) during a subsequent "local" phase (Paperin et al., 2011). Examples of such processes will be offered in the following chapter.

The nature of connections

An important property of most human networks is that they are *complex adaptive networks* (Prieser et al., 2018). In other words, the links between members are such that they permit, and even facilitate, communication. The communication can then change the behavior of one or both members in a pattern that may involve a sequential chain of events and/or feedback loops between the members. These members may be people, institutions, plants, animals, the oceans or the atmosphere. It doesn't matter. *What matters is that this complex web of interacting parts can seem to have a life of its own (its **emergent** behavior), with little or no respect for the lives, or even the survival of its members.*

A simplified diagram of such a network is given in Fig. 8.4.

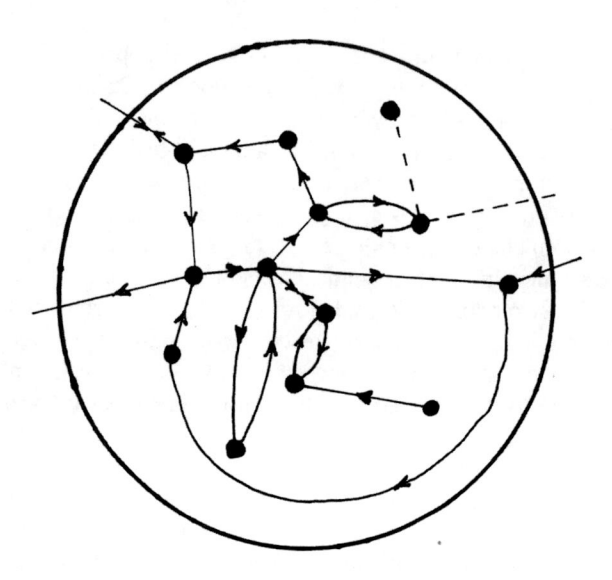

Fig. 8.4 Simplified diagram of a complex adaptive network. The black dots (technically called *nodes*) represent individual members. The lines between them (technically called *links*) represent connections between the members. The arrows represent the direction of communication &/or influence. When there are two different links between a pair of nodes, this represents *feedback* between the nodes. Feedback may positive or negative; reinforcing or damping down; leading to runaway effects or to stability

Note that this is a very simplified diagram. Interactions may be strong or weak (sometimes represented by thicker or thinner arrows). Links may be potential (represented by the dotted lines) or real, and may be long-range or short-range. Surprising feedback processes may occur through sequential &/or multiple interactions. Links may be strengthened, weakened or cut entirely over time, and nodes may appear or disappear.

A very important point, relevant to the goal of the Manifesto, is that the ongoing emergent behavior of a complex adaptive network depends upon, but cannot usually be predicted from, that of its individual members. This is why we need systems thinking (Arnold & Wade, 2015), which "looks at relationships (rather than unrelated objects), connectedness, process (rather than structure), the patterns (rather than the contents) of a system, and context. Thinking systematically also requires several shifts in perception, which lead in turn to different ways to teach, and different ways to organize society" (Ackoff, 2008). Those different ways involve different sorts of network, as well as different forms of interaction between members of the network. The perception and meaning of the system as a whole is also important, with promoters of different perceptions competing for attention, and even dominance (as with the perception of the meaning of democracy in the U.S. at the time of writing). Finally, in discussing the formation and evolution of networks, mention must be made of *directed networks*, where communication between members is essentially one-way. The World Wide Web, to which nearly 90% of people in the developed world, and nearly 50% of those in the less developed world, now have access (Clement, 2020) is an example (Fig. 8.5). It is relatively easy to hop from one page to another via a directed link, but most likely you would have to follow a different route, possibly involving dozens of links, to get back to the original page (Barabási, 2002).

Other examples of directed networks include some food webs (Krause et al., 2003), and even the human heart (Vandersickel et al., 2019). A feature of such networks is that they *all* break up into four "continents" that are not necessarily accessible to each other. The OUT continent of the World Wide Web, for example, is largely populated by corporate Websites. These can easily be reached from the outside, but once you get in there is no way out (try it!).

It is relatively difficult to influence the overall behavior of a directed network, which makes the Web and similar networks unpromising candidates for the program outlined in the *Manifesto* (especially considering the large number of bots and trolls that now inhabit its darker corridors). To achieve real transformation, it is far better to focus on modifying real human interactions within the context of other types of real-life social networks (particularly small-world and preferential attachment networks). In the next Chap. 1 examine how this might be achieved, and the barriers that need to be overcome, including the problem that technically mediated networks (e.g. video conferencing) often remove a lot of the meaning from interactions between participants—so they are good for exchanging information, but rather poor when it comes to working our problems, where networks that involve direct interaction and communication are much better suited.

Fig. 8.5 The world wide web (after Barabási, 2002)

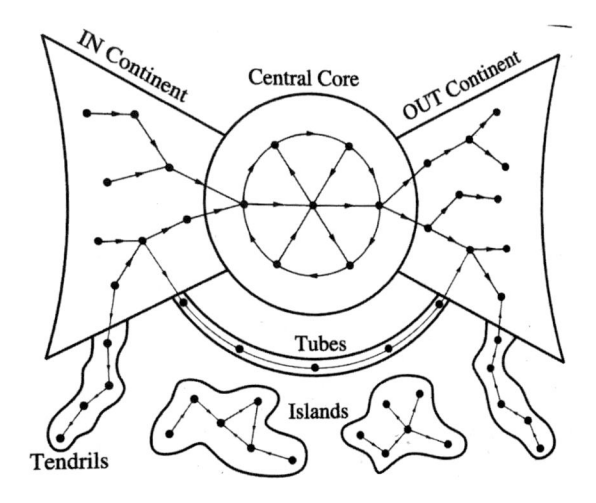

References

Aarstad, J., Ness, H. S., & Haugland, S. A. (2013). In what ways are small-world and scale-free networks interrelated? In *2013 IEEE International Conference on Industrial Technology (ICIT)* (pp. 1483–1487). Cape Town.

Ackoff, R. (2008). *Systems thinking for curious managers.* Triarchy Press.

Anttiroiko, A.-V. (2021). Successful government responses to the pandemic: Contextualizing national and urban resonses to the COVID-19 outbreak in east and west. *International Journal of E-Planning Research, 10,* 1–17.

Arnold, R. D., & Wade, J. P. (2015). A Definition of systems thinking: A systems approach. *Procedia Computer Science, 44,* 669–678.

Avelino, F., Wittmayer, J. M., Kemp, R., & Haxeltine, A. (2017). Game-changers and transformative social innovation. *Ecology and Society, 22,* 41–47.

Barabási, A. -L. (2002). *Linked.* Penguin.

Barabasi, A.-L., & Albert, R. (1999). Emergence of scaling in random networks. *Science, 286,* 509–512.

Barmpoutis, D., & Murray, R. M. (2010). *Networks with the smallest average distance and the largest average clustering.* arXiv:1007.4031.

Bavel, J. J., Van Baicker, K., Boggio, P. S., Capraro, V., Cicjoka, A., Cikara, M., et al. (2020). Using social and 20 behavioural science to support COVID-19 pandemic response. *Nature Human Behaviour, 4,* 460–471.

Beeks, J. C., & Ziko, A. (2018). Internalizing economic externalities on the macroeconomic stage. Exploring and expanding Paul Hawken's the ecology of commerce: A declaration of sustainability for globalized solutions. *European Journal of Sustainable Development Research, 2*(1), 03. https://doi.org/10.20897/ejosdr/76752.

Bodanis, D. (2020). *The art of fairness.* The Bridge Street Press.

Bonar, J. (1926). The theory of moral sentiments, by Adam Smith, 1759. *Journal of Philosophical Studies, 1,* 333–353.

Bowles, S. (2016). *The moral economy.* Yale University Press.

Brannen, P. (2017). Earth is not in the midst of a sixth mass extinction. *The Atlantic.* https://www.theatlantic.com/science/archive/2017/06/the-ends-ofthe-world/529545/.

Broido, A. D., & Clauset, A. (2019). Scale-free networks are rare. *Nature Communications, 10,* 1017–1026. https://doi.org/10.1038/s41467-019-08746-5.

Carney, M. (2020). *From moral to market sentiments.* BBC Reith Lectures. https://www.bbc.co.uk/programmes/m000py8t.

Clement, J. (2020). Percentage of global population accessing the internet from 2005 to 2019, by market maturity. *Statista.* https://www.statista.com/statistics/209096/shareof-internet-users-in-the-total-world-population-since-2006/.

Collins, A., Florin, M.-V., & Renn, O. (2020). COVID-19 risk governance: Drivers, responses and lessons to be learned. *Journal of Risk Research, 23,* 1073–1082.

Conti, M., Passarella, A., & Pezzoni, F. (2012). A model to represent human social relationships in social network graphs. In K. Aberer, A. Flache, W. Jager, L. Liu, J. Tang, C. Guéret (Eds.), *Social informatics. SocInfo 2012. Lecture notes in computer science* (vol. 7710). Springer, Berlin.

Díaz, S., Settele, J., Brondizio, E.S., Ngo, H.T., Agard, J., & Arneth, A., et al. (2019). Pervasive human-driven decline of life on Earth points to the need for transformative change. *Science, 366,* eaax3100.

Diffenbaugh, N. S., & Burke, M. (2019). Global warming has increased global economic inequality. In *Proceeding of the National Academy of Science of the US.* https://doi.org/10.1073/pnas.1816020116.

EASAC (2020) *Towards a sustainable future: Transformative change and postCOVID-19 priorities.* European Academies Science Advisory Council. https://easac.eu/fileadmin/user_upload/EASAC_Perspective_on_Transformative_Change_Web_complete.pdf.

Elliott, C. (2020). *Why are meat factories a coronavirus hotspot?* https://www.newfoodmagazine. com/article/112889/coronavirus/.

Erdös, P., & Rényi, A. (1959). On random graphs. I. *Publicationes Mathematicae, 6*, 290–297.

Farmer, J. D., et al. (2019). Sensitive intervention points in the post-carbon transition. *Science, 364*, 132–134.

Gandica, Y., Charmell, A., Villegas-Febres, J., & Bonalde, I. (2018). Cluster size entropy in the Axelrod model of social influence: small-world networks and mass media. arXiv:1109.oo59v1. Last accessed 1 Sep 2011. (physics.soc-ph).

Haldane, A. (2017). *Rethinking financial stability. Speech delivered to the conference rethinking macroeconomic policy IV.* Peterson Institute for International Economics, Washington, D.C., USA. https://www.bankofengland.co.uk/speech/2017/rethinking-financial-stability.

Haldane, A. G., & May, R. M. (2011). Systemic risk in banking ecosystems. *Nature, 469*, 351–355.

Harangozo, G., Csutora, M., & Kocsis, T. (2018). How big is big enough? *Toward a Sustainable Future by Examining Alternatives to the Conventional Economic Growth Paradigm, Sustainable Development, 26*, 172–181.

Hilgetag, C. C., & Goulas, A. (2016). Is the brain really a small-world network? *Brain Structure and Function, 221*, 2361–2366.

Huang, C. -Y., Sun, C. -T., & Lin, F. -C. (2005). Influence of local information on social simulations in small-world network models. *Journal of Artificial Societies sand Social Simulation, 8*. https:// jasss.soc.surrey.ac.uk/8/4/8.html.

IPBES (2019). https://www.ipbes.net/news/Media-Release-Global-Assessment.

IPCC (2016). *Special report: Global warming of 1.5 °C.* https://www.ipcc.ch/sr15/.

Klein, N. (2007). *The shock doctrine.* Penguin.

Krause, A. E., et al. (2003). Compartments revealed in food-web structure. *Nature, 426*, 282–285.

Krivitsky, P. N., Handcock, M. S., Raftery, A. E., & Hoff, P. D. (2009). Representing degree distributions, clustering, and homophily in social networks with latent cluster random effects models. *Social Networks, 31*, 204–213.

Liu, J., et al. (2015). Systems integration for global sustainability. *Science, 347*, 1258832. https:// doi.org/10.1126/science.1258832.

Lynn, C. W., et al. (2019). Human information processing in complex networks. arXiv:1906.009 26v1. (physics.soc-ph).

Lyytimäki, J., Gudmundsson, H., & Sørensen, C. H. (2014). Russian dolls and Chinese whispers: Two perspectives on the unintended effects of sustainability indicator communication. *Sustainable Development, 22*, 84–94.

MacWilliams, J. J., La Monaca, S., & Kobus, J. (2019). PG & E: Market and policy perspectives on the first climate change bankruptcy. *Columbia SIPA Center on Global Energy Policy Report.* https://energypolicy.columbia.edu/research/report/pgemarket-and-policy-perspe ctives-first-climate-change-bankruptcy.

May, R. M. (1972). Will a large complex system be stable? *Nature, 238*(413–414), 893–895.

May, R. M., Levin, S. A. & Sugihara, G. (2008). Ecology for bankers. *Nature, 451*.

Meitner, L., & Frisch, O. R. (1939). Disintegration of uranium by neutrons: A new type of nuclear reaction. *Nature, 143*, 239–240.

Merton, R. K. (1968). The Matthew effect in science. *Science, 159*, 56–63.

Paperin, G., Green, D. G., & Sadedin, S. (2011). Dual-phase evolution in complex adaptive systems. *Journal of the Royal Society Interfce, 8*, 609–629.

Perera, M., Bell, M. G. H., & Bliemer, M. C. J. (2017). Network science approach to modeling the topology and robustness of supply chain networks: A review and perspective. *Applied Network Science, 2*, 33–58.

Francis, P. (2020). *Let us dream: The path to a better future.* Simon & Schuster.

Postrel, V. (1998). *The future and its enemies.* Touchstone.

Preiser, R., et al. (2018). Social-ecological systems as complex adaptive systems: Organizing principles for advancing research methods and approaches. *Ecology and Society, 23*, 46. https://doi. org/10.5751/ES-10558-230446.

Sayama, H., Pestov, I., Schmidt, J., Bush, B. J., Wong, C., Yamanoi, J., & Gross, T. (2013). Modeling complex systems with adaptive networks. *Computers and Mathematics with Applications, 65,* 1645–1664.

Scheffer, M., et al. (2001). Catastrophic shifts in ecosystems. *Nature, 413,* 591–596.

Scheffer, M. (2009). *Critical transitions in nature and society.* Princeton University Press.

Scheffer, M., et al. (2009). Early-warning signs for critical transitions. *Nature, 461,* 53–59.

Scheffer, M., & van Nes, E. H. (2018). Seeing a global web of connected systems. *Science, 362,* 1357.

Simpson-Porco, J.W., Dörfler, F. & Bullo, F. (2016) Voltage collapse in complex power grids, *Nature communications,* |7:10790|. https://doi.org/10.1038/ncomms10790.

Smith, A. (1759). *The theory of moral sentiments.* London: Andrew Millar.

Thom, R. (1989). *Structural stability and morphogenesis: An outline of a general theory of models.* Reading, MA: Addison-Wesley.

United Nations (2012). *Defining a new economic paradigm: The report of the high level meeting on wellbeing and happiness.* https://sustainabledevelopment.un.org/content/documents/617Bhu tanReport_WEB_F.pdf.

Vandersickel, N., et al. (2019). Directed networks as a novel way to describe and analyze cardiac excitation: Directed graph mapping. *Frontiers in Physiology.* https://doi.org/10.3389/fphys.2019. 01138.

Vespignani, A. (2018). Twenty years of network science. *Nature, 558,* 528–529.

Vorogushyn, S. et al. (2018) Evolutionary leap in large-scale food risk assessment needed. *WIREs Water, 2,* e1266.

Watts, D. J., & Strogatz, S. H. (1998). Collective dynamics of 'small-world' networks. *Nature, 393,* 440–442.

WEF (2017). https://www.weforum.org/projects/inclusive-growth-and-development.

West, G. (2017). *Scale.* Weidenfeld & Nicolson.

Willett, W. et al. (2019). Food in the anthropocene: The EAT-lancet commission on healthy diets from sustainable systems. *The Lancet, 393.* https://doi.org/10.1016/S0140-6736(18)31788-4.

Zscheischler, J., et al. (2018). Future climate risk from compound events. *Nature Climate Change.* https://doi.org/10.1038/s41558-018-0156-3.

Chapter 9
Achieving Transformation in Our Highly Interconnected World II: The Role of the Individual

Len Fisher

Abstract Our global economy is currently driven largely by the pursuit of individual selfinterest. What can we do as individuals to help achieve transformation to an economy where the interests of society and the world as a whole take centre stage? To take effective action, we must see ourselves as nodes in a vast global socioeconomic-ecological complex adaptive network (Preiser et al. in *Ecology and Society, 23*, 46, 2018), where multiple feedback loops and non-linear interactions mean that the network is constantly changing and evolving in response to internal and external pressures. As demonstrated in the previous chapter, such networks can develop emergent behaviours that are more than the sum of their parts, and which may be inimical to the interests of its individual members. To avoid or ameliorate such situations, and to get our global socio-economicecological network functioning for the benefit all its members, human and nonhuman, living and non-living, we need to work together to transform the network as a whole so that it becomes a functionally cooperative unit, with cooperation replacing competition and the interests of others take precedence over the interests of self.

9.1 Summary

Our global economy is currently driven largely by the pursuit of individual selfinterest. What can we do as individuals to help achieve transformation to an economy where the interests of society and the world as a whole take centre stage? To take effective action, we must see ourselves as nodes in a vast global socioeconomic-ecological *complex adaptive network* (Preiser et al., 2018), where multiple feedback loops and non-linear interactions mean that the network is constantly changing and evolving in response to internal and external pressures. As demonstrated in the previous chapter, such networks can develop emergent behaviours that are more than the sum of their parts, and which may be inimical to the interests of its individual members.

L. Fisher (✉)
School of Physics, University of Bristol, Tyndall Ave, Bristol BS8 1TL, UK
e-mail: Len.Fisher@bristol.ac.uk

© Springer Nature Singapore Pte Ltd. 2022
S. Hill et al. (eds.), *The Kyoto Post-COVID Manifesto For Global Economics*,
Creative Economy, https://doi.org/10.1007/978-981-16-8566-8_9

To avoid or ameliorate such situations, and to get our global socio-economicecological network functioning for the benefit all its members, human and nonhuman, living and non-living, we need to work together to transform the network *as a whole* so that it becomes a functionally cooperative unit, with cooperation replacing competition and the interests of others take precedence over the interests of self.

Such a transformation needs action at three nested levels:

(1) The level of individual interactions, and the evocation of trust
(2) The level of governance, and mechanisms to promote awareness and cooperative interactions
(3) The level of network integrity and embedded cultural principles: the earthworm solution.

Here I discuss each of these in turn.

(1) Individual interactions, and the evocation of trust

Our starting point is a world in which many people believe (falsely) that the unfettered pursuit of individual self-interest leads to optimum outcomes for society and the world as a whole, and where economies, societies and individual systems of morality are founded on this assumption.

This is the world of the "free market," promulgated by Adam Smith in his classic text *An Inquiry into the Nature and Causes of the Wealth of Nations* (Smith, 1776). Advocates of the free market principle, however, seldom seem to realize that Smith had earlier argued in *The Theory of Moral Sentiments* (1759) that the unfettered pursuit of self-interest is insufficient in itself without moral guidelines to keep it in check. Here I argue (in line with the major objectives of the *Manifesto*) that we need to go even further, and develop the arguments introduced by Stephen Hill in Chap. 2 that we need not just to control but to *replace* the pursuit of individual self-interest with interactions based on trust and on putting community before self.

The Problem with Self-interest

We now know that the apparently rational pursuit of individual self-interest on its own can *never* lead to optimum outcomes for the individuals concerned.

This is because of a series of paradoxes that were discovered by the mathematicians.

John von Neumann and John Nash in the mid-twentieth century (Nash, 1950; Von Neumann & Morgenstern, 1944). They found that, if people act rationally and independently in pursuit of their own interests, this very logic can draw the participants inexorably into situations where self-interest is the last thing that is being served.

The most important of these situations have acquired evocative names through illustrative stories. *The Prisoner's Dilemma* (Poundstone, 1993) and *The Tragedy of the Commons* (Hardin, 1968) provide over-arching examples. Other more specific cases include *Free Rider* (where people take advantage of a community resource without contributing to it), *Chicken* (where each side tries to push the other as close to the edge of disaster as possible, hoping that they will then back down first) and

The Volunteer's Dilemma (where someone must make a sacrifice on behalf of the group, but if no one does, everyone loses out) (Fisher, 2008).

All of these cases involve situations where the logic of individual self-interest suggests that an individual will benefit by "cheating" on cooperation, but where everyone loses out when all concerned use similar logic. An archetypal example is provided by the Tragedy of the Commons, which describes a situation where a group of people (say a group of farmers) share a common resource (the commons where their sheep are grazing) for maximum cooperative benefit (grazing the largest number of sheep). But then one of them, using the principle of independent self-interest, works out that if he or she adds an extra sheep to the flock, he or she will have a net benefit, even though there will now be slightly less grass available per sheep. So far, so logical. But what is logical for one must be logical for the others. So they all add an extra sheep, and soon the commons are grazed out. By each independently following the principle of self-interest, all have lost out, compared to what they would have gained by maintaining cooperation.

Hardin's example has been criticized as if it were synonymous with the free-rider problem (Frischmann et al., 2019), but the image is nevertheless powerful, and alarmingly relevant to many real-world situations (e.g. Spooner undated). Climate change is a prime example (Barrett, 2018)). Less obvious examples are privatized health care and commercial retirement planning, where individual solutions to shared problems lead in both cases to a modern Tragedy of the Commons (Gross & De Dreu, 2019).

Reciprocity

One potential route that has been suggested for overcoming the paradoxes of self-interest is to use self-interest itself as a motivation for cooperation and the support of others. This is the main route that game theorists have followed since the paradoxes were first uncovered. They have particularly sought ways to use self-interest as a motivation to promote, encourage or even force cooperation by and with others through *reciprocity*.

The power of reciprocity was revealed in a computer game devised by Axelrod in (1984). The game was intended to test whether strategies of cooperation or the pursuit of self-interest provided a better outcome. Competitors could choose to cooperate, or cheat on the cooperation, at each turn, knowing what their opponents had done the turn before. The competition was won by the peace researcher Anatol Rapoport, who used his experience of real-world negotiations to devise a programme where the underlying strategy was "tit-for-tat"—that is, the programme simply "paid back" whatever the opponent had done to it in the previous round.

This meant that cheating was punished, while cooperation was rewarded. One can see obvious problems (strategies become locked in, for example), but more realistic computer simulations of real-life interactions between individuals have produced similar outcomes. Reciprocity promotes cooperation—at least in some circumstances. In particular, reciprocity within small groups is an important factor in the evolution of cooperation when those groups are merged to form a larger assembly[1] (Artiges et al., 2019). Importantly, **successful reciprocity does not require the selfish pursuit of individual interests as a motivation**. This is a key result when it comes to the aspirations of the *Manifesto*. True reciprocity is the basis of a healthy society (Rabinovitch, 2019). It means that small groups of people who each have a drive to cooperate (maybe through a shared spirituality, or a wish to please or belong to a group) can generate a stable cooperative social norm which is not threatened by the paradoxes exposed by game theory. In the terms of these two chapters, such a social norm may then provide a nucleus for the growth of cooperation in a network.

Trust, cooperation and morality as driving forces

From now on in time, morality must either be all-inclusive or it becomes immoral. In our world there is no more room for outsiders. Our sense of belonging must include not only humans, but animals, plants, and all the inanimate furniture of our Earth Household. Nothing will do any more, but the widest possible horizon of belonging. The words in the above paragraph are not mine. They belong to the experimental psychologist David Steindl-Rast (1993), a Benedictine monk and who has also been deeply involved with Zen Buddhism. His arguments for a morally-based sense of belonging fit with those of the *Manifesto* for a spirituality-based, cooperative future.

But how can this future become a reality?

A possible answer for the future lies in the past. Behavioural scientists Samuel Bowles and Herbert Gintis (2011) have advanced persuasive arguments for the evolution of humankind as a cooperative species through the early "evolution of social preferences on which altruistic cooperation is based." Experiments have shown that people shift from cooperation to competition, and to behave like Adam Smith's *homo economicus*, only in market-like situations where contractual agreements are "complete" (i.e. enforceable by private agreement or government fiat). Otherwise kindness (Mackay, 2021) and fairness (Bodanis, 2020) are more common, and more powerful, than is often supposed.

Bowles and Gintis argue that "social interactions in modern societies are at best quasi-contractual"—that is, they *seem* to be contractual, but many essential elements (complete information, efficient allocations, etc.) are missing. There is thus a gap to be filled by different social preferences—in particular, concern for the well-being of others and for the environment that sustains us.

---

[1] It is worth quoting the full conclusions of Atriges et al., since they offer much to think about: "The fitness of … individuals," they say "is related to their group performance, whereas the imitation takes place globally, that is, agents have a global vision and can imitate the most successful behaviors. We have shown that cooperation is maintained by a homogeneous group of cooperators. Note that this fully cooperative group does not necessarily have to be related to a physical group, but a social norm. In this sense, the existence of a cooperative social norm can be interpreted as a non-null probability of cooperation, which in the proposed model is mathematically equivalent to a homogeneous group of cooperators. This social norm can be based either on moral principles or driven by both empirical and normative expectations".

This qualitative summary of a mathematically rigorous study bears some important relationships to the approach proposed in the *Manifesto*—in particular, the emphasis on social norms and global visions as driving forces.

The tools to fill that gap are trust and consideration for others. Game theorists have long recognized that trust between participants obliterates all of the paradoxes of traditional game theory, and many of their efforts to overcome those paradoxes have focused on ways of initiating and maintaining trust.

Unfortunately, most of those ways have involved the motivation of self-interest in some way or another, with all of the baggage that this carries. But the baggage is not necessary. An alternative, spelled out with supporting evidence by political economist Francis Fukuyama in his book *Trust* (1996), lies in the evocation of trust through offering care for others without expectation of reward—what Stephen Hill (this volume) calls "the power of the gift." It is an approach that fits well with the conditions outlined above for the emergence and growth of self-sustaining, cooperative groups, hopefully to spread like fungal mycelia, undetected but influential, through the socio-economic-ecological network. It also fits well with the healing approach of Carl Rogers through "unconditional positive regard" in psychological counseling (REF). Above all, it fits with the underlying foundation of spirituality that lies at the core of this volume.

"Where the invisible hand fails," say Bowles and Gintis "the handshake may succeed."

(2) The level of governance, and mechanisms to promote awareness and cooperative interactions

The development and growth of networked groups based on mutual trust, care and social responsibility is a necessary step in the transformation of our global socioeconomic-ecological network, but it is not sufficient. We need also to transform our modes of decision-making to reflect the realities of the future.

There are two main problems to overcome:

- Allowing for human irrationality
- Choosing between alternatives.

Irrationality

One of the many problems with the "rational self-interest" approach is that this is not necessarily the way in which people make decisions. For one thing, it assumes perfect information, whereas Gerd Gigerenzer and his colleagues have pointed out that we often make better decisions with only limited information (Gigerenzer et al., 1999). Irrational decisions (especially economic decisions) may even be the result of the brain's attempts at efficient encoding, and hence built into our very nature (Summerfield & Tsetsos, 2015).

Professor Lee Cronin[2] argues that "most humans are not capable of making real decisions. Instead, decisions are formed by many small circumstantial nudges until criticality when state flips. Some humans, however, can make lots of decisions & appear to carry most of the agency of the human race ...".

---

[2] Personal communication.

The critical point, based on these and similar observations, is that economic and social systems which assume the rational pursuit of self-interest are unstable, both because of the paradoxes of game theory and because humans often don't think in that way. It needs something more—something that accounts for the reality of human decision-making, and which asks what else we need to ensure a secure and sustainable future.

A new approach to game theory that takes these considerations into account has recently been developed. It is called *behavioural game theory* (Camerer, 2003), and its principle application to date has been in behavioural economics (Kahneman, 2002; Shiller, 2013; Thaler, 2017).

Behavioural game theory could well serve both as a test bed and a source of practical ideas for the approach to transformation proposed in the *Manifesto*. It is in its early stages, and testing its predictions in real-life situations remains a challenging task (McDonald et al., 2019). Nevertheless, it acknowledges the reality of human irrationality, and ask what needs to be added to use and control it.

One answer, according to political economist Francis Fukuyama in his book *Trust* (1996), lies in the evocation of trust through offering care for others. The power of the gift is nowhere more clearly illustrated, and the potentiality for transformation through the principles laid down in the *Manifesto* is nowhere more clearly supported by scientific study and rigorous analysis.

Choosing between alternatives

Supposing that we achieved the requisite spiritual and cooperative ethical environment to promote transformation, there still remains the question of choosing an appropriate, achievable goal in the context of our networked world. What alternative is there to unlimited growth and the pursuit of self-interest? The plot of Goethe's play *Faust* suggests one possibility.

In the first part of the play, the scholar Heinrich Faust sells his soul to the devil in return for satisfaction of his desires—first for understanding, but then for a woman called Gretchen. By the end of the lesser-known second part, however, Faust has rejected the devil's offers of power and fame, and aims instead to build a technological utopia out of land currently under the sea. Angels rescue him from the hands of the devil, proclaiming "He who strives on and lives to strive/Can earn redemption still." (Goethe, 1832).

There are interesting parallels here with the argument in the *Manifesto*. The *Manifesto* strives to establish a new economic order based on human values, where technology and progress are servants rather than masters. Can this approach earn us redemption?

A part of the redemption from continued wastage and over-use of the world's resources depends on the utopian ideal of sharing and cooperation. But we must be careful to distinguish the *Manifesto* proposals, based on spiritual values, from the common notion of the "sharing economy", which has often been touted as "an antidote to the consumer culture of modern society because it supports sharing rather than ownership" (Sigala, 2019). The evidence (Sigala, 2019) shows that "The sharing economy [as commonly conceived] has not changed people's mindsets, values, lifestyles or behaviours. People still wish to consume at the same levels and they do consume for the same reasons, but in a different way. The sharing economy disrupts the traditional economy, but it has not transformed it."

Closer to the ideas of the *Manifesto* is Ernest Schumacher's classic essay on Buddhist Economics (Schumacher, 1973). Schumacher distinguishes Buddhist economics from the economics of modern materialism by the value that is put on labour, whose function is at least three-fold: "to give man a chance to develop his faculties; to enable him to overcome his ego-centredness by joining with other people in a common task; and to bring forth the goods and services needed for a becoming existence." Only the last of these is relevant to Western materialist economics, which aims to minimize the cost of labour, and does not otherwise consider its value except in wealth creation. "It is not wealth that stands in the way of liberation" says Schumacher "but attachment to wealth".

The Beat Generation author William S. Burroughs puts it more succinctly *"money is shit. And what does the money machine eat to shit it out? It eats youth, spontaneity, life, beauty, and above all it eats creativity"* (Odier, 1989).

Our present era has been characterized by environmental historian and sociologist Jason Moore as the *Capitalocene* (Moore, 2019). In Moore's view "the idea[s] that we're all going to cover our footprints, we're going to be more sustainable consumers, we're going to pay attention to population, are really consequences of a highly unequal system of power and wealth".

Moore's alternative is "a democratically controlled accumulation fund…. banking and finance have to be socialized because otherwise you're continually at the mercy of big capital deciding what's profitable or not. What would the ideal world be like? It would integrate town and country, it would have cheap and low-carbon public transportation …".

To achieve such a world requires identifying problems at an overall system level—for example, in a truly circular economy[3] we need to focus on the whole production system, of which waste and its recycling is just one aspect. This means shaping community dialogue so as to incorporate *everyone*, and to take advantage of the different qualities and information that different people (from the top to the bottom in an organization, for example) can bring. Librarians, for example, may become knowledge searchers to link things together, while top executives can act as a linking point rather than simply handing down decisions.

On the economic side, economist Kate Raworth has proposed a switch from free market economics to "doughnut economics" (Raworth, 2017), whose aim is "to ensure that no one falls short on life's essentials (from food and housing to healthcare and political voice), while ensuring that collectively we do not overshoot our pressure on Earth's life-supporting systems, on which we fundamentally depend—such as a stable climate, fertile soils, and a protective ozone layer." It is noteworthy that Raworth has no clear idea on how this ideal might be achieved in practice, and has set up a competition for schemes for its realization (Raworth, 2019).

---

[3] A concept that needs careful definition (Korhonen et al., 2018a, b).

Both Moore's and Raworth's proposals focus on the material aspects of life. So does the World Economic Forum in its analysis of future food scenarios (WEF, 2017). The analysis reaches the dismal conclusion that, of four plausible future scenarios, there is not one in which there not winners and losers.

The closest balance is achieved by two scenarios: "Open-source sustainability" and "Local is the new global". The first consists of "A future linking highly connected markets and resource-efficient consumption [that] has increased international cooperation and innovation but may leave some behind" while the second comprises "a world of fragmented local markets with resource-efficient consumption, [where] resource-rich countries focus on local foods whereas import-dependent regions become hunger hotspots." Interconnection plays a vital role, and it may be that the "small world" concept (see previous chapter) may help to link the two scenarios in a benefical way.

Scenario analysis has its problems (Sitas et al., 2019), but it can nevertheless help to expose fundamental truths. Here, the truth is that the assumptions of traditional economics (competition, self-interest, unlimited growth) can never lead to a fair and just society insofar as essential food supplies are concerned. Similar arguments apply to other areas of our material existence.

The *Manifesto* contends that this situation can only be remedied by moderating the pursuit of individual self-interest through shared human values of compassion, cooperation and care, based on a spiritual approach. This argument is reinforced by the considerations in the present chapter.

With these human values built in, other future scenarios become realisable. That favoured by the authors of the *Manifesto* has the circular economy as its practical goal and human values at its spiritual heart (see chapters by Kosir, Holth, Potocnik, and Kuenkel & Kühn in this volume). Here I list some of the major considerations that need to be addressed for the establishment of a practicable form of governance based on these principles.

Style of governance

Capitalism is broken (see Coyle (2019) for a perceptive review), and with it styles of governance that rely on it. But candidates for an adequate replacement also have their problems (Duit & Galaz, 2008).

Top-down solutions alone do not work (Ostrom, 2010). An alternative, also discussed by Ostrom (especially for the governance of environmental issues) is *polycentric governance*, which involves many centres of authority interacting coherently for a common governance goal. A recent longitudinal study, however (Morrison et al., 2019) "reveals many polycentric systems are struggling to cope with the growing impacts, pace, and scope of social and environmental change. Analytic shortcomings are also beginning to appear, particularly in the treatment of power."

At the heart of these analytical shortcomings is the problem of how to understand, follow, control and respond to the many interlinkages between different social development goals (SDGs), and to develop in-depth analyses of SDG synergies and trade-offs and the impacts of achieving one target on others. An example of such impacts is "biocultural hysteresis" (Lyver et al., 2019), where well-meant conservation policies can "trigger a set of feedback mechanisms that ... diminish the efficacy of local management. These feedbacks, which include knowledge loss and a breakdown of social hierarchies, prevent IPLC from adapting their management to change." A recent web-based tool (SDG, 2019) reveals just how difficult the task may be. The tool aims to develop a systems approach to decision-making in today's complex, highly interlinked environment. It goes well beyond the current use of scenario archetypes (e.g. Sitas et al., 2019), which "allow syntheses of large amounts of information for scientific, practice-, and policy-related purposes, streamline key messages from multiple scenario studies, and facilitate communication" but which are "perceived as subjective in their interpretation, oversimplifying information, having a limited applicability across scales, and concealing contextual information and novel narratives."

It is the contention of this author that responding appropriately to "novel narratives," holds the key to effective governance. As shown in the previous chapter, such narratives may lead sudden and dramatic changes in the system as a whole, especially when those narratives are based on the pursuit of individual self-interest. By building close links based on trust and community welfare, such narratives can be displaced or overcome by those that benefit the community as a whole, particularly in underpinning the cooperation that is essential for fast, flexible action to avoid tipping points and critical transitions in the system.

Resilience

A second consideration in choosing a fresh style of governance is how effective it would be in conveying economic, social and environmental resilience.

The concept is a slippery one. There are over seventy definitions in the literature, ranging from the ability to "bounce back" after disruption to the ability to change and adapt to the new circumstances, with many shades in between (Fisher, 2015). Economists tend to talk in terms of an ability to "bounce back," and have developed sophisticated tools to measure this ability (Klimek et al., 2019). Ecologists and social analysts tend to be more concerned with the capacity of social-ecological systems to adapt or transform in response to unfamiliar, unexpected and extreme shocks (Carpenter et al., 2012).

One potentially useful concept is that of "antifragility" (Taleb, 2012), defined broadly as an ability to benefit from variability and change. An ecosystem, for example, is antifragile if it benefits from environmental variability (Zamora et al., 2019). These authors point out that "antifragility goes beyond robustness or resilience because while resilient/robust systems are merely perturbation- resistant, antifragile structures not only withstand stress but also benefit from it."

But whatever goal we adopt, whether it be resilience, robustness or antifragility, it can only be achieved within a governance system that is itself of equal flexibility and adaptability (Fisher, 2019).

(3) The level of network integrity and embedded cultural principles: the earthworm solution

Planting flowers

We have seen that trust, cooperation, and care and compassion for others (based, in the case of this *Manifesto*, on spirituality) can help the formation and stabilization of small groups that may act as nuclei to spread these principles through a network.

We have also discussed the styles of governance that may incorporate these principles, while having the flexibility and speed of response that is necessary for the governance of complex adaptive networks. There remains the question of whether these are sufficient to achieve the necessary transformation of our global socioeconomic-ecological network *as a whole.*

I believe that they are, so long as the seeding takes place at a sufficient number of sites across the network. The situation is similar to that in a conversation between two characters in an anonymous Internet cartoon:

"Why so optimistic about [next year]? What do you think it will bring? Everything seems so messed up." "I think it will bring flowers."

"Yes? How come?"

"Because I am planting flowers."

"Planting flowers" has an essential role to play in social transformation through complementing and limiting the role of top-down governance (some form of which is still necessary (Lawson, 2019)):

- "First, to counter the power of what Shoshana Zuboff (2019) calls 'surveillance capitalism' through anti-competition, privacy and other laws."
- "And second, to help join up, scale up, accelerate, replicate and project these emerging forms of collaborate action to ensure they become the predominant form of 'deciding and doing' in the 21st century."

"The intersection between … emerging horizontal bottom-up change and the more vertical state [of traditional top-down control]" they argue "is the diagonal fault line through which a new society can and must be born. …" (as described in previous chapter) "… However hard, these new formations will have to form broader alliances, both across civil society and with the state, nationally and locally. They must become a sum that is greater than their parts, if the opportunity and need for a paradigm shift is to be realised."

A closer examination of the behaviour of social organizations (Bar-Yam et al., 2018) supports the contention that "society requires some organizing processes, even if there is no traditional government or hierarchies." At the *Nesta* Innovation Foundation's.

Government Innovation Summit (Nesta, 2019), speakers compared cases for radicalism and incrementalism as approaches to transforming government and governance.

Summarising the discussion, John Burgoyne (2019) brought the two approaches together in the form of "pragmatic radicalism." "Radical" because it involves a big, bold vision that goes beyond incrementalism and acknowledges structural issues with existing approaches; "pragmatic" because people can immediately translate the vision into specific "what can I do now to make this happen" actions. Social entrepreneur Hilary Cottam described this as being an approach where "the role of government [is] to be a gardener who tends to the wellbeing of all of the organisms in the ecosystem. The most important part of the ecosystem", she noted "was the earthworm buried deep down, emphasizing the need to radically redistribute power to the lowest levels."

The earthworm solution

Ultimately, it is we earthworms who must do the job of transformation. We have found that our interactions with each other and with our environment can act as nuclei to initiate change for the better throughout a network, and help to steer that network away from undesirable states, with reciprocity (*not* allied to the pursuit of selfinterest) as a major tool. To carry the job through to complete transformation, we need to achieve four objectives:

- Change community perceptions
- Create a new framework
- Disrupt the present system
- Put a new system in place.

Overlaying all of this is an absolute requirement for attention to detail in individual and small group interactions—serious, concentrated dedicated, creative, ongoing and flexible. For a splendid real-life example see Stephen Hill's *Captives for Freedom* (2017).

Changing Perceptions

Let us begin with a concrete example: why, in the face of all the evidence, do so many people have difficulty in processing the threat of climate change?

Self-interested disinformation campaigns aside, the major reason, according to neuropsychologists, may lie within our own brains (McGonigal, 2019). According to fMRI studies "Your brain acts as if your future self is someone you don't know very well and, frankly, someone you don't care about. And if we view our own selves in the future as virtual strangers, how much less do we care about the lives of generations yet to be born? Economists have a figure for this: the "social discount rate," which quantifies how much value declines as we look into the future." To quote UCLA researcher Hal Hirschfield "Why would you save money for your future self when, to your brain, it feels like you're just handing away your money to a complete stranger?"

This real-life psychology is something that the *Manifesto* approach could help to overcome. In particular, bringing consideration for others to the fore may help to enhance our consideration for our own future selves, and the future selves of others. A major perception that has to change is the dominance of self-interest. This is not just down to game theory, which is concerned with *rational* self-interest. People are not necessarily good at making decisions (Summerfield & Tsetsos, 2015), and often have a commitment, which may be rational *or* irrational, to the set of beliefs that they have built up over a lifetime. The more that those beliefs are challenged, whether by opinion or contrary evidence, the stronger they tend to be held (Kaplan et al., 2016). To break the cycle needs a change in culture, and for this we need to add trust to the mix.

The political economist Fukuyama (1996) has argued that "high trust societies" are essential for our future progress and prosperity. The Organization for Economic Cooperation and Development (OECD) concurs. In 2009 it attempted to *measure* trust—between individuals, within communities, and between communities.

(Morrone et al., 2009). The three are intimately related, as the first paragraph of the OECD report makes clear:

"Trust is the foundation of most personal relationships, which in turn are key determinants of human well-being and economic development. Theoretical and empirical analysis shows that high levels of interpersonal trust make many aspects of life more enjoyable and productive. *Trust, if it is matched by trustworthy behaviour in others, reduces the costs of dealing with risk and uncertainty.*"

Trust is particularly important when it comes to the cooperative governance of global catastrophic risks (Fisher & Sandberg, 2021). Effective governance requires sacrifice of immediate gains at the very least, and we must be able to trust others to share the sacrifice, rather than taking advantage for immediate gain.

But how can we know when trust is well-founded, and when it is misplaced? The answer, reinforced by the OECD study, lies in ourselves. It is to make ourselves truly trustworthy, as a prelude to others learning to trust us. It is an answer that is well understood by Western counsellors of the person-centred persuasion as an answer to the problems posed by game theory (Fisher et al., 2013). It is also an answer that emerges directly from the philosophy of the *Manifesto*.

The concept of Sensitive Intervention Points may come into play here. The idea has been advanced by Doyne Farmer and his colleagues (Farmer et al., 2019) as a way of changing the trajectory of a carbon-based economy towards more sustainable energy sources, but it could have much wider application when it comes to changing the trajectory of community opinion and attitudes. Rather than using a battering ram, such as community activism, we may also on occasion be able to introduce a catalyst for cultural change. The prestigious *Quarterly Journal of Economics*, for example, has never published an article on climate change. It could take just one successful submission about the drastic potential economic damage to open the floodgates. *Information gerrymandering* however, remains a problem. A recent study (Stewart et al., 2019) of the vulnerabilities of collective decision-making to systematic distortion by restricted information flow has made it clear that "the structure of an influence network can sway [a vote outcome] even when both parties have equal size" and that "a small number of zealots, when strategically placed on the influence network, can also … bias outcomes."

So far, so intuitive. But the study also shows that "when multiple parties engage in gerrymandering the group loses its ability to reach consensus and remains in deadlock"—a group-level social dilemma.

The world is facing that dilemma right now. A gridlocked network of fixed opinions, rigid positions and immovable prejudices. To achieve real transformation, the gridlock must be broken. But how?

Creating a New Framework

The first step must be to create a framework that is acceptable, and even attractive, to a sufficient number of people. It must be based on concrete reality, and be achievable in practice.

Complexity scientist Dirk Helbing has argued (Helbing, 2013) that a new global systems science is needed to overcome the governance problems posed by complexity. A part of that science will be working out ways to stabilize global networks and help to steer them away from tipping points.

Helbing was one of the first to point out the dangers of networked risks, and networks of networked risks. But with danger there also comes promise—the promise that a properly constructed network, based on sustainability and the maintenance of human values, may help to maintain stability, rather than destroy it.

The criteria for such a system change were outlined during an online discussion of the Systems Innovation network (@Sys_Innovation). Five major criteria were identified:

(1) The system to be changed needs to be the complex system as a whole, not some simple subset.
(2) The change process should not be imposed by a central entity directly, but guided by a collaboration of multiple parties.
(3) The change should be an intentional response to a wicked problem.
(4) The change to the structure of the system should be such that qualitatively different outcomes emerge over time.
(5) The change should shift the system to a more sustainable state, reducing negative externalities while increasing positive ones.

One system change that fulfils these requirements is a shift to the *circular economy*—a potentially effective toolbox for a sustainable future (Schroeder et al., 2018). The nature of the goal is discussed in detail elsewhere in this volume (see chapters by Kosir, Holth, Potocnik, and Kuenkel & Kühn in this volume). Here I present a few key points and examples relevant to realizing the goal, whose importance is increasingly being realized by major organizations. The Royal Society, for example, recently held a series of workshops on the role of science in establishing the circular economy (Royal Society, 2019), while UK Research and Innovation is appointing a Circular Economy Coordinator.

Much of the effort so far has been concerned with physical recycling, particularly of plastics (e.g. Scottish Government, 2019). Other materials are also on the agenda. Philips Lighting, for example, is changing its business model to provide lighting and fixtures as a service, leasing the equipment and taking responsibility for the recycling or environmentally responsible disposal of lighting and fixtures at the end of their lives (Pincus & Ellman, 2017). This is at least a first step to the "system-level" changes advocated earlier in this chapter.

But, as Mark Miodownik pointed out in a talk at a recent meeting of the Association of British Science Writers, people, not plastics, are the problem. How can we curb industry and consumption patterns?

Psychological factors lie at the heart, and Katherine White and her co-authors (White et al., 2019) have suggested a novel framework for using them to encourage a transformation. The framework goes under the acronym SHIFT, standing for Social influence, Habit formation, Individual self, Feelings and cognition and Tangibility. It will be seen that these correspond quite closely in practical terms with the factors identified in the *Manifesto*.

Another creative idea has been to embed biodegradable coffee cups with tree seeds (Bored Panda, 2019). But eventually we must get past fiddling at the edges, and go for truly radical transformation of our society and the economic values that it has so far embraced.

Disrupting the Present System

The first step is to disrupt the present system so as to make way for the new. There are two ways in—to persuade people that disruption is in their own individual interests, or to demonstrate that group interest, cooperation and sharing offer a more promising way forward.

Some businesses are already using the first approach. The resources company Alderan, for example, argues that "We need *positive* disruption if we're going to meet the 2030 UN Sustainable Development Goals (SDGs). It's obvious why. Having individuals, companies or governments change their stand-alone behavior is crucial. It's also insufficient. To shift our current unsustainable trajectory, we need system-level change. That's the kind that comes from new technologies and new models of organization" (Alderan, 2019).

The authors propose a "disruption stack", consisting of three pairs of layers. At the base there is the "meme layer," where "humans communicate and infect each other with ways of thinking about the world" along with the "structural change layer", where the basic conditions of our society and our economy shift (but more slowly than in the meme layer).

Above these layers lie the "physical technology intervention" layer and the "non-physical innovation" layer. The nature of the first is obvious from the name; the second is concerned with solving problems using physical innovation (e.g. blockchain).[4]

Finally there are the "execution" layers. The "ecosystem" layer is concerned with the way that firms may coordinate and compete with other firms to innovate and solve problems. The "firm" layer, on the other hand, is concerned survival and success: which firms are in the best position, which ones may lose out.

It all makes for rather depressing reading for those of us who are concerned to make the world a better and more equitable place, but there are lessons to be learned. In particular, the "meme" layer may be used (as in the *Manifesto*) to develop and

---

[4] We note here in passing that statistical methods exist for assessing the success of innovation, and that these methods depend very much on whether the innovation is incremental or arises from a "black swan" insight (Azevedo et al., 2019).

drive change that is not solely dependent on technology or competition, but which instead is based on human values of group interest, cooperation and sharing.

How realistic is this possibility? It may depend on the *potentiality* of society for change. Christian Zingg and his collaborators at ETH Zurich have argued, for example, that it is a "question how many different states a social organization can attain" and that "the number of such possible states is an indication of the ability of the organization to respond to various influences. As there can be a vast variety of such influences, the corresponding number ideally should be very large. This indicates that, even for unforeseeable events, the social organization still has many ways to respond. We call such an ability the potentiality of the organization" (Zingg et al., 2019).

In other words, the more diverse a society, the higher its potentiality for change from below. This is an important prerequisite for transformation (Lawson, 2019). Some writers have argued that the only way to achieve such transformation is for outright revolution. Geophysicist and modeller Brad Werner, for example, argues that "global capitalism has made the depletion of resources so rapid, convenient and barrier-free that "earth-human systems" are becoming dangerously unstable in response." He sees only one hope: "resistance"—movements of "people or groups of people" who "adopt a certain set of dynamics that does not fit within the capitalist culture". According to the abstract for his presentation, this includes "environmental direct action, resistance taken from outside the dominant culture, as in protests, blockades and sabotage by indigenous peoples, workers, anarchists and other activist groups" (Klein, 2013).

But perhaps, as with the approach of the *Manifesto*, we can do it by more peaceful means. Bevis Watts, CEO of Triodos Bank UK, argues that the banking sector must take a central role "to take on the existential environmental and social challenges within the UN Sustainable Development Goals and Paris Climate targets" (Watts, 2019). One way in which it can do this is to pay to change the game—a strategy that has its roots in traditional game theory (Wolpert & Grana, 2019).

We may need to pay quite a lot to change the game. Authors Johan Falk and Gaffney (2019) offer an "exponential road map" of twelve actions for tech companies to help halve global emissions. These include low-carbon design, enabling circular business models, and enabling sustainable transportation and travel—all worthy longterm objectives, but all bearing a short-term cost.

Who should bear that cost? Again we run into the *Tragedy of the Commons* dilemma, where rational self-interest dictates that competing firms would rather that others bore the cost while they themselves continued to make short-term profits. One answer is that Governments should provide subsidies so that all competitors are on a level playing field. But this is top-down governance, and (as previously argued) needs to be combined with bottom-up transformation (Lawson, 2019).

A study of fish-buyer networks (González-Mon et al., 2019) offers some clues as to how the transformation may be achieved. The authors find that "adaptability differs substantially amongst [different fish-buyer] types, thus implying that fish buyers' abilities to respond to changes are unevenly distributed." They suggest that an answer, as in mediaeval times, may lie in patronage to support and promote adaptive capacity—patronage that could, and probably should, be provided by government. The distribution of such patronage is the subject of the *fair reward problem*, analyzed in detail by Didier Sornette and his colleagues (2019). The problem is to reward and support merit, rather than luck. The authors propose three different measures to assess merit: (i) *raw outcome*; (ii) *risk- adjusted outcome,* and (iii) *prospective.*

Of particular interest is their emphasis on "the need for the deductive *prospective approach,* which considers the potential of a system to adapt and mutate in novel futures. This is formalized within an *evolutionary system,* comprised of five processes, inter alia handling the *exploration–exploitation trade-off*. Several human endeavors—including finance, politics, and science—are analyzed through these lenses, and concrete solutions are proposed to support a prosperous and meritocratic society."

Those solutions take the form of a five-step process: "Observe, decide, execute, challenge and explore."

- Observe: *Broadly decipher the role of skill, luck, and environmental changes.*
- Decide: *Strive for independent and diverse viewpoints during exploration of alternatives.*
- Execute: *Unite behind a common goal, while allowing local initiative for adaptability.*
- Challenge: *Constantly monitor, and ruthlessly scrutinize both successes and failures.*
- Explore: *Evolutionary learners are open to breakthrough mutations.* These steps correspond rather closely with those discussed here for the implementation of the *Manifesto.*

Putting a new system in place

The new system must take account of the complex realities of our socio-economicecological world—in particular, its capacity for sudden, unpredicted, and unpredictable change, and the propagation of shocks throughout the interconnected system (Startini et al., 2019). Free market thinking is no longer enough—a point emphasized by Adam Smith himself: "People of the same trade seldom meet together, even for merriment and diversion, but the conversation ends in a conspiracy against the public, or in some contrivance to raise prices" (Smith, 1776).

One possible transition phase, which subtly imposes the *Manifesto* philosophy on the present pursuit of self-interest approach, would be to create a market for moral, organizational and cultural values (Senatore, 2019). "Individuals, companies and local communities would exchange documents, each of which would list the benefits that have been experienced through applying a given moral, organizational or cultural value. Values would include: social justice, inclusivity towards minorities, propensity to innovation, environmentalism. The experiences would be certified on the basis of quantitative indicators decided by law. For instance, companies might add an experience to a document referred to environmentalism after reducing CO_2 emissions by a certain percentage; individuals would have the chance to do the same after donating a certain amount of money to "green charities"; local communities may add an experience after increasing green areas by a certain percentage. Quantitative indicators for social justice would include, for instance, a certain reduction of inequality in local communities and of wage disparities in companies."

It is an interesting concept. One would hope that the "market" idea would disappear in due course, to be replaced by the solid moral foundation proposed in the *Manifesto*. Certainly it has been demonstrated by game theorists that co-evolution between the cost of decisions and the strategy contributes to the evolution of cooperation (Ohdaira, 2019). It would be interesting indeed if the end result was that the very basis of classical game theory—the rational pursuit of self-interest—were to disappear in the process! It also fits with the observation that "individuals optimise what happens to them over time, not what happens to them on average in a collection of parallel worlds" (Buchanan, 2019).

The resultant synthesis, if achieved, would go far towards resolving the problem of achieving a form of governance that establishes a viable balance between *uncertainty* and *controllability* (Allen et al., 2011).

The important point to note here is that all four forms of governance will be made more effective by "polyphonic coexistence" within the governed and governing community. Some modern innovations, such as blockchain, may also act as enablers (Lin & Liu, 2019).

In the end, a harmonious cooperation between all parties provides the best chance for the world to achieve an appropriate and necessary balance between resilience, contingency, risk and governance (Zebrowski, 2009). This cannot be achieved in the context of the pursuit of individual self-interest, which can produce paradoxical negative outcomes and which lies at the heart of many of the world's woes. Rather, it needs transdisciplinary collaboration, adaptability, and a polyphonic transformation of bodies and minds so that individuals can act as one in a collaborative effort to solve problems. By seeing ourselves as nodes in a vast global socio-economic-ecological complex adaptive network, interacting with others to promote change, trust and awarenss, we can help to achieve such a transformation.

References

Alderan (2019). A new disruption framework. https://medium.com/@alderanimpact/alderans-new-disruption-framework-383112fc2a60.

Allen, C. R., et al. (2011). Adaptive management for a turbulent future. *Nebraska Cooperative Fish & Wildlife Research Unit—Staff Publication, 80.* http://digitalcommons.unl.edu/ncfwrustaff/80.

Artiges, E., et al. (2019). Replicator population dynamics of group (n-agent) interactions. Broken symmetry, thresholds for metastability and macroscopic behaviour. arXiv:1909.06858v1. (physics.soc-ph).

Axelrod, R. (1984). *The evolution of cooperation.* Basic Books.

Azevedo, E. M., et al. (2019). A/B testing with fat tails. https://eduardomazevedo.github.io/papers/azevedo-et-al-ab.pdf.

Barrett, S. (2018). Choices in the climate commons. *Science, 362,* 1217.

Bar-Yam, T., Lynch, O., & Bar-Yam, Y. (2018). Inherent instability of disordered systems. arXiv: 1812.00450v1.

Bodanis, D. (2020). *The art of fairness: The power of decency in a world gone mean.* The Bridge Street Press.

Bored Panda. (2019). Biodegradable coffee cups embedded with seeds grow into trees when thrown away. https://www.boredpanda.com/biodegradable-plantablecoffee-cup-reduce-reuseg row/?utm_source=google&utm_medium=organic&utm_campaign=organic.

Bowles, S. & Gintis, H. (2011) *A Cooperative Species: Human Reciprocity and its Evolution.* Princeton University Press.

Buchanan, M. (2019). How ergodicity reimagines economics for the benefit of us all. *Aeon magazine.* https://aeon.co/ideas/how-ergodicity-reimagines-economics-for-thebenefit-of-us-all.

Burgoyne, J. (2019). A reflection on Nesta's government innovation summit: A case for pragmatic radicalism in the face of government's legitimacy crisis. https://medium.com/centre-for-public-impact/a-reflection-on-nestas-governmentinnovation-summit-a-case-for-pragmatic-radicalism-in-the-face-c19d4ed4ced4.

Camerer, C. (2003). *Behavioral game theory: Experiments in strategic interaction.* Russell Sage Foundation Princeton University Press.

Carpenter, S. R., et al. (2012). General resilience to cope with extreme events. *Sustainability.* https://doi.org/10.3390/su40x000x.

Coyle, D. (2019). When capitalisms collide. *Nature, 574,* 323–324.

Duit, A., & Galaz, V. (2008). Governance and complexity—emerging issues for governance theory. *Governance: An international Journal of Policy Administration and Institutions, 21,* 311–335.

Falk, J., & Gaffney, O. (2019) 12 ways for tech companies to ½ global emissions in 12 years. https://exponentialroadmap.org/wpcontent/uploads/2019/01/190121_ShortSprint_FINAL_REV.pdf.

Farmer, J. D., et al. (2019). Sensitive intervention points in the post-carbon transition. *Science, 364,* 132–134.

Fisher, L. (2008). *Rock, paper, scissors: Game theory in everyday life.* Basic Books.

Fisher, L., et al. (2013). How can I trust you? Encounters with Carl Rogers and game theory. In J. H. D. Cornelius-White (Ed.), *Interdisciplinary handbook of the person-centred approach* (pp. 299–317). Springer-Verlag.

Fisher, L. (2015). More than 70 ways to show resilience. *Nature, 518,* 35.

Fisher, L. (2019). Global challenges: Personal reflections on the Stockholm "New Shape" competition. *Journal & Proceedings of the Royal Society of New South Wales, 151,* 213–231.

Fisher, L. R., & Sandberg, A. (2021). Necessary conditions for the governance of global catastrophic Risks. *Global Policy* (submitted).

Frischmann, B. M., Marciano, A., & Ramello, G. B. (2019). Retrospective: Tragedy of the commons after 50 years. *Journal of Economic Perspectives, 33,* 211–228.

Fukuyama, F. (1996). *Trust: The social virtues and the creation of prosperity.* Free Press.

Gigerenzer, G., Todd, P.M. and the ABC Research Group, 1999.Gigerenzer, G., Todd, P. M., & ABC Research Group. (1999). *Simple heuristics that make us smart.* Oxford: Oxford University Press.

Goethe, J. W. V. (1832). *Faust part II, scene V.* English Translation. https://www.poetryintransla tion.com/PITBR/German/FaustIIActIScenesItoVII.php.

González-Mon, B., et al. (2019). Small-scale fish buyers' trade networks reveal diverse actor types and differential adaptive capacities. *Ecological Economics, 164,* 106338.

Gross, J., & De Deu, C. K. W. (2019). Individual solutions to shared problems create a modern tragedy of the commons. *Science Advances, 5,* eaua7296.

Hardin, G. (1968). The tragedy of the commons. *Science, 162,* 1243–1248.

Helbing, D. (2013). Globally networked risks and how to respond. *Nature, 497,* 51–59.

Hill, S. (2017). *Captives for freedom.* University of Papua New Guinea Press.

Kahneman, D. (2002). Maps of bounded rationality a perspective on intuitive judgment and choice. *Nobel Memorial Lecture.* https://www.nobelprize.org/uploads/2018/06/kahnemann-lecture.pdf.

Kaplan, J. T., Gimbel, S. I., & Harris, S. (2016). Neural correlates of maintaining one's political beliefs in the face of counterevidence. *Nature*. https://doi.org/10.1038/srep39589.

Klein, M. (2013). How science is telling us all to revolt. *New Statesman, October 29th*. https://www.newstatesman.com/2013/10/science-says-revolt.

Klimek, P., Poledna, S., & Thurner, S. (2019). Quantifying economic resilience from input-output susceptibility to improve predictions of economic growth and recovery. *Nature communications, 10 (1)*, e1677. https://doi.org/10.1038/s41467-019-09357-w.

Korhonen, J., Nuur, C., Feldmann, A., & Birkie, S. E. (2018a). Circular economy as an essentially contested concept. *Journal of Cleaner Production, 175*, 544–552.

Korhonen, J., Honkasalo, A., & Seppälä, J. (2018b). Circular economy: The concept and its limitations. *Ecological Economics, 143*, 37–46.

Lawson, N. (2019). Transforming society from below and above. http://www.compassonline.org.uk/wp-content/uploads/2019/02/Compass_45-degreechange-1.pdf.

Lin, C. -F., & Liu, H. -W. (2019). Disruptive technologies and sustainable development. *International Centre for Trade and Development*. https://www.ictsd.org/sites/default/files/research/disruptive_technologies_and_southeast_asia_-_liu_and_lin.pdf.

Lyver, P. O'B., Timoti, P., Davis, T., & Tylianakis, J. M. (2019). Biocultural hysteresis inhibits adaptation to environmenta change. *Trends in Ecology and Evolution, 34*, 771–780.

Mackay, H. (2021). *The kindness revolution*. Allen & Unwin.

McDonald, K. R., et al. (2019). Bayesian nonparametric models characterize instantaneous strategies in a competitive dynamic game. *Nature Communications, 10*, 1808. https://doi.org/10.1038/s41467-019-09789-4.

McGonigal, J. (2019). Our puny human brains are terrible at thinking about the future. *Slate*. https://slate.com/technology/2017/04/why-people-are-so-bad-atthinking-about-the-future.html.

Moore, J. (2019). The capitalocene. *Wired magazine*. https://www.wired.com/story/capitalocene/?utm_brand=wired-science&utm_socialtype=owned&mbid=social_tw_sci&utm_medium=social&utm_source=twitter.

Morrison, T. H., et al. (2019). The black box of power in polycentric environmental governance. *Global Environmental Change, 57*, 101934.

Morrone, A., et al. (2009). *How good is trust? Measuring trust and its role for the progress of societies* (OECD Statistics Working Paper). https://www.oecdilibrary.org/docserver/220633873086.pdf?expires=1572664168&id=id&accname=guest&checksum=4D4605D78BA840C1D1B5ECADEEBC73EA.

Nash, J. (1950). Equilibrium points in N-person games. In *Proceedings of the National Academy of Sciences of the U.S.A.* (vol. 36, pp. 48–49).

Nesta (2019). *Government innovation summit*. https://medium.com/centre-for-publicimpact/a-reflection-on-nestas-government-innovation-summit-a-case-for-pragmaticradicalism-in-the-face-c19d4ed4ced4.

Odier, D. (1989). *The job: Interviews with William S. Burroughs* (pp. 73–74). New York, Penguin.

Ohdaira, T. (2019). Coevolution between the cost of decision and the strategy contributes to the evolution of cooperation. *Scientific Reports, 9*, 4465. https://doi.org/10.1038/s41598-019-41073-9.

Ostrom, E. (2010). Polycentric systems for coping with collective action and global environmental change. *Global Environmental Change—Human Policy Dimensions, 20*, 550–557.

Pincus, C., & Ellman, K. (2017). Philips lighting, WM transition to the circular economy. https://www.greenbiz.com/article/philips-wm-transition-circular-economy.

Poundstone, W. (1993). *Prisoner's dilemma*. Anchor Books.

Preiser, R., et al. (2018). Social-ecological systems as complex adaptive systems: Organizing principles for advancing research methods and approaches. *Ecology and Society, 23*, 46. https://doi.org/10.5751/ES-10558-230446.

Rabinovitch, S. (2019). What is wrong with tolerance? https://aeon.co/essays/reciprocity-not-tolerance-is-the-basis-of-healthysocieties?fbclid=IwAR0-4wsOQJ_CS-2_IcwjrlcRD7QPyutYaYxO6rL9K9IJzN3QxfSQLctY4k0.

Raworth, K. (2017). *Doughnut economics: Seven ways to think like a 21st-century economist.* Chelsea Green Publishing.

Raworth, K. (2019). https://www.kateraworth.com/2019/01/28/8thwaycompetition/.

Royal Society (2019). Science to enable the circular economy. *Discussion Meeting, London.* https://royalsociety.org/science-events-andlectures/2019/06/circular-economy/. https://royalsociety.org/science-events-andlectures/2019/06/circular-economy-priorities/.

Schroeder, P., Anggraeni, K., & Weber, U. (2018). The relevance of circular economy practices to sustainable development goals. *Journal of Industrial Ecology, 23,* 77–95.

Schumacher, E. F. (1973). *Small is beautiful: Economics as if people mattered.* Blond & Briggs Ltd.

Scottish Government (2019). Driving a circular economy: social and economic benefits of deposit return. https://www.gov.scot/news/driving-a-circular-economy/.

SDG. (2019). *Sustainable Development Goals Web-Based Tool.* https://sdgtool.com/.

Senatore, M. (2019). Should we create a market for values? *The Philosophical Salon.* https://thephilosophicalsalon.com/should-we-create-a-market-for-values/.

Shiller, R. J. (2013). Speculative asset prices. *Nobel Memorial Lecture.* https://www.nobelprize.org/uploads/2018/06/shiller-lecture.pdf.

Sigala, M. (2019). The 'sharing economy' simply dresses up our consumerist tendencies in a more palatable ideology. *The Conversation.* https://theconversation.com/the-sharing-economy-simply-dresses-up-ourconsumerist-tendencies-in-a-more-palatable-ideology-99090?utm_medium=email&utm_campaign=Latest%20from%20The%20Conversation%20for%20January%2028%202019%20-%201221611230&utm_content=Latest%20from%20The%20Conversation%20for%20January%2028%202019%20-%201221611230+CID_7e4295f703904a652cb9187d52eeb031&utm_source=campaign_monitor&utm_term=The%20sharing%20economy%20simply%20dresses%20up%20our%20consumerist%20tendencies%20in%20a%20more%20palatable%20ideology.

Sitas, N., et al. (2019). Exploring the usefulness of scenario archetypes in sciencepolicy processes: Experience across IPBES assessments. *Ecology and Society, 24,* 3559. https://doi.org/10.5751/ES-11039-240335.

Smith, A. (1759). The theory of moral sentiments. In A. Millar, A. Kincaid & J. Bell (Eds.), *Strand.* Edinburgh.

Smith, A. (1776). An inquiry into the nature and causes of the wealth of nations. In R. H. Campbell & A. S. Skinner (Eds.), *Glasgow edition of the works and correspondence of Adam Smith* (vol. 2, p. 154). Oxford: Oxford University Press, 1976.

Sornette, D., Wheatley, S., & Cauwels, P. (2019). The fair reward problem: the illusion of success and how to solve it. *Swiss Finance Institute Research Paper Series 19–25.* https://papers.ssrn.com/sol3/papers.cfm?abstract_id=3377177.

Spooner, A. M. (undated). Ten real-life examples of the tragedy of the commons. https://www.dummies.com/education/science/environmental-science/ten-real-lifeexamples-of-the-tragedy-of-the-commons/.

Startini, M., Boguñá, M., & Serrano, M. A. (2019). The interconnected wealth of nations: Shock propagation on global trade-investment multiplex networks. *Scientific Reports.* https://doi.org/10.1038/s41598-019-49173-2.

Steindl-Rast, D. (1993). Precepts. In *Thich Nhat Hanh for a future to be possible?* (p. 125). Berkeley; Parallax Press.

Stewart, A. J., et al. (2019). Information gerrymandering and undemocratic decisions. *Nature, 573,* 117–121.

Summerfield, C., & Tsetsos, K. (2015). Do humans make good decisions? *Trends in Cognitive Science, 19,* 27–34.

Taleb, N. N. (2102). *Antifragile: Things that gain from disorder.* New York: Random House.

Thaler, R. H. (2017) From cashews to nudges: The evolution of behavioral economics. *Nobel Prize Lecture.* https://www.nobelprize.org/prizes/economic-sciences/2017/thaler/lecture/.

Von Neumann, J., & Morgenstern, O. (1944). *Theory of games and economic behavior*. Princeton University Press.

WEF (2017). Shaping the future of global food systems: A scenarios analysis. https://www.wef orum.org/whitepapers/shaping-the-future-of-global-food-systems-ascenarios-analysis.

White, K., Habib, R., & Hardisty, D. J. (2019). How to SHIFT consumer behaviors to be more sustainable: A literature review and guiding framework. *Journal of Marketing, 8*, 23–49.

Wolpert, D., & Grana, J. (2019). How much would you pay to change a game before playing it? *Entropy, 21*, 686–703.

Zamora, M. E., et al. (2019). Ecosystem antifragility: Beyond integrity and resilience. *Peer J Preprints*. https://doi.org/10.7287/peerj.preprints.27813v1.

Zebrowski, C. (2009). Governing the network society: a biopolitical critique of resilience. *Political Perspectives, 3*. http://www.politicalperspectives.org.uk/wpcontent/uploads/2010/08/Vol3-1-2009-4.pdf.

Zingg, C., Casiraghi, G., Vaccario, G., & Schweitzer, F. (2019). What is the entropy of a social organization? arXiv:1905.09772v1. (physics.soc-ph).

Zuboff, S. (2019). Surveillance capitalism and the challenge of collective action. *New Labour Forum, 28*, 10–29.

Chapter 10
Transdisciplinary Study of How to Integrate Our Shattered World: The Self–nonself Circulation Principle of "Living" Wholeness

Masatoshi Murase and Tomoko Murase

Abstract The present transdisciplinary study shall challenge the long-standing problem: What is life? Indeed, it is often mentioned that we will not be able to answer this problem satisfactorily even in the future. However, it is possible to provide an ostensive definition of life based on a self-consistent way. It is clear that the self–nonself circulation theory developed by Masatoshi Murase in 2000- characterized by the 5-NECTE principle—provides a useful model not only for understanding the dynamics of living cells and the origin of life, but for realizing the co-existence or being of the self and nonself in a circulation way. Here, we need a paradigm shift from the outdated materialistic and reductionist view of life to the process-centric and holistic view of life. Life must be considered as emergent properties driven by circular processes, but not linear processes, leading to self-nested hierarchical evolution. Only then, we will be able to understand how to integrate our shattered world leading to the circle of wholeness.

Masatoshi Murase (✉)
Yukawa Institute for Theoretical Physics (YITP), Kyoto University, Kyoto, Japan

International Research Unit of Advanced Future Studies (IRU-AFS), Kyoto University (2015–2020), Kyoto, Japan

International Research Unit of Integrated Complex System Science (IRU-ICSS), Kyoto University, Kyoto, Japan

T. Murase
Japanese Red Cross Toyota College of Nursing, Toyota, Japan
e-mail: murase@yukawa.kyoto-u.ac.jp

Masatoshi Murase · T. Murase
2021 Project of Challenges of Advanced Future Studies, Kokoro Research Center, Kyoto University, Kyoto, Japan

S. Hill et al. (eds.), *The Kyoto Post-COVID Manifesto For Global Economics*, Creative Economy, https://doi.org/10.1007/978-981-16-8566-8_10

Brief Historical Background

Tracing the evolutionary history of life over time back to its origin, we can realize the *self-consistency principle* at the fundamental level as the *fundamental homology*. Simple principles of complex "living" dynamics can be, therefore, deduced from the demand that the underlying principles should be self-consistent, regardless of the scale with which we are concerned. It is *the self–nonself circulation principle* detailed in Kyoto Manifesto (KM-I) by Murase (2018) that would provide us with an integrated world view, often called a systemic view, rather than a shattered world view, which is responsible for co-existence, co-evolution, and co-creation between Nature and Humanity.

Such a unified view is urgently needed today to deal with our current global crisis and make Nature, together with all Life on Earth, sustainable and persistent, because our perceptions are constantly shaping our world and are being shaped by the world itself. For this purpose, first of all, we have to appreciate the co-existence—referred to as the logic of *both A and not-A*—of so many contradictions between differentiation and integration, between reductionist view and holistic view, between self-consistency and self-transcendence, between order and disorder, between change and constancy, and so on. Then, we should not only consider the possibility of *either A or not-A*, like the traditional way of logical thinking, but also think about the possibility of *neither A nor not-A*, realizing the situation of *nothingness* or *emptiness*. The set of the logics is known as *tetralemma*.[1] Besides the tetralemma, finally, we should consider the possibility of *self-transcendence*: that is, the reaching out beyond the tetralemma itself.

The multiple perspective of this kind must be especially important because—just as *Polyphony* introduced by Stomu Yamash'ta from music in KM-I and of course central in KM-II, as emphasized by Stephen Hill (Chaps. 1 and 2), is the necessary concept for admitting difference into consideration of harmony—when dealing with current shattered world phenomena, assertion and maintenance of difference, instead of attempt either at isolation or at sameness, in the context of harmony allows a far more constructive dialogue and resolution, leading to realization of hidden dimension for further co-evolution and co-emergence of Humanity and Nature.

In our living world, indeed, life and death are always appearing at various hierarchical levels. Seemingly contradictory oppositions are, however, considered as merely different aspects of the same "life" phenomena. In such an all-embracing world, what we have to realize is *the circle of "life"* or *the circle of wholeness* beyond our limited perceptions. We can hardly access the realization of the circle of wholeness, without mystic or meditative experience, which is one of the most challenging problems. According to artist Jacques Debs, upon encountering with *silence,*

---

[1] The idea of the *tetralemma* was developed by Indian logic. There are four logical possibilities of the tetralemma as follows: (1) "A" (affirmation); (2) "not-A" (negation); (3) "both A and not-A" (both); and (4) "neither A nor not-A" (neither). Of these, the fourth case corresponds to nothingness (neither held nor not held).

he began to appreciate the feeling of spirituality or infinity, essential to *Buddhist religion*, along with intuition, resolution, determination and synchronicity.[2]

Astonishingly, this was already experienced scientifically when the ancient Indian culture discovered the number *zero*, based on the concept of nothingness, as it resulted in the invention of the counting system generating infinite numbers! In the present paper, a *transdisciplinary* scientific study was introduced to approach how we can realize the circle of wholeness of this kind for *inventing the future.*

From front to the back; Stephen Hill, Juichi Yamagiwa, Masatoshi Murase, Jacques Debs

At Divinity Hall Chapel in Doshisha University on June 4, 2017.

10.1 Introduction

The new scientific understanding of life at all levels of living systems—organisms, social systems, and ecosystems—is based on a perception of reality that has profound implications not only for science and philosophy, but also for politics, business, healthcare, education, and many other areas of everyday life.

> Fritjof Capra and Pier Luigi Luisi
> "The Systems View of Life: A Unifying Vision" p. 12
> Cambridge: Cambridge University Press, 2014

What is life? It is widely understood that, despite the advanced studies of Western science and the progress of modern technology, it is impossible to answer this problem satisfactorily even in the future. *We shall challenge this misunderstanding! What we are facing with is not the difficulty of the problem itself, but the difficulty of finding*

---

[2] There was the panel discussion with President Juichi Yamagiwa of Kyoto University in the international symposium at Doshisha University on June 4, 2017. http://www2.yukawa.kyoto-u.ac.jp/~future/news/20160604-1.html.

a methodology of how to understand life itself. Indeed, most of us agree with the fact that within the strong constraint of linear written natural and even scientific language, it is often impossible to describe the complex nonlinear networks and hierarchical dynamics typical of life. However, arts and Eastern religious philosophy can get rid of the difficulty, because they are totally free from the constraint of linear cause-and-effect constraint of Western thinking.

There appears a strong hope for answering the problem of "What is Life?" Indeed, genetic information is written in the DNA language within its linear constraint. Life is, however, solves this constraint so that it is emerging as life itself. Here, we should realize *the self-consistency principle: life is emerging whenever it is consistent with itself and with everything else.* We may encounter with a sort of tautology because life is used as a method to understand life. However, this is the exact point that we can solve the problem at once. There appears *the circle of wholeness.* At its center, Stephen Hill (Chap. 2) focused on Humanity whereas we will focus on life. There is no essential difference, however, between them because of the self-nested hierarchy.

It is, therefore, possible to provide an ostensive definition of life based on a self-consistent way. Of course, we need a paradigm shift from the outdated materialistic and reductionist view of life to the process-centric and holistic view of life. Life must be considered as emergent properties driven by circular processes, but not linear processes, leading to self-nested hierarchical evolution. Besides life and human beings, the surrounding environment involving all the emergent problems, such as the COVID-19 pandemic, economic crises, food security, and so on, must be also considered as life phenomena. *It is now time to reconsider our world and all the emerging problems based on the new conception of life.*

In this Introduction, we describe the limits of modern science and a paradigm shift necessary for understanding life itself toward a new synthesis.

10.1.1 *"Collapsologie" Arrived but Pandemic Returned: From Reductionist View Toward the Circle of Wholeness*

On March 11 in 2020, the coronavirus pandemic was declared by the World Health Organization. Since this COVID-19 pandemic, we have moved from a world where everything seemed certain and nothing changed largely to an extremely shattered world where nothing seems certain and everything changes so radically. Ironically, such a worse scenario was already presented as *"Collapsologie"* by Servigne and Stevens (2015). No one had ever paid much attention to the *self-disorganization* of our world (cf. Jantsch, 1980, p. 26). We began to realize that, although modern science is true in its validity, it is not the only way to access "ultimate reality".

It turns out that we, human beings, appear no longer as ultimate evolving organisms in the world, and also that the world itself becomes increasingly *alive* and thus evolving. Both are evolving into the *co-evolution* through the interplay processes, just like emerging complex life (Jantsch, 1980). We need, therefore, a radically new thinking way or a *holistic* perception for a deep understanding of life itself or *wholeness*. Here, we are confronted with the problems of wholeness (cf. Schrödinger, 1958): How can we perceive wholeness? What is life as a whole? What is *the circle of wholeness?*

As we shall discuss later, we must have not only intellectually logical thinking, but also nonlogical intuition or even an evolutionary perspective responsible for *novelty* or *creativity*, which is needed for how to understand and how to survive our *unpredictable* world (cf. Goldberger, 1996). Modern science has developed and accumulated a vast knowledge of the Universe including Humans and their histories. We can now realize, however, that *the fact that modern physics is true—which it certainly is—does not mean that it is fundamental* (Bortoft, 1996).

10.1.2   Exploring a Deep Understanding of "What is Life?": Ostensive Definition as a Compensation for a Lack of Its Scientific Definition

Indeed, physical reality like nonliving things has been understood based on a reduction to composite elements, and even to physical laws. It is a common understanding, however, that it is *impossible* to provide a *scientific definition* of life based on traditional reductionism, simply because *living processes* cannot be defined based on a reduction to *nonliving structures* (Capra & Luisi, 2014; Murase, 1996, 2000, 2018). Life is not a *thing*, but instead an *emergent property*. Through *holistic* approach, nevertheless, it is *possible* to provide an *ostensive definition* of life by raising several instances such as cells, species, and so on (Bateson, 2002; Bortoft, 1996; Murase, 1996, 2000).

There must be *homologous* dynamics among different kinds of life phenomena, as they have evolved from the same origin. This is the *self-consistent* way of how to understand ourselves, our perception, and our world simultaneously (Jantsch, 1980; Murase, 2018; Murase & Murase, 2020). It is difficult to specify the beginning and ending of the circular processes between a holistic perception and wholeness of life. However, the circular processes exist definitely. In other words, there seems to be a serious dilemma: without a holistic perception, we cannot deeply understand life as a whole, whereas, without a deep understanding of the wholeness of life, we cannot get a holistic perception. It is a developing and dialectical process that would operate through the interaction between perceiving subjects and perceived objects. This results in a circle of wholeness.

What does this mean? Besides a reductionist approach, there is a *phenomenological* approach which is based on observations made at the level of our experience. This approach can be applied to the definition of life: the *complex* life phenomena are understood based on the *ideal* or *typical* life (Murase, 1996, 2000). Such a definition is called an ostensive definition (see Sect. 10.4.2). As Bortoft (1996) mentioned, nature can manifest in more than one way. This means that, besides modern science, there must be different ways toward "ultimate reality", without assuming that one way is more fundamental than another.

10.1.3   Co-Existence of Structural Thinking and Process Thinking

We have been so familiar with *structural thinking*, in which nonliving things are tried to be understood based on their composite elements. Similarly, structural thinking has also been applied to living things to understand life, based on their composite elements, although it would lead to the concepts of an outdated view of life.

It is now clear that all living things including our world are no longer considered as the machinery composed of elementary building blocks. But instead, there is the holistic and *process thinking* that an existence of life is being, being is living, living is learning, learning is a developmental process, which is itself in an evolutionary process of life as becoming. Thanks to Stephen Hill's suggestions, there is no contradiction between being anchored in the local area (i.e., self-consistency) and at the same time becoming open to a greater opportunity (i.e., self-transcendence). Life should not be, therefore, considered as a merely localized object. Once again, life must be an emergent property.

When we are looking at life at its ascending and descending levels, it turns out that life is not present in the parts but originates only when the parts are together. This leads to the concept of life as *self-transcendence* or *meta-evolution*: the open evolution of evolutionary processes, characterized by reaching out beyond the boundaries of its existence (Jantsch, 1980). A deep understanding of life, thus, requires an *emergentist* view, in addition to a traditional reductionist view. Only then, by courtesy of Stephen Hill again, we realized the argument by Francis (2020, p. 57): that is, "There is no contradiction between being solidly rooted in the truth and at the same time being open to a greater understanding." Here, we should emphasize the possibility that there could be a different science for understanding life itself, not contradictory but complementary to the science of nonliving things.

10.1.4   Parallel Between Development and Evolution

Piaget (1950) noted the striking consistency between the two processes: one is the *developmental process* of knowledge arising from the interaction of perceiving subject with perceived objects, and the other is the *evolutionary process* of their structure and function arising from the interaction of organisms with their environment. The parallel relationship between the development of knowledge and adaptation of life occurs because both the perceiving subject and the perceived object share the same kind of reality through evolution (see Lorenz, 1973).

In other words, humans are at once objective physiological entities and experiencing subjective entities: this dual capacity leads to the blurring of boundaries between self (or the endo-system) and nonself (or its environment), between the parts and the whole, and many other dichotomous oppositions. It turns out that the world we experience outside and the world we recognize inside are converging into the "living" world or the "experiencing" world (Gottwald, 2002).

Surviving a shattered world, therefore, requires a holistic or emergentist view of the "living" world by integrating fragments of knowledge at various levels and scales. Only then, we can find meanings or values; although when there appear differences of values, there appear conflicts of interest, which in turn are the causes of different power relationships (Capra & Luisi, 2014). We will be faced with the shattered world, again!

This is actually the entry points given by Stephen Hill in Chap. 2. He mentioned as follows: *The 'Circle of Wholeness' represents the full power of our existential being as social human persons—inclusivity of our full sharing and care for others, of guidance from the many domains of human knowledge connecting in overall harmony, with caring and knowledge held into relationship by the 'circle's' central point, integrity and trust.*

The circle of wholeness, therefore, must enhance its own power whenever it is based on the self-consistency principle. Only then, it is possible to integrate living individuals and social dimensions simultaneously.

10.1.5 Paradigm Shift from a Non-nested Hierarchical to Nested Hierarchical View

For having a holistic conception of life, we need a paradigm shift in our thinking, from a stable structure-oriented perspective to an unstable process-oriented one, just like the Copernican revolution (Capra & Luisi, 2014; Taleb, 2007). This means that the view of the world as a non-nested hierarchical structure composed of "nonliving" materials should be replaced by one that sees it as the self-nested hierarchical "living" systems (cf. Feinberg, 2001; Murase, 2018). This must be, in a deep sense, a paradigm shift from material sciences to life sciences (Capra & Luisi, 2014; Murase, 1996, 2000).

Since special emphasis has been placed on the transient process but not on the stable structure, then, even the existing structure can be simply viewed as a stationary state of the *recurrent* process. This leads to a new synthesis capable of studying self-transcendental "living" nature: that is, as we mentioned, the reaching out beyond the boundaries of its existence due to the evolution of evolutionary mechanisms and principles (Jantsch, 1980); because the seemingly contradictory perspectives due to the radical shift in our thinking turn out to be merely different aspects of the same wholeness, regardless of the scales with which we are concerned.

Indeed, no living structures can be permanently stabilized. Immune cells, for example, are continually being created and destroyed within our body, which is important for keeping the balance of health and disease. Even an adult nerve cell is continuously renewing itself through the simultaneous running of upgrading (anabolic) and downgrading (catabolic) processes (cf. Murase, 1996, 2018). Living cell, thus, involves a recycling "economy" (or circular economy in our modern terminology) instead of linear one-way (throw-away) processes. Similarly, *learning* is not a linear one-way process, but a circular process between the system and its environment (Murase & Tsuda, 2008; Varela et al., 1991). Besides the evolution (i.e., *becoming*) of life, therefore, its existence (i.e., *being*) in a specific structure appears to be dissolved into processes.

It now turns out that there must be the common dynamical process among being, becoming and learning, regardless of the details with which we are concerned. Furthermore, it should be emphasized that, concerning the adaptive stability, slight instability or *failure* is necessary for the stability or *resilience* of the living organism (Cannon, 1929). This generally implies that order and disorder have to be considered complementary with each other in the evolving complex systems. The same is true for our social "living" system: if it is designed to be sustainable and even resilient, we should take account of the complementarity principle, together with the circular economy.

10.1.6 Toward a Symbiotic or Integrated Relationship Between Nature and Humanity

Even before the COVID-19 pandemic, our overpopulated and globally interdependent world has been confronted with so many difficult problems such as climate change, financial security, energy, environmental pollution, food security, education, and so on. They cannot be understood in isolation, because they are all interconnected and interdependent, characterized as systemic problems just like living systems (Medows, 2008; Zolli, 2012; Capra & Luisi, 2014). What is worse, in scientific communities, there is a common understanding as follows: it is impossible to define life precisely in terms of material science, and thus we could not possess a reliable concept of life itself. This must be the main reason why most of us have failed to recognize how the emerging problems themselves involve the self-transcendental "living" nature.

Beyond the diversity and difficulty of these complex problems typical of living systems, however, there appears the hope that there are rather simple solutions based on principle, *self-consistency*. Within this framework, we need no longer a precise definition of life because life could be considered not only as an elementary process but also as a whole, just like the fractal dynamics (Murase, 2018). Once we have developed a new conception of life, a sustainable and resilient "living" society could be designed on the condition that we are taking care of the economy, business, structures, technologies, and humanity in order not to interfere with originally emerging "living" nature (Capra & Luisi, 2014).

In other words, the universe, the world, the human body, and mind should not be considered as non-nested hierarchical structures composed of elementary material components; but instead, they should be thought of as the self-similar dynamic systems typical of the self-transcendental "living" nature conducted by the *self–nonself circulation principle*, discussed in Kyoto Manifesto by Murase (2018).

The present chapter extends the previous paper to advance a *transdisciplinary* study of how to integrate the shattered world in a coherent wholeness. We have to develop a rather coherent world involving co-existence, co-evolution, and co-creation between Nature and Humanity, in the face of serious conflicts and oppositions in our current crisis. A new synthesis is needed for integrating all-embracing dynamics such as the self–nonself circulation, the circular economy, the circular balance between differentiation and integration, the circle of wholeness, and so on; as they are only different facets of the same emerging phenomena in the world based on the self-consistency principle.

10.2　What is the Wholeness of Nature?

Spiritual things can be 'fixed' as little as living things. Where growth ceases, there nothing but the dead form remains. … Even the best food, if preserved too long, becomes poison. It is the same with spiritual food. Truths cannot be 'taken over', they have to be rediscovered continually. … This is the law of spiritual growth, from which results in the necessity to experience the same truths in ever new forms, and cultivate and propagate not so much the results, but the *methods* through which we obtain knowledge and experience Reality.

Lama Anagarika Govinda
"Foundations of Tibetan Mysticism" p. 38–39
Martino Publishing, Mansfield, U.S.A. 2002

Being confronted with the shattered world, we have often asked so many questions: What is conflict? What is life? What is evolution? What is wholeness? What are the parts? What is spirituality? What is humanity? What is the ultimate reality? What are health and disease?

Despite seemingly different questions, it turns out that they are merely different facets of "the same truths". What is important is not the results, but the *methods* through which we obtain knowledge and experience Reality (Govinda, 2002). Before discussing some of the above questions, therefore, we had better think about "the methods" in two ways: one is about perception and another is philosophy.

10.2.1 Incomplete Perception

Nobody would doubt that we know the facts and the world through experience. This is the philosophy of *empiricism*. But perception cannot be making a copy of the object. Understanding is neither a static knowledge nor a linear process, but a circular process between an observer and an object. Expanding the philosophy of empiricism from static view to a dynamic one, it is possible to understand how we can experience reality: that is, it is not the obtained knowledge but the methods or processes of obtaining knowledge that must be important for living the unpredictable world (Goldberg, 1996).

Look at the Necker cube in Fig. 10.1. This is one of the well-known ambiguous figures used by *gestalt* psychologists. When you are observing the cube shown in the top panel, you can see alternately the two different objects as indicated in the bottom left and right panels. Although in the top panel, the sensory experience is the same in both cases, we can realize alternately the two different objects because of the *organization*: it is not an element in the visual field, but rather how elements are appreciated. Please remind the phrase given by Govinda (2002) once again that not the results but the methods through which we obtain knowledge and experience Reality are important.

In a complex system, principally, just as every perturbation in any one point can affect the entire system, we can experience that knowing even the simplest case goes beyond the purely sensory (Jantsch, 1980; Murase, 1992). Let us experience some examples. Recognizing one of the two different objects (shown in the bottom left and right in Fig. 10.1) is the perception of *meaning* (Bortoft, 1996). It is a sudden switch in the meaning that is experienced. Even if we investigate a set of lines on this page, we cannot see the different meanings associated with the organizations of reversing cube. This occurs because meaning is an *emergent* property just like reality and even life.

In the previous experience, we realized a switch in the meaning that is seen at the level of the three-dimensional cubes. It is also possible to make a sudden change in our image world when a very tiny change is applied to the object. Look at Fig. 10.2, where the Necker cube and its deformed patterns are shown. When we look at the left

Fig. 10.1 Necker cube. The reversing cube (top) and the two different organizations (bottom left and right)

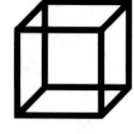

Fig. 10.2 Necker cube and deformed patterns

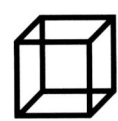 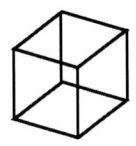 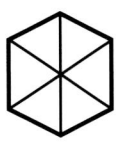

or middle panel, we can see the three-dimensional cube as usual. However, we will see the right panel as a two-dimensional hexagon, instead of a three-dimensional cube. Once you see the three-dimensional cube in this figure, it is hard to hold it. There is the tendency to switch back to a two-dimensional hexagon (Solso, 1996). Anyway, we have experienced that we perceive the spontaneous appearance of new forms. Such an experience must be a key property of life, for it is relating to emergence or *creativity*. Concerning our incomplete perceptions, there is no fundamental difference between seeing objects and seeing facts, which will be discussed next.

10.2.2 Dialectical Philosophy, Bootstrap Philosophy, and Systemic Thinking

From a point of view of dialectical philosophy, nothing is absolute or established for all time. Nothing can resist the unceasing process of construction and deconstruction. *One without the other is poor and, ultimately sterile*, as clearly mentioned by Nicolescu (2002). Holding the self-consistency principle, there now arise great challenging perspectives: indeed, such dialectical philosophy itself is viewed only as a simple reflection inside our concepts; but at the same time, our outside world is viewed also as a complex of *processes* (but not merely a complex of *objects*), where stable objects are undergoing incessant changes. What does this mean?

According to Weinberg (1977), *there is a parallel between the history of the universe and its logical structures.* Such a parallel suggests that the reality of evolution appears from a complex of processes, not only through the emergence of *dynamical* structures *outside* us but also through the creative imagination *inside* us. The parallel perspective of this kind is reasonable because fundamental process dynamics may be found not only in the physical and cosmological history of the universe but also in the history of biological and mental life in our world (Jantsch, 1980).

Since Democritus for over 2000 years, the main interest of Western science has been devoted to recognizing *static* structure, especially based on reductionism, exploring fundamental building blocks of matter on the assumption that the essential properties of matter may be traced back to these fundamental building blocks, and also that the whole may be completely reduced to its parts. According to the reductionism, physical reality has also been reduced to basic laws or even to equations describing the motion of certain entities, just like Newton's equations for macroscopic bodies, Maxwell's equations for electric and magnetic fields, and Schrödinger and Dirac's equations for atomic systems.

Despite the triumphs of these classical physics, *bootstrap philosophy* has emerged against such classical realism during the formation of *quantum mechanics* (see Nicolescu, 2017). Bootstrap means self-consistency, just as "pulling ourselves up by our bootstraps". Whereas the view of classical realism assumed that the fundamental principles of matter may be completely deduced from its components, the bootstrap philosophy considered that nature's laws can be deduced from the demand that they are self-consistent. In other words, the bootstrap assumed that *the part appears simultaneously as the whole.*

In bootstrap, a part plays a role of a whole system, thus it is closely relating to *systemic thinking.* It is very instructive to realize the difference between the view of classical physics and bootstrap or systemic thinking. Encounter with a complex system, the former considers the system as being developed in the ways from the bottom up. The latter, in contrast, implies the simultaneous integration and differentiation, associated with from the bottom-up (or *induction*) and from the top-down (or *deduction),* which can shape the hierarchical levels from both sides.

10.2.3 Single Question Simultaneously Relating to All Other Questions

Now return to the questions raised at the beginning of this section, relating to the question: "What is the Wholeness of Nature?" According to the self-consistency principle, there is no question in itself defined differently from others, for all of the questions have to be understood as different aspects in the emergence of life in Nature. From a recycling process view of life, the entire matter of an organism as well as every single molecule returns to the earth after death, and then is reused for a new life. For all the questions, there will be simply common answers based on the process-centric view of life. The realization of this emerging view of life would require a radically new way of thinking in terms of relationships, patterns, and context (Murase, 1992, 1996, 2000, 2008, 2011, 2018; Bortoft, 1996; Bateson, 2002; Capra & Luisi, 2014).

Let us first think about the question "What is conflict?" Indeed, conflict-whether it is at the individual level or the group level—was previously viewed as a negative meaning relating to a destructive force. There appears, however, the possibility that conflict is not always *destructive,* but even *constructive.* How we deal with conflict would determine whether or not the outcome will be constructive or destructive (Hough & Chaney, 2005; Haidt, 2013, p. 253; Zolli, 2012). The notion of such a dual outcome must be taken into account seriously especially in the current pandemic situations.

Geertz (1973, p. 108) mentioned:

The effort is not to deny the undeniable—that there are unexplained events, that life hurts, or that rain falls upon the just—but to deny that there are inexplicable events, that life is unendurable, and that justice is a mirage.

Now, let us consider the question: "What are Health and Disease?" Usually, medical textbooks define health as the absence of disease and vice versa. Indeed, these definitions rest on the assumption that the two conditions are opposites of each other. There must be, however, an alternative view that health and disease are only different in degree of balance between the *direct action* of the external agent (i.e., the apparent pathogen) and the *indirect reaction* due to the internal *inhibitory* or *facilitatory* factors (i.e., the body's active responsiveness). Searching for a *unified theory*, Selye (1978) proposed the new concept of "diseases of adaptation": that is, different adaptation occurs due to different balanced blends of direct and indirect factors. It is the dynamical process interacting among factors, but not individual factors in isolation that must play an important role in re-organizing diseases of adaptation. But, at this point, we should realize the fact that there is usually a *trade-off* as another dimension of dual outcome: that is, what is adaptive in one situation (e.g., in a short time scale or a certain condition) is less adaptive in another (e.g., in a long time scale or a different condition) (cf. Gilbert, 2009). This is the main reason why most of us have failed to recognize simple rules behind seemingly complex phenomena.

In all these examples—whether we deal with the problems of intra-individual conflict, with those of inter-individual conflict, with those of inter-group conflict, or seemingly conflicting religious notions typical of Buddhism—there appears a unified vision that the dynamical balance between the two extremes must be essential for various kinds of "living" phenomena when we are taking account of time scales and related conditions. Conflict must be, therefore, considered as a driving force for dual outcomes depending on the relationships, patterns, and context. In the next section, we shall discuss healthy cardiac dynamics poised between too much order and total randomness.

10.3 Fractal Dynamics in Physiology: Unpredictable Dynamics as a Hallmark of Healthiness

It has long been assumed that a very steady and regular heartbeat is a sign of healthiness. However, closer inspection shows that variability of the interbeat time interval, even under constant conditions, is not the only characteristic of healthy and not too old persons but that a lack of variability can be an indication of some malfunction.

An Der Heiden, U.
Chaos in Health and Disease: Phenomenology and Theory
In: Self-Organization and Clinical Psychology, 1992, p. 56

According to classical concepts of *homeostasis*, healthy biological organisms are self-regulated to reduce variability and maintain physiological constancy. Contrary to these traditional thoughts, however, a wide range of biological systems show complex dynamics known as *chaos* or *fractal* dynamics (Heiden, 1992; Goldberger, 1996; Goldberger et al., 2002; Murase, 1992).

Figure 10.3 shows 30-min heart rate time series from four subjects. One record is normal (b), the other three represent severe pathologies (a, c, and d). (a) and (c) are from patients in sinus rhythm with severe congestive heart failure. (d) is from a patient with a cardiac arrhythmia, atrial fibrillation, producing an erratic heart rate.

Interestingly, the healthy record (b) is notable for its visually apparent non-stationarity, which is far from a homeostatic equilibrium state. Its characteristics can show self-similar temporal patterns typical of the fractal. Indeed, the concept

Heart Rate Dynamics in Health and Disease: A time Series Test

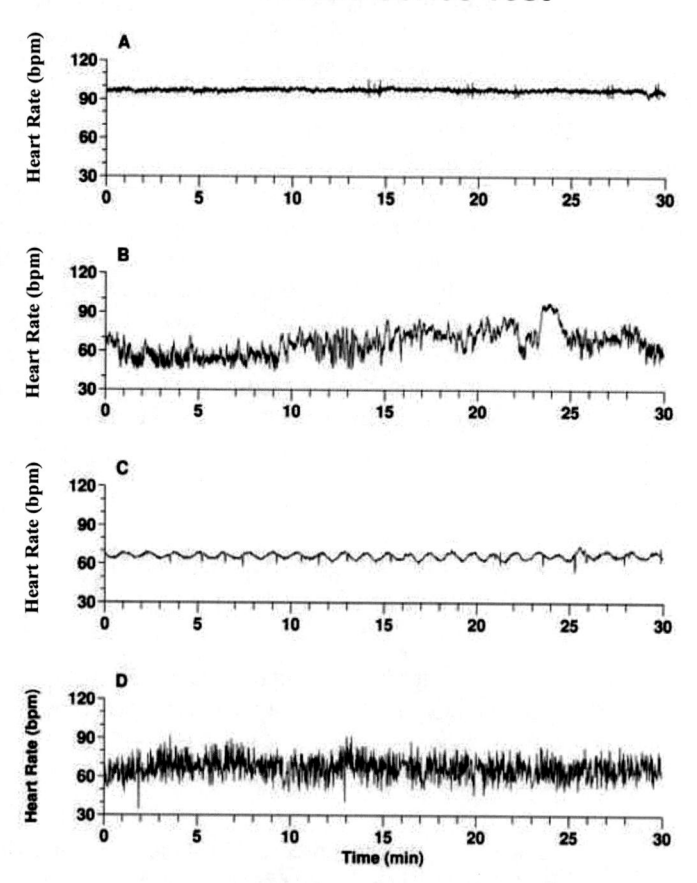

Fig. 10.3 Heart rate patterns of four subjects from (**a**)–(**d**). From Goldberger et al. (2002): Copyright (2002) National Academy of Science, U.S.A.

of fractal was originally developed in association with irregular geometric objects (Mandelbrot, 1977). The most striking property of fractal shapes is that their characteristic patterns are found repeatedly at descending scales as shown by Fig. 10.4 (left). Every part looks like the whole. The fractal concept can be applied to certain complex processes. A fractal temporal process may generate fluctuations on different time scales that are statistically self-similar, just like healthy heart rate as shown in Fig. 10.4 (right).

There arises a question: why is it healthy to be fractal? The healthy function requires adaptability, the capability to respond to unpredictable environments. In

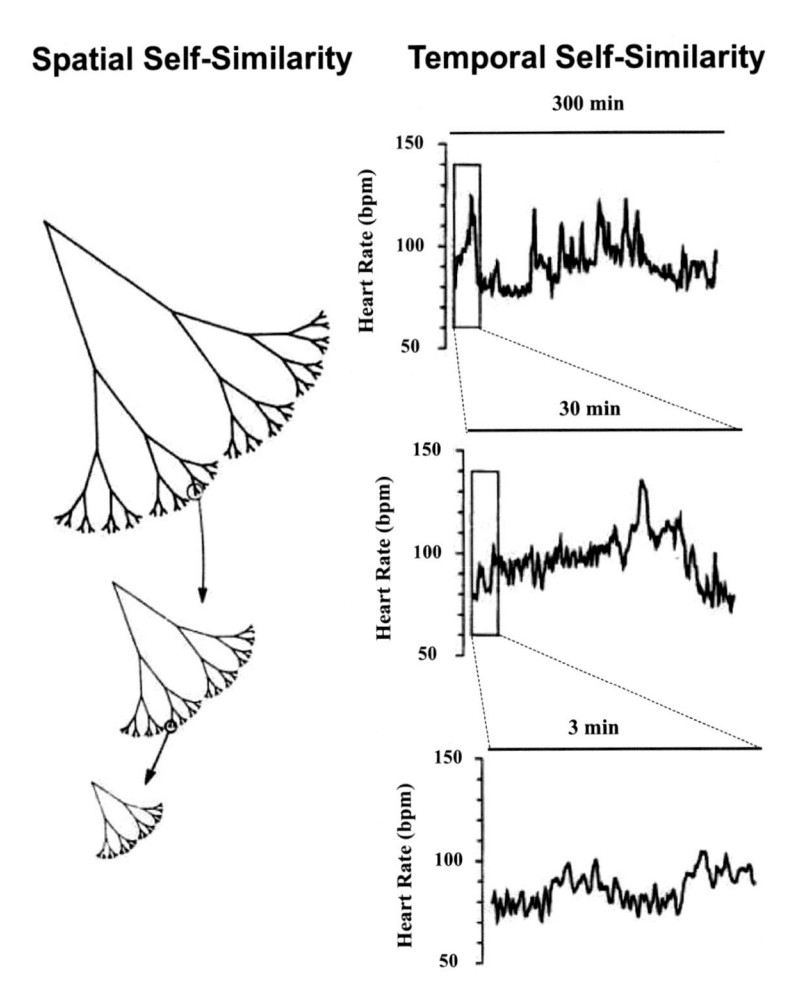

Fig. 10.4 Spatial self-similarity (left) and temporal self-similarity (right). From Goldberger (1996): Copyright (1996) Published by Elsevier Ltd.

response to unpredictable stimuli and stresses, fractal dynamics would generate fluctuations across a wide range of time scales. Such a broad range of responses is necessary for adaptation and *functional plasticity*. Surprisingly, the output of physiological systems often becomes more regular and periodic with disease and aging. Although physiological systems are complex, there appear a certain general explanation independent of their details: that is, whereas loss of complexity must be a hallmark of disease and aging, restoration and/or maintenance of complexity could provide a new framework for therapeutics.

As we realized in Sect. 10.2.3, health and disease are not the opposed physiological states, but they are only different in the degree of fluctuations. Certain degrees of fluctuations must provide us with the adaptability in response to the unpredictable environments, just as the continuous local instability furthers the global stability of the whole system (Jantsch, 1980; Murase, 1992). Based on the fractal nature of our world, the same arguments can be applied to the social, sociocultural, or ecological systems as well, to further sustainability, persistence, and resilience. Because of the limits of our knowledge and foresight, we have to take the possibility and even the necessity in an extreme sense, of failure seriously to sustain Nature and Humanity simultaneously.

10.4   Goethe's Way Toward a New Science How to Perceive the Wholeness of Nature

Almost two hundred years ago, Goethe discovered the historicity of science for himself, expressing it succinctly when he said, "We might venture the statement that the history of science is science itself". He came to this understanding as a result of his struggle with science which had fundamentalist pretensions in his day, i.e., the science of Newton. This understanding makes Goethe our contemporary. We realize now that nature can manifest in more than one way, without needing to argue that one way is more fundamental than another.

Henri Bortoft
The Wholeness of Nature:
Goethe's Way Toward a Science of Conscious Participation in Nature
Lindisfarne Press, New York, 1996

We have just learned, in the previous section, how important it is for living organisms to have a wide range of variabilities in unpredictable environments. The same is true for our perception and our science, to realize emerging problems. Let us think about the following possibility. From a wide range of perspectives, there may be a different science of nature, not contradictory but complementary to modern science. Both can be true, simply because they reveal nature in different ways. Of course, modern science has indeed discovered the *causal order* in nature. It does not mean, however, that it is the only fundamental science toward ultimate reality.

10.4.1   Exact Sensorial Imagination

What is the significance of Goethe's legacy? It is Goethe's alternative methodology that offers a complement to *positivistic* reductionism relating to its fragmented knowledge. Relying on the accuracy of our senses, instead of adopting our intellectual thinking, Goethe's methodology begins with the exact observation of the phenomenon in question: it is what he calls "exact sensorial imagination". The exact sensorial imagination not only involves the observational stage, characterized by an active seeing rather than our habitual passive reception of the object but also contains an *intuitive* and almost *meditative* experience, characterized by an exact image of the object internally until reaching an element and realizing its relationship to others without imposing subjective mental constructs or preconceived theories externally.

Please be reminded of the bootstrap philosophy discussed in Sect. 10.2.2: that is, the properties of any one particle are determined by all the other particles; therefore, every particle is a reflection of all the others. In other words, every particle consists of all other particles. The whole, therefore, cannot simply be the sum of the parts: the whole is reflected in the parts, which in turn contribute to the whole. Perceiving the whole could be possible by going further into the parts instead of by *standing back from them*. This must be a sense of a different kind of *dimension* in nature. Bortoft (1996) mentioned, "it turns out a habitual way of thinking inside out".

Just as there are no independent elementary particles simply interacting with one another through fields of force on the small scale, there are also no independently separate masses on the large scale. We used to think about the universe of matter as being made up of separate and independent masses merely interacting with one another through the force of gravity. However, it is now understood that mass is not an intrinsic property of a body, but instead, it is a reflection of the whole of the rest of the universe in that body. We have been trying to understand the universe by extrapolating from the local environment to the universe as a whole. Reversing the relationship, we would understand the local environment as being the result of the rest of the universe. In the next subsection, we will discuss this perspective.

10.4.2   Ostensive Definition

Goethe's Way toward a New Science seemed to be unusual to most of us. However, we have often appreciated almost the same type of understanding procedure in everyday lives. It is called *ostensive* definition (Bateson, 2002). If a mother says to her small child, "That's what a cat looks like", pointing to the cat. The mother uses the cat as an example of an ostensive definition. After perceiving a few examples, the child begins to recognize cats. Some specific instances become like *mirrors* in which any cats are seen reflected. As Bortoft (1996) mentioned, this process does not involve empirical generalization or *induction* (i.e., abstracting what is common from several cases). The concept of cats is derived directly from the sensory experiences of the child, which is also known as *abduction* given by Charles Peirce (cf. Bateson, 2002).

The same procedure has been used to understand wholeness, which is often unrecognized. Let us begin with a very primitive example. When we see a redwood tree standing up out of the ground, we can also know the roots under the ground. The whole and its parts are closely related to each other, whether or not they are visible. Then, let us think about the *anthropic principle* (*anthropic* comes from the Greek word *anthropos* meaning man). The essential idea of the anthropic principle is that there is a correlation between the emergence of the human on Earth and the physical conditions governing the evolution of the universe (see Nicolescu, 2017).

Such a seemingly strong correlation suggests that if the value of certain physical constants is changed a little, the physical, chemical, and biological conditions, allowing the appearance of human beings on Earth, are no longer satisfied. Likewise, if gravity is too strong or too weak, the formation of planets is impossible. Let us recall Fig. 10.2. A slight change of the object orientation triggered the sudden appearance of the different meanings of the object, which is known as the *phase transition*. As we have experienced the current pandemic and related emerging problems, Nature is full of various phase transitions.

It is a vast self-consistency that seems to govern the evolution of the universe involving galaxies, stars, planets, humanity, quantum world, and even our usual world. Here, we should not recognize the whole as a thing. The whole comes into presence within its parts. Therefore, we cannot encounter the whole in the same way that we encounter the pars, because it is the *emergent whole*. The human being is not the center of our world, for the center is everywhere. Nevertheless, the human being is necessary for the self-consistency of the whole. *Whatever comes into being has to be consistent with itself and everything else.*

10.4.3 The Emergent Whole: Active Absences

Imagine a situation that we read a written text. What is *successful reading*? It is not just a matter of following the words. It is an act of *interpretation* that imparts the real meaning, but it is not an interpretation that puts the biased meaning based on the reader's personality. Now, the question arises: what or where is this meaning?

Thinking of this question, we encountered similar problems discussed above, concerning the relationship between the whole and its parts. The meaning of the text is considered as the whole, which is emerging from all of the text, and even from its any part. This is the reason why we suddenly see meaning all at once in an instant like a phase transition, even if we read a part of the full text. We should not think of the whole of the meaning as if it were a thing, because the whole of the meaning comes into present not only in the full text but in its parts.

This is the experience we go through to understand the meaning of the text. It is also the exact experience we go through in *creative writing*, where the need is to find the "right" expression to let the meaning appear. We now realize the *reciprocal relationship* of part and whole in either case of reading or writing.

Bortoft (1996, p. 14–15) mentioned as follows:

... our everyday awareness is occupied with things. The whole is absent to this awareness because it is not a thing among things. ... The whole becomes present within parts, but from the standpoint of awareness which grasps the external parts, the whole is an absence. This absence, however, is not the same as nothing. Rather, it is an active absence since we do not try to be aware of the whole, as if we could grasp it like a part, but instead let ourselves be open to being moved by the whole.

Whereas we are accustomed to think of going from parts to whole in some sort of summative way, we often understand the whole meaning of the text in advance to read the parts. This is a contradiction to *logic* and the *order of reasoning*. Now, we should begin to understand the whole and the part, the one and the many, the universal and the particular, in a radically new way. Indeed, we used to adopt logical thinking to search for reasoning based on the choice of *either A or not-A*: that is, we must go either from part to whole or from whole to part. However, the paradox arises not only because the whole (or the meaning as a whole) is holistic and an active absence, but also because understanding cannot be reduced to analytical logic (Edwards, 1986; Jullien, 1999). Understanding is not a linear process, but a circular process between the part and the whole (Jantsch, 1980). Because of this "circle" of the reciprocal relationship between the whole and the parts, it is called the *hermeneutic circle* (Bortoft, 1996).

Before ending Sect. 10.4, it is very instructive to reconsider "circle". Indeed, without 'right' perception, we cannot obtain 'right' knowledge. Without 'right' knowledge, however, we cannot have 'right' perception. It is possible that there appear two different kinds of circle: one is vicious circle, and another is virtuous circle or the circle of wholeness. Vicious circle appears and persists as long as we keep a traditional paradigm for a long time, as if it were unchangeable dogma. It seems to be 'undesirable' because there is little possibility for co-existence and co-emergence of differences and oppositions. Ironically, we can hardly consider how we have been trapped in such a vicious circle. It is, therefore, important to distinguish between the two kinds of circle. Only then, we can attack the challenging problem: *How can we transform the vicious circle to virtuous circle?* Please recall the above-mentioned *emergent dynamics*: that is, Goethe's exact sensorial imagination, ostensive definitions, and active absences. Regardless of their details, there appears the common criterion that every single part is consistent with the wholeness and with itself. This must be the circle of wholeness.

10.5 The Self–nonself Circulation Theory of Life

Drawing is full of paradox, as is creativity itself. And dealing with paradox requires that one be able to hold in the mind simultaneously two diametrically opposed ideas

... One must search outside oneself for whatever is related to the first insight, testing confidence in the rightness of the initial question or insight by constantly checking information for *fit*. But at the same time, one must acquiesce to being completely unsure of the next move, or in fact of the whole process.

Betty Edwards
"Drawing on the Artist Within", p. 134
Simon & Schuster, Inc. New York, 1986

The present scientific thinking is often described as 'Western', for it is based on ancient Greek thought. A clear distinction between subject and object is characteristic to the so-called Western scientific paradigm. It is assumed that we obtain knowledge about a given natural object in strict isolation from other objects and from ourselves as perceiving subjects. This is our scientific world picture. How accurate a world picture does this present?

François Jullien (1999, p. 11) offers us a good summary of our present situation:

We start with a distinction. On the one hand there is the disposition of things—their condition, configuration, and structure. On the other there is force and movement. The static versus the dynamic. But this dichotomy, like all dichotomies, is abstract. It is a temporary means for the mind to represent reality, one that simplifies as it illuminates. The question we should thus ask is: ... How can we conceive of the dynamic in terms of the static, in terms of "disposition"? Or, to put it another way, how can any static situation be simultaneously conceived in terms of historical movement?

Let us think about the serious paradox: knowing everything and nothing at the same time. This implies spirituality essential to the Eastern world. In our daily lives, the spirituality of this kind seems to be very useful, not only because there seems to be too many oppositions in our world, but also because we have to realize the notion of such dual outcome merely depending on the combination of various contexts. This is the reason why the essential nature of *Buddhism* in Eastern world cannot be found in abstract thought, nor dogma, but only in the immensity of its movement and development (Govinda, 2002). Depending on how we handle conflict or opposition, there could appear constructive and/or destructive outcome.

By moving away from the traditional scientific world picture, therefore, we take part in an evolving and dynamic process in which knowledge is produced through the interaction between thinking subject and observed objects. The dialectical process that results is common both to the history of scientific evolution and the history of development in an individual's life cycle.

Fig. 10.5 *Yin-Yang* symbol

The ancient Chinese philosophers believed that the ultimate reality is intrinsically dynamic. It was called *Tao*: that is, the path or the process of the universe (Puett, 2016). For example, as shown in Fig. 10.5, *yin* and *yang* refer to any pair of seemingly opposing forces that are complementary and interdependent. God and devil are not enemies, nor are good and bad, day and night, male and female. We need both, often in an alternating balance (Haidt, 2013). According to Stephen Hill, furthermore, *yin* and *yang* are continuously transitioning into each other as the symbol suggested. This immediately allows us an alignment with the dialectic, where the antithesis emerges out of the thesis, rather than is an opposing 'attacking' force. This matters enormously if we try to understand social change: there is an intrinsic *emerging weakness* within the thesis or system from which change will occur. Such a weakness turns out to be constructive!

The Self–nonself Circulation theory (Murase, 2000, 2018) is illustrated in Fig. 10.6. A self (or a subject) has its own consciousness and unconsciousness mind. Likewise, a nonself (or an object) has its actuality in the visible world and its latency in the invisible world. The dynamic interactions between the self and nonself are conducted by the 5 successive processes:

① Negation, ② Expansion, ③ Convergence, ④ Transference, and ⑤ Emergence.

From the first characters of each name, it is called *5-NECTE Principle* (Murase et al., 2021). We shall discuss how the NECTE Principle works in the final Section. Note that the essential features of this theory, as illustrated in the bottom panel of Fig. 10.6, involve the dynamics of *yin-yang* symbol shown in Fig. 10.5.

In Fig. 10.6, we can realize that there are both horizontal and vertical bidirectional relationships. It is true that the hypothesis can turn into reality through complex evolutionary dynamics. This means that mental anticipation can pull the future into the present. The direction of causality thus seems to be reversed, which evokes the deductive process. As time proceeds in inductive ways, we have an example of circular dynamics between present (or past) and future, as shown by the top-down as well as bottom-up arrows in Fig. 10.6. We now realize that there are two different kinds of bidirectional relationships between the oppositions: one is the horizontal circulation, and another is the vertical circulation. Therefore, the essence of the dynamics in Fig. 10.6 can be represented by the coupled dynamics of *yin-yang* symbols as illustrated in Fig. 10.7.

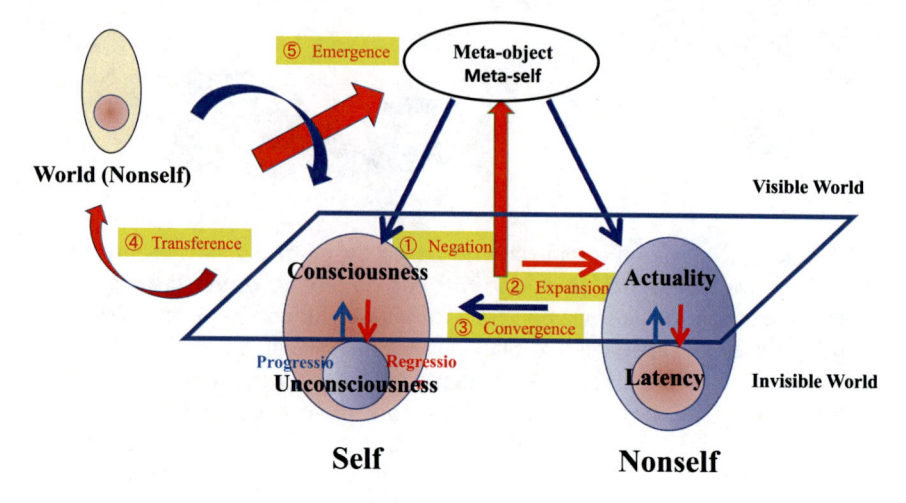

Fig. 10.6 The self–nonself circulation theory

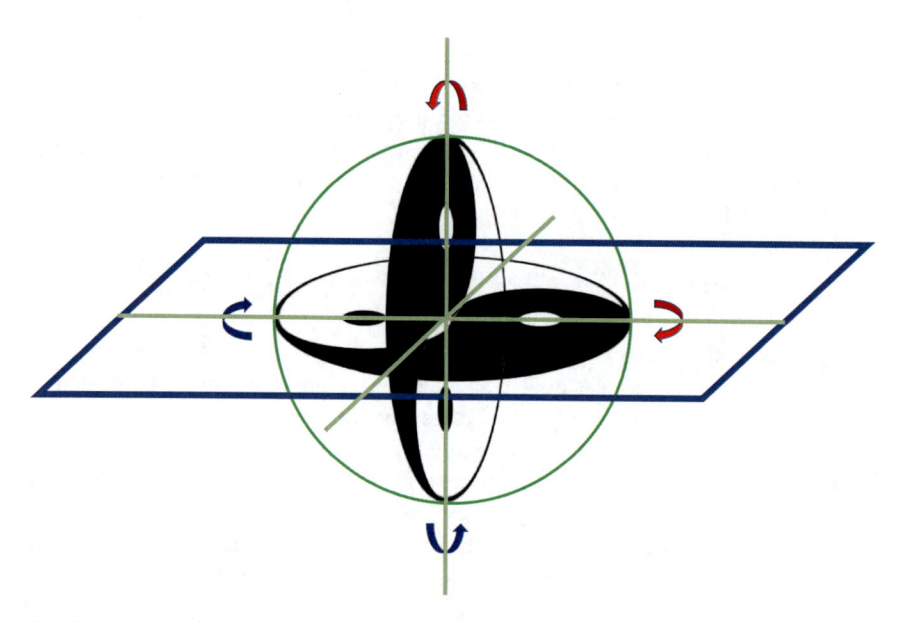

Fig. 10.7 The coupled dynamics of *yin-yang* symbols

10.6 A New Synthesis: Toward an Integrated View of Being, Evolving and Learning

Human nature was produced by natural selection working at two levels simultaneously. Individuals compete with individuals within every group, and we are the descendants of primates who excelled at that competition. · · · But human nature was also shaped as groups competed with other groups. As Darwin said long ago, the most cohesive and cooperative groups generally beat the groups of selfish individualists. · · · We're not always selfish hypocrites. We also have the ability, under special circumstances, to shut down our petty selves and become like cells in a larger body, or like bees in a hive, working for the good of the group.

Jonathan Haidt
"The Righteous Mind: Why Good People Are Divided by Politics and Religion"
p. xvi

Penguin Books, New York, 2013

It is now clear that the self–nonself circulation theory—characterized by the 5-NECTE principle—provides a useful model not only for understanding the dynamics of living cells and the origin of life (Murase, 2000, 2008, 2018), but also for realizing the co-existence or being of the self and nonself in a circulation way (Murase et al., 2021).

In the present Sect. 10.6, let us explore how the 5-NECTE principle works conduct evolving and learning processes.

10.6.1 *Evolutionary Processes Conducted by the 5-NECTE Principle*

In 1959, Charles Darwin published "On the Origin of Species", by which he provided the evolutionary theory based on natural selection. Interestingly, the underlying dynamics turned out to be conducted by the 5 NECTE Processes, although it is necessary to reframe the terminology of each process. Figure 10.8 illustrates how the 5-NECTE principle works during the evolution of species.

① Negation is relating to the occurrence of mutation at the level of individual organisms. After the mutation, ② Expansion of many different kinds of organisms occur. Then, some of the organisms disappear due to the maladaptation to the environment, leading to ③ Convergence. When the remaining organisms change their habitats from say sea to land, and from land to sky. This is the case of ④ Transference. Finally, new species would appear, known as the process of ⑤ Emergence.

Ironically, we should realize here that the COVID-19 pandemic is also the evolutionary processes conducted by the same 5-NECTE principle. From a virus-oriented perspective, of course, there appears the *virtuous circle* at the level of virus-human relationships. From a human-oriented perspective, however, this must be exactly the case of the vicious circle. *The same principle serves as a double-edged sword!* This is the main reason why we should learn based on the same 5-NECTE principle.

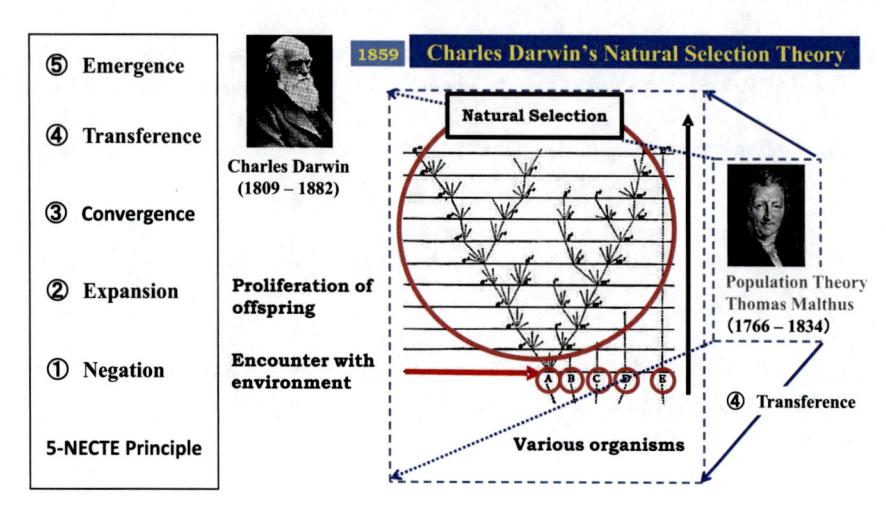

Fig. 10.8 Evolution conducted by NECTE Principle

10.6.2 Learning as an Evolution Process Conducted by NECTE Principle

It is very exciting to realize that the same 5-NECTE principle would conduct the quite different dynamics such as learning and evolution. This means that the 5-NECTE principle could be understood as the scale-invariant principle among the diverse life

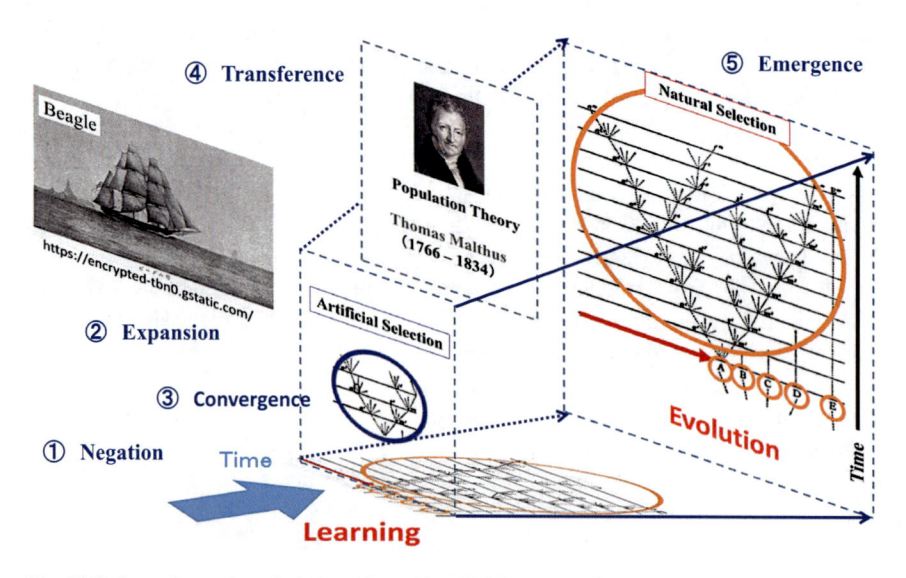

Fig. 10.9 Learning and evolution conducted by NECTE principle

phenomena. Figure 10.9 shows that the leaning process by Charles Darwin and his theory of evolution are both conducted by NECTE Principle.

① Negation, often known as *unlearning*, of preexisting perspectives is required for developing new theories of biological evolution. ② Expansion of perspectives is also important for understanding the essential features of biological phenomena through the accumulation of vast knowledge. ③ Convergence of a particular hypothesis among the collected perspectives is required. Then, ④ Transference of the hypothesis between the different discipline is important, which is called as *learning of transfer*. Finally, ⑤ Emergence of the new theory occurs.

The dynamics of all these NECTE processes would be found in the evolutionary as well as learning processes, which is not so surprised because both are biological processes. Again, we should realize how the same principle serves as a double-edged sword: there appear both the virtuous and vicious circles even at our learning processes. The remaining problem is how we can contribute to develop the circle of wholeness.

10.6.3 Beyond Glocalization: Advanced Future Studies

Almost 15 years ago, the Vice-president Toshio Yokoyama of Kyoto University let us know the importance of paradoxical term *Glocalization*: that is, *think globally and act locally*. The Glocalization is somewhat different from the *Global Localism* developed by Stephen Hill. Whereas Global Localism emphasizes the developmental process, in which social or environmental change happens from local or community action; Glocalization emphasizes the power of paradox, through which we can keep both the global perspective and local action at the same time being necessary for inventing the future.

In 2015, Masatoshi Murase developed *the International Research Unit of Advanced Future Studies at Kyoto University* and developed a *Grand Unified Theory of Life* in the book (Japanese Edition), which was co-edited with President Juichi Yamagiwa of Kyoto University and was published in 2020. What we need is the methods of how to develop the concepts reliable to the future. Murase suggested that one of the methods can be the self–nonself circulation theory involving the 5-NECTE principle. That is, it is true that Glocalization means *think globally and act locally*. However, we should *think globally and think locally or intensively*, and also we should *act globally through multiple connective methods and act locally at School, University, and even at Home*.

This kind of consideration must be especially important based on the consistency principle, because as we discussed in the above Sections, there are common dynamics among being, becoming (or evolving) and learning. All the dynamics must be kept in polyphony. Only then, there appears the circle of wholeness. Sander and Murase (2021) suggested that the present is constructed by interaction between past and future. Here, we should consider ourselves and our world at the same time. It is true that no one could any longer assume that the structures in the universe were built up one-sidedly, bottom up, from elementary particles and atoms to stars, galaxies and so on (Jantsch, 1980). There must be a mutual co-evolution of the conditions for simultaneous differentiation and complexification between the microscopic and macroscopic levels of co-evolution.

Through such meta-evolution or self-transcendental dynamics, a novel mental system may emerge within an individual person. As indicated by Murase (2018, Fig. 13 on p. 278), the individual person carries the additional dimensions in the form of the macro-world within oneself. Societies could then enter into a new phase such as coevolution with themselves (Jantsch, 1980). This leads to the reversal of the time series typical of Western thinking, because humans can imagine and plan. The plan can turn into reality through advancement of science and technology, meaning that *mental anticipation can pull the future into the present*. The direction of causality is reversed, which evokes the deductive process. As time proceeds in inductive ways, we have an example of circular dynamics between present (or past) and future.

Maatoshi Murase have founded the new course "*Introduction to Advanced Future Studies: From the Philosophical Foundation of Natural Science to the Artistic Expansion of Psychology*" for graduate students at Kyoto University since 2018.

Acknowledgements The authors would like to thank to Prof. Stephen Hill for his intensive efforts on careful reading of this manuscript and giving us an invaluable comments and suggestions.

References

Bateson, G. (2002). *Mind and nature: A necessary unit*. Hampton Press Inc., Cresskill, USA. (Originally Dutton edition published 1979).

Bortoft, H. (1996). *The wholeness of nature: Goethe's way toward a science of conscious participation in nature*. Lindisfarne Press.

Cannon, W. B. (1929). Organization for physiological homeostasis. *Physiological Reviews, 9*, 399–431.

Capra, F., & Luisi, P. L. (2014). *The systems view of life: A unifying vision*. Cambridge University Press.

Edwards, B. (1986). *Drawing on the artist within*. Simon & Schuster, Inc.

Feinberg, T. E. (2001). *Altered egos: How the brain creates the self*. Oxford University Press.

Francis, P. (2020). *Let us dream: The path to a better future*. Simon & Shuster.

Geertz, C. (1973). *The interpretation of cultures: Selected essays*. Basic Books Inc.

Gilbert, S. F. (2009). *Ecological developmental biology: Integrating epigenetics, medicine, and evolution*. Sinauer Associates Inc., Sunderland, USA.

Goldberger, A. L. (1996). Non-linear dynamics for clinicians: Chaos theory, fractals, and complexity at the bedside. *Lancet, 347*, 1312–1314.

Goldberger, A. L., Amaral, L. A., Hausdort, J. M., Ivanov, P. C., Peng, C. -K., & Stanley, H. -E. (2002). Fractal dynamics in physiology: Alterations with disease and aging. *PNAS, 99*, 2466–2472.

Gottwald, F.-T. (2002). Life—a problem inherent in the research context. In H.-P. Dürr, F.-A. Popp, & W. Schommers (Eds.), *What is life? Scientific approaches and philosophical positions* (pp. 25–37). World Scientific.

Govinda, L. A. (2002). *Foundations of Tibetan mysticism*. Martino Publishing.

Haidt, J. (2013). *The righteous mind: Why good people are divided by politics and religion*. Penguin Books.

Heiden, U. A. (1992). Chaos in health and disease: Phenomenology and theory. In W. Tschacher, G. Schipek, & E. J. Brunner (Eds.), *Self-organization and clinical psychology* (vol. 58, pp. 55–87). Springer Series in Synergetics.

Hough, L., & Chaney, S. (2005). Chapter 10: Thomas' conflict theory. In S. M. Ziegler (Ed.), *Theory-directed nursing practice* (2nd ed., pp. 223–246). Springer.

John, D. (2017). Portrait of an artist today. http://www2.yukawa.kyoto-u.ac.jp/~future/news/201 60604-1.html. Last accessed 4 June 2017.

Jantsch, E. (1980). *The self-organizing universe: Scientific and human implications of the emerging paradigm of evolution.* Pergamon Press, Oxford.

Jullien, F. (1999). *The propensity of things: Toward a history of efficacy in Chin* (J. Lloyd, Trans.). Zone Books, New York.

Lorenz, K. (1973). *Behind the mirror: A search for a natural history of human knowledge* (R. Taylor, Trans.). Methuen and Co Ltd., London.

Mandelbrot, B. B. (1977). *The fractal geometry of nature.* W.H. Freeman and Company, New York.

Medows, D. (2008). Thinking in systems: A primer. Chelsea Green Publishing, White River Junction, USA.

Murase, M. (1992). *The dynamics of cellular motility.* John Wiley & Sons.

Murase, M. (1996). Alzheimer's disease as subcellular 'Cancer': The scale-invariant principles underlying the mechanisms of aging. *Progress of Theoretical Physics, 95*(1), 1–36.

Murase, M. (2000). *Life as history: The construction of self-nonself circulation theory* (pp 369–376). Kyoto University Press, Kyoto (in English). https://repository.kulib.kyoto-u.ac.jp/dspace/bitstream/2433/49765/1/Murase2000b2.pdf. (in Japanese).

Murase, M. (2008). Environmental pollution and health: An interdisciplinary study of the bioeffects of electromagnetic fields. *SANSAI, An Environmental Journal for the Global Community, 3,* 1–35.

Murase, M. (2018). A self-similar dynamic systems perspective of "Living" nature: The self-nonself circulation principle beyond complexity. In S. Yamash'ta, T. Yagi, & S. Hill (Eds.), *The Kyoto Manifesto for global economics the platform of community, humanity, and spirituality* (pp. 257–283). Springer.

Murase, M., & Murase, T. (2020). A grand unified life theory: An extension of the self-nonself circulation theory. *Journal of Integrated Creative Studies.* https://doi.org/10.14989/259183.

Murase, M., & Tsuda, I. (Eds.), (2008). What is life? The next 100 years of Yukawa's dream. *Progress of Theoretical Physics Supplement, 173,* 1–370.

Murase, M., Mori, A., & Murase, M. (2021). Chapter 22: A unified theory and practice of creative complex systems: challenging to the systemic problems spanning the inside and outside world. In: K. Nishimura, M. Murase, Kazuyoshi, Yoshimura (Eds.), *Creative Complex Systems* (pp.373–424). Springer-Nature.

Nicolescu, B. (2002). *Manifesto of Transdisciplinarity (Suny Series in Western Esoteric Traditions).* State University of New York Press.

Piaget, J. (1950). *The psychology of intelligence (M. Piercy & E. E. Berlin, Trans.).* Routledge.

Puett, M., & Gross-Loh, C. (2016). *The path: What Chinese philosophers can teach us about the good life.* Simon & Schuster Paperbacks.

Schrödinger, E. (1958). *Mind and matter.* Cambridge University Press.

Selye, H. (1978). *The stress of life.* McGraw-Hill Paperbacks.

Servigne, P., & Stevens, R. (2015). Comment tout peut s'effondrer: Petit manuel de collapsologie à l'usage des générations présentes.

Solso, R. L. (1996). *Cognition and the visual arts.* The MIT Press.

Taleb, N. N. (2007). *The black Swan: The impact of the highly improbable.* Penguin.

van der Leeuw, S. E., & Murase, M. (2021). Chapter 21: Ignorance, creation, destruction. In K. Nishimura, M. Murase, Kazuyoshi, Yoshimura (Eds.), *Creative complex systems* (pp. 351–372). Springer-Nature.

Varela, F. J., Thompson, E., & Rosch, E. (1991). *The embodied mind.* The MIT Press.

Weinberg, S. (1977). *The first three minutes: A modern view of the origin of the universe*. Basic Books.

Zolli, A., & Healy, A. M. (2012). *Resilience: Why things bounce back*. Simon and Schuster.

Masatoshi Murase received his Ph.D. degree from The University of Tokyo in 1987. Since 1992, he has been an associate professor at the Yukawa Institute for Theoretical Physics, Kyoto University. In 1987 and 1988 he was a visiting scientist at the Duke University Medical Center, USA. Since 2010, he has been a member of the Cooperation Promotion Committee of the International Research Unit of Integrated Complex System Science, Kyoto University. Between 2015 and 2020 he was a director of the Research Promotion Strategy Office of the International Research Unit of Advanced Future Studies, Kyoto University.

Tomoko Murase graduated from the School of Nursing at Chiba University, Japan, in 1985 and received a Master's degree from Chiba University in 1987. In 1987, she became an assistant professor at the Japanese Red Cross College in Tokyo, Japan. She was a lecturer at the Japanese Red Cross College in Tokyo from 1989–1991, Between 1991 and 1993, she was a visiting researcher at the University of Tokyo (Division of Health Science and Nursing, Department of medicine). After spending almost 10 years for caring Children, she entered the doctoral course of the Graduate School at Chiba University and got Ph.D. in 2010. In 2011, she became an associate professor of the Faculty of Nursing, Himeji University at Himeji, Japan, and in 2012, she became a professor and Dean of Nursing at Himeji University. In 2013, she was a professor of the School of Nursing at Japanese Red Cross Toyota College of Nursing, Japan. Since 2016, she has been a Dean of School of Nursing at this College.

Chapter 11
The Self-nonself Circulation Principle of "Living" Nature: How to Survive Shattered World

Masatoshi Murase and Tomoko Murase

Abstract The present paper challenges the traditional concepts in our daily lives. That is, when we are surviving our shattered world, we cannot realize how we are deeply influenced by the traditional way of Western thinking. The reason may be very simple: owing to the dichotomy of subject (or endo or self) and object (or exo or nonself), together with its corresponding reductionism, Western science has been so dominant in our daily lives. We usually consider that opposites are mutually exclusive and even contradictory.

What is Life? Besides this problem, there is another problem that we cannot realize how we are deeply influenced by the traditional way of Western thinking in attacking the problem of life. Owing to the dichotomy of subject (or endo or self) and object (or exo or nonself), together with its corresponding reductionism, Western science has specified more and more the detailed components of a living system and has also required the reproducibility principle that the living system shows the same responses to the same stimuli under the same conditions. A dichotomy perspective of this kind, which has been central to modern science, stands on the assumption that opposites are mutually exclusive and even contradictory.

M. Murase (✉)
Yukawa Institute for Theoretical Physics (YITP), Kyoto University, Kyoto, Japan
e-mail: murase@yukawa.kyoto-u.ac.jp

International Research Unit of Advanced Future Studies (IRU-AFS), Kyoto University (2015–2020), Kyoto, Japan

International Research Unit of Integrated Complex System Science (IRU-ICSS), Kyoto University, Kyoto, Japan

T. Murase
Japanese Red Cross Toyota College of Nursing, Toyota, Japan
e-mail: tmurase@rctoyota.ac.jp

M. Murase · T. Murase
2021 Project of Challenges of Advanced Future Studies, Kokoro Research Center, Kyoto University, Kyoto, Japan

S. Hill et al. (eds.), *The Kyoto Post-COVID Manifesto For Global Economics*, Creative Economy, https://doi.org/10.1007/978-981-16-8566-8_11

Contrary to this dichotomy perspective, there is an alternative complementarity perspective typical of Eastern philosophy. It suggests that opposites are not mutually exclusive, but merely complementary to one another in such a way that opposites are only different aspects of the same wholeness. This means that there is no clear distinction between subject (or endo or self) and object (or exo or nonself). As there is no definitely isolated object, we must pay much attention to the transients—or processes—during the history of life and even the present moment.

Based on this complementarity idea, we are encouraged to have a holistic view by integrating fragments of knowledge at various component levels and time scales throughout life phenomena including their evolutionary and/or developmental histories. Along these lines, a process of self-nonself circulation is considered as a radically new conception of life. As a living organism is engaged in challenges from both its internal and external environments, it contains unlimited conflicts and oppositions, which in turn must be the driving force for its evolution and development. It is such reconstructive dynamics that can give rise to an identity of the living organism. The resultant identity of life is represented by the Eastern image of the Mandala as an emergent symbol generated by the process of self-nonself circulation.

11.1 Systemic Thinking of Life for Approaching Systemic Problem in the World

As science has increasingly adopted a systems perspective in investigation and analysis, the understanding has emerged that our mental and emotional functions stem from the activity of *systems*—organized pathways interconnecting different organs and areas of the brain and body—just as do any of our physiological functions. Moreover, our mental and emotional systems cannot be considered in isolation from our physiology. Instead, they must be viewed as an integral part of the dynamic, communicative network of interacting functions that comprise the human organism.

Rollin McCraty, et al.
"The Coherent Heart: Heart-Brain Interactions, Psychophysiological
Coherence, and the Emergence of System-Wide Order", p. 19
Integral Review, Vol. 5, 2009.

In science, the integrative way of thinking is called "systemic thinking" or "systems thinking" (Capra & Luisi, 2014). Note that the emerging problems within us, around us, and without us are all interconnected and interdependent, characterized as systemic problems. There arises, therefore, the only way that we should apply the systemic thinking to approach systemic problems, just like the easy case of fighting like with like.

Why should we take a systemic approach to systemic problems? To answer this question, let us reconsider the notion of "system". A system is no longer considered as a complex structure involving merely interconnected characteristics. Rather, a system itself is evolving through the interplay between differentiation and integration dynamics, which reveals ever new dimensions of novelty and exchange with the environment. Of course, it must keep its self-identity. Otherwise, we cannot understand what we observe. Ironically, this is the exact point how we have often failed to recognize the systemic problems, for they seem to have a little identity at their origins.

Such a system is just like life, or the whole as an active absence. In other words, the emerging problems behave like living systems, and therefore, it is difficult to predict their behaviors. This is the reason why we have to take a systemic and evolutionary approach for the emerging and evolving systemic problems. The systemic thinking and systemic problems are merely different aspects of the emerging wholeness, which can be described as *the circle of wholeness.*

11.1.1 Active Absence: A Complementary View to Western Scientific Reductionism

The previous section discussed that the whole meaning of the text comes into presence within its parts, and that, from the standpoint of our everyday awareness, the whole is an absence. We cannot recognize the whole as a thing, because it is emerging only when we have open eyes. For this reason, the whole is an active absence. Similar discussions are available in so many different situations involving systemic problems and systemic thinking.

Let us consider for instance the question: where is cellular life located? When we look at particular composite molecules within a cell, the cellular life is absent, after all, they are only nonliving things (Murase, 1996). It turns out that life is not localized, but globally distributed. Cellular life is an emergent property, which is arising from the collective interactions of the molecules in the cell. This is true not only for the simple cell but for any other living organisms. Life is, thus, considered as an emergent property, which is not present in the parts, but instead arises only when the parts are together (Capra & Luisi, 2014; Murase, 1996). Western scientific reductionism has failed to answer the question: "What is life?" because life is an emergent property and thus an active absence.

11.1.2 Active Absence: The Enacting of a Play Familiar to Eastern Philosophy

The enacting of a play provides another example of active absence. The play is constructed well only when the whole play comes into presence within the parts, where actors encounter the play through their roles. However, actors do not encounter the play whenever they rely on intellectual knowledge as an object. Once actors encounter the play in their part as an active absence, it can in turn begin to move them. Instead of actors, the play itself is becoming the origin of the acting. When this happens, an actor no longer acts the play, but rather the actor is to be acted by the play. The play is thus emerging as a whole, not as an objective something but as an active absence (Bortoft, 1996). This is the main reason why most of us have often failed to understand the ultimate reality of Nature, just as the beginners have often failed to achieve the ultimate skills of the play.

Because of the self-consistency principle, it is not surprising for us to encounter the "homologous" arguments concerning the nature of mind and consciousness. Many cognitive scientists indeed agree that the notion of "I" is again an active absence, or in other words, an emergent property, as it is arising from the simultaneous appearance and resonance of memories, feelings, and thoughts. "I" is organized without a center, but not is localized anywhere (Capra & Luisi, 2014).

Now we shall realize that "novel" problems, whether they are benefits or risks, are again active absence or emergent phenomena. They cannot be ascribed to the individual parts when we observe the parts in our usual way.

11.2 Information Dynamics: From Sequential Processing to Context Dependence

The relationship between subject and object is explained most effectively with the help of the circle of function. It shows how subject and object fit together and form a methodical whole. Imaging that a subject is tied to the same or several objects via the circle of function, allows for an insight into the first basic principle of environmental teaching: all animal subjects, the most simple as well as the most complex, fit perfectly into their environments. The most simple animal is equated to a simple environment, the most complex to a respectively varied one.

Quoted from Franz-Theo Gottwald
Life: A Problem Inherent in the Research Context, p. 33.
In: What is Life? Scientific Approaches and Philosophical Positions
World Scientific, 2002.

11.2.1 Visual Pathways of the Brain

It was believed in the 1970s that the information is transferred in a one-way direction sequentially like a chain of command. Figure 11.1a shows the sequential way in the visual pathways of the brain. Here, visual information enters through the eyes and is relayed sequentially via the thalamus called the lateral geniculate nucleus to the visual cortex. The information in the visual cortex is then sent to other parts of the cortex for higher-order processing in the brain.

Fig. 11.1 Connections in the visual pathway of the brain: **a** sequential pathway; **b** interactive pathway

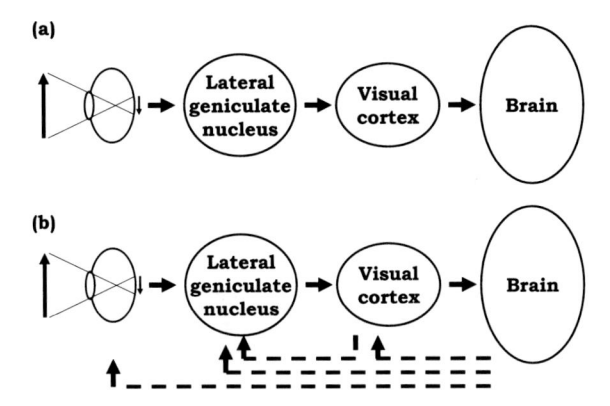

According to the animal experiments by Varela et al. (1991), it was investigated how neurons in the visual cortex respond to specific visual stimuli. When an animal was anesthetized, a simple stimulus–response relationship was observed in such a highly controlled 'internal' and 'external' environment. The animal was next studied without the use of an anesthetic, under rather more usual conditions. In this case, the animal was awake and able to move. It turned out that the same visual stimulation gives rise to different neural responses in the primary visual cortex. The change in response to the same stimulus occurred because a small change in the animal's posture took place. In other words, the animal's responses were highly "context-dependent". This experiment demonstrates that seemingly remote motion is in resonance with sensation. This revises our understanding of the sequential pathways of the brain, and also suggests that mind and body are a unified whole like the highly cooperative system.

Figure 11.1b illustrates the visual pathways of the brain as they are understood today. The lateral geniculate nucleus is now shown embedded within the brain network. It is receiving information not only from the eyes but also from the visual cortex and other parts of the cortex, as indicated by broken lines. This interactive pathway model offers a better description of reality than the sequential information-processing model that was originally thought about as a brain function.

Because of the complex networks in the brain, there seems to be the constitution principle: if a region A connects to B, then B connects reciprocally back to A. This principle holds not only for the subsystems of the brain but also at the descending and ascending levels of connections among various subsystems. The resulting dense interconnections among various components in the brain give rise to both coherence and cooperation within the system: what a local component within a given subsystem does depend on what all the other components of all the subsystems are doing. Here, we have encountered the self-consistency principle again. Viewing the brain as a nested hierarchy of interconnected subsystems, we could understand 'mind' as emergent dynamics, which extends beyond the material brain. In the next subsection, we will discuss how the nested hierarchy appears from the non-nested hierarchy.

11.2.2 *From Non-nested to Nested Hierarchy*

There are two different types of hierarchies: non-nested and nested hierarchy. Let us first consider the non-nested hierarchy. Figure 11.2 represents a typical non-nested hierarchy, in which a pyramidal or inverse tree-type structure is shown with a clear-cut top and bottom. The top and bottom ends of the hierarchical structure remain independent, though the neighboring levels of the hierarchy connect directly. Five elements from 1 to 5 appear at the bottom ends and three nodes are assigned a series of numbers, denoted by 12, 34, and 345. The top end is assigned by 12,345. The assigned numbers indicate the geometrical structure of the non-nested hierarchy.

Since the various levels of a non-nested hierarchy are not closely connected, information transmits unidirectionally either from the top to the bottom or from the bottom to the top (see Feinberg, 2001; Ichikawa, 2001). Note that one simple example of a non-nested hierarchy is the sequential pathway diagram depicted in Fig. 11.1a.

An alternative framework is offered by the nested hierarchy model. What are the differences between nested and non-nested hierarchies? Fig. 11.3 helps us realize the differences by showing how we can construct a nested hierarchy from a non-nested hierarchy. Figure 11.3a shows the non-nested hierarchy depicted in Fig. 11.2,

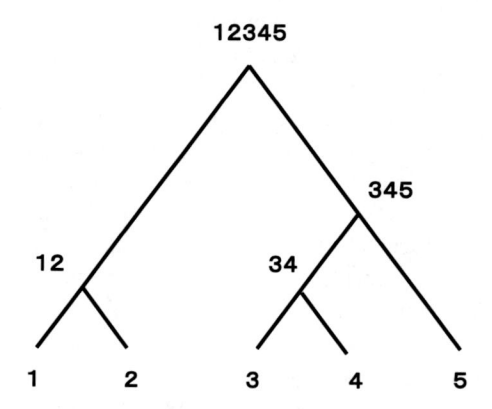

Fig. 11.2 The non-nested hierarchical model

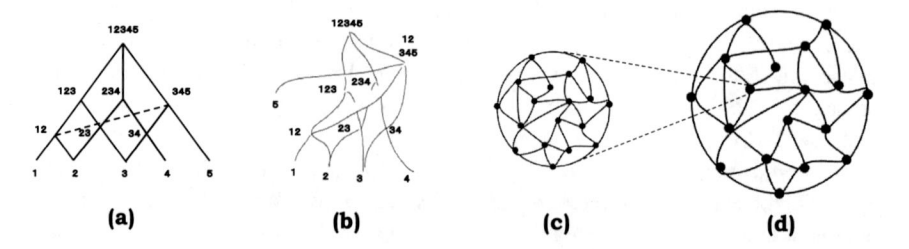

Fig. 11.3 Transformation of a non-nested hierarchy to nested hierarchy: **a** A non-nested hierarchy; **b** Deformed structure; **c** A nested whole; **d** A nested hierarchy

where each element (or node) ordinarily connects with its nearest neighbor *only* at the next hierarchical level. If an intra-level connection takes place—as shown by the broken line connecting node 12 and node 345—the structure begins to transform. Figure 11.3b shows this state.

The more the number of connections among the elements increases, the more the pyramidal structure becomes deformed. Finally, the fine pyramidal structure collapses, and instead, the now-nested whole appears as shown in Fig. 11.3c. Here, the elements composing the lower levels of the original non-nested hierarchy are connected or nested within higher levels. An increasingly complex whole emerges without top nor bottom. There is no unidirectional command pathway at all, for control within this nested whole is embodied within itself.

Let us remember the constitution principle at this point. If *A* connects to *B*, and *B* connects reciprocally back to *A*, as we saw in Fig. 11.1b, we might expect each component of our nested whole to connect not only with neighboring components but also to the different components of different subsystems. It is now clear, as shown in Fig. 11.3c and d, that nested whole connects with other nested whole through repeated cycles of connection and collapse, resulting at last in the construction of a complex nested hierarchy. There appears to be the circle of wholeness, again.

We have seen how transformation appears from non-nested hierarchy to nested whole to nested hierarchy. While each level of a non-nested hierarchy is physically independent of all higher and lower levels and the control of the hierarchy transmit unidirectionally, the various levels of a nested hierarchy are composed of each other and the control of the hierarchy is embodied within the entire hierarchical system (see Feinberg, 2001; Ichikawa, 2001). This seems to be the case of life because any living organism is a nested hierarchy within which every part of its system is connected and interdependent.

The brain is considered a deep connection with the mind, while both connect with everything involving the environment that makes up life. The mind cannot be reduced to the physical, material brain, just as life cannot be reduced to mere physical and material substances. In the nested hierarchy of mind and body, the immaterial mind can cause material events to happen in the brain and body while the opposite is also true: bodily events can influence the mind. There is, in short, no clear distinction between mind and body. Mind and matter are the same. This must be instructive as follows.

Let us recall again the constitution principle. We have realized that an additional increase in the number of physical connections leads to the nested hierarchy via the nested whole, which could give rise to emergent properties like "mind". If this is true, then the reciprocal relationship is also true, as mentioned above. Let us think about this issue from a point of view of neuroscience. It is well acknowledged that neuroplasticity—the change of connectedness between functioning neurons—occurs depending on the use or disuse of neurons.

Surprisingly, physical practices and/or mental attention or focusing are all the sources of such neural plasticity. Relying on such neural plasticity as medical methodology, Doidge (2016) has shown that *many brain problems thought to be incurable or irreversible can be improved, often radically, and in several cases cured.* It seemed to be a miracle, because it was thought that *the brain, unlike other organs, could not repair itself or restore lost functions.*

Here, we can find out the key feature of how to recover the lost functions at different levels of different organizations such as social systems, education systems, economics, politics, and so on, for we can now realize the self-consistency as a guiding principle for understanding and resolving the complex problems. In cultural history, it is Mandala that has been a method of meditation and/or of curing mental illnesses, which will be described in the next section.

11.3 Mandala as a Symbol of Life: Beyond the Linear Constraints of Written Language

The theories of the *mandala* took their origin in India and then penetrated Tibet and these theories, expressed in symbols, allegories and connotations, have, as it were, colour of the spiritual world in which they developed…. So these symbols are uncertain and doubtful like writing in books to whose language we no longer possess the key. Still, they are symbols which, when we do learn to interpret them, share with the writers of the Upanishads the same noble aspiration: *Tamaso ma jyotir gamaya*—'Let me pass from the darkness to the light.'

Giuseppe Tucci (Translated by Brodrick AH)

"The Theory and Practice of the Mandala:
With Special Reference to the Modern Psychology of the Unconscious"
Dover Publications, Inc. New York, 1961, pp. viii–ix

From the view of life—whether it is being or learning—as a thinking subject and observed object, we can generalize the self-nonself circulation principle for 'living' nature (Murase 2000, 2008, 2018). We began to understand how the major problems of our time are all interconnected known as systemic problems, because tentative solutions, in turn, cause unpredictable side-effects on future generations like a trade-off. As we have pointed out in Sect. 11.5, we have to have systemic thinking in understanding systemic problems. But how can we do it?

First of all, we have to realize that living life, our systemic thinking, and even systemic problems are all obeying the self-nonself circulation principle, for all of them have the 'living' nature. Note that the circle of wholeness is one of the realizations of the self-nonself circulation principle. Then, we must understand how life is characterized by unlimited conflicts and oppositions. Finally, we have to remember the self-transcendental nature of life, together with the self-consistency principle. When all these characteristics can be converted into a coherent picture, known as Mandala, we begin to understand who we are, what there are, why things happen, and so on. In the present section, we will try to draw our original Mandala.

Before drawing the Mandala, let us summarize our current understandings. According to the Japanese Philosopher, Nishida (1987), an emphasis was placed on the co-existence of conflicts, oppositions, contradictions in our everyday experience and thoughts. Indeed, individual human life, in general, seems to contain conflicts and oppositions within itself such as the struggle between evolving cancer cells and defending immune systems (Murase, 1996), regulation between on and off states, and so on (Murase, 2008). Besides conflicts within individuals, there appear different kinds of conflicts between individuals and without individuals through the emerging systemic problems. They are all connected as nested hierarchies.

How do we describe this situation? Figure 11.4 illustrates our Mandala. Historically, Mandala has been considered as tools or methods for the religious to see the reality behind complex features through meditative experiences. Despite its almost infinite variations, most Mandala has a very universal meaning and structure: it is a symbol of wholeness that represents a synthesis of endless conflicts. Jung (1968) realized that Mandala can be a good tool for mental patients to recover from their mental illnesses.

Let us now explain how we draw this Mandala. Almost 20 years ago, one of us (Murase M) suddenly started to draw the Mandal shown in Fig. 11.4 without noticing what is going on, but after the Mandala was completed, uncertainty was replaced by the certainty with satisfaction.

During drawing 5 steps were required. (1) Negation: A single unit, $\circ$, was placed in the center on the white paper. (2) Expansion: The single unit, $\circ$, placed in the center starts to divide into opposing units, $\circ \Leftrightarrow \circ$. (3) Convergence: The opposing units in turn build up a higher unit as a synthesis of opposition, $\boxed{\circ \Leftrightarrow \circ}$. (4) Transference: The same process continues. (5) Emergence: A whole system is emerging. These 5

Fig. 11.4 Mandala. There are intra-, inter- and trans-subsystem conflicts

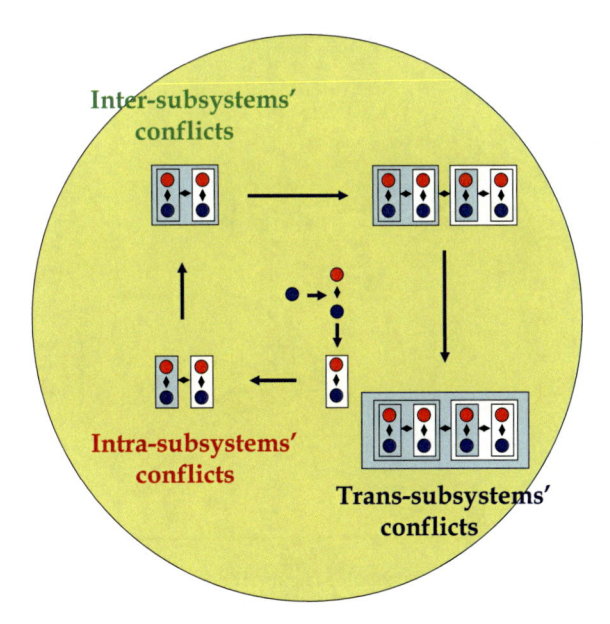

steps are called 5 *NECTE* processes based on the first character of each name (see previous Chapter).

This is driven by the circulation between self (or endo-system) and nonself (or exo-world). The targeting whole system is the same as the beginning unit, though there is a difference in size and complexity. So, the Mandala shows historical processes of both division (and differentiation) and synthesis (or integration). At the same time, the Mandala is also a picture representing spacio-temporal arrangements of different kinds of subsystems, in which there are intra-, inter- and trans-subsystems' conflicts. Each unit is indicated by a closed line. The Mandala is therefore the nested hierarchical structure, but not the non-nested one, as there are no edges just like the case of an open tree-type structure.

A mandala can be a good tool for us to acquire an improved understanding of the Universe including Nature and Humans because we can speculate missing things or hidden dimensions behind complex features. Under the given constraints or frameworks of thinking ways, it is rather difficult to understand the 'outside' world beyond the traditional constraints or frameworks. However, it is relatively easy to get rid of them by taking their *negation*.

Figure 11.5 illustrates how we can realize the oppositions outside the constraints. Since the Mandala is based on intra-, inter- and trans-subsystems' conflicts, we have to expect that conflicts also appear beyond the whole system. This may reflex the idea of an *inverse relationship* given by Kitaro Nishida. A set of two opposing whole systems, represented by clockwise and anti-clockwise rotational arrows would play an important role in predicting the emergent phenomena. Interestingly, there are self-similar structures at any level of this symbol like the fractal.

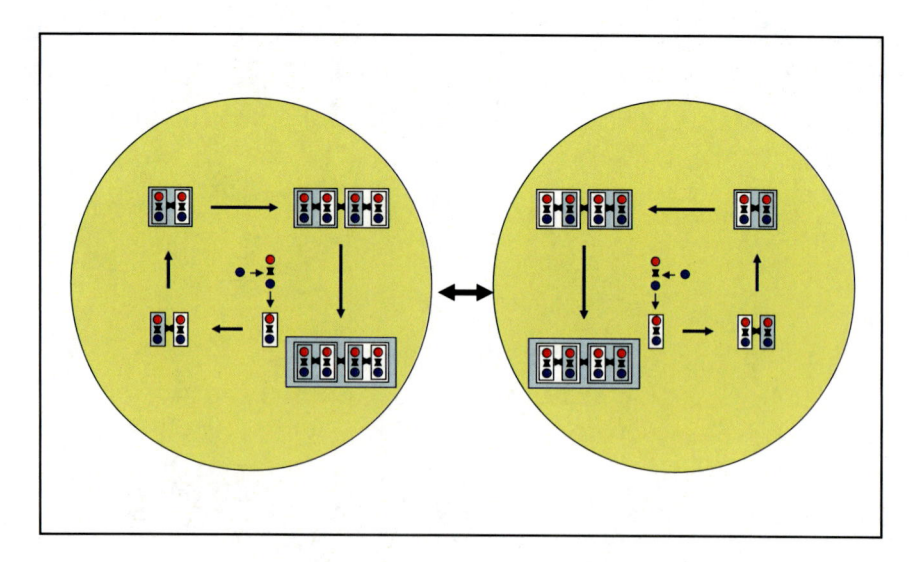

Fig. 11.5 Set of two whole systems. There is self-similarity at any level of the symbol

The self-nonself circulation principle can provide a symbol of life like a Mandala. Mandala is not only the symbol of life but also mind and even the Universe. Because of the self-consistency principle, Mandala is also the tool to understand key features behind complex phenomena involving the major emerging systemic problems. The resulting complex picture shows opposed phenomena, sometimes observed as conflicting results. But such opposed phenomena are merely the two sides of a double-edged sword. In other words, the self-nonself circulation can be considered as a radically new paradigm of life, mind and nature. A transdisciplinary perspective based on Mandala would be required to advance this idea for co-creating the future, for infinite possibilities are emerging from the Mandala forever.

Mandala is very interesting because of its potentially infinite polymorphism: that is, there are infinitely different kinds of Mandala beyond its fundamental self-consistency, which means that there are infinite variations within individual whole Mandala as well. This seems to be very interesting because such polymorphism is based on the co-existence of oppositions, while there is polyphony introduced by Stomu Yamash'ta from music which is the necessary concept for admitting difference into consideration of harmony.

Surprisingly, Mandala can take any process not only as an emergent pattern, but also as a harmonious music, which is considered to be resonant with Human body and mind. When we deal with current shattered world phenomena, assertion and maintenance of difference or namely polymorphism, instead of attempt at monism, in the context of harmony allows a far more constructive dialogue and potential resolution, leading to realization of hidden dimension for further co-evolution, co-emergence and co-creation of Humanity and Nature.

Before closing this Section, let us make the following remarks. Concerning the linear constraints within the written 5 NECTE processes. The 5 NECTE processes begin with (1) Negation until the end at (5) Emergence, which resembles the fact that the discovery of nothingness leads to the invention of counting system of infinite numbers. Between the two ends, (2) Expansion occurs due to so many trials and errors for inventing the counting system. Then, (3) Convergence happens, when the final system is established, and (4) Transference occurs as it is exported to the different cultures.

The same is true not only in the case of the COVID-19 pandemic in our external world, but in the case of creative thinking in our internal world. We can realize that 5 NECTE processes are universally found elsewhere. Although 5 NECTE processes are formed in linear way, it can be transformed into Mandala as a symbol of life.

11.4 Discussion

Globalization is, in some sense, the mother of all coupled systems, and for all its benefits and wonders, it has often accelerated the loss of adaptive capacity by spinning incomprehensibly vast and interconnected webs across the planet, increasing the latent dependencies between far-flung entities of all types.

Andrew Zolli and Ann Marie Healy
Resilience: Why Things Bounce Back, p. 19
Simon and Schuster, New York, 2012

11.4.1 Revisiting the Question "What is Life?"

At the level of molecules in living organisms, it is true that physics, together with chemistry, plays an essential role in understanding the structures and functions of molecules, contributing many detailed findings toward the classification of life's component materials. At the level of living systems, however, physics and conventional material science are no longer sufficient enough to describe life processes and their self-transcendental dynamics, toward a holistic understanding of life itself.

In order not only to survive our shattered world but also to deal with the current global crisis, we must have an integrated view of "life" or a radically new conception of "life" because Nature is full of life phenomena: such as life on Earth involving Human beings and even the emerging systemic problems. The new conception of "life" requires new systemic thinking and vice versa: that is, there is no center in our world, but instead, the self-consistency principle, such that we must have systemic thinking in terms of patterns, relationships, and contexts. For one example, we proposed our original Mandala as a symbol of life.

According to Mandala, we can realize how self-nested hierarchy appears infinitely, characterized by horizontal and vertical relationships within and without hierarchical levels, respectively. A slight perturbation at one single point, therefore, can be detected in the entire whole system, as each interaction depends on all the others. Here, unpredictability is always the case, and thus the contemporary material science has given up a holistic understanding and scientific definition of life.

However, this is exactly the point, that we can get rid of such difficulties. Because of the self-nested hierarchy, it is clear that the same arguments and considerations are valid, not only at the level of the simplest microorganisms but also at the level of the higher organisms and even at the level of the social and ecological systems on the Earth. It is the self-consistency principle underlying life that must be the same at all levels. Instead of a lack of scientific definition, we could use the ostensive definition to understand complex life phenomena. A Mandala can be a powerful lens or methodology through which we can view major emergent problems afresh. Due to the self-consistency principle, we now realize that not only life itself but also the emerging problems and even a methodology must be all life. It turned out that Mandala is a symbol of life to understand the complementary aspects of all the oppositions and contradictions within us, around us and beyond us.

11.4.2 Unfolding of Enfolding: Co-evolution of Macro- and Microcosmos

According to Jantsch (1980, p. 75), "the evolution of the Universe is the history of an unfolding of differentiated order or complexity". Here, unfolding is not the same as building up. Indeed, we are familiar with the description that hierarchical levels emerge by the joining of systems "from the bottom up" on the assumption that the hierarchical structures are non-nested as illustrated in Figs. 11.2 and 11.3a. Unfolding, however, implies complex processes that lead to simultaneous and interdependent structuration of hierarchically different levels just like the transformation described in Fig. 11.3.

There appears, nevertheless, a simple question: Why do we draw Mandala from the small unit to the whole? When we drew Mandala (see Fig. 11.4), we put the unit at the center and then expanded it toward the whole. It seemed to us, however, as if we had realized that the emergent whole will come forth into the parts. Bortoft (1996) described the character of this emergence as the "unfolding of enfolding". We should not consider the parts and the whole as separate things, but instead, the parts are the place of the whole where it embodies forth into presence.

Let us consider our thinking. Whereas we are accustomed to thinking of going from special parts to the general whole in some sort of induction, we often start with rather general considerations and then focus more and more on special questions known as deduction. Likewise, hierarchically higher levels of structure form "from the top", where the top furthers the manifestation of higher levels, while the lower levels are included in their scope (Jantsch, 1980). The hierarchical structures are shaped from both sides, but not in a single direction, either from bottom to top or from top to bottom.

It turns out that the emerging reality is coordinated at many levels. In other words, it is the interplay between seemingly opposed processes, whether they are integrations or differentiations, that conduct the evolution of life and the emergence of systemic problems. We should therefore adopt the same emerging dynamics toward the systemic problems. As Capra and Luisi (2014) emphasized, "the only viable solutions are those that are *sustainable*". Such sustainability can be phrased by the circle of wholeness.

11.4.3 Self-interest (or Selfishness) Versus Integration (or Altruism)

From an emergentist view, the co-emergence of a whole and its parts asks important questions about the balance between self-interest and altruism, for the two tendencies are both essential aspects of all living systems. Of course, neither of them is intrinsically good nor bad. What is good is a dynamic balance between them, whereas what is bad is a lack of balance.

This is relating to the social question about how to balance the needs of individuals and groups (Haidt, 2013). There seem to be two different kinds of answers to this question: one is the socio-centric answer that the needs of groups are placed first and those of individual second; another is the individualistic answer that individuals are placed first and groups are second. Individuals of humans and many other animal species exploit the experiences and works of others by learning things from them socially. There appear to be both individual learning and social or cultural learning.

As Tomasello (2009) mentioned, humans have spread out all over the Earth, while the nearest great-ape relatives live in limited areas such as Africa or Asia. Then, Tomasello (2009) emphasized the role of social and cultural learning in the evolution of humans: just as individual humans biologically inherit genetic information that has been adaptive in the past; they also culturally inherit collective information of their ancestors through their accumulated products and experiences. Because social and cultural learning is the result of evolution, we will co-evolve toward the future.

Here, we have to pay much attention to the quality of life and social interactions concerning power. As Capra and Luisi (2014) pointed out, there are two different kinds of power at the level of individuals: one is the power that dominates others based on excessive self-interest, and another is power as the empowerment of others. The former seems to be the case of non-nested hierarchy, while the latter the nested hierarchy. In such a nested hierarchy, people are empowered by being connected to the nested hierarchy. This difference not only explains the difference between self-interest and altruism, but also suggests how to make a dynamic balance between them, which is urgently needed today in the COVID-19 pandemic. As we begin to understand, non-specialists and volunteers play important roles for developing the enlightened society, for there is no established center in our world.

11.5 Conclusion

Nature is full of phase transitions, known as abrupt appearance and/or annihilation of orders and/or disorders, often ascribed to 'miracles'. In other words, our universe is full of self-organization and self-disorganization from an elementary particle to a huge galaxy. There is no permanently stable structure. The same is true for our mind.

How could you imagine the appreciation of the presence of 'nothingness' changed the world so radically, through the invention of counting system leading to 'infinite' numbers in the history (Barrow 2001). Although 'silence' was considered the cause of fear for our inability to focus it, 'silence' is now considered precious tressure because it is the best tool toward spirituality with 'infinite' depth and width (Debs, 2017). A tiny 'invisible' information or almost 'ignored' event has not only triggered vast creativity in our mind like eureka, but also caused the COVID-19 pandemic! In an extreme sense, we should mention that nature is full of 'pandemics' at any level of our universe, although we have not fully recognized them.

Most people have been, indeed, astonished by individual 'miracles' or 'pandemics' themselves. A little people, however, has paid much attention to the process how the phase transitions happen. There must be no essential difference among all the above phenomena. Consider, for instance, the counting system. It can generate numbers infinitely like a 'pandemic'. As long as we know the counting system, we no longer remember infinite numbers. Because of this convenience, the counting system spread out all over the world, like a 'pandemic' again!

What we have to realize is, therefore, not the details of individual things, but instead a self-consistency principle, through which infinite things happen forever. Based on the self-nonself circulation theory (Murase 2000, 2008, 2018), a sustainable society and resilient individuals could be desirable on the condition that we are taking care of the economy, business, structures, technologies, and humanity in order not to interfere with originally emerging "living" nature.d

Let us remember the vicious and virtuous circle mentioned in Sect. 11.4.3 of the previous chapter. The remaining problem is how to transform the vicious circle to virtuous one. It is the new conception of life exploring in this text that must be taken into account as a reliable method for our perception. Once we have such a perception based on vital living nature, then we can enjoy virtuous cycle: this is exactly the circle of wholeness.

In conclusion, the present transdisciplinary study presents the important roles of horizontal and vertical relationships within the nested hierarchy for the co-evolution of Nature and Humans. We are not only empowered by Nature but also empower Nature. This must be the circle of wholeness, which is driven by the self–nonself circulation principle developed by Murase (2000, 2008, 2018).

Acknowledgements The authors would like to thank to Prof. Stephen Hill for his intensive efforts on careful reading of this manuscript and giving us an invaluable comments and suggestions.

References

An Der Heiden, U. (1992). Chaos in health and disease: Phenomenology and theory. In W. Tschacher, G. Schipek, & E. J. Brunner (Eds.), *Self-organization and clinical psychology* (Vol. 58, pp. 55–87). Springer Series in Synergetics.

Barrow, J. D. (2001). *The book of nothing: Vacuums, voids, and the latest ideas about the origins of the universe.* CPI COX & Wyman Ltd.

Bateson, G. (2002). *Mind and nature: A necessary unit.* Cresskill, USA: Hampton Press, Inc. (Originally Dutton edition published 1979).

Bortoft, H. (1996). *The wholeness of nature: Goethe's way toward a science of conscious participation in nature.* New York: Lindisfarne Press.

Cannon, W. B. (1929). Organization for physiological homeostasis. *Physiological Reviews, 9,* 399–431.

Capra, F., & Luisi, P. L. (2014). *The systems view of life: A unifying vision.* Cambridge: Cambridge University Press.

Debs, J. (2017, June 4). *Portrait of an artist today.* http://www2.yukawa.kyoto-u.ac.jp/~future/news/20160604-1.html.

Doidge, N. (2016). *The brain's way of healing: Stories of remarkable recoveries and discoveries.* Viking Press.

Edwards, B. (1986). *Drawing on the artist within.* New York: Simon & Schuster, Inc.

Feinberg, T. E. (2001). *Altered egos: How the brain creates the self.* Oxford: Oxford University Press.

Francis, P. (2020). *Let us dream: The path to a better future.* London: Simon & Shuster.

Geertz, C. (1973). *The interpretation of cultures: Selected essays.* New York: Basic Books Inc.

Gilbert, S. F. (2009). *Ecological developmental biology: Integrating epigenetics, medicine, and evolution.* Sunderland, USA: Sinauer Associates, Inc.

Goldberger, A. L. (1996). Non-linear dynamics for clinicians: Chaos theory, fractals, and complexity at the bedside. *Lancet, 347,* 1312–1314.

Goldberger AL Amaral LAN Hausdort JM Ivanov PCh Peng C-K and Stanley HE (2002) Fractal dynamics in physiology: Alterations with disease and aging. *PNAS, 99,* 2466–2472.

Gottwald, F.-T. (2002). Life—A problem inherent in the research context. In H.-P. Dürr, F.-A. Popp, & W. Schommers (Eds.), *What is life? Scientific approaches and philosophical positions* (pp. 25–37). Singapore: World Scientific.

Govinda, L. A. (2002). *Foundations of Tibetan Mysticism.* Mansfield, USA: Martino Publishing.

Haidt, J. (2013). *The righteous mind: Why good people are divided by politics and religion.* New York: Penguin Books.

Hough, L., & Chaney, S. (2005). Chapter 10: Thomas' conflict theory. In S. M. Ziegler (Ed.), *Theory-Directed Nursing Practice* (2nd ed., pp. 223–246). New York: Springer.

Ichikawa, H. (2001). Shintairon-Shusei (in Japanese), Gendai Iwanami Bunko

Jantsch, E. (1980). *The self-organizing universe: Scientific and human implications of the emerging paradigm of evolution.* Oxford: Pergamon Press.

Jung, C. G. (1968). Psychology and alchemy. In H. Read, M. Fordham, G. Adler, & W. Mcguire (Eds.), *The collected works of C. G. Jung* (Vol.12). Princeton: Princeton University Press.

Jullien, F. (1999). *The propensity of things: Toward a history of efficacy in China* (J. Lloyd, Trans.). New York: Zone Books.

Lorenz, K. (1973). Behind the mirror: A search for a natural history of human knowledge (R. Taylor, Trans.). London: Methuen and Co Ltd.

Mandelbrot, B. B. (1977). *The fractal geometry of nature.* New York: W.H. Freeman and Company.

McCraty, R., Atkinson, M., Tomasino, D., & Bradley, R.T. (2009). The coherent heart: Heart-brain interactions, psychophysiological coherence, and the emergence of system-wide order. *Integral Review 5,* 10–115.

Medows, D. (2008). *Thinking in systems: A primer.* White River Junction, USA: Chelsea Green Publishing.

Murase, M. (1992). *The dynamics of cellular motility.* Chichester: Wiley.

Murase, M. (1996). Alzheimer's disease as subcellular "Cancer": The scale-invariant principles underlying the mechanisms of aging. *Progress of Theoretical Physics, 95*(1), 1–36.

Murase, M. (2000). *Life as history: The construction of self-nonself circulation theory* (in Japanese) (pp. 369–376). Kyoto: Kyoto University Press. https://repository.kulib.kyoto-u.ac.jp/dspace/bit stream/2433/49765/1/Murase2000b2.pdf.

Murase, M. (2008). Environmental pollution and health: An interdisciplinary study of the bioeffects of electromagnetic fields. *SANSAI: An Environmental Journal for the Global Community* (3), 1–35.

Varela, F. J., Thompson, E., & Rosch, E. (1991). The embodied mind. The MIT Press.

Murase, M. (2018). A self-similar dynamic systems perspective of "Living" nature: The self-nonself circulation principle beyond complexity. In S. Yamash'ta, T. Yagi, & S. Hill (Eds.), The Kyoto Manifesto for global economics the platform of community, humanity, and spirituality (pp. 257–283). Springer.

Nishida, K. (1987). *An inquiry into the good* (translated by Abe M and Ives C). Yale University Press

Tomasello, M. (2009). *Why we cooperate.* MIT Press.

Chapter 12
A Case Study of the Self-nonself Circulation Principle in Action: Toward a New Synthesis Beyond Division Between Inside and Outside World in Nursing

Tomoko Murase and Masatoshi Murase

> *The Nature is living because it is there that life is present in all its degrees and because its study demands the integration of lived experience.... The study of living Nature asks for a new methodology—transdisciplinary methodology—which is different from the methodology of modern science and from the methodology of the ancient science of being.*
> —Basarab Nicolescu
> "Manifesto of Transdisciplinarity" p. 64
> State University of New York Press, 2002

Abstract We have been confronted with too many contradictions, oppositions, or paradoxes in our daily lives inside us, around us and even beyond us. Previously, from a dichotomous perspective, such emerging paradoxes were considered only as negative and destructive forces. The authors challenge this traditional view, because there appears the resilience or negative capability that constructive outcomes can be developed. Whether constructive or destructive outcomes appear depends on how we deal with paradoxes. Actually, in the history, paradoxes and even unpredicted failures have been the mother of creativity. Since the COVID-19 pandemic, most of us, even

T. Murase (✉)
Japanese Red Cross Toyota College of Nursing, Toyota, Japan
e-mail: murase@yukawa.kyoto-u.ac.jp; tmurase@rctoyota.ac.jp

T. Murase · M. Murase
Kokoro Research Center, Kyoto University (2021), Kyoto, Japan
e-mail: murase@yukawa.kyoto-u.ac.jp

M. Murase
Yukawa Institute for Theoretical Physics (YITP), Kyoto University, Kyoto, Japan

International Research Unit of Advanced Future Studies (IRU-AFS), Kyoto University (2015–2020), Kyoto, Japan

International Research Unit of Integrated Complex System Science (IRU-ICSS), Kyoto University, Kyoto, Japan uninfected people, not only live in the shattered outside world, but also suffer the mental illness in the inside world because of lower social resources, lower economic resources, and so on. The previous Chapters dealt with how to integrate shattered outside world based on the self-nonself circulation theory of life. The remedy was clear: it was necessary to consider multiple issues together rather than step by step. Then, the present Chapter not only discusses how the same theory can provide us with a better understanding of the mental problems arising inside us, but also describes how it can work in a practical way during nursing.

12.1 Introduction

The recent report suggests that prevalence of depression symptoms in the US was more than threefold higher during COVID-19 compared with before the COVID-19 pandemic (Ettman et al., 2020). A greater burden of depression symptoms was reported in individuals with lower social resources, lower economic resources, and greater exposure to stressors such as job loss. Such a tendency is worldwide. Post–COVID-19 plans should take into account for the probable increase in mental illness to come, particularly among at-risk populations. It is urgently needed today that, because of the worldwide crises, the nursing theory and practice caring patients with depression are redeveloped from a global perspective.

12.1.1 Historical Background: Increase in the Number of Patients with Depression

The World health Organization (WHO) developed a health index called "Disability Adjusted Life Years (DALYs)" in order to evaluate population health under the health and welfare policy. In the past, it was predicted based on DALYs that the incidence rate of depression becomes second highest next to that of malignant neoplasm in 2020, leaving behind those of cerebral vascular disease and ischemic cardiac disease (Health, Labor and Welfare Statistics Association, 2009).[1] Even before the COVID-19 pandemic, depression has been increasing.

The number of suicide and self-destructive behaviors such as self-mutilation has been rapidly increasing as well. As a reason behind this, there seems to be a link to depression (Rosen, 1993; Tsutsui, 2004). Tendency of depression is also changing its clinical picture such as chronic depression, protracted and treatment-resistant depression (Kasahara, 2005; Takaoka, 2003; Kaiya et al., 2008). Besides patient him/herself, it has a profound economic and psychological damage on his/her family and/or co-workers because of prolonged course of treatment, recrudescence and exacerbation. Especially, suicide and self-injury behaviors caused under depressed

---

[1] Health, Labor and Welfare Statistics Association (2009).

mood have a potential to leave serious aftereffects on the patient and also on his/her family and acquaintances.

It should be realized that the economic crisis is *neither* exterior *nor* interior: it is simultaneously *both* exterior *and* interior. As a result, the studies of the social economy and of the human being should sustain one another.

12.1.2   Contemporary Nursing Care for Patients with Depression: Limited Understandings Despite Its Potential Seriousness

In general, depression is called the *common cold* of the mind and it is considered rather mild case of other psychiatric illness. This makes it difficult to understand the seriousness of depression. In reality, however, patients with depression are going through serious physical and mental distress and each patient has each trouble (Widlocher, 1987). Moreover, patient with depression can talk about his/her torments only when he/she is under the relaxed state of mind. While patient with depression is in serious condition, he/she is strictly restricted expression of emotion and drive, which unable for him/her to talk about him/herself even though he/she wants to (Abe, 2008). Therefore, it is necessary to take the patient's physical and mental condition sincerely and provide detailed as well as effective nursing care appropriate to individual pathological condition in the course of onset to cure.

However, nursing guidelines for patients with depression described in the existing textbooks of nursing science and case studies entirely focused on classic and typical description; for example, providing safety of life with no threatening for suicide prevention, giving advice to have enough rest, encourage to have a sense of self-affirmation, avoiding easy cheering-up and so on. These detach the meaning of illness for patients from the context of life and livelihood of them (Nakai et al., 2004; Sakata, 2005; Shiraishi et al., 2006).

In addition, previously, few studies brought out about sufferance which patients with depression went through. There are the studies reporting what is like to be a patient by conducting semi-structured interviews to patients after discharge (Yamakawa, 2006; Okada, 2006a; Sai, 2009). These previous studies revealed some aspects of cognition and realization of living experience of depression by patients themselves. However, the interviews were conducted after discharge and therefore the data are mainly based on what the patients recalled. Because of that, it could not capture thoroughly the circumstantial changes of recognition on his/her illness and also the mental changes along the course of conversations with nurses during the hospital stay. All such studies concluded their findings as empirical knowledge via medical practice, simply saying that patients keep balancing by being depressed. There, indeed, is little study that questions the meaning of experience being depressed for patient's life (Moroboshi, 2005; Otsumura, 2008).

In the field of research on nursing care for patients with depression, there has several study-focus as follows; research which are recognized its usefulness by patients for his/her recovery (Yamakawa, 2003, 2004), research incorporating the tidal model interview method (Sonehara 2005), research introducing patient-participating style care (Tokuhara et al. 2005), research which applied group cognitive therapy on female patients (Okada 2006b, c).

These previous studies pointed out three effective cares; (1) together with patient reviewing patient's experiences of being depressed through interview, (2) help to getting back means to support him/herself in accordance with patient's lifestyle, (3) working upon cognitive and behavioral phases by utilizing group dynamics.

However, regarding cognitive behavior therapy and group approach method, there is limitation on the effects of nursing care depending on the competence of nurse in charge.[2] Our study, therefore, focused on the recognition of nurses who have been taking care of patients with depression.

In medical services, it tends to place much value on maintenance and advancement of health in general. It is observed, however, that patients achieved further growth and development in the course of recovery while accepting and co-existing the disease rather than being healthy at the opposite of being sick. Therefore, it seems necessary to have a view-point considering suicidal attempts and self-injury behavior as positive experiences to facilitate his/her recovery and personal growth rather than considering self-destructive behavior as entirely negative. But, at this point, there is no such theoretical study has done yet.

Under this circumstance, we conducted nursing care based on "Self-nonself circulation theory" of the integrative life theory proposed by Murase (2000, 2006). That is, at clinical site, we aimed to develop nursing care model which enables patients with depression to place suffering experiences of being sick into his/her life properly and give it meaning onto his/her life.

With the evolution of methodologies such as tools, measuring devices, and complex systems, we have observed an example of the spectacular relationship between the levels of *inner* human perception and those of *outer* physical reality. This leads us to realize the inverse relationship: it is the co-evolution of the *inner* human being and of the *outer* society that ask for a new methodology; and thus, the self-transcendental meta-evolution must emerge. This must be a study of *transdisciplinary ecology* (Nicolescu 2002, p. 65).

---

[2] There is one study which focused on one nurse who had given nursing care to three patients who have a risk factor for depression after being cerebral vascular disease (Sato, 2007). However, in that study, there is limitation on its application in a clinical setting in the following two points; (1) target patients are limited to whom have cerebral vascular disease, (2) what revealed on the targeted nurse's cognition was mainly acquired from the view of assessment and there is no explanation on how the meaning of the sickness and suffering experience relate to his/her life.

12.2 Theoretical Considerations: Emergent Perspective Requisite for Emergent Problems

In Western scientific thinking, the general principle is to divide huge problems into constituent, smaller problems and then reason about them and continue to divide them forever until they are of a magnitude that is considered to be solvable. Along this line, in physics, matter or a nonliving thing has been understood and defined based on a reduction to basic building elements or even to physical laws. However, this approach has failed to understand the problem of What is Life?

Why does this happen? There is the simple reason behind this situation: life or a living thing is not the structures of *timeless matter*, but the processes of *evolving matter* in which the self (or endo-system) and nonself (or exo-world) are complementary to each other.[3] In other words, life always depends on its context and thus something *circular processes* always come into play (Murase, 2018). Among the diverse emerging phenomena, there must be the common problem of our incomplete perception, which will be briefly mentioned in this section.

12.2.1 The World as Full of Dichotomies: Too Many Oppositions and Too Little Syntheses[4]

What is Life? What is Death? These are, of course, long-standing problems. It is a common understanding, however, that it is impossible to provide a materialistic or scientific definition of life and death. Such an understanding is also universally accepted. What we need is not the continuing increase in the vast knowledge of materials supposed to be essential to life and death; but instead, a paradigm shift from reductionist-physical view to emergentist-holistic or systemic view. Life and death should not be viewed as simple *beings* like definite *things*, but *emerging properties* driven by the dialectical *circular processes* between oppositions or contradictions.[5]

It is the self-nonself circulation principle by Murase (2000, 2018) that would provide a complex system with the emergent properties. Here, not only a new paradigm but also a paradigm shift must be considered as emergent properties, again! Such emergent properties are "alive" so that they are suitable for understanding

---

[3] According to von Uexküll (1934) and Bateson (2002), Life (or Mind) and Nature were classified as a functional circle (or a necessary unit).

[4] In the previous chapters, we intensively discussed the problem "What is Life?" In this chapter, however, we will discuss additionally two other problems: "What is Death?" and "What is Cognition?", because all of them are merely the different facets of the same emergent phenomena of life itself and thus they are closely related to each other.

[5] Death or aging has been understood as a progressive process or an intra-individual evolutionary process, corresponding to the destruction of the emergent properties of the various levels characterizing the complexity of the entire organism (Murase 1996, 2000). The death of a living organism has been thus described in terms of "neg-emergence" (see Capra and Luisi 2014, p. 139).

life and death. Now, we are arriving at the third long-standing problem: *What is Cognition?*

It is clear that the three different problems mentioned above are converging into the self-consistent view of life itself, for *being*, *developing* and *learning* are merely the different facets of the same life's reality (Nishida, 1987). There must be, therefore, self-consistency among *subjects*, *objects* and *methods*; that is, it is essential to realize how *subjects* understand *objects* through *methods* in a self-consistent way (Murase, 2018). Without realizing such all-embracing relationships, we cannot understand what life really is (Jantsch, 1980). This is the main reason why most of us have failed *not only* to understand the emergence of systemic problems, as such systemic problems are "alive"[6] again (Capra & Luisi, 2014), *but also* to survive depression and related self-destructive behaviors.

12.2.2 Synesis and Change Management

Why have we been seriously confronted with so many different crises? How can we understand and deal with them? The reason is very simple: it is the problem of our incomplete perceptions. Think about our social system. There is the enormous complexity connecting economics, organizations, businesses and humans among different countries. It is therefore impossible to understand such huge complexity based on monolithic thinking.

The classic *divide and rule* principle is well known, for decomposition has been an attractive approach by dealing with problems part by part rather than together to make an appropriate management. Of course, it worked effectively until almost a century ago, because organizations until then were rather simple in such a way that it was rather possible to understand what happened and acknowledge how it worked. It is therefore realized that a pathological organization focuses on a single issue. In our time, many things have changed too quickly like innovations or too slowly like global warming to realize what happens within us, between us and beyond us. It is essential to possess an integrated view of how an organization functions resiliently to manage changes.

According to Hollnagel (2021), "*synesis* represents the mutually dependent set of priorities, perspectives and practices that an organization needs to carry out its activities as intended". The advocated approach was to think in terms of *functions* rather than structures, to think in terms of *processes* rather than outcomes (or products), and to think in terms of *change* and *dynamics* rather than stability and statistics (Hollnage 2021, p. 10).

---

[6] Stephen Hill mentioned, through the personal communication on February 21 in 2021, "attacking an emergent problem will construct another problem". This strongly suggests how such an emergent problem seems to be "alive". Concerning this point, Hollnagel (2021) mentioned "Socio-technical systems are active rather than passive, i.e., they try to understand us as we try to understand them", simply because we as humans are part of these systems.

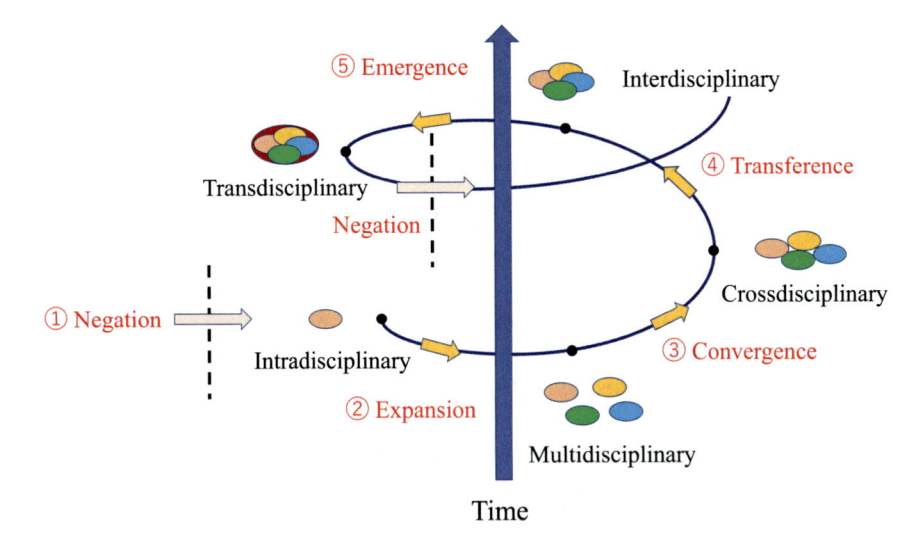

Fig. 12.1 Transdisciplinarity conducted by NECTE Principle. NECTE means the five different processes: ① Negation (indicated by broken lines), ② Expansion, ③ Convergence, ④ Transference and ⑤ Emergence

Organizations have to be dynamic, creative, and resilience to cope with environmental changes. To comprehend such environmental changes, of course, we have to develop concepts of meaning or mental patterns. Based on this paradigm of *change management* (Hollnagel, 2021), however, it is not enough to simply *modify* the mental patterns when required. We have to radically *destroy* and *create* the mental patterns to permit us not only to shape but also to be shaped by the changing environment.[7] Such alternating cycle of *destruction* and *creation* triggers higher and broader levels of elaboration, corresponding to an improved understanding of what is essential for change management.[8]

12.2.3   Transdisciplinarity and Levels of Reality

In Chap. 2 of this book, Stephen Hill emphasized the key new concepts of *transdisciplinarity* introduced by a theoretical physicist, Nicolescu (2002) and *polyphony* stimulated by Stomu Yamash'ta. Figure 12.1 illustrates how transdisciplinarity is conducted by *NECTE principle* (see the previous chapters in more details).

---

[7] This is a sort of *co-evolution* between the individual's mental patterns (or parts) and the changing environment.

[8] Ironically, a higher level of organization performance is often *short-lived*. A successful *change* seems to involve paradoxical capability, for it intend to keep the elevated level frozen or *unchanged*. But here is the origin of our problems how to survive our shattered world and how to integrate our shattered mind, which will be discussed in the rest of this chapter.

According to Nicolescu (2002, p. 8), "The challenge of *self-destruction* has its counterpart in the hope of *self-birth*". In Fig. 12.1, this is indicated by broken lines: through *Negation*, problem finding takes place. In the traditional fragmented approach, indeed, distinct subjects are intensively studied within discipline namely intradisciplinary approach. Through *Expansion*, multidisciplinary approach appears, which concerns studying a certain topic not in just one discipline but in several at the same time. Through *Convergence*, crossdisciplinary approach appears, in which different disciplines begin to contact directly together for further cooperation. After *Transference*, interdisciplinary research appears, which concerns studying transfer of methods from one discipline to another.

It is true that difference from multidisciplinary to interdisciplinary approach is only the difference of the degree of overflow among disciplinary boundaries, while the goal of individual approach limited to the framework of disciplinary approach. Through *Emergence*, however, transdisciplinary approach occurs like the *disciplinary big bang* called by Nicolescu (2002, pp. 43–44): that is, "transdisciplinarity concerns that which is at once between the disciplines, across the different disciplines, and beyond all discipline". Its goal is, therefore, no longer remains within the framework of discipline, but instead is the understanding of the *world* or *universe*.

Here, Nicolescu emphasized the *levels of Reality*. Whereas disciplinary research concerns at most one and the same level of Reality, transdisciplinary approach concerns the dynamics triggered by the action of several levels of Reality at once. It should be realized that the relationship between disciplinarity and transdisciplinarity is not antagonistic but *complementary*: that is, while disciplinary research is clarified by transdisciplinary study, transdisciplinarity is nourished by disciplinary study.[9]

Besides the important goal of transdisciplinarity (i.e., the understanding of the world), another important characteristic must be research going beyond academia and involving stakeholders from civil society, policy and so on, leading to change or transformation towards higher levels of group performance, relating to levels of Reality. This characteristic is important because, in the traditional intradisciplinary (or just disciplinary) approach in any subject, the motivation originated from productivity and efficiency concerns rather than a concern for the well-being and happiness of people or the greater goodness of society (Hollnagel, 2021). It turns out that individuals can contribute to make the world sustainable and vice versa like *co-evolution* between humans and the world. This must be a special case of *global localism* (Stephen Hill, Chap. 2).

12.2.4 Negative Capability and Creativity

Despite the advanced development of modern science and technology, we have been struggled with complexity, uncertainty and 'not knowing' in our everyday lives.

---

[9] This is also a sort of *co-evolution* between disciplinary studies (or parts) and transdisciplinary research (or a whole).

Surprisingly, more than 200 years ago, the poet John Keats (1795–1821) coined *negative capability* in a letter to his two brothers, although he did not revisit this term again after his single use of it (see Cornish, 2011). Negative capability is the attitude of mind and the approach that facilitates creative power of *imagination* to reach the truth.[10]

Why do we need negative capability? Because negative capability can facilitate imagination, which can then allow us to identify and acknowledge potential risks and crises. Without such *requisite imagination*, we have never understood and specified any organization in our world (Hollnagel, 2021). In other words, as there is no formula which can explain everything, uncertainty and unexpected things always appear in our life.

Nicolescu (2002, p. 54) provided a new "Principle of Relativity": *no level of Reality constitutes a privileged place from which one is able to understand all the other levels of Reality.* Nicolescu (2002, p. 55) then continued as follows.

This Principle of Relativity is what originate a new perspective on religion, politics, art, education, and social life. And when our perspective on the world changes, the world changes. Reality is not only multidimensional, it is also multireferential.

The different levels of Reality are accessible to human knowledge thanks to the existence of different levels of perception, which are found in a one-to-one correspondence with levels of Reality. These levels of perception permit an increasingly general, unifying encompassing vision of Reality, without ever entirely exhausting it.

As in the case of levels of Reality, the coherence of levels of perception presuppose a zone of nonresistance to perception.

These statements lead to an important conclusion: we can understand paradoxical nature of destruction and construction in our world only when we perform requisite imagination based on the similar paradoxical nature. It is the co-evolution of the human being and of the universe that would require us to have a new methodology. Nicolescu (2002, p. 64) called it *transdisciplinary methodology*, whereas the authors introduced the *self-nonself circulation theory of life* (Murase, 2000, 2018). Despite their seemingly different characteristics, both methodologies share the common nature: that is, *subject, object* and *method* must be considered simultaneously within all the phenomena of *living nature*, and in this sense, both are radically different from the methodology of traditional material science.

12.3 A Self-nonself Circulation Theory of Nursing and Its Practice

How can we understand a wholeness behind complex emergent phenomena? In change management, Hollnagel (2021) took into account multiple issues at once:

---

[10] Negative capability could be not only the method to reach the truth, but also the skill in art, religion, business and so on to enter completely into other worlds, other minds or personality (see Cornish, 2011).

that is, he first emphasized the synesis of *productivity, quality, safety, and reliability,* and then thought *functions, processes* and *dynamics* rather than structures, outputs and stability, respectively. In modern physics, Nicolescu (2002, p. 62) mentioned "matter is far from being identical with substance" and continued "matter is associated with a *substance-energy-information-space–time* manifold". New radical approaches have been always required to understand a wholeness behind complex emergent phenomena.

12.3.1 Construction of the Nursing Theory Based on the a Self-nonself Circulation Theory of Life

Concerning organizations in general, most of us have an obvious interest in understanding *why* pathological situations happened and *how* they could be prevented or cured once happened, *no matter what* the organizations are and *regardless of whether* they are developing individuals or elderly persons. These problems have been also the challenging problems in nursing science.

Murase (2006), who worked at a psychiatric hospital as an executive nurse leader, started to investigate the complex human relationships as a graduate student, School of Nursing at Chiba University, and developed a new nursing theory based on the self-nonself circulation theory of life as a theoretical framework (Table 12.1 in Appendix). During the development of a new nursing theory, she obtained data from 10 patients with depression and got 148 scenes of relationship between nurses and patients (Table 12.2).

The resultant data were reconstructed to specify 5 different characteristics for patient cognition: (a) condition of self,[11] (b) balance of harmony between mind and body,[12] (c) level of energy,[13] (d) human relationship,[14] and (e) life history[15] (labelled (a–e) in Table 12.3). Based on the same data, it is also possible to specify 5 different

---

[11] This is a condition of living self here and now. *Collapsing self* contains denial of existence and *redeveloping self* contains affirmation of existence.

[12] This is circulating *inharmonic body* and *harmonic mind–body,* closely related with the living self here and now, which is swinging between disintegrating self and reorganizing self.

[13] This is a circulation factor of *limit of energy* and *increase in energy* that patients acquire during activity, transforming relationships with others from *introvert relationship* to *extrovert relationship,* or vice versa.

[14] This is a circulation of the characteristic cognition for patients that introverted and extroverted relationships are in confrontational coexistence.

[15] This is a history of the patient's life. *Past life* contains review and *future life* contains hope for life.

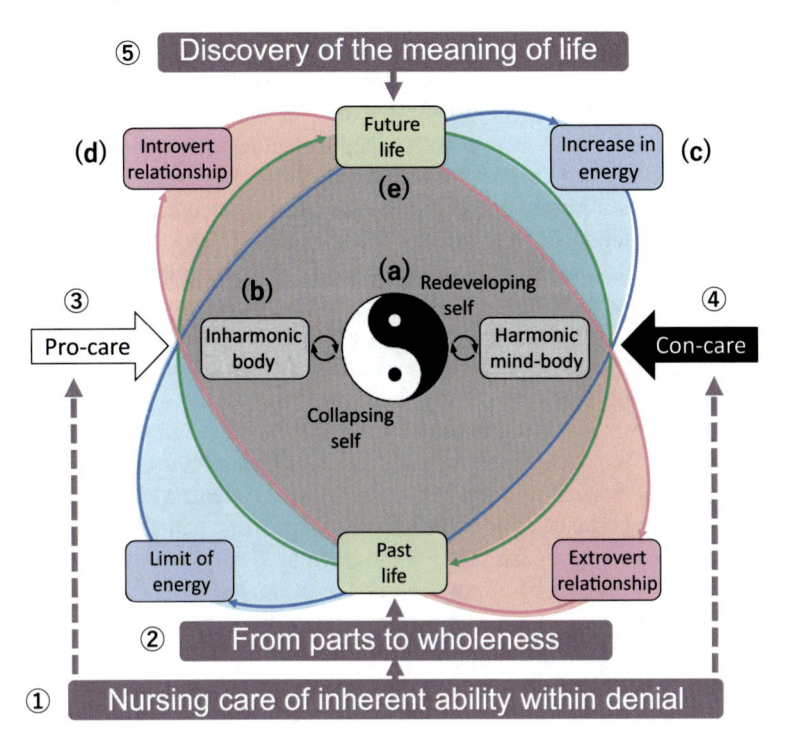

Fig. 12.2   The Mandala Nursing Theory (After Murase, 2006)

patterns for nursing care: ① inherent ability (resilience or negative capability), ② parts-to-wholeness relationship, ③ Pro-care (sympathetic care), ④ Con-care (critical care), ⑤ discovery of the meaning of life (labelled ①–⑤ in Table 12.4).[16]

Figure 12.2 illustrates the new mandala nursing theory involving all the five circulation processes in the patient's (self) physical–mental characteristics labelled (a)–(e) and all the five circulation processes of nursing care (nonself) patterns (numbered ①–⑤).

The nature of nursing care for patients with depression is the circulation process which changes and improves the patient's condition through mutual and reciprocal interaction between a patient as "self" and a nurse as "nonself". This circulation process is not a mere interaction but the repetitive process in which a patient introjects "nonself" into "self" and integrates it into "self". In this process, it includes not only recovery and growth but also risks such as being sick and attempt of self-injury and/or suicide. This is also related to the time course of spiral process.

Through this study, we found that two types of nature of nursing care exist for patients with depression; *pro-care* and *con-care* (see ③ and ④ in Fig. 12.2). That is, we offer not only "pro-care" (sympathetic care) to patients but also "con-care"

---

[16] Note that the labeled characteristics from ① to ⑤ correspond to 5 NECTE processes, respectively.

(critical care). On the contrary to the "pro-care" which we normally provide, "con-care" undermines the recognition of the disease and the patient as well and thus it is a confrontational *coexistence* between "self" and "nonself".

This care is similar to a psychotherapeutic method through dialogue called "*Yusaburi* (shaking)" proposed by Kandabashi (2001). According to Kandabashi, "*Yusaburi*" induces a movement in motionless states, which can be happened due to an inherent function of the patient. When medical care workers send signals to the patient as "*Yusaburi*", it is important to keep "holing Environment" for its preparations. A nurse (as "nonself" for a patient as "self") needs to recognize the confrontational coexistence between "self" and "nonself" and thus support patients to exert their potential vital force for themselves. This is *the inherent ability within denial* (see ① in Fig. 12.2).

A human being is an indecomposable and holistic being, and parts are contained in the whole and vice versa. Therefore, we can think that minute change of behavior (part) may indicate recognition and perspectives in the patient (whole). Narita (1998) pointed out the importance of *palpation* for psychosomatic patients: it is possible to vocalize inherent voices of the patients by touching them. During this care, at the same time, it is a process of going deep inside of nurses' own mind according to Narita. This can be applied to the situation of nurses with patients with depression. By paying attention and facilitating the expression of patients with depression such as "comfortable", nurses can plan a care policy for each patient with depression individually (Kandabashi, 2007).

Patients with depression deeply adhere to a past and therefore they are living in emptiness (Binswanger, 1960). By applying repetitive characteristics of "Self-nonself circulation theory", nurses should help patients with depression and support them to admit historicity of life that proceeds to *redeveloping self* (see (a) in Fig. 12.2). Ultimately, this process can lead to *discovery of the meaning of life* (see ⑤ in Fig. 12.2). Along the course of this process, nurses provide assistance through this symbolic collapsing process which patients with depression themselves review and restructure "self". And eventually, nurses support a new life of patients with depression. This is "nursing care".

In conducting nursing process, based on "Self-nonself circulation theory", nurses need to capture the unconscious parts in a deep mind of patients with depression as well as conscious ones. In our study, we found that every patient can share the changing process of *redeveloping self*, if patients themselves and their family and even nurses together can find meanings of being depressed. That is, not only patients with depression but also family members of patients with depression as well as nurses would change their "self" accordingly. This must be again a special case of *global localism* emphasized by Stephen Hill in Chap. 2 of this book *Kyoto Manifesto II*.

12.4   Historical Consideration of Depressive Person's Cognition

Rosen (1993) valued depression as an archetype and found creativities within depression. He emphasized that depression had double-sided characteristics, affirmation and negation. His interviews with survivors of jumps from the Golden Gate Bridge and San Francisco-Oakland Bay Bridge revealed that all of them experienced transcendence and spiritual rebirth phenomena. Based on Jungian Psychology, he developed new therapeutic method called *Egocide and Transformation* and went on group therapies. He was sure that iconic death of falsehood (Egocide) lead to reproduction of true self and new life (transformation). He talked about depression as below, with an idea that true nature of depression must be understood for the recovery of patients with depression.

I am suggesting that depression is an archetype—an effectual predisposition, as old as life itself that expresses itself in biological, psychological, social, and existential/spiritual ways. As with any archetype, it has both a dark side and a light side. In this respect, depression resembles the Chinese principal of yin/yang, an archetype of all existence as a balance of opposites. The dark (yin) and the light (yang) function are together to make a whole. Within each is a little of the other; they can't be separated by drawing a straight line (Rosen, 1993).

Bin Kimura presented that depression and manic are the same pathology, along with his clinical experiences, in a dialog with a philosopher (Kimura, 1992; Kimura & Higaki, 2006). This idea accords with the philosophy of "Self-nonself circulation theory". Even a phenomenon that appears to conflict externally, the biological reaction is the same. He mentioned that the depression was the urgent rest reaction of nervous system occurred at both sides of a body and the consciousness when a physical rest function failed. That is, the depression is a very proactive action, general diseases as they are, to try to rebuild a principal in emergency basis. He thought affirmatively that physical symptoms associated with depression were the body-specific adjustment process. This way of thought must have in common with the words of Nightingale (1859): "All disease is a reparative process".

It is clear that the importance of attention focused on the body in all stages of depression is also suggested, not only care for mental and cognitive side. Takei (2004) mentioned that physical cares in psychiatry promoted the functional recovery of patients as direct approaches to the self by "therapeutic touch". Harmony between non-verbal communication (physical care) and verbal communication enables empathic relationship between a patient and a nurse, understanding unconscious communication with patients.

12.5 The Meaning of Application with 'The Self-nonself Circulation Theory' for a New Nursing Care Model

The two-dimensional diagram of Fig. 12.2 can be represented by the three-dimensional view (Fig. 12.3) when the past–future time axis is taken horizontally. As we have mentioned in our previous chapters, we human beings can make plans by imagination to the future. This leads to the reversal of the time series of simple causality, because the plan can turn into reality through advancement of science and technology. This means that mental imagination can pull the future into the present. The direction of causality is reversed, which evokes the deductive process. As time proceeds in inductive ways, we keep present through circular dynamics between past and future, just as the hierarchical structures are shaped from both sides from bottom to top and from top to bottom.

The quintessence of "self-nonself circulation theory" lies in its view that the oppositions are co-existent: reorganizing and disintegrating processes of the self are inextricably linked together. It is because there is always a risk of disorganization when the nonself in the exo-world is assimilated into the self in the endo-world during the process in which the self and the nonself circulate maintaining their confrontational co-existence. By constructing a nursing care model based on this theory one is able to recognize that "health and illness", "normality and abnormality" and "life and death" are two sides of the same coin and think that there are meanings even in depressive behaviors which often trigger suicide and self-mutilation out of pessimism and remorse.

The very effort to find such meanings leads to the ability to counter depression or loss of hope (Rosen, 1993). Through our theory, nurses can show compassion for the patient sensing the deep cognition behind suicide and self-mutilation, and support patients with depression now believing in the future existence of health, normality

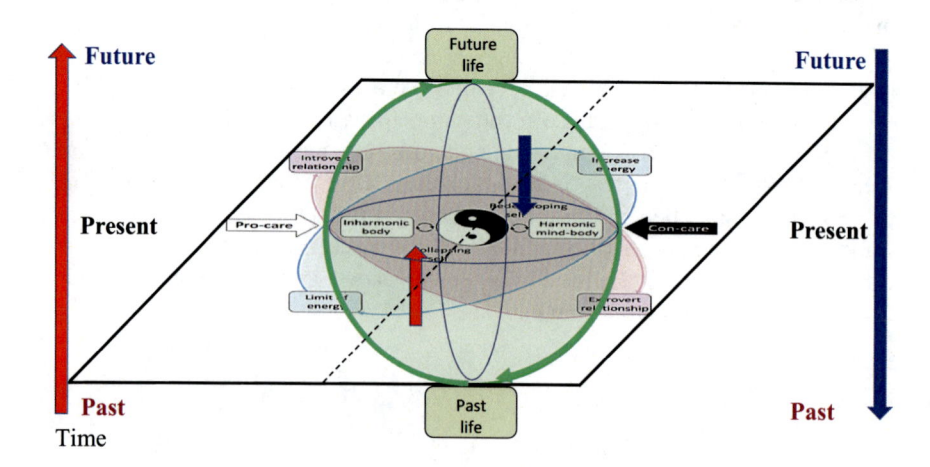

Fig. 12.3 The three-dimensional view of the Mandala Nursing Theory

and life, despite the current disability by illness, abnormality and death. The situation that patients with depression likely to give rise to self-destructive behaviors can be understood different ways: they have enough energy for self-reorganizing and can exercise their creativity. This gives them the opportunity for transforming themselves.

In summary, a nursing care model constructed based the "Self-nonself circulation theory" helps patients discover the fact that there is another aspect in the experience of anguish caused by illness, find meaning in that experience and position that experience in their life. In addition, it offers patients with depression and nurses in another ways of thinking the illness which helps them to reorganize related nursing phenomena.

12.6 Discussion

Think about problems, regardless of whether they are about our society or ourselves. It is commonly acknowledged that we deal with problems when they happened but never in advance. Solutions not only are incomplete but also make them worse. This quickly create a *vicious circle* that makes the problems even more serious.

It is therefore worthwhile to consider deeply why this situation happens and how we can get rid of this vicious circle. As we have realized through our chapters, the answer is very simple: we have had limited perspectives and thus we should change our perception dynamically. The self-nonself circulation theory of life proposed by Murase (2000, 2018) could provide us such a dynamical perception. In other words, the theory is not only the methodology how to understand emergent problems typical of life, but also the living Nature and even Life itself.

Why have not we understood these things? Again, the answer is fairly simple. We have been blind due to the *biological evolution* of human beings. As Nicolescu (2002, p. 73) clearly mentioned, biological evolution has reached full term. A new kind of evolution is actually emerging linked to culture, science, and consciousness. Individual evolution and social evolution condition each other, leading to the emergence of co-evolution characterized as a *self-transcendence*.

We should therefore appreciate such self-transcendental characteristics typical of ourselves and Nature itself. The authors have experienced *miracles* at Universities, Hospitals, Societies and so on. Even in our everyday lives, we have experienced miracles without our serious concerns: for example, bipedal walking, speaking and hearing language, counting infinite numbers, swimming, and so on. Besides the diverse phenomena listed above, there must be the common principle behind them. The authors declared that they are all conducted based on the same principle of self-nonself circulation. It is our hope to make us happy, which must be the most reliable power inherent in all the human beings.

Acknowledgements The authors would like to thank Stephen Hill for his continuous encouragements and invaluable discussions. A part of the current work was conducted by the project of Kokoro Research Center at Kyoto University approved in 2021, whose project leader is Masatoshi Mursae.

Appendix

See Tables 12.1, 12.2, 12.3 and 12.4.

Table 12.1 Relations between self-nonself circulation theory and framework for intervention study

The self-nonself circulation theory	Framework for intervention study
Life phenomenon can be taken as the "Self-nonself circulation". In this dynamic 'process', a closed structure "self" and outer "nonself" persistently circulate. It continues changes of growth and development based on the "Self-nonself circulation"	Care based on the idea of circulation between self and nonself. Patients with depression (self) take a closed structure against surroundings (nonself). In the process of making relationships, nurses and patients with depression mutually affect each other and encourage transformation
As the whole dynamics can be the "Self-nonself circulation process", whole phase can go into every part. This will produce Nested Structure. This process continues persistently	Care based on the idea that whole phase can go into every part. Patients with depression often show their restraint in the mental and physical malfunction. A minute change of behavior (part) may indicate recognition and perspectives in the back (whole)
In the life process, "self" and "nonself" persistently circulate. There is no definite boundary between "self" and "nonself". In this historic process of circulation after circulation, evolution takes place despite the appearance of repetition characteristics and similarity	Patients with depression deeply adhere to a past and have a thought separated from the future. Based on the thought that the life process circulates with historicity, caretakers need to receive their sufferings of becoming empty. Support to find power that can be resilient to illness in the experience of the past life process, and the review of the life pattern to show enough power
In life phenomenon, 'self-reorganizing process' and 'self-disorganizing process' are both in confrontational coexistence. Hence these processes are of inside and outside unification, keeping permanent structuration. 'Self-reorganizing process' means the process of generation and development of biological order, such as the origin, ontogeny, recognition, evolution of the life. 'Self-disorganizing process' means the process of extinct and collapses of biological order, such as cancer, aging, and death. Although health and illness, normal and abnormal, life and death seem to be opposed phenomena, it only reflects a vital reaction mechanism of delicate environmental difference inside and outside of the working living life	In life phenomenon, 'self-reorganizing process' and 'self- disorganizing process' are both in confrontational coexistence. Support to promote development of cognition by showing a different thought to bring confrontational coexistence. This helps patients with depression find implication of the illness called depression, and they come to find their new life

Table 12.2 Summary of patients for the intervention study on 148 scenes

Example	Age	Diagnosis	Suicidal ideation	Hospitalization form	Period of help
Sex				Period of affection	Number of scenes
Ms. A M	50s	Unipolar depression	Y	Voluntary commitment 2 years	A month 12 scenes
Mr. B F	30s	Depression with mental disorder	Y	Hospitalization for Medical Care and Protection 5 years of hospitalization	3 months 15 scenes
Ms. C F	20s	Postpartum depression Mental retardation	Y	Voluntary commitment 1 year	3 months 10 scenes
Ms. D F	40s	Unipolar depression	N	Voluntary commitment 1 year	2.1 months 17scenes
Ms. E F	60s	Recurrent depressive disorder	Y	Voluntary commitment 5 years	2 months 17 scenes
Ms. F F	60s	Unipolar depression Rheumatoid Arthritis	Y	Voluntary commitment 15 years	2 months 19 scenes
Mr. G M	40s	Unipolar depression Alcoholism	Y	Voluntary commitment 5 years	3 weeks 10 scenes
Ms. H F	70s	Late-life depression Slight Dementia	Y	Voluntary commitment Half a year	4 months 18 scenes
Ms. I F	70s	Late-life depression	N	Voluntary commitment 20 years	A month and 3 weeks 14 scenes
Mr. J M	40s	Paranoid depression	Y	Hospitalization for Medical Care and Protection Half a year of hospitalization	2.5 months 16 scenes
				Total 148 Scenes	

Table 12.3 Synthesis about characteristics of cognition of patients with depression based on their words and actions

Characteristics of cognition for patients with depression from a point of view of "self-nonself circulation theory"	Characteristics of negative cognition		Characteristics of positive cognition	
(a) Collapsing self versus developing self	Denial of existence		Self who push to the edge of life and death	
(b) Inharmonic body versus harmonic mind–body	Pain	I have a painful body I can't eat anything I have no feces I can't sleep	Comfort	I am at ease in mind–body Eating any food taste good I had feces I had a good sleep
(c) Limit of energy versus increase in energy	Pessimistic view	I am lacking energy I can't recover from illness A nameless anxiety	Prospective view	I am in full activity I have good felling of recovery from illness Hope for be able to discharge
(d) Introvert relationship versus extrovert relationship	Shut oneself up	Keeping away from personal relationship	Association	Association with person
	Distrust	Rock trust from an enemy to a supporter	Trust	Spread spectrum of trust
	Solitude	Nobody understands my felling	Asking for help	I want to understand my felling
	Hold in one's arms	I must do by myself I discharge my duty	Let go one's hold	I wonder asking someone for help I wonder releasing my duty
(e) Past life versus future life	Alteration that meaning of life	A life style till now	Grope for life	A life style from now

Table 12.4 Synthesis about nature of nursing care for patients with depression

Nature of nursing care from a point of view of "self-nonself circulation theory"	Synthesis about nature of nursing care	Synthesis about nature of nursing care
① Inherent ability within denial	Trusting patient's abilities which exists in the depth of one's consciousness	Not to disturb expression of underlying vitality, vital energy of patient oneself
		To affirm the self of a patient denying self
② From parts to wholeness	Understanding oneself under the minute expression	Grasp of the perspective with observation of minute expressions as a clue
		Accumulation of small physical care
③ Pro-care (sympathetic care)	Coexistence with persons coming closer to one's cognition	Acceptance and parry of the uneasiness
		Not to threaten environmental security
		To wait for increase in energy
		To make use of the experience in the conventional life process
④ Con-care (critical care)	Coexistence with patients in contrary to one's cognition	Promotion to develop recognition by presenting different viewpoints
		Infusion of relaxation to depressed mood by offering humor
⑤ Discovery of the meaning of life	Reviewing patient's own life style with illness	To support new way of life acquired by oneself
		To look back together about the way of life which lead to disease

References

Abe, T. (2008). Talks of persons with depression. In S. Kato (Ed.), *Talks and hearings* (pp. 136–149). Nakayama Shoten.

Bateson, G. (2002). *Mind and nature: A necessary unit*. Cresskill, USA: Hampton Press, Inc. (Originally Dutton edition published 1979)

Binswanger, L. (1960). *Melancholie und Manie*. Pfullingen: Neske.

Capra, F., & Luisi, P. L. (2014). *The systems view of life: A unifying vision*. Cambridge: Cambridge University Press.

Cornish, S. (2011). Negative capability and social work: insights from Keats, Bion and business. *Journal of Social Work Practice, 25*(2), 135–148.

Ettman, C. K., et al. (2020). (2020) Prevalence of depression symptoms in US adults before and during the COVID-19 pandemic. *JAMA Network Open, 3*(9), e2019686. https://doi.org/10.1001/jamanetworkopen.2020.19686

Health, Labor and Welfare Statistics Association (2009) Trend of the nation hygiene, *51*(9), 71, 110, 114.

Hollnagel, E. (2021). *Synesis: The unification of productivity, quality, and safety and reliability.* London and New York: Routledge.

Izutsu, T. (1973). The interior and exterior in Zen Buddhism. In A. Portmann, & R. Ritsena (Eds.), *Correspondence of man and world* (Vol. 42). Eranos Yearbook.

Jantsch, E. (1980). *The self-organizing universe: Scientific and human implications of the emerging paradigm of evolution.* Oxford: Pergamon Press.

Jullien, F. (1999). *The propensity of things: Toward a history of efficacy in China* (J. Lloyd, Trans.). New York: Zone Books.

Kaiya, M., et al. (2008). Atypical depression (in Japanese).

Kandabashi, J. (2001). The art of the psychotherapy interview (in Japanese).

Kandabashi, J. (2007). The art of the psychiatric therapy (in Japanese).

Kasahara, Y. (2005). Mild depression: Psychopathology of "depression" (in Japanese).

Kimura, B. (1992). Form of the life (in Japanese).

Kimura, B., & Higaki, T. (2006). Life and reality (in Japanese).

Moroboshi, N. (2005). From a case of studying cares for depression patients. *The Japanese Journal of Clinical Nursing, 31*(1), 73–76 (in Japanese)

Murase, M. (1996). Alzheimer's disease as subcellular 'Cancer'—The scale invariant principles underlying the mechanisms of aging. *Progress of Theoretical Physics, 95*, 1–36.

Murase, M. (2000). *Life as history: The construction of self-nonself circulation theory* (in Japanese) (pp. 369–376). Kyoto: Kyoto University Press (in English). https://repository.kulib.kyoto-u.ac.jp/dspace/bitstream/2433/49765/1/Murase2000b2.pdf.

Murase, T. (2006). Toward construction of new nursing theory based on self-nonself circulation theory (First Report). *Journal of Chiba Nursing Academy, 12*(1), 94–99.

Murase, M. (2018). A self-similar dynamic systems perspective of 'Living' nature: The self-nonself circulation principle beyond complexity. In: S. Yamash'ta, T. Yagi, S. Hill (Eds.), *The Kyoto manifesto for global economics the platform of community, humanity, and spirituality* (pp. 257–283). Springer.

Nakai, H., et al. (2004). *Psychiatry for nursing* (2nd ed.), Japanese version.

Narita, Y. (1998). Mental and physical psychotherapy (in Japanese).

Neuman, M. A. (1994). *Health as expanding consciousness* (2nd edn.). Sudbury, MA: Jones and Bartlett (NLN Press).

Neuman, M. A. (2008). *Transforming presence: The difference that nursing makes.* Philadelphia, Pennsylvania, USA: F. A. DAVIS.

Nicolescu, B. (2002). *Manifesto of Transdisciplinarity.* State University of New York Press.

Nightingale, F. (1859). *Notes on nursing* (Facsimile of 1st edn.). J.B. Lippincott Co.

Nishida, K. (1987). *An inquiry into the good* (M. Abe & C. Ives, Trans.). New Haven: Yale University Press.

Nishida, K. (1997). Kitaro Nishida's essays on philosophy, II: Logic and life (in Japanese).

Okada, Y. (2006a). Patterns of cognition of female depression patients and relations with symptoms. *Journal of Japan Academy of Nursing Science, 26*(4), 93–101.

Okada, Y. (2006b). Relationships between cognition and condition of female patients of depression. *Journal of Japan Academy of Nursing Science, 26*(4), 93–101.

Okada, Y. (2006c). Group cognitive behavioral therapy introduced to female patients of depression. *Psychiatric & Mental Health Nursing, 9*(6), 16–23.

Otsumura, Y. (2008). Study of nursing and hospital experience of a self-critical female depression patient: Analysis of the content by the semi-structured interview method and participant observation. *Journal of Japanese Psychiatric Nursing Society, 51*(3), 13–17.

Rosen, D. (1993). Transforming depression: Healing the soul through creativity.

Sai, F. (2009). Situations and self-cognition in outbreak: Depression patients of middle or higher age. *Proceedings of Japan Academy of Nursing Science: Region, 39*, 143–145.

Sakata, M. (2005). Life and nursing care for persons with schizophrenia or mood disorder (in Japanese)

Sato, Y. (2007). *Literature review on the image of nurses in the assessment to develop a nursing process for persons suffering depression after Cerebrovascular disease.* Master's thesis of The Graduate School of Nursing, Chiba University.

Shiraishi, H., et al. (2006). Comprehension and care of depression from cases (in Japanese).

Sonehara, J. (2005). Fact of nursing as seen from cases: Facing the depression with the patient through tidal model interview. *Japanese Journal of Clinical Nursing, 31*(1), 84–88.

Takaoka, K. (2003). New depression theory (in Japanese).

Takei, A. (2004). Mental nursing notes (in Japanese).

Tokuhara, S., et al. (2005). Changes in behavior when the convalescent patients overcome depression set along with the nurse challenges to be overcome towards the discharge. *Proceedings of Japan Academy of Nursing Science, Psychiatric & Mental Health Nursing, 36*, 101–103.

Tsutsui, S. (2004). Suicide and depression (in Japanese).

von Uexküll, J. (1934). Instinctive behavior: the development of a modern concept. International Universities Press, Inc.

Widlocher, D. (1987). Les logiques de la depression.

Yamakawa, Y. (2003). Cognition during in recuperation of patients admitted to psychiatric by depressive state. Report of Grants-in-Aid for Scientific Research, 2001–2003

Yamakawa, Y. (2004) Depressed patients' recognition of their own recovery process. In *Proceedings of Japan Academy of Nursing Science, Adult II* (Vol. 34, pp. 287–289).

Yamakawa, Y. (2006). Self-recognition of improvement in depression patients during in recuperation. *Journal of Kawasaki Medical Welfare Society, 16*(1), 91–96.

Zolli, A., & Healy, A. M. (2012). *Resilience: Why things bounce back.* New York: Simon and Schuster.

Tomoko Murase graduated from the School of Nursing at Chiba University, Japan, in 1985 and received a Master's degree from Chiba University in 1987. In the same year,she became an assistant professor at the Japanese Red Cross College in Tokyo, Japan. She was a lecturer at the Japanese Red Cross College in Tokyo from 1989 to 1991. Between 1991 and 1993, she was a visiting researcher at the University of Tokyo (Division of Health Science and Nursing, Department of Medicine). After spending almost 10 years caring for children, Murase entered a doctoral course at the Graduate School of Nursing at Chiba University and was awarded her Ph.D. in 2010. In 2011, she became an associate professor at the Faculty of Nursing, Himeji University, Japan, and in 2012, became a professor and Dean of Nursing at Himeji University. In 2013, she was appointed professor at the School of Nursing at Japanese Red Cross Toyota College of Nursing, Japan, and has been Dean of the School of Nursing since 2016. In 2021 and 2022, she was a Project Member of Kokoro Research Center, Kyoto University.

Masatoshi Murase received his Ph.D. degree from The University of Tokyo in 1987.Since 1992, he has been an associate professor at the Yukawa Institute for Theoretical Physics, Kyoto University. In 1987 and 1988 he was a visiting scientist at the Duke University Medical Center, Durham, NC, USA. Since 2010, he has been a member of the Cooperation Promotion Committee of the International Research Unit of Integrated Complex System Science, Kyoto University. Between 2015 and 2020 he was a director of the Research Promotion Strategy Office of the International Research Unit of Advanced Future Studies, Kyoto University. In 2021 and 2022, he was a Project Leader of Kokoro Research Center, Kyoto University.

Chapter 13
Taiji:—Philosophical, Cultural and Educational Views from Tian Zhen Yuan

Xing Qi-Lin

Abstract For many people, the term "Taiji" 太极 is synonymous with "Taijiquan" 太极拳, a style of martial arts based on Taiji philosophy. In Chinese culture, Taiji is much more than a set of physical exercise. It is an all-encompassing universal concept from which a complete culture has developed over thousands of year of Chinese civilization. This article explains the philosophical foundation of Taiji and uses the "Taijitu" (Taiji diagram) to illustrate the concepts of Taiji. The important role of "He" (harmony) as the core foundation of Taiji is identified and the means to attain "He" through Taiji cultural education and practice is discussed. Next, the practical steps to learn Taiji culture according to the curriculum at "Tian Zhen Yuan" (see Appendix 1), designed by its founder Xing Qi-Lin, is explained. Finally, various case studies are presented as real-world examples of Taiji culture applied in diverse community contexts.

Keywords Taiji · Taijiquan · Tian Zhen Yuan · Community education

The content of this article is based on a lecture given by Taiji Master Xing Qi-Lin at the Kyoto Manifesto II on Kyoto Symposium V conference in Kyoto, Japan on June 11th, 2019. The lecture was delivered in Chinese with Japanese translation by Dr. Cui Ai-Ling. Content and presentation advice was given by Takahiko Maruyama. The article is translated into English and edited by Dr. Corinne Koo. Diagrams and additional details have been added as visual aids and for clarification and reference purposes.

Translation by Dr. Cui Ai-Ling and Dr. Corinne Koo. Diagrams provided by Tian Zhen Yuan.

Dr. Cui Ai-Ling is the co-founder of Tian Zhen Yuan. She completed her studies in Japan, and holds a Ph.D. degree in Engineering. Following her successful career as a scientist with many publications, she became an entrepreneur, managing numerous companies.

Since 2000, Dr. Cui has focused on the study of traditional Chinese culture and values, teaching and management of Tian Zhen Yuan. Her classes combine traditional values and modern concepts. She teaches at Tian Zhen Yuan and around the world.

Xing Q.-L. (✉)
Tianzhen Traditional Culture Training School, Tianjin, China

13.1 Introduction

13.1.1 Overview

The history of Taiji culture is as long as that of Chinese civilization. It is an expression of distinguished traditional Chinese culture. Whilst it is vast and profound, it is presented in a form which is accessible and relatively easy to comprehend.

Taiji philosophy encompasses the essence and summary of Chinese cosmology. These include the formation of the universe; the laws governing its transformation and the route, the path, the sequence and the methodology of its transformation.

In Chinese philosophy, the universe is formed by Yin and Yang. And the interaction and transformation of Yin and Yang represents the fundamental and the most salient way the universe revolves and transforms. Taiji itself is the continual, dynamic process in which Yin and Yang change and transform.

The core of Taiji philosophy is the Taijitu; the guiding principle of Taiji is the transformation between the unmanifest and the manifest; the laws governing the changes in Taiji is creation, transformation and return; and the root foundation of Taiji is profound harmony. Taiji culture is the sum of traditional Chinese wisdom:—it reveals the laws of human and the universe; explores the origin of life; reveals the path of return to the source of life; and unites theory with real-life practice. In an increasingly divided world today, Taiji, rooted in harmony, may be the invaluable remedy that can bring health, happiness, kindness and wisdom.

Taiji culture is the consecrated wisdom of ancient Chinese ancestors. It is deeply rooted, systematic, and has its own lineage. Today, its theories are often supported by modern science. Since Taiji culture is directly connected to the origin of life and emphasizes in experiential practice, it is infused with a continuous flow of life force. Hence it will continue to grow and strengthen along with human development and contribute to the harmonious evolution of humankind.

13.1.2 What is Taiji

Taiji is an all-encompassing, universal concept which has been studied and practiced throughout Chinese civilization over several thousand years. Taiji represents the Chinese view of the cosmos and of the world (Louis, 2003), and serves as their methodological foundation. 太极是一种宇宙观, 世界观和方法论。

Defined by Master Xing Qi-Lin (2017):-

Taiji represents the infinite interchanging order of Yin 阴 and Yang 阳 in the universe. It is the source of all human virtues (Dao 道 and De 德) and life. Taiji pervades in every aspect of existence and it is the core of universal order. It represents the rhythm and harmony of Dao 道 (the ultimate truth) and Fa 法 (the order of nature) which arises from the interaction between heaven and earth. Taiji regulates the infinite cycles of life and the ever-changing nature of all things. Within the immense, infinite and all-encompassing sphere of Taiji, heaven, earth and man are all in perfect balance and harmony.

This philosophical concept will be further explained in the next section, with reference to the Taijitu (Taiji diagram).

13.2 Taiji is Not Simply a Form of Martial Arts

First, it is important to make a distinction between the terms "Taijiquan" 太极拳 and "Taiji" 太极.

"Taijiquan" is a style of martial arts or exercise which, as a symbol of Chinese culture, has made a deep impact around the world for many years. It was developed when Taiji concepts were adopted and applied into physical movements (Horwitz, 2003). Since Taijiquan is often simply referred to as "Taiji" by the general public and by many academic researchers, it can be rather confusing.

The scope and depth of Taiji is impossible to be covered by the confines of martial arts. Taijiquan is only a form of physical expression of Taiji, and even the most advanced practice of Taijiquan cannot fully represent Taiji.

Whilst the origin of Taiji concept and culture can be traced back to the time of primeval sage Fuxi at the beginning of Chinese civilization almost 5000 years ago (Perkins, 1999), Taijiquan has a much shorter history. It is commonly believed to be created by the mythical Daoist sage Zhang San Feng around AD 1000 in Song Dynasty (Delza, 1961) and was not popularized until the seventeenth century (LaRochelle, 2014).

13.2.1 Taiji Culture

On a cultural level, Taiji can be expressed in many forms. These include physical movements (exercise), arts, music, literature, mind–body practices such as meditation, breathing exercises as well as diet and lifestyle. In relation to individual wellness, the aim of Taiji is to bring about mental, physical and spiritual growth; and to improve health, longevity and awareness.

13.3 Taijitu 太极图

The core concept of Taiji can be illustrated in the "Taijitu" 太极图 (Taiji diagram). The term Taijitu refers to a number of "tu" or diagrams which are visual representations of the concept of Taiji (Wang, 2005).

Whilst the early history of the Taijitu is unclear, a common view is that it is a divine revelation from the ancient past by the mythical sage Fuxi. Sages such as Confucius also mentioned references to the diagram in the book Yijing (Louis, 2003). The Taijitu is believed by many scholars to be transmitted in secret by certain Daoists and NeoConfucian thinkers of the Song period before becoming more widely known in the Ming period (Hu, 1985). There are many versions of the Taijitu associated with individual thinkers and schools of thoughts (Louis, 2003) and the pictorial representation continues to evolve over time.

The Taijitu used here to represent and explain the concept of Taiji is one that has three key elements: Wuji, Taiji and Huangji.

13.3.1 The Three Key Elements of Taijitu

Taijitu has three key elements: "Wuji" 无极, "Taiji" 太极 and "Huangji" 皇极 (see Fig. 13.1).

"Wuji" corresponds to the "Yuan Yin" dimension 原音层 or primordial sound dimension; "Taiji" corresponds to the "Yuan Qi" dimension 元气层 or primordial Qi dimension; and "Huangji" corresponds to the "Yuan Guang" dimension 元光层 or primordial light dimension. See Fig. 13.2.

According to Taiji philosophy, Yuan Yin 元音 (primordial sound), Yuan Qi 元气 (primordial Qi), and Yuan Guang 元光 (primordial light) are the three primordial substances which give rise to the universe and all manifested phenomena. "Qi" has no exact translation but can be regarded as a vital and dynamic force or energy.

Fig. 13.1 **a** Taijitu, **b** Taijitu with annotated Wuji, Taiji and Huangji

Fig. 13.2 Diagrams illustrating the three key elements of the Taijitu: Wuji, Taiji and Huangji

Table 13.1 Summary table of the three key elements in Taijitu

In Taijitu	Corresponding element	Equivalent scientific term
Wuji 无极	Yuan Yin 元音 (Primordial Sound)	Signal or information 信息
Taiji 太极	Yuan Qi 元气 (Primordial Qi)	Substance 物质
Huangji 皇极	Yuan Guang 元光 (Primordial Light)	Energy 能量

Modern scientific terms can be used to help promote understanding. Yuan Qi 元气 (primordial Qi) can be described as substance (物质), meaning all the phenomena of the manifest world; Yuan Guang 元光 (primordial light) can be described as energy (能量), and Yuan Yin 元音 (primordial sound) can be described as information or signal (信息). See Table 13.1.

- Wuji 无极

Wuji is the undifferentiated, unmainfested primordial state. It is formless, shapeless and limitless. It is the state prior to differentiation into Yin and Yang and is the state which gives birth to all manifested phenomena (Reninger, 2019), (5). Wuji is represented by an empty circle in Taijitu (Taijitu Shuo). See Fig. 13.3. Wuji represents Yuan Yin, and is a system of information and signals.

- Taiji 太极

Yuan Yin (primordial sound energy) of Wuji gives birth to the universe by separating into the duality of Yin and Yang (Taiji). Then, within this Taiji Yuan Qi (primordial Qi) dimension of Yin and Yang, there is further manifestation of the essence of Yang

Fig. 13.3 Diagrams illustrating Wuji dividing into the duality of Ying and Yang by the motion of Yuan Yin and the formation of Yin within Yang and Yang within Yin

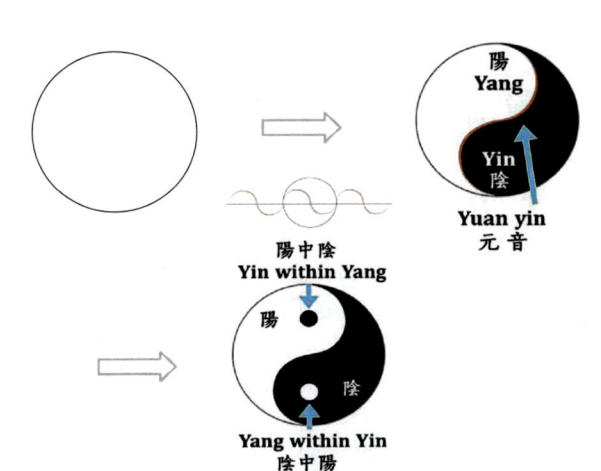

within Yin, and the essence of Yin within Yang. They are represented by two small circles within Yin and Yang. See Fig. 13.3.

The flow of Yin and Yang, abiding by the law of nature which existed since the beginning of time, are constantly transforming, developing, interconnecting and interlinking. This gives rise to the universe and all natural phenomena in the manifested world.

Yin and Yang in the Taijitu are similar to the 0 and 1 in the binary system which forms the basis of modern computer language. The 17th-century philosopher and mathematician Leibniz who developed the modern binary number system made direct references to the yin-yang and the cosmological ideas in the Chinese classic I-Ching (Perkins, 2004). He believed that "ones" and "zeros" are capable of expressing any possible value and that Chinese cosmology shows how the universe can be created from "unity" and "nothingness" (Doroudi, 2007).

- Huangji

When the highest level of harmonisation takes place between the two polarities of the essence of Yin and Yang, Huangji (the Yuan Guang/primordial light dimension) is formed. The light of Huangji is the illuminated essence of Taiji, becoming a new system from which all phenomena can be created. In the classic "The Emperor"s Eternal World" 皇极经世书 written in Song Dynasty, the character "Huang" 皇 is described as "large" or "immense" and "Ji" 极 as center or middle "至大之谓皇, 至中之谓极". The vastness of Huangji can permeate the entire universe and encompass everything; and the center is the source of all manifested phenomena.

13.3.2 How the Taijitu Relates to "Dao De Jing"

The law of nature which guides the flow of Yin and Yang is called "Dao" 道, which is the core concept described in the Chinese Classic, "Dao De Jing". As Laozi, the author of the five-thousand word "Dao De Jing" explains, "Dao gives rise to 'one', 'one' gives rise to 'two', 'two' gives rise to 'three', and 'three' gives rise to all natural phenomena" (Dao De Jing, Chap. 42).

This is fully illustrated in the Taijitu where Wuji is one, Taiji is two and Huangji is three (Fig. 13.4). The way Dao, or the law of nature, gives rise to all natural phenomena from the unmanifest (Wuji) will be explained in more detail below.

13.3.3 The S-Shaped Curve in Taijitu

As we can see in the Taijitu, Yin and Yang are separated by a smooth S-shaped curve, shaped like a flowing stream (Fig. 13.3). This wave form can be described as a "sine wave" in scientific language.

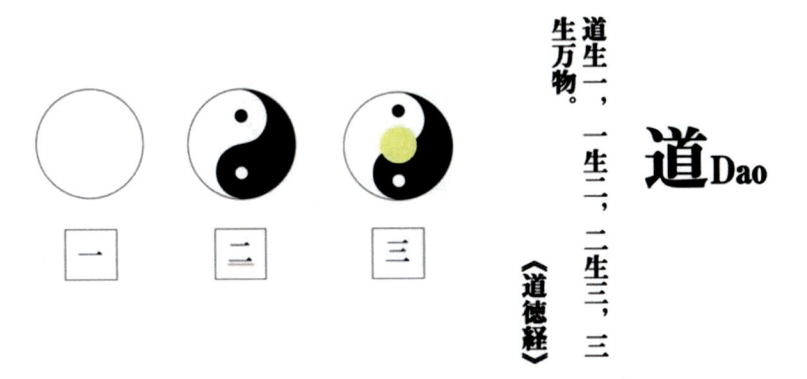

Fig. 13.4 Diagrammatic representation of, "Dao gives rise to 'one', 'one' gives rise to 'two', 'two' gives rise to 'three', and 'three' gives rise to all natural phenomena" according to Laozi

Sine wave is a continuous wave or a mathematical curve that represents a smooth periodic oscillation. It is the fundamental waveform from which other waveforms may be generated and it is also the simplest wave form that can be generated naturally. This wave pattern often occurs in nature, including wind waves, sound waves, light waves, electromagnetic waves, and the motion of all subatomic particles. The movement or flow of primordial Qi (vital energy), Guang (light) and Yin (sound) in the Taijitu follow the same fundamental wave form.

Scientifically, waves are sums of signals and wave motion is a propagation of disturbances, that is, deviations from a state of rest or equilibrium in a regular and organized way (see Encyclopedia Britannica). In the same way, it is the sum of signals (Yuan Yin) of Wuji which initiates the wave motion, represented by the s-shaped curve in Taijitu, and separates the Wuji state of equilibrium into the duality of Yin and Yang. See Fig. 13.5.

When sine waves interact and flow, the shape ∞, the symbol for infinity, appears. And infinity is the scientific definition of the origin of the universe. All the changes

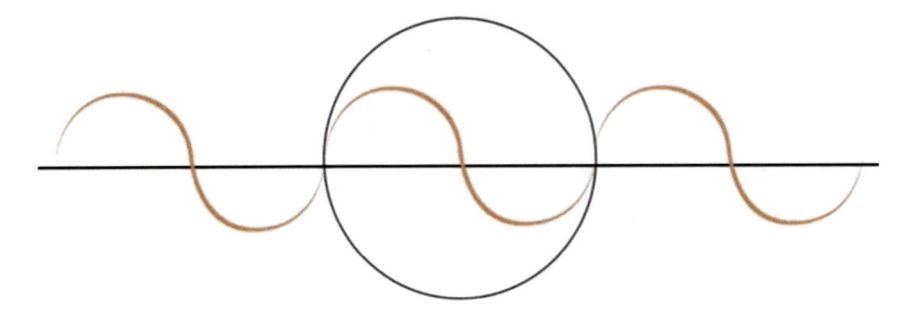

Fig. 13.5 Visual representation of a sine wave passing through Wuji

in the universe follow the flow and movement of this S-shaped curve. It represents the path of the endless transformation and manifestation from "one" in the Taijitu.

13.4   The Guiding Principles of Taiji

There are two main principles which guide the dynamic changes of the constantly revolving universe of Taijitu:-

(1)   The unmanifest gives birth to all manifested phenomena and all manifested phenomena dissolves back to the unmanifest. 无中生有, 有化于无。

In Taiji philosophy, all tangible matters are part of Yuan Qi 元气 or "primordial Qi": Heaven and earth, sun and moon, mankind and all the phenomena of the manifest world are formed through the mutual interaction and union of Yin Qi 阴气 and Yang Qi 阳气.

Prior to the birth of the universe, "Hun Yuan Yi Qi" 混元一气 is contained within the primordial state of Wuji. "Hun Yuan Yi Qi" (translated as the undifferentiated, primordial, singular Qi) is sometimes erroneously interpreted as "nothingness". It is not "nothingness" because contained within this "Hun Yuan Yi Qi" are the formless and intangible primordial substances which give birth to all things, namely: Yuan Guang, Yuan Yin and Yuan Qi. The character "Wu" 无 in "Wuji" 无极 represents the unmanifest. Taiji principles tell us that there is "something" within "emptiness" and the unmanifest is not truly "empty" 空中真的有, 无中原不虚.

The primordial substances follow the oscillation of Yuan Yin (primordial sound), the S curve, to give rise to the duality of Yin and Yang. Yin Qi and Yang Qi then interact to give birth to Heaven and Earth and all the phenomena in the manifest world. This is the journey wherein the un-manifest gives birth to the manifest.

When a life-form is born in its dimension of existence, it follows the changes in Yin and Yang through the passing of time and goes through many stages in life: conception, growth, flourishing, reaching its prime, decline/deterioration, and finally, death. This is the dynamic process through which manifested phenomena dissolves back into the un-manifest.

This cyclic transformation between the manifest and un-manifest is the foundation of Taiji. It is rooted in "Dao" 道 and "De" 德. "Dao" 道 is the basic principle of existence and "a metaphysical first principle that embraces and underlies all beings"; it is intangible and "lies beyond the power of language" (Lee, Yang & Wang, 2009). "De" 德 is the tangible manifestation of "Dao". It also represents specific humanistic behaviors and moral virtues which one acquires through being in accordance with Dao (Lee et al., 2009). When De becomes infinitely small or "zero", it is "Dao". "Dao" and "De" are the un-manifest and the manifest, and there is no differentiation between the two in their origin.

In "Dao De Jing" 道德经, the ancient sage Laozi 老子 confers a secret message within which the ultimate truth hides; a message that has yet to be truly deciphered:-

Man follows the laws of the Earth; The Earth follows the laws of the universe; The universe follows the laws of Dao; And Dao follows the laws of nature.

人法地, 地法天, 天法道, 道法自然。(Dao De Jing, Chap. 25).

The law of nature is the true guiding principle of Dao, of the manifest and un-manifest.

This seemingly abstract notion of cyclic transformation between the manifest and un-manifest is actually constantly taking place in our daily lives. As Master Xing explains, "Having practiced Taiji for several decades, I have direct experience to prove that these words are true. My Taiji lineage, Li-style Taiji, emphasizes on experiential practice. During my sixty years of Taiji practice, I can constantly feel the flow of Qi between my body and mind; and the transformation and union between Qi, Guang and Yin is continually taking place."

To illustrate this concept of cyclic transformation, here is a real-life example:

When two strangers meet, they become immediately connected as they are constantly exchanging the air that they breathe. When they start a conversation, the voice of the speaker, following the rhythm of his or her breathe, travels through space into the other person's ears. The sound waves which carry the signals of the words, convey information. This information elicits exchange between the two individual's minds and bodies and conveys emotions and understanding. They get to know each other and start to build a relationship with physical and mental exchange. This process can lead to changes in their emotions and focus and so on. After a while, their bodies may relax and become less anxious. This is a real-life example of transformation and interaction between the manifest (tangible) and un-manifest (intangible).

(2)　The relationship between thought and matter

Chinese writing is hieroglyphic. The character for "thought" (意) consists of 2 parts: "mind" (心) and "sound" (音). Thought can be described as the sound of the mind at any given moment in time; it is the message or information from the mind. This is called "Yuan Yin" (primordial sound) in Taiji culture.

It has already been explained that "Qi", "Guang" and "Yin" are the primordial substances contained in "Hun Yuan Yi Qi". And it is the oscillation of Yuan Yin which gives birth to the universe and all things within. Here, the relationship between thought and matter is similar to that between the un-manifest and the manifest. And contained within thought (the un-manifest), there is the transference of energy which conveys information (a manifested phenomenon). Hence, within the un-manifest, there is also the essence of manifested phenomena.

13.5 The Laws Governing the Changes and Transformations of Taiji

13.5.1 Dynamic System of Taiji

Taiji is a dynamic system where constant changes take place. These changes and transformations are not random, but follow a set of law or pattern.

(1) Taiji: Creation, Transformation and Return 太极的生化反

The laws governing the changes and transformation of Taiji between the un-manifest and the manifest are the three stages of creation/birth 生, transformation 化 and the return to origin 反. Wuji gives rise to Taiji; Taiji transforms into Huangji; and Huangji returns to Wuji.

The cycle of "Wuji giving rise to Taiji, transforms into Huangji and returns to Wuji" 无极生太极, 太极化皇极, 皇极返无极 is the fundamental cosmic law of order governing the universe, nature, as well as the inner workings of society and science. It not only guides the relationship between heaven, earth and man but also the internal relationship an individual has within himself and the external relationship with society. The infinite cycle also governs the interactions between different nations, ethnicities, religious groups and so on. See Fig. 13.6.

In practice, this pattern of change can be observed in the life cycle of human individuals; in the growth cycle of plants and even in the growth and changes of corporate companies.

The infinite process of of Creation, Transformation, and Return.

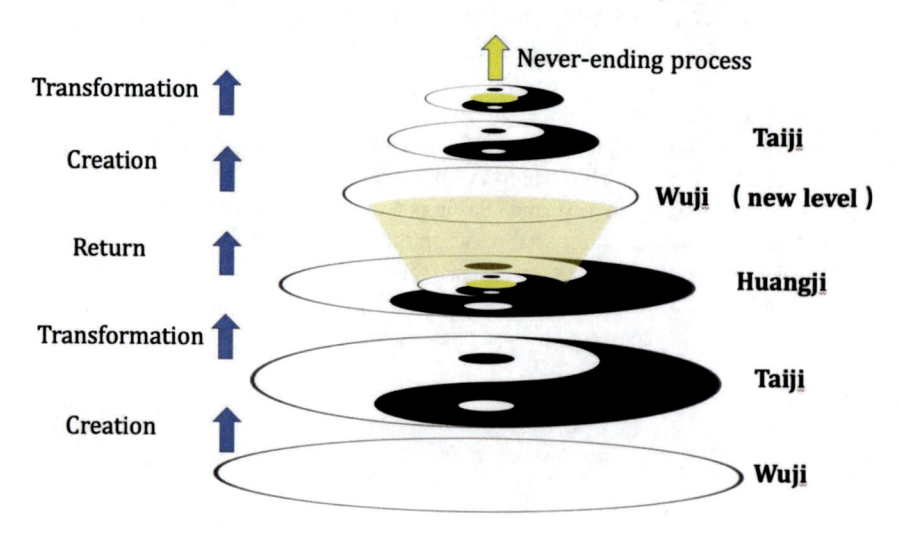

Fig. 13.6 Diagram showing cyclic infinite process of "creation, transformation and return"

The concept of Wuji and Taiji and Huangji is very abstract. To aid understanding, below are two real-life examples:-

a. The growth cycle of plants can be used to illustrate this process of creation, transformation and return. When a plant is still a seed, it is in the stage of Wuji. Existing within the small seed are all the information (coded in the DNA) and vital substances necessary for its development into a plant. Wuji is not empty of everything, it actually contains everything but has not manifested into form. Then the seed starts to sprout and adapts to its environment, receiving nourishment from sunlight and water. This process of growth and transformation is Taiji. Yin and Yang are interacting, interconnecting and harmonizing within this plant. Through the passage of time, given the right conditions, its root grows deep and its foliage becomes full. Beautiful flowers start to blossom, eventually bringing succulent fruits. This process is the formation of Huangji. This is the stable form that is achieved when the harmonization between Yin and Yang reaches a high level. And each seed inside the fruit contains within itself a new life. When the fruit is ripe and drops onto the ground, the seeds are released back into the soil (nature) and begin a new cycle of life. This is the process of 'return'. The seed is now the new Huangji, at a new level. See Fig. 13.7.

b. The second example is a lecture. Before the lecture starts, the hall is empty with nobody there, but everything has been set up and organized, waiting for the talk to take place. We will just call this state Wuji.

When the lecture starts, the speaker stands on the stage talking and the listeners sit below the stage listening. There are now the duality of a lecturer and the audience:— Yin and Yang are born.

Fig. 13.7 Diagram showing the life cycle of a plant illustrating the infinite process of "creation, transformation and return"

Whilst the lecturer is speaking, he is sensing the audiences " condition as they listen. Changes in their bodies and minds are perceived and continuously integrated into the speech of the lecturer, affecting what he says (Yin within Yang). Whilst the audience are listening, they are continuously receiving energy and information from the lecturer; absorbing the essence and relating it with their past experiences, transforming it into their own learning and gains. The listener may also become curious and inquisitive in new and unfamiliar territories (Yang within Yin). Hence through the interaction arises Yin within Yang and Yang within Yin. This process can be likened to Wuji giving rise to Taiji.

As the lecturer and the audience delve deeper and deeper into the subject, their minds and bodies begin to resonate and connect, developing deep understanding between each other, sharing a harmonious relationship and experience. At this time, Taiji is transformed into Huangji.

When the lecture is over, both the lecturer and the audience leave the hall and it will again return to its original, empty state. This is Huangji returning to Wuji. However, this new Wuji is different from the one at the start when there was nothing. It now contains the transmission and exchange of energy and information between the speaker and the audience. Both parties have developed new insights and understanding. This is the new Wuji that arises from the return of Huangji.

(2) Changes are initiated when extremes are reached 极则生变

    a.   The process of creation, transformation and return is initiated extremes are reached.

        This is the second law governing the changes in Taiji. As one approaches the fullness of yin, yang begins to emerge in the horizon and vice versa. In everyday language, it can be described as quantitative change leading to qualitative change.

        Yin and Yang are born together, transform together and return together, they are from the same source and inseparable. The cycle is dynamic, continuous and never-ending.

    b.   The process of birth, transformation and return can be further divided into 2 types:

- the process that take place within one-self 自生自化自返 and
- the process that take place through interaction with others 互生互化 互返.

13.5.2 *The Meaning of the Chinese Characters Taiji* 太极

Understanding the meaning of the two Chinese characters "Taiji" (太极) helps the comprehension of Taiji concept.

In ancient texts (白虎通义。五行), the character "Tai" 太 means "big" or "large" 大: so big that it is boundless and infinite, representing the whole universe. "Tai" can also be small, so tiny that it cannot contain anything inside, at a point so near zero that it cannot be further divided. This primordial substance "Tai" (太) which can be boundlessly large and infinitely small is what gives birth to all things, man and nature. It is the origin of the universe. It is called "Yuan" 元 in Taiji culture and "Dao" 道 according to Laozi. And this primordial substance, which is the source of the universe, is formed from the combination of Qi, Guang and Yin.

"Ji" (极) is described as the "centre" 中 (Five Classics of Justice 孔颖达《五经正义》). It is the pattern of "Wuji giving rise to Taiji; Taiji transforms into Huangji; and Huangji returns to Wuji"; the law which governs creation, transformation and return.

13.6 The Core Foundation of Taiji Dynamics

The ideal picture of the Tai Chi diagram is perfect and beautiful, representing the ultimate fruit of the endless cycle of creation, transformation and return. The crucial question is: what it the core foundation of this natural and perfect process?

13.6.1 The Core Foundation of the Process of Creation, Transformation and Return

In order to identify the core foundation of Taiji, one needs to first observe and understand nature. As described by Li Shui Dong, the founder of Li-style Taiji in "Taiji Milu" 太极秘箓:-

i.   Observe the Changes in Nature 观自然之变化

Quietly observe the changes in nature:—the never-ending cycle of birth of all phenomena of the manifested world from the unmanifest; and the return of the manifest to the unmanifest.

ii. Connect with and Follow the Laws of Nature 通自然之法规

One must always act according to the laws of nature and not against them. Take the different seasons as an example: spring is the season of birth; summer is the season of growth; autumn is the season of harvest; winter is the season of concealment/containment; and the "long summer" is the season of transformation. If a person truly connects with the laws of nature, he or she must follow the characteristics and changes of each season and act accordingly.

iii. Realize the Concepts of Nature 明自然之定理

Fig. 13.8 Taijitu illustrating
"He"/harmony as its core
foundation

The transformation and changes between the three essential cosmic elements Yuan Guang, Yuan Yin and Yuan Qi involves constant interaction and integration. The essence of each element is within one another and there is no separation (the concept of "me within you and you within me"). This smooth, unobstructed and instantaneous interaction and integration between matter, energy and information is the guiding principle of nature that is leads to creation, transformation and return.

iv. "He" 和 is the Dao of Immortality 和乃长生之道也

The secret of immortality is "He" 和/Harmony. It is the core foundation of the process of birth, transformation and return (see Fig. 13.8).

13.6.2 "He"/Harmony: Its Changes and Transformation

"He" 和 is probably the most cherished ideal in Chinese culture. The word "He" can be translated as "harmony" but it is probably more appropriate to be described as harmonization (Li, 2006) in the context of Taiji philosophy. This is because it is a dynamic process of interaction of Yin and Yang as opposed to a static condition.

He (harmony) has always been the root of all life cycles in nature. Man and all things are created by this process of dynamic harmonization:-

- He (harmony) in Wuji gives birth to Yin and Yang;
- He (harmony) between Yin and Yang gives rise to Heaven and earth; and
- He (harmony) between Heaven and earth creates all things.

Fig. 13.9 Using the Taijitu to illustrate the "three harmonies"

This is the process through which the manifested world is born from the unmanifest.

On a human level:-

- He (harmony) between the body and mind brings health and long-life;
- He (harmony) between human beings and all other living things results in intimacy, kindness and happiness.

We rely on our environment for all our basic necessities of life including food and shelter. In order to live, we cannot be separated from our environment. Human and all living things must have mutual respect, sustain and nourish one another, in order to develop intimacy and kindness.

- Wisdom arises when there is He (harmony) between man and heaven and it purifies human minds which results in a state where:—"the skies are clear; the land is safe and peaceful; and human minds are clear and luminous". In this harmonious state, man can connect with the information from the cosmos; his breath and life resonating with that of the universe and receiving the ultimate wisdom. This is the path of the return to the un-manifest (see Fig. 13.9).

13.6.3 How to Achieve "He"/Harmony

When Dao follows the law of nature; human and the universe become one. 道法自然, 天人合一。

In order to achieve harmony, there are three inner qualities of harmony which one must understand and practice:

i. Harmony Arises from the Mind

A person"s mind has to be continuously cultivated and nourished. First, one must quiet down the mind; then slowly empty the mind of thoughts; and eventually focusing on the mind. It will gradually purify to become clear and uncontaminated. Then harmony between Man and the cosmos will be attained and the two will become one.

The capacity and flexibility or the heart and mind will increase, allowing room not only to embrace oneself, but also others. Tolerance, understanding and kindness will result. By adapting to changes instead of resisting or fighting them, a person's heart and mind are strengthened. By being compassionate and moral, the heart opens up, bringing happiness and contentment.

ii.   Harmony Arises from the Body

One has to constantly protect and nurture his or her own body. As a human being, the mind and body are one and inseparable. Only through practice and training of both the mind and body together can one achieve self-harmony and health. In order to achieve this goal, a person has to:

- look after one's health;
- cultivate one's moral character;
- cherish one's body;
- continually removing impurities from the body;
- harmonise the major organs;
- cultivate Qi that is of good quality, centered and harmonious.

iii.   Harmony Arises from the State of Mind

The process of regulating the body and mind is also the process of removing one's ego/self. Erogenous views of the truth and obstacles such as greed, hatred, stupidity, pride and doubt; attachment to the self and to manifested phenomena are obstacles preventing a person from genuine communication with the universe. This is why one must aspire to achieve a state free of being controlled and driven by desires, selfishness, and sensory fulfilment.

There is a Taoist saying: "The Dao mind can only be born when the human "mind is defeated." 人心灭处道心. Here, the "human mind" refers to the modern mind that is driven by desires and habitual thinking; and the "Dao mind" refers to the primordial mind which is luminous and complete in itself."

The wisdom of the universe will be experience by those who can truly connect, understand and be in harmony with the laws of nature without obscuration. True happiness will be attained, and finally leading to the great completion of life. Harmony is the root of all the paths and laws of nature 和是万法之宗.

13.7   The Purpose of Learning Taiji

The purpose of learning Taiji philosophy, culture and practice is to help transform the body and mind in order to attain the state of "He" or harmony.

We live in an increasingly divided world. A vast array of disharmonies exists, from the individual level to groups, societies and to the natural world. There is mind–body disconnection within individuals; communicative difficulties between people; conflicts within families; clashes between different factions of society; racial and ethnical conflicts; opposing stances between countries; misunderstanding between different schools of thought; intolerance between religious groups; damage to the environment caused by man and the harm that man inflicts on other living things……the list goes on. These issues seem to be intensifying and spiraling out of control.

Human desires are growing in a troubling manner despite the level of comfort, convenience and affluence we enjoy today; people are always yearning for more. Anxiety, fear and depression have become common ailments. People's sense of unhappiness and discontent seems to grow by the day in spite of abundant of material comforts and possessions.

All these can be seen as the consequences of the absence of "He"/harmony: when harmony is lost, there is misfortune, destruction and death; when harmony is achieved, there is health, prosperity and happiness. In order to achieve the "three harmonies": harmony between the mind and body; between man and all things; and between man and the universe, one must genuinely cultivate one's life and practice according to Taiji teachings sincerely with all your heart, under the guidance and protection of authentic teachers, using authentic methods and with the support of a community. Only then can we return to the arms of our parental universe.

Taiji culture, rooted in harmony, is an invaluable antidote to the problems of this generation. Learning and practicing Taiji culture can restore balance and harmony, bringing health, happiness, wisdom and help resolve inner and outer conflicts.

Human beings are ultimately children of the universe; of Heaven and Earth. It should be a person's innate ability to connect with and to resonate with the cyclic changes of the universe. However, people today are generally too egocentric, only focusing on the self. Many have lost the connection with nature. Learning and practicing Taiji culture will help re-establish the bond. When true understanding of Taiji is established within a person, his or her desires will gradually decrease and eventually be able to attain harmony and return to authenticity.

13.8 Taiji Education at Tian Zhen Yuan 天真园

The path to harmony is through education and commitment to the study and practice of authentic teachings. Tian Zhen Yuan 天真园 (see Appendix 1) offers a complete educational path for learning and experiencing Taiji culture. It is a place where Taiji culture is a way of life, practiced and incorporated into daily living.

A basic holistic education curriculum, with Taiji culture as its foundation, has been developed by its founders Master Xing Qi-Lin, Dr. Cui Ai-Ling and like-minded individuals over the past twenty years. It is suitable for people of all ages, from age one to a hundred. The guiding principle of this education is to harmonize and to cultivate the whole-person: mind, body and spirit. There are existing Taiji-cultural practitioners of different age groups at Tian Zhen Yuan.

13.8.1 Educational Structure

Based on traditional Chinese educational principles, Tian Zhen Yuan believes that education should start from the prenatal stage. As a person grows up, there should be different educational emphasis and objectives through different stages of life, listed below are the details: See Fig. 13.10.

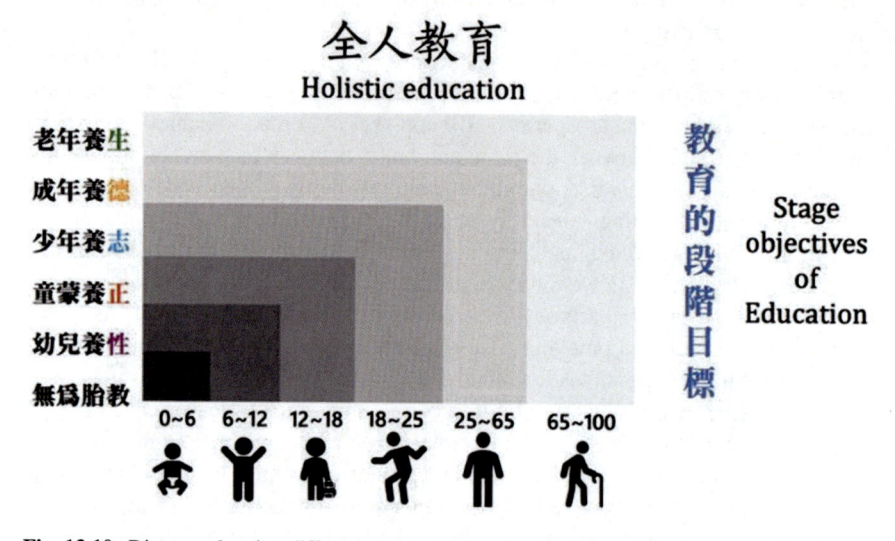

Fig. 13.10 Diagram showing different stages of education in Chinese, English translation is given in the paragraph below

- Infancy: nurture and cultivate an infant's innate, wholesome virtues and traits
- Childhood: nurture the sense of righteousness, establish honorable, upright and virtuous behaviors and habits
- Youth: establish and cultivate noble aspirations
- Adulthood: cultivate "De" (morality) and lead ones' life accordingly
- Old age: cultivate health, well-being and longevity.

These objectives are focused on the cultivation of "De"; the tangible manifestation of "Dao". If a person can truly cultivate "De" throughout life, he or she will be connected to "Dao", the ultimate truth. And this will bring harmony and wisdom.

De is cultivated at Tian Zhen Yuan through five main mediums: (i) the study of Chinese Classics and literature including Dao De Jing and Confucius texts; (ii) martial arts with Taijiquan as the main focus, (iii) Chinese medicine, (iv) agriculture (there is ann on-site organic farm where most of the food consumed in the center is grown); (v) art including Chinese calligraphy and painting.

13.8.2 Practical Methods to Cultivate "He"/Harmony

The practical methods to cultivate "He" are:—quiet meditative practice (静修), movement practice (动修) and practice through doing/daily life (事修). All three methods are incorporated into the daily routine at Tian Zhen Yuan.

a. Quiet Meditative Practice

　　There are 10 levels of internal practice in quiet meditative practice, that is, a 10-step practice method. If an individual follows the step-by-step instructions given by an authentic teacher who has genuine understanding of the teachings, the mind and body will reach a basic level of harmony over time.

b. Movement Practice

　　Movement practice includes the Taiji standing pose/exercise, Taiji massage and Taijiquan (martial arts). The methods are simple, easy to follow and to keep up regularly. If one commits to regular, long term practice, treating it as a daily necessity like eating and sleeping, one would experience the joy and beauty that comes when the body and mind are serene and harmonious.

c. Practice through Doing

　　Practice through dong means cultivating De (tangible manifestation of Dao)/morality in our daily lives—through every action (including walking, standing, sitting and lying down), every arising thought; and through the way we deal with others and handle matters.

13.8.3 The Importance of an Authentic Teacher

It is important to realize that it is almost impossible to complete the study and practice of Taiji without an authentic teacher. This is because a person would not be able to recognize or understand the different states of meditation and practices without guidance by an authentic teacher who has received direct transmission from his or her lineage teachers. The teacher must have personal experiences of these states of practice. To start the journey, one needs to first receive direct teaching and transmission by a teacher. The next step is to start cultivating harmony of the body and mind to become balanced and healthy. Mind and body cultivation and nourishment will eventually open up the hidden potentials and powers of the person; opening up the chakras and the Qi breathing system to become connected to the energy/Qi of the cosmos; and restoring the innate ability to connect with and to resonate with the energy and cyclic changes of the universe.

　　According to Master Xing, there are nine "levels" in our body which need to be opened up one by one. And this process relies on the teacher's instructions and guidance at every step.

　　In order to achieve harmony, one must genuinely cultivate one's life and practice according to Taiji teachings sincerely and whole-heartedly, under the guidance of authentic teachers, using authentic methods and with the support of a community. Only then can we return to the arms of our parental universe.

Tian Zhen Yuan is an ideal environment for experiencing, learning and practicing Taiji culture. Anyone wishing to cultivate harmony is welcomed to pay a visit to Tian Zhen Yuan.

13.9 Taiji and Community

In its practice of Taiji culture over the past 20 years, Tian Zhen Yuan has hosted numerous activities in community, industrial and academic environments. By achieving harmony of mind and body, such activities not only promoted mental and physical health, but also enhanced interpersonal cohesion, creativity and team unity of the groups involved. The following cases feature a diverse range of locations: local communities in Beijing, Chinese listed companies, Japanese-invested companies and preschool education groups; outside of China, Hong Kong-based initiatives and Taiwanese organizations.

13.9.1 Mainland China

13.9.1.1 Unika

UNIKA is a Japanese company with investments in China. As early as the year 2000, Master Xing Qilin and Dr. Cui Ailing gave seminars to company management on the practical application of Taiji philosophy, with the goal of achieving harmony and unity in interpersonal relations. At the same time, Tian Zhen Taiji Dance was introduced as a work-break exercise to maintain physical and mental health. By popularizing these practices in UNIKA, good practical results were achieved: employees at all levels of UNIKA were positive in mood and engaged harmoniously with one another, whilst working efficiently towards common goals in the workplace; and not only did they enjoy their spare time, they loved the workplace as their home.

Outside of 9-to-5 work hours, Dr. Cui also used Taiji philosophy to teach employees how to become an ideal family member: topics included the role of the woman in the family as a wife, a mother and a daughter-in-law, or the role of the family man in making himself a figure of respect to his children, as well as an effective middleman for the communication between his mother and his wife. In addition, Dr. Cui Ailing also set up a night-time childcare station at the company and personally oversaw the care of children whose parents were working overtime. This initiative taught employees' wives by example the following ideal: if one develops the child's spirituality, activity and intellect whilst protecting a child's naivety, the child would grow up physically and mentally healthy.

Thanks to applied Taiji philosophy, UNIKA was the most dynamic of the foreign-funded enterprises in the Langfang Economic Development Zone of China at that time. In light of this achievement, UNIKA repeatedly invited Dr. Cui as a guest speaker to their Japanese headquarters; they were curious of the techniques by which a native Japanese enterprise could operate and manage in China with such efficiency, whilst maintaining high employee morale. UNIKA's example also attracted inspections by a range of national, provincial and municipal leaders of China's governing body, and enterprises from all over the country visited in order to gain advanced experience in company management. In recognition of her efforts, Dr. Cui was awarded the title "Friend of Employees" by the All-China Federation of Trade Unions.

13.9.1.2 Suzhou Good-Ark Electronics Co. Ltd.

Founded in 1990 and listed in 2006, Suzhou Good-Ark Electronics Co. Ltd. is one of the largest diode manufacturers in the world. Good-Ark has always been advocating the concept of "family culture" as the core of their enterprise management. In 2018, Good-Ark's chairman visited Tian Zhen Yuan; upon coming into contact with Taiji culture, he had a revelation, saying: "If my progress so far were a field, my 30 years of family culture at Good-Ark was like only loosening the soil. The Taiji culture of Tian Zhen Yuan are the seeds, nutrients and environment that can brighten every life and bring harmony to every individual. I must bring those at Good-Ark to Tian Zhen Yuan to learn this kind of Taiji philosophy that can be used in daily life."

In 2019, about 40 core members of the management team of Good-Ark came to Tian Zhen Yuan to learn Taiji culture; they stayed for a week, learning both theoretical and practical aspects of Taiji as well as practicing the simple, yet beautiful Tian Zhen Taiji Dance. Initially, the atmosphere of the learners from Good-Ark had started out serious and rigid; however, by the end, all were smiling and exuded an positive aura from the inside out.

When the learners returned to Good-Ark, they shared their experiences and Taiji Dance to all levels of the company; as a result, the Good-Ark employees became more positive and full of energy. Since then, Good-Ark has also brought Taiji Dance to their branch in Malaysia to continue spreading the benefits of applied Taiji philosophy.

13.9.1.3 Tongcheng Mingli (TCML) Preschool Education Group

Founded in 2010 by Dr. Cui Ailing's former student, TCML is a preschool education group with 13 kindergartens. This group has engaged in the practical application of Taiji culture in the management of preschool teachers and the teaching of students at their kindergartens.

In 2019, TCML sent five batches of approximately 40 six-year-old children to Tian Zhen Yuan to learn how the concept "In Infancy, Cultivate Human Nature" in Taiji culture could be applied to daily life. The children were taught about Taiji through activities that challenged their minds and bodies, and learned how Taiji could help them in daily activities such as eating, sleeping and even making friends. The consensus from kindergarten teachers regarding students who returned from Tian Zhen Yuan was that these children showed significantly improved focus and hands-on abilities during learning; in social situations they were more lively and were observed to be at harmony with other students, and at home they were said to be more well-behaved.

Therefore, TCML asked for two six-year-old students of Tian Zhen Yuan to teach and demonstrate Taiji Five-Finger Exercise, Taiji Five-Step Stance, Taiji meditation, Taiji diet, Taiji breathing technique and other such practical Taiji applications at 5 kindergartens. Through this exchange between children of the same age with Taiji as the medium, all parties experienced first-hand the happiness that Taiji culture brought to young bodies and minds.

The directors of all 13 kindergartens under TCML have also come to Tian Zhen Yuan to experience and train in Taiji culture. As a result, they felt that coming into contact with Taiji culture had given them vitality in body and flexibility in mind; they were more able to feel harmony in their lives and were more creative in work situations.

13.9.1.4 Taoran Academy (Taoranting, Beijing)

The Taoran Academy in Taoranting, Beijing has held a weekly Taiji culture class since 2018; each class typically has about 20 people. Participants learn about the Taiji theory of "Harmony" and practice applied Taiji forms such as Taiji Thirteen Stances, the Taiji ceremony of tea and the Taiji ceremony of incense. After more than one year of study and practice, common feedback taken from members of Taoran show increased peace of mind and smoother interpersonal relations; in the family, there is harmony among family members, especially in cases of parent–child understanding. Due to its simplicity and effectiveness, class participants believe that Taiji culture could easily be applied to all aspects of work and life.

13.9.1.5 Daxing Rixin School (Beijing)

For two consecutive years from 2019 to 2020, Master Xing Qilin's students were invited to carry out intensive teaching sessions on Taiji culture for children aged 7–11 at the Winter Camp and Summer Camp of the Daxing Rixin School in Beijing. The aim of these sessions was to enhance the children's perceptive and concentration abilities. To this day, the cumulative number of students has reached 500.

Campers experienced Taiji theories through the following activities: the campers were taught Taiji meditation to improve concentration; they were guided to understand the Taiji concept of "All living things originate from the same root" by using plants; finally, campers tried an experiment demonstrating the importance of harmony using rice. These Taiji culture winter and summer camps have generally been welcomed by students and parents alike.

13.9.2 Hong Kong, China

At present, there are four Taiji cultural learning communities in Hong Kong: the Hong Kong Tian Zhen Taiji class, the Master Nan Taiji class, the Ten-Mile Peach Blossoms class and the Hong Kong Chinese Orchestra workshop. These four groups were founded at different times: the earliest in 2012 and the latest in 2018. Combining their experience of Taiji culture, they have had the following four gains.

13.9.2.1 Learning to Manage Emotions

Health and happiness are common goals for many people. However, more often than not, the education many have received since childhood did not teach us how to manage our emotions so as to achieve these goals; now we understand the importance of such an ability to anyone on the road of life.

Over the process of learning and practicing Taiji culture in Hong Kong, the learners have begun to perceive that they are becoming more skilled in emotional management. To describe the process, they refer to active Taiji practice: through practice, the learner gradually understands the parts of one's own body, and by extension learns the body's needs and how to correctly use each part; by accepting that the body is a product of heaven and earth, one begins to understand the natural principles by which parts of the body interact and respond. This process of introspection is one of the most important foundations of emotional management.

13.9.2.2 Learning to Alleviate Stress

All kinds of things can happen on the path of life, and these things may give rise to troubles and unhappiness within the self. Learning to properly resolve and release stress without side effects, and allow the body and mind return to equilibrium is an essential lesson for everyone's life path.

Passive Taiji practices teach us to let go: under a correct meditative state, we can empty our hearts and return to a blank slate, and we can soothe our frustrations with the peaceful melodies of Taiji music. The effects may seem infinitesimal, but with consistency and repetition, even small strokes can feel great oaks: the group members who have practiced Taiji for 7–8 years have felt improvement in their ability to alleviate stress.

13.9.2.3 Learning Taiji is for All Ages

From when we are born to when we become adults, very few of us will begin to think about the inevitable end of our lives; and among this minority, even fewer will decide to go against the flow and proactively plan for life's final destination.

Therefore, preserving one's health is a lifetime endeavor, yet it is never too late to start.

The Hong Kong learners consist mostly of family groups. Therefore, the age diversity of these families allows for the study and practice of all parts of the Holistic Education system of Taiji culture, that is: "In infancy, cultivate nature; in childhood, cultivate integrity; in adolescence, cultivate aspirations; in adulthood, cultivate virtue; in old age, cultivate longevity." Common feedback from these families is that in maintaining their children's nature, they have grown up healthy and brimming with positivity. The women are good housewives who can happily manage their families, while the men are good husbands, good sons and good dads (fathers) in their families while also seeing success in their careers. Finally, despite some more experienced members entering the age group of elders, they continue to learn and practice the applications of Taiji culture.

13.9.2.4 Cultivating Wisdom

In a world where we cannot claim to know everything, can we truly say that we have finished learning?

Through the study and practice of Taii culture over the years, the learners in Hong Kong gradually reached the revelation that the human body is in itself a small universe, and the wisdom we seek was right before our very eyes. To cultivate wisdom is to reach harmony between oneself and the world; to know oneself is to know others and to walk the path of wisdom. Such methods to cultivate wisdom are an integral part of Taiji culture, and are expressed in its more artistic applications.

The Hong Kong learning communities often study and practice Tian Zhen Taiji ceremonies of tea, incense and flower arrangement. Through the lens of aesthetics and art, learners can understand how one's body and mind is connected to the nature of heaven and earth, thus achieving harmony both physically and mentally.

13.9.3 Taiwan, China

Taiwan's Cixin Group has been learning and practicing Tian Zhen Yuan's Taiji culture since 2014. Every year, 20 members of Cixin go to Tian Zhen Yuan for 15 days of study, then return to Taiwan to share what they have learned. The Cixin Group is based in many counties of Taiwan and has a diverse membership: the age of its members range from elementary school children to 70 year olds. Moreover, Cixin's membership contains people of varied career backgrounds: these include volunteer teachers at Cixin who are in charge of etiquette and scripture reading courses, entrepreneurs, real estate traders, financial insurance personnel, elementary school teachers, housewives and more. Typically, these members consist of families as units as they study and practice Taiji culture together.

Cixin's branches in Tainan and Taipei have regularly arranged sessions for different aspects of Taiji practice: 1 hour of Taiji dance group training every week, a monthly gathering to practice Taiji meditation and learn Tian Zhen Taiji culture, and encouragement of Cixin members to carry out active and passive Taiji practice at home every day. Starting from January 2020, Cixin also began daily mass group meditation practice by video conferencing from 9:15 to 10:00 pm.

Through seven years of constant learning and practicing Taiji culture, the team cohesion of Cixin has become stronger as its individuals become unified and at harmony with one another. Moreover, the concept of Taiji culture has been used to create innovative community activities. With the vitality of the community growing more vigorous and an influx of young people joining its ranks, Cixin shows potential for the future.

As shown by the above case studies of learning and practicing Taiji culture, Taiji philosophy has had a profound and positive influence on their respective platforms.

The Taiji culture practiced in Tian Zhen Yuan over the past 20 years has been simplified for the layman and adapted for integration into our daily lives. Its practice is not limited by time nor space: during short breaks or after meals, indoors or outdoors, or in all four seasons; Taiji culture has corresponding practice methods for each situation, with cumulative progress that is measurable both physically and mentally.

In addition, Tian Zhen Taiji culture has been designed to interest newcomers with aesthetics and artistry. With detailed instruction on each aspect of practical Taiji methods, all applications can play a role in achieving harmony in body and mind with consistent practice. At the same time, these Taiji cultural arts can also become a tool by which interpersonal relations and community cohesion can be improved.

The learning and practicing of Tian Zhen Taiji is an exercise in introspection: by looking into ourselves more clearly, we understand our needs so as to gradually become a more harmonious and consistent self. Only in this way can one engage others in effective communication through understanding and empathy. As the individual nears this ideal, one then influences those around them; from families to communities, and from societies to nations. Only then can harmony be achieved between races, religions and ethnicities; by accepting that all living things originate from the same root, the people of the Earth become an existence with a shared destiny to face an unpredictable future.

Appendix 1

Introduction of Tian Zhen Yuan

- Founded in the year 2000 by Master Xing Qi Lin and his wife, Dr. Cui Ai Ling, Tian Zhen Yuan is an institution for the education and application of Taiji culture. It is located in former ancient town Yongyang, now known as Chengguan in Wuqing, Tianjin. With Taiji culture as its main focus, the curriculum includes literature, martial arts, traditional Chinese medicine, agriculture and the arts; the institution hopes to ensure the continued research, development, innovation and inheritance of 5000 years' worth of traditional Chinese culture, which will be achieved by cultivating talent of able body and mind, through methods that are both innovative, yet also acceptable by modern people.

References

In English

Delza, S. (1967). The Art of the Science of T'ai Chi Ch'uan. *The Journal of Aesthetics and Art Criticism, 25*(4), 449–461. https://doi.org/10.2307/428394

Doroudi, S. (2007). On Leibnitz and the I Ching. Ramix.org. (Digital Library: On Leibnitz and the I Ching - Doroudi.pdf).

Horwitz, T. (2003). Tai Chi Ch"uan, the Technique of Power. Cloud Hands. 0974201308 (ISBN13: 9780974201306).

Hu, W. (1985). Yitu mingbian 易图明辨. Congshu jicheng chubian (vol. 438–439, p. 81). Beijing: Zhonghua shuju.

LaRochelle, D. (2014). Making the new appear old: the Daoist spirituality of Chinese martial arts in Taiji Quan manuals published in North America. *Nova Religio: The Journal of Alternative and Emergent Religions, 17*(3), 64–83. https://doi.org/10.1525/nr.2014.17.3.64

Lee, Y.-T., Yang, H., & Wang, M. (2009). Daoist harmony as a Chinese philosophy and psychology. *Peace and Conflict Studies, 16*(1). Article 5.

Li, C. (2006). The confucian ideal of harmony. *Philosophy East and West, 56*(4), 583–603. Retrieved from http://www.jstor.org/stable/4488054.

Louis, F. (2003). The genesis of an icon: The "Taiji" diagram's early history. *Harvard Journal of Asiatic Studies, 63*, 145–196. https://doi.org/10.2307/25066694

Perkins, D. (1999). *Encyclopedia of China: the essential reference to China, its history and culture.* New York: Facts on File. ISBN 0816026939 ISBN 9780816026937.

Perkins, F. (2004). *Leibniz and China: A commerce of light* (p. 117). Cambridge: Cambridge University Press.

Reninger, E. (2019, May 22). The Meaning of Wuji (Wu Chi), the Un-manifest Aspect of the Tao. Retrieved from https://www.learnreligions.com/wuji-wu-chi-3183136.

Tzu, L., & Legger, J. (2009). Tao teching. Digireads.

Wang, R. (2005). Zhou Dunyi's diagram of the supreme ultimate explained (Taijitu shuo): A construction of the Confucian metaphysics. *Journal of the History of Ideas, 66*(3), 307–323. University of Pennsylvania Press. Retrieved September 13, 2019, from Project MUSE database.

Watson, B. (1968). *The complete work of Chuang Tze* (vol. 80). Cambridge University Press.

Yang, Z. (2001). A comparative study of confucianism and taoism interpretation on "the Annotations to Taijitu". *Journal of Nanchang University* (Social Science), 2001–01 (in Chinese).

In Chinese

邵雍.《皇极经世书》年代: 北宋.【ISBN:9787510814358】·九州出版社·2012 周敦颐 .《太极图
说》年代: 北宋.【ISBN:7532511499】·上海古籍出版社·1992 郑玄释义.《易纬是类谋外四种
》年代: 西汉.【ISBN:9925000029817】·台湾·新文丰出版社公司·1987.

郭顺紅:太極圖解説 (三) 應用篇(四) 太極明辨 2016-02-16 發表于文. https://kknews.cc/culture/
p4ezk4e.html.

先秦诸子·《尚书》【ISBN 978-7-5090-0090-8】·北京: 环球印刷 (北京) 有限公司, 2007.

姬昌.《周易》【ISBN 978-7-5508-0388-6】·杭州: 西泠印社出版社, 2012. 李耳.《道德经》
【ISBN 978-7-5508-0043-4】·杭州: 西泠印社出版社, 2011. 孔子后学.《易传》年代: 战国
【ISBN 978-7-5508-0388-6】·杭州: 西泠印社出版社, 2012. 郑玄释义.《易纬是类谋外四种
》年代: 西汉.【ISBN:9925000029817】·台湾·新文丰出版社公司·1987 陈抟.《太极阴阳说》
年代: 晚唐·古籍.

邵雍.《皇极经世书》年代: 北宋.【ISBN:9787510814358】·九州出版社·2012 周敦颐 .《太极图
说》年代: 北宋.【ISBN:7532511499】·上海古籍出版社·1992.

朱熹.《周子太极图》年代: 清朝·【ISBN:9787800607219】·学苑出版社·1990 李瑞东 .《太极
秘笈》年代: 清朝·古籍.

《黄帝内经》年代: 先秦至汉.【ISBN:978896596596596】·辽海出版社·2016.

安冈正笃《易学入门》【ISBN 978-4-89619-002-1】·东京: 明德印刷出版社, 平成二十年四月
十日.

Xing Qi-Lin Master Xing Qi-Lin was born in Tianjin, China and started learning Taiji and traditional Chinese culture at the age 5 under the tutelage of the third-generation Master of "Li-style Taiji". Founded by Master Li Rui-Dong, "Li-style Taiji" was originally taught exclusively at the imperial palace. "Li-style" Taiji has now been recognized as a National Intangible Cultural Heritage of China. Mr. Xing is currently the fourth generation lineage holder of "Li-style Taiji"; the honorary president of both the "Beijing Institute of "Li-style Taiji" and "Wu-Qing Martial Arts Association".

Mr. Xing graduated from the Tianjin University of Sport and the Beijing Sport University. In the late 80s, Mr. Xing spent twelve years travelling to auspicious mountains including Wu-Dong, Jiu-Hua and E-Mei where he met and studied under several accomplished masters. During the latter part of this period, he entered into a retreat in Mount Wu-Dong where he developed deep understanding and experience in the arts of Taiji, Xingyi, Bagua, Shaolin and assimilated their essence into "Li-style Taiji". He integrated his profound insights into the Taijitu.

In addition to teaching at Tian Zhen Yuan, as a distinguished expert appointed by the Ministry of Culture and Tourism, he frequently gives talks on Taiji and traditional Chinese culture in mainland China, Hong Kong and overseas, including Taiwan, Japan, Malaysia, Australia, Europe and the United States. Master Xing has composed a number of Taiji musical scores for health preservation practices. He has also created a series of simple and popular Taiji practices to suit the needs of different groups and ages, including "Taiji Five-Finger Exercise", "Taijiquan", "Taiji Sword", "Taiji Fan" and "Taiji Dance".

Part III
Achieving Sustainable Life—The Circular Economy Movement

Chapter 14
Systemic Change Driven by Circular Change

Ladeja Godina Košir

Abstract Challenged by climate and health crisis—we need a profound systemic change to enable our society and economy to survive. Starting with paradigmatic shift in our mindset—from linear to circular thinking, adding radical collaboration based on trust and transparency, and nourishing sense of community. Interdependent and interconnected as we are, we have a unique opportunity to manage all our global resources in a sustainable way, by respecting the planetary boundaries and making SDG's a reality. Circular change shall be in the core of our daily decision making.

The statue of the "Looking-back Amida" at Zenrin-ji temple (twelfth century), completely captivated me back in 2019, during my stay in Kyoto, when I have got the privilege to join the "Kyoto Manifesto" on Kyoto Symposium V" and spend a month as the visiting professor at the Doshisha University. Amazingly beautiful statue with such a strong and meaningful message. The explanation note next to the statue says: "Catching up the moment from a static pose to a dynamic one/To wait for the people behind/To think back on his own position/To show mercy to neighbors/To watch the people with mercy/To pay attention to the people, as a leader to step forward together."

Perfectly captured message for the so much needed leadership in these challenging times of the twenty-first century. Throughout our life and work we shall lead and engage at the same time—pay attention to the people as individuals and strive for the harmony of the whole. As the European New Green Deal is saying—we shall make a world a better place by not leaving anyone behind.

L. Godina Košir (✉)
Circular Change & ECESP, Institute for Circular Economy, Ljubljana, Slovenia
e-mail: ladeja@circularchange.com

© Springer Nature Singapore Pte Ltd. 2022
S. Hill et al. (eds.), *The Kyoto Post-COVID Manifesto For Global Economics*,
Creative Economy, https://doi.org/10.1007/978-981-16-8566-8_14

14.1 The Circular Economy as an Instrument to Drive Prosperity

The world's population is growing and resource use is increasing. The gap between abundance and scarcity is deepening. The existing model of production and consumption does not contribute to the wellbeing of everyone on the planet. On the contrary, the world has become extraordinarily unequal. As of 2020, the world's richest 1% own twice as much as the bottom 90%.[1] Human activity is putting unprecedented stress on Earth's life-giving system.[2] Humans will need two Earths to support our lifestyles by 2030 because we are draining the world's resources so quickly.

While facing climate and health (COVID-19) crisis, our approach towards the nature, based on "mastering" it and "fighting" against changes, is seriously challenged. We, humans, have always been and still are the part of nature, as vulnerable and as interdependent as the whole eco-system. We are more interdependent and interconnected than ever and through the pandemic times we have learned, how important it is to nourish core values that bind us—humans, and how very much needed is the collaboration not only on local, but also on global level. Economic, social and ecological dimension of problem solving are strongly connected and the concept of circular economy can be used as a kind of "guiding principle" for exploring approaches towards the co-creation of more resilient economy and society, that is not leaving anyone behind.

As Albert Einstein once said, "We cannot solve our problems with the same thinking we used when we created them." It is time to rethink our business models and focus on the future of the global economy and how to replace our current linear "take, make, dispose" model with a new, circular one. But we cannot channel our economies and societies in the sustainable direction without implementing systemic approach. Engagement of different stakeholders is needed and re-evaluation of different kinds of capital (financial, natural, human, social …) is crucial. We face a host of systemic challenges beyond the reach of existing institutions and their hierarchical authority structures. We have to revalue what really matters and adjust our structures and systems accordingly.

The concept of a circular economy as such is not new. It has its roots in the1960s, when several authors recognized the boundaries of global industrialization. *Limits of Growth (1972)* a report published by the Club of Rome considered certain aspects of sustainability for the first time. As the authors explained, we have gone from an Empty World, dominated by natural ecosystems in which labor and infrastructure were the limiting factors of human wellbeing to a Full World. A world dominated by humans and human activity where diminishing natural resources and environmental sinks are now the limiting factor of human wellbeing. Such ideas have now been developed further by several authors. Biomimicry, Performance Economy, Cradle to Cradle, Blue Economy and other concepts have been introduced.

---

[1] https://philanthropynewsdigest.org, 19th January 2020.
[2] Raworth (2017).

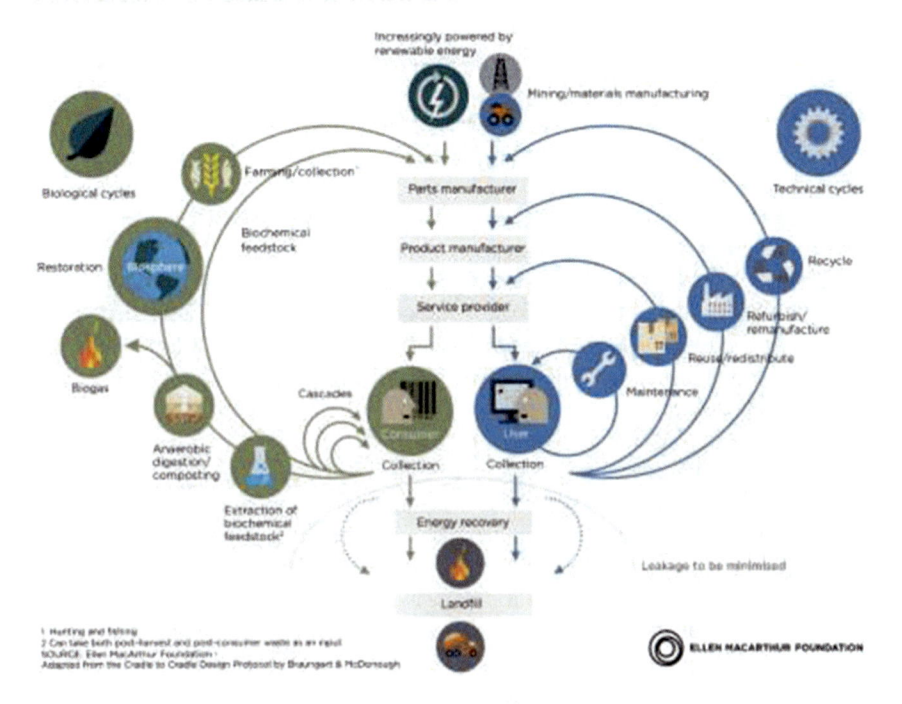

Fig. 14.1 Circular economy—Ellen MacArthur Foundation

The way we understand circular economy is based on the Ellen MacArthur Foundation's "butterfly" diagram that illustrates a continuous flow of technical and biological material. It is based on the three pioneering principles for a circular economy: design out waste and pollution, keep products and materials in use and regenerate natural systems. The Circular Economy focuses on maintaining the value of materials in the production and consumption cycle for as long as possible. On designing products in a way that they can be maintained, refurbished, repaired, reused and at the end of their life cycle recycled. In biological terms, the reintroduction of biomaterials into the biosphere is a key for circularity (Fig. 14.1).

14.2 A Collaborative Mindset—Lost in the Linear Economy Decision Making Paradigm

Christiaan Kraaijenhagen defines a circular economy as "An economy in which stakeholders collaborate in order to maximize the value of products and materials and as such contribute to minimizing the depletion of natural resources to create positive societal and environmental impact". This perfectly highlights the importance of collaboration for a successful circular transition. It also includes three interdependent dimensions—economic, social and environmental—all of them being equally important. Without a shift in the mindset that collaboration is the key to the creation of a circular economy model, the circular journey cannot start. We must identify the drivers and pressures causing the primary problems and address them with appropriate responses. This requires a complete paradigm shift. It is up to us to make change happen.

The concept of "prosocial behavior" has been introduced earlier in Chap. 3, and several categories have been explained. As we can see, the relationship between social obligation and profit is in the essence of the decision-making process and behavior. Understanding collaboration is the key for circular transition. Consequently, our social ability to respond to the complexity and interdependency of the modern world seems to be our main challenge. We have a lot of knowledge, scientific evidence, reports, measurements, new technologies but it is new forms of collaboration and more systemic approaches that we are lacking.

In the Kyoto Manifesto for Global Economics Hugh Mackay pointed out that: "We used to live in a society. Now we live in an economy."[3] Janez Potočnik (former European Commissioner for the Environment who first presented The Circular Economy Package in June 2014, a revised version of which was adopted in December 2015) said:" The problem is that financial capital is overvalued, human capital is undervalued, and natural capital is not valued at all." Economy (oeconomicus) as defined by the philosopher Xenophon in Ancient Greece consisted of oikos = household, nomos = norms. Household management, leads us back to the roots of an economy that is not detached from society, but on the contrary, rooted in the primary cell of it—the household. Today individual, as well as collective responsibility towards the community and the environment, are increasing with globalization. We are becoming aware that we have lost a sense of the planetary interdependency of systems. Without this sense of individual and collective responsibility for our prosperity and wellbeing, true collaboration cannot emerge. As long as we are driven by financial benefits, and the short-term nature of decision-making focused on GDP growth, as primary driving forces of our economy, we cannot co-create the society we aspire to live in.

14.3 Sustainable Development Goals in the Context of Circular Transformation

In the need to develop a model of progress that can improve (or at very least, maintain) the quality of life on our planet, it is crucial that we consider economic, environmental and social factors and encourage innovation and new solutions. As an answer to the need for a change in the current economic paradigm, and the call for a more holistic systemic approach to the development of our planet, the United Nations adopted a set

---

[3] Yamash'ta et al. (2018a).

of 17 Sustainable Development Goals[4] (SDGs) in 2015. In response 193 countries have committed to uphold the agenda. This global societal contract is calling for global collaboration.

Circular economy is one of the instruments addressing particularly Goal #12, responsible consumption and production, calling for a systemic change for the realization of this as well as of all other SDG's. The commitment is in place but how about the implementation? The transformation is not addressing only the economic aspect, it is also an essential part of a societal and cultural change. Stephen Hill has presented The Social Paradigm "Global Localism" based on the power of individual action and the power of inter-subjective community. It emphasizes that our culture is not produced elsewhere, which encourages us to concentrate the attention on helping the local community to transform itself and, in so doing, to create economic benefit for society.[5]

In Europe, next to the European Green Deal, a concerted strategy—Circular Economy Action Plan (2020) was launched by the European Commission. This document has the ambition to contribute to the ambitious goal, climate-neutral and resource-efficient Europe in 2050, cutting emissions by 55% by 2030. Together with the Green Recovery Program, Fit for 55 Strategy and European New Bauhaus— all three adopted in 2021—the European Union is clearly demonstrating a strong determination to achieve economic and social progress by turning climate and environmental challenges into opportunities.

14.4 From Shared Values to Shared Socio-economic Models

As the Chair of the European Circular Economy Stakeholder Platform, which was born as a joint initiative by the European Commission and the European Economic and Social Committee (EESC) in March 2017, I have been engaged in numerous activities, promoting the transition to a circular economy by facilitating policy dialogue among different stakeholders, by disseminating good practices and strategies as well as by mapping and encouraging circular economy pioneers in different countries. For the leadership expressed also through the activities delivered by Circular Change, the platform I have founded back in 2016 in Slovenia, I was recognized as the finalist in the Leadership category at the international award program The Circular 2018, organized by the World Economic Forum and Accenture in Davos. In 2020 I was selected as one of the #EUwomen4future. What I have learned on this explorative circular journey is, that there are no "simple recipes" that we can simply "copy paste" from one community or country to another when leading the

---

[4] https://www.undp.org/sustainable-development-goals?utm_source=EN&utm_medium=GSR &utm_content=US_UNDP_PaidSearch_Brand_English&utm_campaign=CENTRAL&c_src= CENTRAL&c_src2=GSR&gclid=Cj0KCQAt8WOBhDbARIsANQLp955L5No1qehVSxcRBLk CRJGjsRLrQ-1NFuA3LCfSPAAvXN1l2qoMc4aAjYfEALw_wcB.

[5] Yamash'ta et al. (2018b).

transformation from linear to circular economy. Why? Because we have to understand people, their values and behavior, their cultural and historical background first. What is, for example, a "good life" for someone in Norway is not necessarily a "good life" for someone in Serbia. Being sensitive and open to listen and hear, to learn and co-create, that is of great importance when working on the ground.

Let's take the example of "sharing economy" as one of the elements of the boarder context of circular economy. In Norway, sharing a car (probably electric one) is something what is highly acceptable—it contributes to low carbon emissions, it lower costs on personal level, it enables people to more from point A to B in an accessible and affordable way. Same solution in Serbia would not be accepted so enthusiastically. Why? Since owning the car (most often German brand) is the status symbol. The more expensive the car, the more reputation you get in the society. Sharing, instead of owning, would be understood as not being capable of earning enough money for a "good life". Sharing is also related to the historical context of socialism, where private property was not acceptable—forms like cooperatives, public (instead of private) ownership were promoted. In such a context, sharing gets completely different connotation than in the case of Norway. This kind of insights lead us to the development of the "Circular Triangle".

14.5   Three Aspects of the Circular Transition—The Model of the Circular Triangle

With the co-authors I described three aspects of the circular transition through the Circular Triangle model. This was first published in the Roadmap towards the circular economy in Slovenia in 2018,[6] which also explored the relationship between a local and global perspective, bottom-up and top-down driven activities, value-driven versus money-driven decision-making processes …

A systemic transition from a linear to a circular economy is only possible if we successfully maintain the balance between the various policies while simultaneously rearranging our values so as to promote the transition to new economic patterns and individual behavior. We need a new kind of leadership and new coalitions for change to emerge. The aspects of a systemic circular transition are interdependent, the process is long-term and complex, and bottom-up and top-down approaches have to be aligned to navigate through this challenging transformation (Fig. 14.2).

The Circular Triangle is comprised of the following:

- Circular Economy—from linear to circular business models/companies
- Circular Change—comprehensive policies to support the transition/public sector
- Circular Culture—reflection on values and behaviors and a new future narrative/citizens

---

[6] https://circularchange.squarespace.com/projects-1/2018/11/8/roadmap-towards-the-circular-economy-in-slovenia.

Fig. 14.2 The circular triangle (Adapted from Gm-Circular Change 2017)

14.6 Circular Economy—Companies as the Core

The transition from linear to circular economic models brings numerous changes. These are reflected on various levels, which is why the transition is difficult, and generally only possible with the full support and trust of corporate leaderships, validating and justifying the notion that the economic model needs to change. By collaborating with the stakeholders, the vision will lead to new value chains, which will in turn bring new risks, new circumstances and a renewed need to adapt. By the end of the transition, everyone involved should have gained more than they would if there had been no collaboration. Altered forms of collaboration can mean the involvement of new suppliers, the development of new technologies, the restructuring of organizational culture, forays into new markets, etc.

Circular Economy offers a variety of opportunities for innovation, including social innovations. Addressing the SDG #12—sustainable consumption and production—opens the possibility of questioning our values and purpose (individual vs. social), the concept of ownership (from owning to sharing), leadership (long term stewards instead of short-term maximizers), silo focused thinking with a systemic and holistic approach (sense for interdependency and interconnectivity). The power of a circular economy lies in its contribution to sustain humanity and its prosperity, to address people not as consumers but as citizens encouraged to pro-actively contribute to the positive change.

According to experiences with the business sector, the main challenge is the understanding of systems thinking which is essential for trust and a fruitful collaboration. Being able to first articulate the interests of your organization, then to consider the multiple stakeholder interests and finally to accept and evaluate success based on the triple bottom line: business, society, the environment, is not easy to achieve. As Table 3.1 in Chap. 3 "The Summary of merits and demerits of three types of prosocial behavior"—shows, motivation for altruistic behavior is sustainable only when a dominant portion of the organization's members recognize the importance of such behavior and when the positive profit levels are kept stable. Quite often a lack of leadership skills and the knowledge needed for this "mindset transition" prevent the collaboration that would lead to the transition of the business and revenue model, and in consequence to the multiple positive results. The approach presented in the book "Circular Business—Collaborate and Circulate" by Christiaan Kraaijenhagen[7] offers very practical tools to encourage much needed collaboration based on long term partnerships and trust.

14.7 Circular Change—Public Sector as the Core

It is important that policies for the circular transition are coordinated and comprehensive. Interdepartmental collaboration is crucial, as is considering the principles of circular economy when determining all policies. National circular economic roadmaps and action plans can be a great start for encouraging governments to strategically and systematically approach the transition. On the international level linking the achievements of SDG's, mitigation of climate change, protection of biodiversity, development of bio-based economy, implementation of digitalization and blockchain technologies, introduction of new green financial instruments and other initiatives and agreements must be linked.

On the global level, capitalism has not led to harmony. As described in chapter 27 of the Kyoto Manifesto for Global Economics, the need for change is inevitable. However, a circular economy should not be understood as another western economic model, being "exported" to less developed countries, and by so doing protecting their own interests and competitiveness. What we need is a global leadership based on shared values and respect towards humanity and the wellbeing of everyone. A "global localism" based on wisdom and respect towards different cultures offers an extraordinary challenge and opportunity to engage local "disruptors" who are contributing to the solutions that work on a local and national level and to connect them to the global network, to the new coalition for change. "Listening"—across cultural differences—is the basis of bridging our personal and local domain with the world as a whole.[8]

14.8 Circular Culture—Citizens as the Core

We individuals, acting as responsible, active and engaged citizens, shape society as a whole with our systems of values, our choices, our decisions and our behaviors. It is crucial for the transition that the role of the consumer is abandoned in favor of the role of the user. We must improve our understanding of the role of the user. We must improve our understanding of the repercussions that the choices that we make every day have and strive to manage our resources better. The home, the household is the basic cell in which we can enact circular principles and reinforce a circular culture.

---

[7] Kraaijenhagen et al. (2016).

[8] Yamash'ta et al. (2018c).

As already highlighted, it is of great importance to understand the cultural context in which the circular solutions are developed and implemented. Already within the EU, differences exist between "eastern" and "western" countries. Those, who were under the communist regime in the twentieth century, have developed completely different attitudes towards ownership to those who are used to capitalism. Therefore, sharing concepts or models of cooperatives or of usage of services instead of ownership might be understood as something negative, as something, that recalls bad memories, related to the times when private ownership was very restricted.

In addressing culture, we are touching the values and the value system of a society, as well as the question of identity. Sensitivity for different cultural contexts and understanding the construction of personal identity in the modern world is needed to address these issues. This in order to facilitate the introduction of sustainable, circular solutions in an effective way, empowering people to feel engaged, fulfilled and valued. "Not owning" might be still understood as not being capable of buying, of not being successful according to existing marketing norms.

Active citizens, who are willing to explore new ways of living, producing, consuming … are those, who can significantly contribute to the circular culture. Cities are becoming the driving force of circular transition, systems on a city level adjust faster than those on a national one. City governance is also more agile than national governments, which brings us back to a "local globalism". Several researches, initiatives, measurements, reports, programs on circular cities[9] are indicating that cities are becoming more relevant for the implementation of sustainable solutions than ever before. Approximately 50% of the world's population now live in urban areas and 70% is expected to live in cities by 2050. Increasing urbanization is sparking the need for more jobs, housing, transportation, energy, water, and food, which, in turn, leads to increased consumption and ultimately increased amounts of waste and greenhouse gas emissions. These pressures make cities an ideal hotbed and key inflection point for innovation and change. The circular economy provides solutions for many of the environmental, economic and geopolitical challenges that cities worldwide are facing. As it continues to gain exposure at the political, social and commercial level, future-proofing cities is the next step in creating sustainable solutions for our planet's future.[10] Meaning, that local circular stories can inspire global circular transformation.

---

[9] Some relevant sources: https://www.ellenmacarthurfoundation.org/our-work/activities/circular-economy-in-cities; http://www.oecd.org/regional/regional-policy/circular-economy-cities.htm.

[10] https://www.circle-economy.com/tool/cities/#.XMc3C-gzbIU.

14.9   The Value of the National Circular Economy Roadmaps

The model of the Circular Triangle has been practically implemented in the processes of national circular economy roadmaps co-created by the Circular Change—Institute for Circular Economy team—in different countries (Slovenia, Serbia, Chile, Montenegro). Enabling space for discussions and engaging different stakeholders, coaching and orchestrating the process, co-creating recommendation for the roadmap design, and at the very end supporting communication and implementation of the document is what we have been working on.

As I have explained in the interview for Eurochile: "In whichever country I have been engaged in the circular economy transition exercises—from Japan to Brazil—I have been looking for the "DNA" of the nation, for those core values that are embedded in culture and behavior. We, human beings, are those who are designing our present and future—by decisions we make, by choices we take. I find it crucial that circular economy transition of the country is harmonized with the culture of the country. Therefore, I am always super curious. Trying to understand people, in our case representatives of Chile, first. Being humble and opened for what you have to propose, share, introduce—that is how I navigate through the joint process of road mapping."[11]

Saying that, I wanted to emphasize the need for turning the "Circle of Wholeness" into new normative business practice which is only possible, if based on values and understanding of our existential being as social human persons—inclusivity of our full sharing and care for others, of guidance from the many domains of human knowledge connecting in overall harmony, with caring and knowledge held into relationship by the 'circle's' central point, integrity and trust.[12] This "magic of collaboration" happens in the process of circular economy roadmaps, since the focus in on engagement of different stakeholders and on equal value of their contribution, no matter if they are coming from big multinational companies or simply contribute their point of view as citizens.

14.10   Intuitive Transformative Networks—The Invisible Power of Our Civilization

Without bridging top-down and bottom-up approach, identifying, engaging and enabling changemakers, radical transformations cannot happen. It is not about revolution, but rather about evolutionary process addressing and including the existing institutional structures as well as newly established platforms and networks.

---

[11] https://www.eurochile.cl/en/noticias/transferencia-tecnologica/ladeja-godina-es-una-responsab ilidad-colectiva-hacer-realidad-una-vision-circular/.

[12] Chapter 20.

Based on shared values, intuition, empathy, playfulness, trust and transparency, the purpose driven individuals and organizations are contributing their key competences, resources, knowledge and wisdom for the emergence of the new type of global networks. Through systemic collaboration and hearty actions, they transcend the boundaries of the existing structures and overgrow them with the emerging collaborative forms based on AEIOU principles that are nurturing Ecocivilisation.[13]

Without this "invisible societal glue" civilization can hardly function as a coherent ecosystem. Even more, throughout them are we, humans, uncapable to co-exist and co-create while honoring the planetary boundaries. Circular economy roadmaps are serving as a tool helping us to navigate towards a more sustainable future. They are inviting stakeholders from different organizations, cities, countries, to join this challenging journey, following their intuition and fulfilling their purpose in the process of systemic transformation of society and economy.

As stated by Prof. Jacqueline Cramer, the author of the book How Network Governance Powers the Circular Economy, the "network governance" is key in effectuating a circular economy. It bolsters the positive forces in a democratic society, thereby making a crucial contribution to the circular objectives of countries and regions.[14] Having the privilege to collaborate with Prof. Cramer, inviting here to share her experiences with the members of the ECESP (European Circular Economy Stakeholder Platform) in a fruitful dialogue, we have learned, how important "transition brokers" —those, who are leading complex circular transformation on the ground— are. Often overlooked and not valued, they are actually those change agents, who orchestrate complex processes among different stakeholders as well as leading the dialogue between the government (public governance) and other relevant partners (network governance). They help align different interest and orchestrate the transition process, overcoming the practices of working in silos with more systemic and interdisciplinary approach. Specific competences are needed, blended with enthusiasm and persistence, leadership and wisdom.

Once we let our wisdom to connect all of our potentials and our planet is offering, enriched by collaboration and evolutionary transformation, the network governance will prevail and Ecocivilisation powered by the AEIOU leadership will thrive. To get there, we need to nourish the existing and encourage the emerging networks. This is only possible if we open our hearts and humbly recognize what each of us is already contributing to the wellbeing of our communities, and if we value and respect this contribution with gratitude.

---

[13] https://www.circularchange.com/circular-insider, p. 81.

[14] https://hollandcircularhotspot.nl/wp-content/uploads/2020/12/How-Network-Governance-Powers-the-Circular-Economy-Ten-Guiding-Principles-for-a-Circular-Economy-Jacqueline-Cramer.pdf.

14.11 New Narrative Powered by Creativity and Empathy

Communication is not a neutral exchange of messages; it is more or less an intense relationship with the ability to build community. A true dialogue enables community to "emerge". For a circular economy and sustainable development, we have to nourish a dialogue based on a new vocabulary.

Firstly, we need to rethink terms such as growth, development, competition, capital, productivity etc. It is becoming increasingly obvious that the current economic model is not fit for purpose as it does not contribute to the prosperity of our planet or of our human race. Global "development" is depleting the natural capital on which our survival depends. Climate change and several crossed planetary boundaries are proof that the economic development model of the developed world is unsustainable. We are destroying our lifegiving natural resources and there is increasing and accelerating evidence that under the existing economic model, we will need another planet by 2035.[15]

Messages that different stakeholders can identify with, are of great importance if we want everyone to take part in this circular journey. The art of storytelling, usage of right metaphors, capability to identify with the audience and speak their "language", pictures instead of words—all, and more, is needed to engage different audiences. Empathy and creativity are too often overlooked. Given the hyper production of messages, delivered daily via social media and the internet, it is hard to get attention. At the same time—increasingly living in an age when almost everyone is a "medium"—we have a potential that can be used purposefully.

With the COVID crisis, the narrative became very "top down" oriented and often a kind of "war jargon" has been experienced. Selected and centralized information, less space for an open dialogue, spread of fear, authoritative addressing of the citizens—this is not enabling the space we need to embrace and overcome crisis. Neither the health, nor the climate one. Judging is dividing us and so much present polarization between those "vaccinated" and those "anti-vaxxers" is so far away from what this book aims to nourish—the Polyphony. The symphony of our civilization is in "in the air", by mindfully opening our hearts we can sense the wholeness, the miracle of not being a drop in the ocean, but the entire ocean in a drop, to paraphrase a great Sufi poet Rumi.

References

Circular Economy Action Plan. (2020). https://ec.europa.eu/environment/pdf/circular-economy/new_circular_economy_action_plan.pdf.

Kraaijenhagen, C., van Oppen, C., & Bocken, N. (2016). *Circular business: Collaborate and circulate* (p. 15). Amsterdam: Circular Collaboration.

---

[15] https://www.static1.squarespace.com/static/5b97bfa236099baf64b1a627/t/5beabb62f950b773950d1ce7/1542110.257669/ROADMAP+TOWARDS+THE+CIRCULAR+ECONOMY+IN+SLOVENIA.pdf.

Raworth, K. (2017). *Doughnut economics: Seven ways to think like a 21st-century economist* (p. 5). Random House.

Yamash'ta, S., Yagi, T., & Hill, S. (2018a). *The Kyoto Manifesto for global economics: The platform of cummunity, humanity, and spirituality* (p. 4), Singapore.

Yamash'ta, S., Yagi, T., & Hill, S. (2018b). *The Kyoto Manifesto for global economics: The platform of cummunity, humanity, and spirituality* (p. 326), Singapore.

Yamash'ta, S., Yagi, T., & Hill, S. (2018c). *The Kyoto Manifesto for global economics: The platform of cummunity, humanity, and spirituality* (p. 285), Singapore.

Chapter 15
The New Natural State of the Market

Einar Kleppe Holthe

Abstract A New Natural State of the Market, The economic consequence of Awareness. The market ideological appraoch of Natural State is suggesting a more meaningful holistic, and neutral value perspective and methodolgy for value creation. Where a new natural state of the world markets can be obtain with a, spheric and new economic language for the future and aware market. Sustainability over time must become the core market ideal for fostering a sustainable global market culture as key to make sustainability the core quality in any value creation and value transactions, in any value chain, value system or value-spheres for the transparent and aware market spheres of the 21th. century. As a contribution to the second Kyoto Economic Manifesto. The Natural State-theory of market-and value spheres represents a market ideological and practical approach to seek a, more natural and holistic value perspective to secure sustainable value development in any kind of places, markets and aware economis.

Keywords Market ideology · Aware economy · New economic language · Natural state of the market · Sustainability economies · Evolving Value-sphere · Holistic Market-sphere

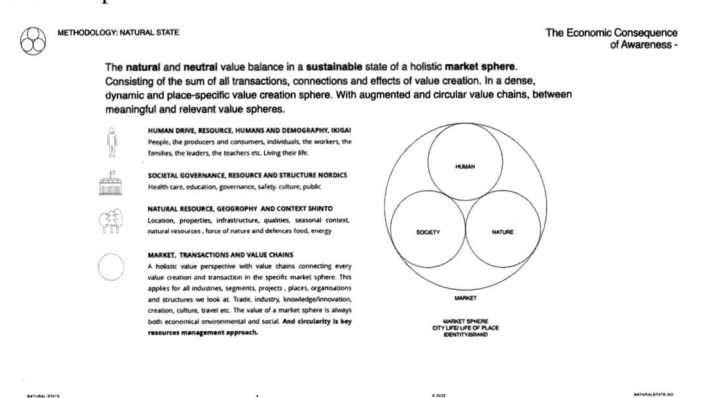

E. K. Holthe (✉)
Natural State As, St. Halvardsgate 33 Bygg H, 0192 Oslo, Norway
e-mail: einar@naturalstate.no

© The Author(s) 2022
S. Hill et al. (eds.), *The Kyoto Post-COVID Manifesto For Global Economics*,
Creative Economy, https://doi.org/10.1007/978-981-16-8566-8_15

15.1   A Personal Perspective and Practical Approach
to the World of Economics

To be invited to contribute to the KM II is a great honour to me as a practical economist. I am very glad to share my experience-based, creative and strategic economic theory and market ideology in this context. The market ideology and this economic language of relevant value spheres and holistic market spheres is a tool for co-creation of future values as base for future holistic, transparent and sustainable markets.

We now need to work actively for an understanding where the key goal of growth in the historic consume and growth economy, is replaced with sustainable value evolvement over time. And it is understood that the markets plural, augmented and synergetic value chains is in a constant state of systemic, cultural and natural change.

We must radically alter our values towards sustainability because then the market itself will evolve in to a new and natural state. And we must make a new economic language to better describe the holistic values and the augmented value chains that are indescribable in today's narrow economical languages.

As a person that has experience in value-creation in both the Nordics of where I origin, as a Norwegian citizen, Japan of where my second home is and the base of the biggest part of my companies and in several projects in Eu and the US, I personally believe and support the stand of KM II fully. We must combine Eastern philosophy with the Western economic methodology of the modern market. And I suggest also looking to the unique Nordic practice as an added dimension.

We must expand the values we account for in our economically described world. A description of what values that will be important in a future aware, holistic and sustainability-oriented market. And we must regard time as our only linear value and constant, and everything else as circular, regenerative or evolving value that just changes in a sustainable way over time, as the only constant over time is change, or evolvement, as in nature itself.

For me Natural state´s spheric evolving economic language represents a strategic tool for systemic description and as such, understanding of all the values in the world. And a way to describe this and thus speak economically about them in a universal way.

It is developed as a strategic and creative economic language for collaboration across borders, across cultures, between rural and urban areas and between private and public economic spheres especially, of where there is often radically different value perspectives, and often hard to obtain mutual agreement and balance in the state of evolvement, as also between the humans and nature itself today.

Through speaking the same economic language, agreeing on what values that matter for our collective future value creation and which spheres that must be in a natural balance, we can change the core of any relevant market sphere.

Maybe this is a small piece in the collective undertaking of changing the worlds markets as well, as KM II sets out to do.

15.2 A New Market Ideal, a New Market Idealism A New Market Ideology

We need to define sustainability over time as the new market ideology, and this must replace growth as ideal, and as the only indicator of prosperity in any economic description of any market.

This can be a collective, neutral and natural stand to evolve values from, values that then evolve in the right direction of sustainable development. We can move from an unaware market, to a aware market and then in the future to a conscious market through always focusing on the holistic totality and effect of any value-creation process.

15.3 Collaboration Ability Will Replace Competition Force as Driver

Meaningless growth of one, can be the de-growth of another, and this in itself is a destructive path from the past. Co-evolvement is a better goal for any value of the future. And the key quality of sustainability must replace scalability as key quality indicator of any solution. We seek meaningful evolvement of values in this new and aware market.

The last 200 years of idealism, of which the economic language of the global markets, and ideals of our societies was formed, has been 200 years of constant change. And now we are becoming aware of this, and we understand that the old theories of economics are dated. A new and digitally augmented awareness, and a new enlightenment of cause and effect is now changing everything faster than ever.

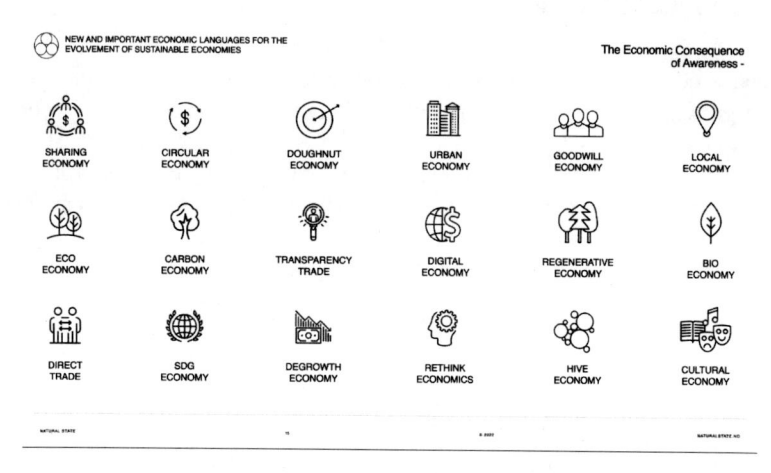

The ways of the nineteenth century is simply not able to describe the world as we know it today. And new economic languages rapidly form. As and example, Circular Economy. The key to sustainability is Circularity, and the key to Circularity is Collaboration.

15.4 We Need a Global Sustainability Culture and as Such the Worlds Sustainability Economies Will Form

The world population, all soon to be 8.000.000.000 of us, the natural being of humans, is the world market.

We are natural, emotional and individual beings with natural and emotional needs both for our body and mind. A value-chain in any market is started by one human cognitive factor, the choice we take. Both individually, or culturally in a society.

This is a fact of which we cannot escape, and as such we need to reorient towards the human perspective on nature and our collective societal structure and form a culture of taking the sustainable choice in the markets. Then it all changes.

To obtain this new state of a sustainability, we must also connect to the cultural aspect, and form sustainability cultures. Because the cultural context of your life, defines which qualities you value.

Today culture change is a societal task. The only societal global entity of any integrity and trust today is the UN, and the UN SDG campaign is an important step for making a global market-culture for sustainability. We need to look at how each value-chain offsets in the SDG´s and adjust them towards synergetic value-creation for all relevant value sphere.

15.5   A New and Aware Market and New Economic Languages for the Plural Sustainable Economies in Dense and Transparent Market-Spheres

The market-sphere. Qualities of a market-sphere is indicated by the density, dynamics and durability of value chains and value transactions. Transparency, trust and synergies is also examples of quality indicators of a market, and not just growth potential and scalability. We need to look at regeneratively, innovation-value, sustainability-value, and resilience structures in plural, local and dense market structures as strengths and qualities of a market sphere.

HIVE ECONOMY: THE 8TH WAY TO THINK LIKE A 21ST CENTURY ECONOMIST

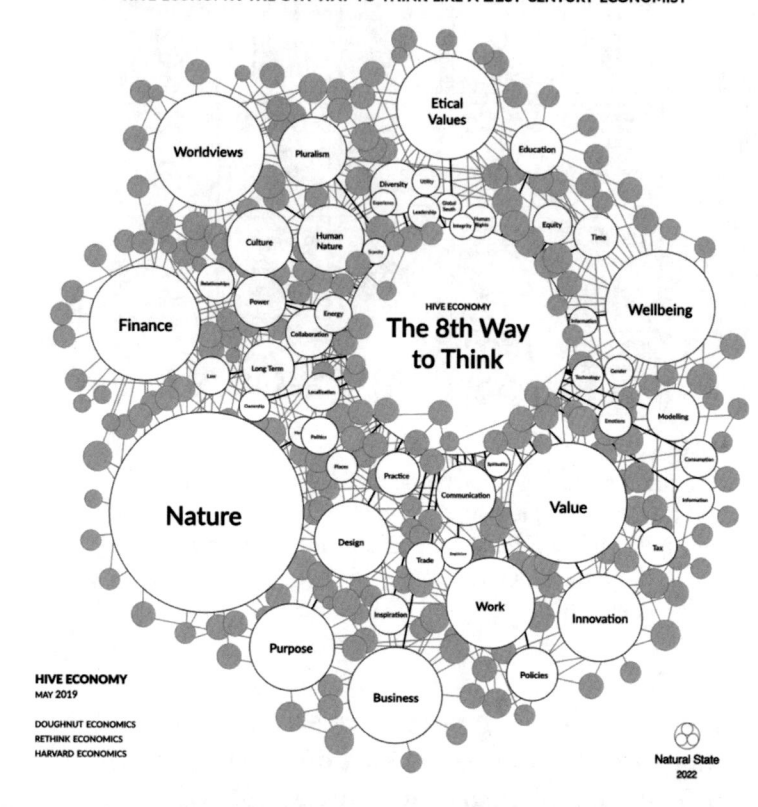

The plurality, complexity and density of the sustainability economics in any market sphere is very well illustrated by the HIVE ECONOMY model produced and presented by Doughnut economies and Kate Raworth organisation, in collaboration with Rethink Economics and Harvard Economics in May 2019.

This is brings a clear visualisation of the value perspectives present as well.

15.6   The Natural State Model and Market Ideology

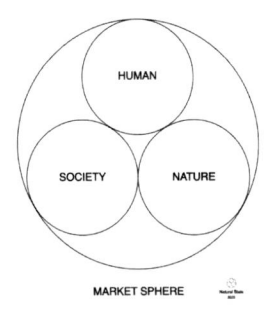

This is a simplified holistic frame for all the values you choose to describe. When you look at all transactions of all the values, the value picture becomes extremely complex and it becomes hard to describe and communicate efficient about it. This is why the Natural State model suggest making less accurate but then more meaningful descriptions of values as holistic value spheres. We describe the spheres as active dense spheres of value.

The key value-spheres of any market-sphere is the human, societal and natural sphere as all transactions involving us humans effects these spheres.

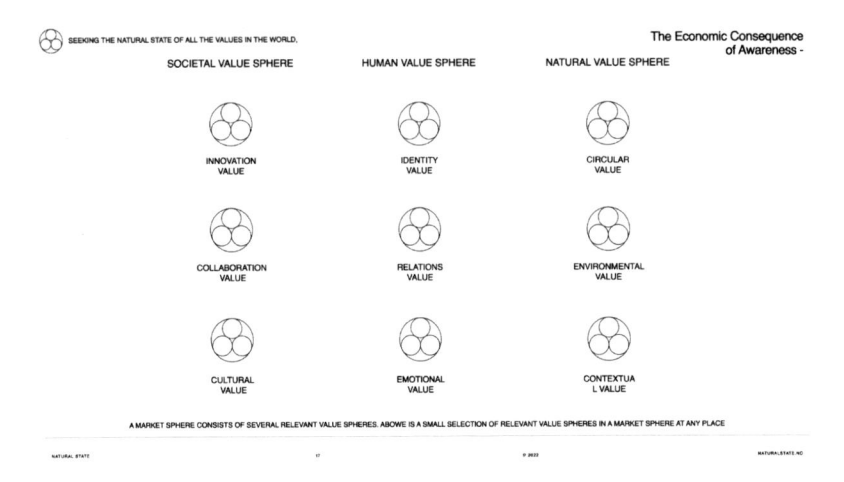

15.7 Segmenting value-Spheres Within the Key Value-Spheres Layering Multiple Values in Any Market Sphere

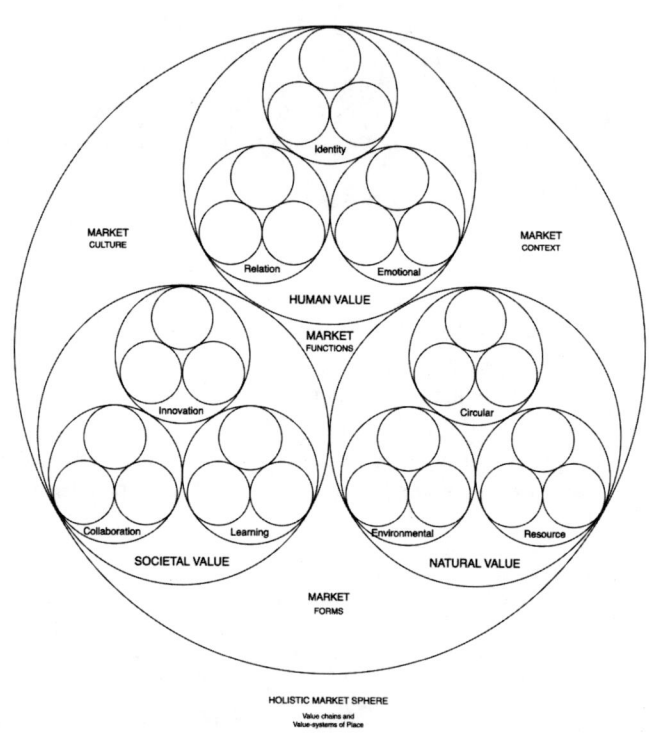

HOLISTIC MARKET SPHERE
Value chains and
Value-systems of Place

MULTILAYERED VALUES OF ANY MARKET SPHERE,
FORMULATING A NATURAL STATE OF ANY PLACE

Natural State
2022

As an example of how this value-language works we can look at examples of multiple layers of value-spheres within the key value spheres. This is an economical formulated tool to start to ask questions about which values are present in any development of any value. The holistic market sphere consists of all the values of a place, and all the value chains forming value systems between all the value spheres. It is the dynamics of tranasactions that are the the interesting element to see and work with in any market sphere, of any place. From local to global context. The basic valuespheres in any market sphere can always be sortet in three elements, the natural sphere, the human sphere and the societal sphere with the market structure and systems of valuechains embedding all of the key factors of value transactions in the holistic market sphere of a place—the market functions and forms and the market context and culture.

Within the natural value-sphere we look at the natural sphere and effects on this. This is important in relation to the natural impact the chain of development has. Key value sphere for natural resources today is circularity value / circular economy principles. How we take out any natural resources needs to be evaluated in any value-development. Also, the environmental impact as climate accounting and co2 emissions needs to be addressed. This can be described as environmental value.

Within the societal value-sphere of any project of place in development you can ask the questions of how any value development also includes innovation for driving society and humans further, how one manages collaboration efforts in the value chain, and key societal value of any development is what the societal and collective learning is. The learning value of anything needs to be addressed and learning needs to be documented for all to learn from.

Within the human value-sphere the key value is the **identity-value**. How we identify ourselves as a human, is our personal key value. And it is also how we identify anything that gives value to anything. If we humans start to value sustainability as a key identity value and quality in any development of any value, we are moving things in the right way. How we identify anything is also an important factor of how we feel, or what emotional value one creates in any development. A good example of emotional value in the markets today, is the volatile emotion of trust. The key emotional value for future value development in the world and base for all investments done in the world finance markets.

15.8   The New Natural State of the Markets and Time as Constant

To obtain a new natural state of the market we must be seeking to find a new, natural and neutral approach to the market itself. And see the markets as neutral, transparent and a natural force and order of the world today. Where time is the only constant, and at the same time recognise that the only constant over time is change. And it is in the dynamics of change, with the transactions in the augmented and interconnected value chains you create the value of where we all relate and belong to.

In this simplified picture of the world order, it is important to maintain a human perspective, for us living today and in the foreseeable future there is four truths of today's markets and economics that need to be recognised.

– The only actual global world order we have today is the market, in its natural and neutral form. With a plurality of segments, societal diversities and economic descriptions.
– The only truly universal language we have today is economics. There is no other universal languages then the number languages of economics, physics, music and the digital bin-ear system.

- Humans are a part of nature, not above nature. As humans are natural beings, there is no other force of nature effecting everything then nature itself. And the market is defined by humans emotional choices.
- There is no global societal structure, order, state of sphere. The UN is as close as it gets, and global communication technology (Internet) is the closest thing to a global community there is.

Culture is key, to sustainability. And sustainability will be the key quality and have the highest identity-value in a future market in a natural neutral and balanced state. To make a humane and sustainable market, we need to reorient the market it selves.

In the historic perspective of trade and markets, humans have always been infinitely tied to nature. A natural market in its neutral and natural form or state is in its pure form simply a function of value or resource transactions, value-chains in nature of natural resources and biomass.

A sphere of value-chains where values described or recognised is completely up to the perspective of the observer. But the key value for any human is how we identify anything. Also, the market it selves. This is why we need to change the identity of the market. Or rename it. We need a market that relate to sustainability as idea, in a holistic matter. This type of market we can rename to a market-sphere. And as such we give an alternative way and an alternative name on the market. And if this is spread as we can start to rebrand the market it selves over time.

The function of a market-sphere is to become a market based on the holistic sustainability of long-term evolvement of values that generate positive impact on all the key value-spheres. A market-sphere is as such a rebranded, or a market with adjusted core ideal, a market, where key idea, identity and goal for evolved values is sustainability. If the market is a 2 dimensional platform, a market-sphere is 7 dimensional. We need to understand 7 dimensional value description to be able to interact with all the values in a holistic and sustainable market evolvement. And obtain sustainability as key quality, in any market.

And like that, we change the ideal of the market.

Then we change the value and qualities of the market.

Then we change the market culture,

and then we change the market it selves. Going from short term, to long term, from linear to circular, from quantity to quality, from meanigless growth, to sustainable dvelopment from and from un-aware to aware.

Culture is key to sustainability. and sustainability is quality, for the future and aware market, in a new natural state.

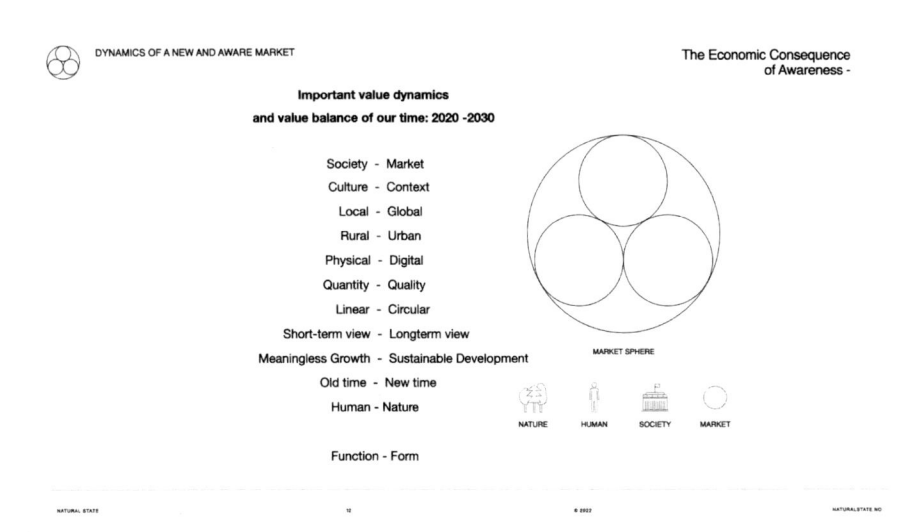

Natural State
Einar K. Holthe
Market Ideolog and Strategist.
2020

Acknowledgements GLOBAL: John Maynard Keynes; Gro Harlem Brundtland, Ellen McArthur Laura Storm, Kate Raworth, Doughnut economies; Mariana mazzucatoThomas Piketty Ladeja Godina Košir-Circular Change Rethink Economics, Fuglen.

NORWAY: Cathrine Barth. Circularities & Nordic Circular Hotspot: Raymond Johansen-Mayor of Oslo.

JAPAN: Kenji Kojima JapanTakashi Murakami: Jesper Koll.

Reference

My references is my companies, my projects and my development strategies. As this is a practical method of value creation that has been developed over 20 years of business modelling, www.naturalstate.no.

Chapter 16
The Role of Sustainable Resource Management in an Economy We Want

Janez Potočnik

Abstract Economic model we have created is unsustainable and transition to a more sustainable economy and society is unavoidable. The way we manage our natural resources to a large extend determines, on one hand, our economic success and, on the other, influences climate, biodiversity and pollution challenges. Decoupling economic growth from resource use and environmental impacts is central ingredient of the necessary change in the way we produce and consume. Circular economy should be seen as an instrument to deliver decoupling in practice and as a part of the bigger picture of economic, societal and cultural transformation needed to implement the SDGs. Complexity and scale of the challenges requires more systemic approaches as well as new forms of collaboration, including on a global level.

Keywords Sustainability · Resource management · Circular economy · Transition

16.1 New Reality–Rethinking Economic Model

For the first time in human history we face the emergence of a single, tightly coupled **human social-ecological system of planetary scope**. We are more interconnected and interdependent than ever and our individual and collective responsibility for our future has enormously increased.

The Club of Rome nicely summarizes this by arguing that we are moving from an empty world, dominated by nature to the full world, dominated by humans. In the empty world, labor and infrastructure were the limiting factors of human wellbeing. In the full world, the limiting factors of human wellbeing are the natural resources and environmental sinks.

Our Economy and Society are built on a system which has resulted in the remarkable socio-economic development of some people but also in an unequal, and arguably, unjust distribution of wealth; inequalities in health and well-being; and an increase in environmental and climatic pressures on parts of the world which are least equipped to deal with them.

J. Potočnik (✉)
UNEP International Resource panel, 1 Rue Miollis, Paris, France

© Springer Nature Singapore Pte Ltd. 2022
S. Hill et al. (eds.), *The Kyoto Post-COVID Manifesto For Global Economics*,
Creative Economy, https://doi.org/10.1007/978-981-16-8566-8_16

It is not difficult to argue and agree that most of the challenges we face can be attributed to the **increasing economic activity of the growing human population**. And it is also not difficult to argue and agree that the currently prevailing linear economic system is not natural and organized in way, which is contradicting the laws of nature.

It is now more or less widely accepted that using (only) **Gross Domestic Product (GDP)** as an indicator of wellbeing and development is no longer appropriate.

One could maybe best summarize GDP by saying, that one will not reach the goal by walking faster, if walking in the wrong direction! We, therefore, have to change the measurement of our growth, wellbeing, success … starting with the GDP, which may help to explain our past achievement, but is of little use in guiding our future priorities and efforts.

This is clearly borne out by the Inclusive Wealth Index (Fig. 16.1).

The Index shows that between 1992 and 2014, the Production Capital (PC) per capita has almost doubled, Human Capital (HC) per capita has only slightly increased and Natural Capital (NC) per capita has fallen for almost 40%. As we can see from the graph, production capital was, during this period, more or less on the same growth path as GDP per capita, which leads us to the conclusion that growth of GDP in the last decades has been achieved at the cost of depleting natural capital and that not all growth we are recording using the GDP measurement is actually a "good" growth. To a large extent this could be explained by the already mentioned fact that the core mechanism defining the equilibria on the markets are price signals and that natural capital is undervalued or not valued at all.

We should aim to **redefine and reorganize our economic model to be consistent with the SDGs**. This is an enormous challenge, in particular if social considerations are taken into account, but it would also clearly provide us with new economic

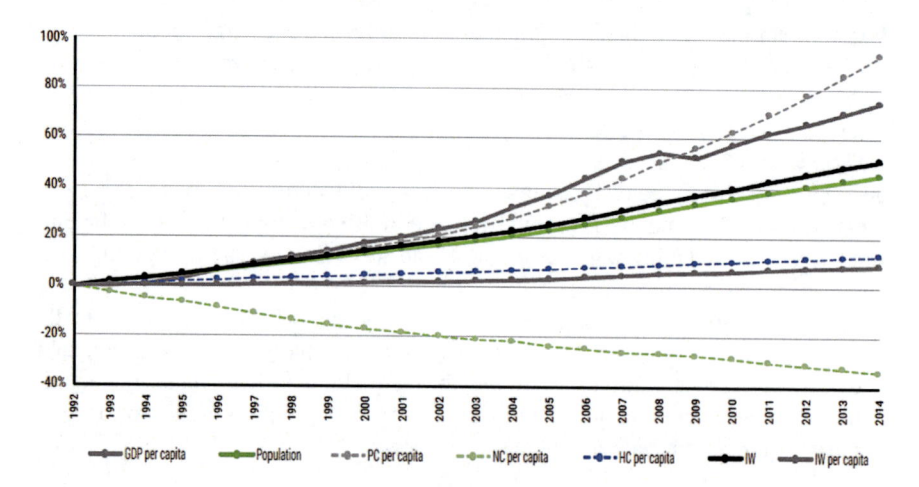

Fig. 16.1 Inclusive Wealth (IW) Index (its components) evolution–1992 to 2014. *Source* Inclusive Wealth Report 2018, Routledge, Edited by S. Managi and P. Kumar

opportunities and jobs. Our economic model has been created and is maintained by governments, international organizations, as well as by education and social institutions. The model has been created with good intentions and it is difficult to change it, because by now it is perceived as almost 'natural'–however, humans have created it and humans can, and must, change it.

16.2   The Missing Link–The Role of Natural Resources

It will require, however, a clear focus on **natural resource use and its impacts**, in order to fix the compass and provide a new guiding framework for truly sustainable growth, accounting for all the externalities, and minimizing the trade-offs between SDGs.

Until now, resources and resource management has by and large, been the missing link in policy making. Yet the delivery of 12 out of 17 SDGs is directly linked to natural resources and their importance is clearly revealed in the recent UN International Resource Panel (IRP) **Global Resource Outlook 2019, (GRO)**.[1]

Global resource use (biomass, fossil fuels, metals, non-metallic minerals, land and water) has more than tripled since 1970 and global material demand per capita grew from 7.4 tons in 1970 to 12.2 tons per capita in 2017, which means that an important part of the increased demand could be linked to higher economic activity. **Material productivity**, the efficiency of the use of resources, was growing until the end of the century and then started to decline and has stagnated in recent years. Even if material productivity was growing in all countries during that period, it was declining on the global level. How could that be possible? It can be attributed to the structural shift of production from countries that are more resource efficient to countries that are less resource efficient. To put it differently, more products we are buying today compared to few decades ago, are produced in Indonesia, China, and India and less in countries like Japan, Europe or U.S.

Consumption of materials is unequally distributed. If measured by **Domestic Material Consumption** per capita, (i.e., all materials, domestic or imported, which are used on in a country), then upper-middle income countries are already the highest consumers. The key drivers are the huge material requirements, in particular of non-metallic minerals in fast developing countries like China, which are needed for the development of new infrastructure and the construction of entire cities.

If measured by per capita **Material Footprint**, (i.e., where materials and products are actually consumed), then high-income countries are still consuming 60% more than the upper-middle-income countries and 13 times the level of the low-income countries. The reason for that is outsourcing of material and resource intensive production, including all connected direct environmental pressures, from high-income countries to other parts of the world.

---

[1] IRP–Global Resource Outlook, UNEP, March 2019.

One of the conclusions following the previous IRP work is also that: "In the mid-term, except in specific cases, resource shortage will not be the **core limiting factor** of our economic development. The core limiting factors are, and will be even more in the future, environmental and health consequences caused by this excessive and irresponsible use of resources." It is not the shortage of oil that brought together the national leaders in Paris to agree the necessary, (although arguably insufficient), steps to address climate change, but the dramatic consequences of the changing climate. It was not the shortage of steel or any other material, which forced the Chinese government to close around 2000 companies around Beijing a couple of years ago, but rather the polluted air in Beijing, (to which these same companies have contributed with their activities).

The Global Resources Outlook 2019 also includes the analyses of **environmental impacts** in the value chain related to resource extraction and processing. 90% of global land-use related biodiversity loss and water stress can be explained by resource extraction and processing. Over 80% of both is linked to biomass, the majority to agricultural activity. Indeed, there is no solution to land-use related biodiversity loss and water stress without the transformation of the current agriculture model, and the broader food system, to one which is more sustainable.

Resource use and management are the **linking elements behind the major problems and solutions** of all major environmental and health challenges. They are the bridge between drivers and pressures caused by human activity (economy, competitiveness, jobs) and the states and impacts visible in a dangerously changing climate, biodiversity loss and increasing pollution of various types. It is therefore essential to decouple the growth of human wellbeing and economy from the use of resources and from environmental pressures and impacts. This theoretical concept is called decoupling and it is the essential ingredient for reorganizing economic activity into a more sustainable model.

16.3   Circular Economy–Let's Mimic Nature

Circular economy is an instrument to deliver decoupling a reality. Circular economy is becoming a concept, which no longer needs explanation. The concept is known by many and in principle already also accepted by many. Saying that does not mean that it is, and it will be, easy to adopt it in practice, in particular on a large scale. The need for redefining the current understanding of circular economy certainly exists. Current approach is to a large extent organized around waste logic and recycling. But when the resources are used, the damage has already been done and it is essential to refocus from the end of pipe solutions to the whole product cycles, from legislating waste to legislating products and services.

Circular economy is not a new concept. It is the **oldest concept on the earth**. All nature is organized based on the principles of the circular economy. Nothing is lost and everything has its purpose. That is why it would make sense to embrace it, reorganize our societies and economies and start to behave accordingly. In essence there is only one question we have to answer. **Do we agree that we humans are part of the nature too?** To answer this question, we probably do not need help of the most famous Belgium detective Hercule Poirot, but his advice is always useful. When asked why he is speaking about himself in a third person he replied something like that: "If one is such a genius like me, it is very important to establish a healthy distance to himself." Intelligence is distinguishing humans from other living beings and putting us in a dominant position. But are we also intelligent enough to establish a healthy distance from ourselves and behave as we are part of the Nature? And, are we intelligent enough to bear the burden of responsibility given to us, and organize ourselves in a way, which will to a full extent respect also all other living beings we share the planet with? Huge responsibility, which is at the same time responsibility to our own existence and next generations.

Circular economy is in the first place about **system change** and about **reorganizing** some of the **fundamentals ruling our societies and economies**. Starting with the prevailing economic theory still being taught in our schools, reviewing the prevailing concepts we use for measuring success in the companies and progress of the societies, to rethinking some of the core ingredients of our quantity driven market economies where more products means higher profits, but at the same time also higher and growing use of natural resources and more environmental and health impacts. Dematerialization, rethinking ownership concepts, better connecting products with producers and shifting from resource efficiency to resource sufficiency are necessary ingredients of the transition in the direction of sustainable economies and societies. We do not need cars, we need mobility; we do not need chairs, we need to seat; we do not need light bulbs, we need light; we do not need CDs, we want to listen to the music; we do not need refrigerators, we need chilled and healthy food; farmers do not need pesticides, they need healthy plants … and I could continue.

What is the difference for the producer selling you the **light** and not **light bulbs**? If selling you light bulbs, producer's interest and profit are based on selling you as many of them as possible, if selling you the light, it is just the opposite, producer would want to use as few of light bulbs as possible. In the first case light bulbs sold to you are the base for the profit in the second they become the costs. And what is the difference for the consumer? None, in reality life for a consumer just gets less complicated. This model is not a fiction, it already works in practice, for example on the Amsterdam airport Schiphol. It is not difficult to see consequences of shifting the logic in the direction of saving resources and lowering environmental and health impacts.

It is time to **refocus from the waste to the product, from the end of pipe approach to the life cycle approach**. What is needed is a product framework legislation introducing for example product hierarchy, focusing on establishing product value retention systems, dealing with end of product status, addressing design for sustainability and public procurement requirements, introducing product passport, registration for market access etc. All that with rethinking the producer ownership concept in the center–connecting responsibility and opportunity of producers to the products they produce. Retaining the value of the products is essential if we are to change incentives which are currently driving producers and consumers behavior.

An important enabler for that to happen is ongoing **digital revolution** allowing wide introduction of the concepts of servitisation and virtualization in practice.

16.4 Transition is Unavoidable–Rethinking the Fundamentals

And **why** are the changes to a more sustainable economy and society **so difficult in practice**? Five important reasons linked to economic behavior:

- While the challenges we face require a deep systemic change and long-term rethinking of the way how we govern our societies, political cycles, public and financial institutions, to a large extent also private companies, have inbuilt **short-term focus, logic and interests**. This inconsistency limits our ability for efficient and strategic action and needs to be addressed urgently.
- Production and consumption systems are based on the logic of **consumerism fueled by quantity-driven profits and growth** measured in GDP. More means more profits, but also more natural resources used and more environmental and health impacts. We have to fix a broken compass!
- Markets are core mechanism for the interaction among economic actors, producers and consumers. Production capital is over-valued and over-rewarded, labor capital is undervalued and under-rewarded and natural capital is in many cases not valued at all. This cannot lead to economic, social and environmental balance. **Signals to economic actors** should change.
- The **existing lock-ins, and vested interests**—economic, social, political, geographical ... create strong resistance to change. Companies are indeed thinking strategically, very likely more than policy makers, their success and survival depends on that. They know where they would like to be in the future, but they also know where they are now. But they clearly struggle how to make a transition, stay profitable and ensure future existence.
- A **transition** to a more sustainable economy and society will **only** be **possible** if it is **just, fair and inclusive**. Social unrest is growing even in high-income countries and it is high time to hear the echo of the streets and the voice of sometimes frustrated young generation. Transition means change and change means some will benefit, and some will lose on a personal base. This will be particularly difficult for vulnerable parts of the society. They need to be helped and the ownership for the transition should be carefully crafted in advance. We have to make our societies more equitable and do more in the fight against poverty.

Good management of the transition depends on good **governance**. System change we are witnessing request mobilization of all the society. It requests clear political and private sector leadership, it requests broad understanding and ownership of the transition, it request more cooperation and coordination on all the levels, including global, it request major innovation efforts and the power of co-creation, and it requests an agreement and a clear inter-generational agreement, a contract for the future we want and need.

Transition will be only successful if going to fundamentals and reaching all. On a **global level** important questions like carbon leakage, trade policy considerations, and the importance of creating level playing field will have to be taken into account.

Back to the baseline thoughts. For the first time in human history we face the emergence of a single, tightly coupled human social-ecological system of planetary scope. Inevitably the challenges we are facing can only be solved by more cooperation, by **sharing our national sovereignty** more–like it was done after the second world by the nations of Europe to avoid future conflicts and wars. Can we avoid major conflicts and wars in an ever-populated world tackling the challenges we face, and we see but growing? Clearly some gaps are existing when it comes to global governance of natural resources, which could be addressed by exploiting the option of establishing a **Convention on Natural Resource Management**.

Transition to a more sustainable economy and society is **unavoidable**. The alternative is of course existing, but I would rather avoid talking about it. It could be fatal; it would likely be fatal.

German philosopher and statesman Johann Wolfgang Goethe:»Knowing is not enough; we must apply. Willing is not enough; we must do.« Let's do it.

Chapter 17
Stewarding Systems Aliveness—Pathways to Transformation

Petra Kuenkel and Elisabeth Kühn

Abstract The strategic transformations that the KM II posits require collective stewardship capacities across the globe inspired by a system's view of life that puts our shared humanity back at the center of attention. Based on more than 20 years of experience in transformation and change initiatives, and grounded in transdisciplinary thinking that draws from, among others, physics, system's theory, organizational theory and ecology, we put forward the 'transformation enablers', part of a meta-level approach for a stewardship architecture fostering multi-level collaboration for sustainability. Integrating a balance of all enablers in design and implementation of strategic transformative action ensures a contribution to shifting the grammar, not just the language, towards a new global socio-economic system serving life.

Keywords System aliveness · Transformation enablers · Aliveness principles · Transformative change interventions · Multi-level collaboration

17.1 System Aliveness and the Transformation Enablers

As the authors of the KM II clearly state, our dominating global perspective is an economic template that is falling short of addressing the climate crisis and other global problems of our time. Not only does it fail to provide solutions to challenges like the 17 Sustainable Development Goals or the increasing global inequality and social fragmentation, but it actively contributes to maintaining the dangerous status quo. Yet, if—as many scientists and sages predict—we need to rise up to our capacity for a collective stewardship approach to stabilize the trajectories of our planet including our global society (Steffen et al., 2011, 2018), we need to become more humble partners of life's potential to renew and replenish. The strategic transformation that KM II asks for, requires a profound transformation that changes the

P. Kuenkel (✉) · E. Kühn
Collective Leadership Institute, Kurfürstenstraße 1, 14467 Potsdam, Germany
e-mail: petra.kuenkel@collectiveleadership.com

E. Kühn
e-mail: elisabeth.kuehn@collectiveleadership.com

© Springer Nature Singapore Pte Ltd. 2022
S. Hill et al. (eds.), *The Kyoto Post-COVID Manifesto For Global Economics*,
Creative Economy, https://doi.org/10.1007/978-981-16-8566-8_17

grammar of how we observe reality. We need to practice the new view of the world, when we define what is needed for a shift of our dominant economic and social paradigms.

Transformative actions that intend to contribute to the realization of KM II needs to be firmly anchored in such a system's view of life. We need to look at our challenges as nested in the complex adaptive systems that constitute human socio-economic-ecological developments. Understanding our world from a systemic perspective is central to conceptualizing transformative change. Moreover, understanding what gives life to systems must become a guiding force for approaching the large systems change we so deeply need. Starting from this perspective, any strategic transformative action needs to put what we call 'systems aliveness' at the core, access our shared humanity, tap into the human desire to contribute to improving life and foster our capability to engage with a bigger picture. We define 'systems aliveness' as the capability of small and larger systems to gain resilience, regenerate and maintain their vitality in mutual consistency with other systems. This capability is, according to our in-depth transdisciplinary research (Kuenkel, 2019; Kuenkel, 2017; Waddock & Kuenkel, 2019), based on six what we call 'aliveness principles'. They constitute a pattern of relational interaction, and work together, like a musical composition, in their effect on the system—fostering aliveness in the system, subsystems and complementary systems. The idea is that the capacity to create the transformative change such as that envisioned by aspirational goals like the United Nations' Sustainable Development Goals (SDGs) can be enhanced by understanding these principles, and translating them into the design and implementation of transformative collective action. Like fractals of the envisaged future pattern of relational interaction, attending to these six principles and translating them into strategic actions contributes pathways to a new civilization with human and ecological flourishing.

One way of translating the essentially non-linear and mutually supportive 'aliveness principles' into the linear planning modalities required by today's institutions is to look at them as strategy elements in large systems change. The principles then become 'transformation enablers', which serve as a quality check for designing transformative change interventions. In their togetherness, attention to the six 'transformation enablers'—enlivening narratives, enabling structures, sustainability-oriented innovation, multi-level governance, guiding regulations, empowering metrics—pave the way for 'systems aliveness' to emerge. At the same time, they provide guidance and inspiration for conceptualizing strategic transformative action in organizations, social change, and global sustainability transformation in the spirit of KM II. A balance of all enablers ensures the polyphonous combination of the elements, and thus a contribution to shifting the grammar, not just the language, towards a new global socio-economic system serving life.

The 'transformation enablers' are part of a meta-level approach for a stewardship architecture (see Fig. 17.1) fostering multi-level collaboration for sustainability based on the Collective Leadership Compass (Kuenkel, 2016), derived from more than 20 years of experience in transformation and change initiatives, and grounded in transdisciplinary thinking that draws from, among others, physics, biology, architecture, system's theory, organizational theory and ecology.

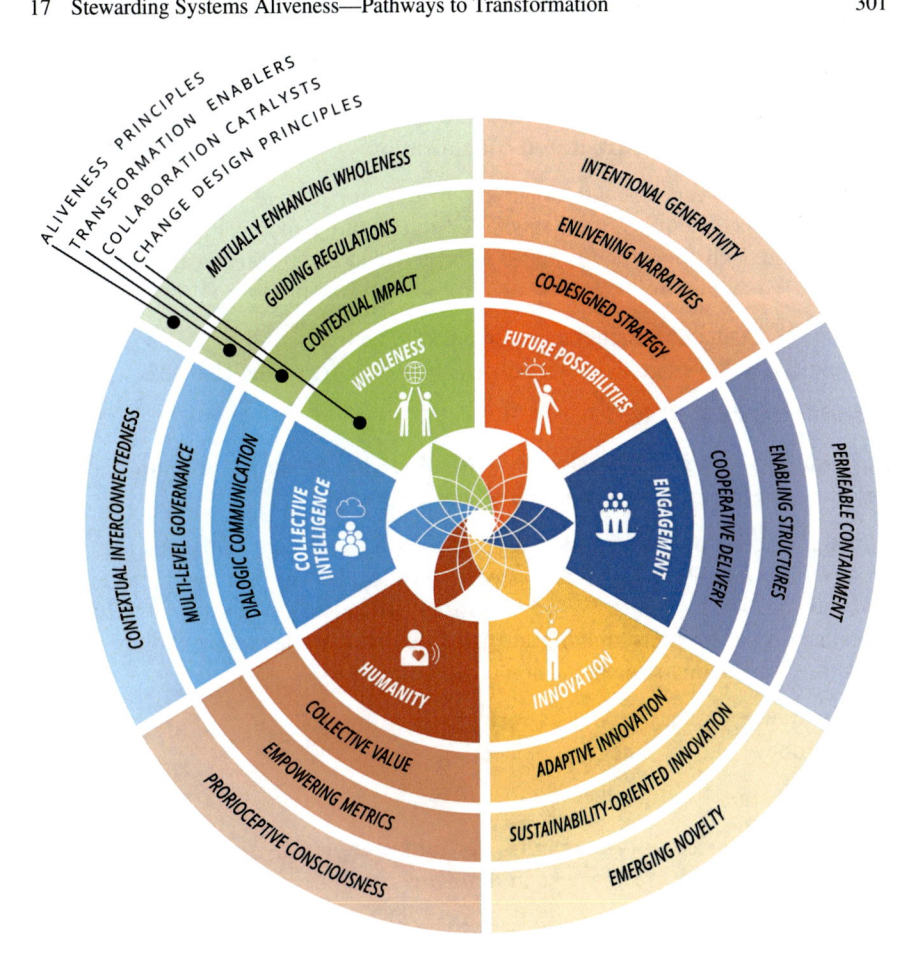

Fig. 17.1 The Collective Leadership Compass as a stewardship architecture: connecting 'aliveness principles' and 'transformation enablers' in a meta-level approach (*Source* Kuenkel 2019)

Transformation Enabler #1:

Enlivening narratives—invigorating the human capability to collectively shape the future

Efforts to bring about the necessary shift in our socio-economic paradigms need compelling and collectively shared narratives for that envisioned future. This enabler encourages stories of future possibilities and creates narratives that inspire minds and hearts for sustainability. It helps identify and co-develop emotionally compelling visions and goals. Exemplary guiding questions for shaping strategic action could be.

- How do we build resonance for transformative change?
- How do we invigorate the capacity to shape the future collectively?

Transformation Enabler #2:

Enabling structures—engaging the human desire for belonging, meaning-making exchange, and structured collaboration

Change makers need to build dynamic networks for change that others can identify with. Engagement is a prerequisite for co-creating structures that enhance self-organization. Existing structures need to be revisited and institutional arrangements adjusted. Exemplary guiding questions for shaping strategic action could be.

- How do we enable structures that enhance collective action of stakeholders?
- How can we leverage the potential of networks for dynamic change?

Transformation Enabler #3:

Sustainability-oriented innovation—building change on the human desire to venture into the unknown and create new pathways

Strategic actions need to nurture existing innovative change initiatives and foster creative new pathways. Resources need to be allocated for prototyping technological and social innovations. We need to foster and amplify pioneering advances for sustainability, so that new thinking and new solutions can emerge. Exemplary guiding questions for shaping strategic action could be.

- How do we accelerate the discovery of new pathways?
- How do we nurture emerging pioneering approaches?

Transformation Enabler #4:

Multi-level governance—leveraging the human capability to thrive on diversity and act in networks of networks in dialogue

As transdisciplinarity and dialogue need to be the primary mode of action, new and contextually relevant forms of harvesting collective intelligence in sense making and co-creation need to be established in multiple stakeholder settings, so that knowledge can be drawn from across difference. Change makers need to attend to the interconnectedness of change initiatives and avoid silo approaches. Exemplary guiding questions for shaping strategic action could be.

- How do we leverage multiple perspectives and expertise?
- How do we establish structured dialogue to negotiate future pathways?

Transformation Enabler #5:

Guiding regulations—tapping into the human desire to contribute to improving life and foster our capability to engage with a bigger picture

This enabler ensures that the systemic perspective is maintained at all levels of transformative action. Seeing the wholeness reminds change makers of the need to create frameworks that safeguard the larger system, set both voluntary and binding rules, reallocate resources to sustainability efforts, and establish steering systems that change behavior. Exemplary guiding questions for shaping strategic action could be.

- How do we assess the well-being/life of the system as a whole?
- How do we codevelop behavioral guidance and adequate resource flows?

Transformation Enabler #6:

Empowering metrics—promoting the ability of humans to become aware of the emergence, evolution, and interdependence of systems

As noted in KM II, our criteria for measuring progress and human welfare are in urgent need of change. We need to revisit what gets measured and create measurements focused on shared values of humanity. Creating awareness of future pathways, and codesigning metric-based feedback systems for iterative learning will promote a shift towards the 'circular triangle'. Exemplary guiding questions for shaping strategic action could be.

- How do measurements support the shift in mindsets?
- How do we develop meaningful measurements of progress?

The translation of the 'systems aliveness principle' into the 'transformation enablers' as quality check for planning transformative change bridges the gap between old and new thinking. It acknowledges current capacities, while ensuring that strategic planning is not merely reinforcing the known approaches of the status quo, but contributing to a deeper transformation of our socio-economic value systems, institutions and structures. The strategic transformations that the KM II posits require collective stewardship capacities across the globe inspired by a system's view of life that puts our shared humanity back at the center of attention.

References

Kuenkel, P. (2019). *Stewarding sustainability transformations: An emerging theory and practice of SDG implementation.* Cham. Switzerland: Springer.

Kuenkel, P. (2017). A pattern approach to sustainability transformation–How the 17 SDG can become a starting point for systemic change. *Collective leadership studies*, Vol. 5. ISSN 2569–1171. Potsdam/Germany: The Collective Leadership Institute.

Kuenkel, P. (2016). *The art of leading collectively–co-creating a sustainable, socially just future.* Vermont. USA: Chelsea Green.

Steffen, W., Rockström, J., Richardson, K., Lenton, T.M., Folke, C., Liverman, D. Summerhayes, C.P., Barnosky, A.D., Cornell, S., Crucifix, M., Donges, J.F., Fetzer, I., Lade, S.J., Scheffer, M., Winkelmann, R., & Schellnhuber, H.J. (2018). Trajectories of the earth system in the anthropocene. *Proceedings of the National Academy of Science* U S A. 2018 Aug 14;115(33):8252–8259. https://doi.org/10.1073/pnas.1810141115. Epub 2018 Aug 6.

Steffen, W., Persson, A., Deutsch, L., Zalasiewicz, J., Williams, M., Richardson, K., & Svedin, U. (2011). The anthropocene: From global change to planetary stewardship. *AMBIO: A Journal of the Human Environment*, 40, 739–761.

Waddock, S., & Kuenkel, P. (2019). What gives life to large system change? *Organization & Environment*. https://doi.org/10.1177/1086026619842482SAGEPublishing.

Chapter 18
From Sustainability to Thrivability: Transforming Systems with Purpose

Alexander Laszlo, Karin Huber-Heim, and Stefan Blachfellner

Abstract The contemporary landscape of challenges to survival, sustainability, and the possibility of flourishing on and with Earth are not the same today as when the Kyoto Manifesto was first written. Fortunately, neither are the tools at our disposal to deal with them. From conceptual to technological to behavioral, the systemic responses being developed appear to be appropriate to the task. However, it is critical that these responses be neither under-conceptualized nor over-constrained in their design and implementation. Through the power of collective intelligence and driven by the very experience of a global pandemic, a new norm for collective wellbeing is emerging in action. This chapter explores the key aspects of both the imperatives for this type of response as well as the practices emerging at the cutting edge of society. These focus not only on the necessary-but-not-sufficient objectives of survival and sustainability, but on the true potential of regeneration and thrivability to create the conditions for flourishing through the dynamics of circularity and inclusion of living systems in all our relations—with ourselves, each other, nature, past and future generations, and the underlying evolutionary dynamics of change.

Keywords Thrivability · Systems · Circularity · Humaning · Metrics · Covid19 · Pandemic · Regenerative economy · Regenerative systems · Behaviour · Behavioural change

A. Laszlo (✉)
Bertalanffy Center for the Study of Systems Science (BCSSS), Laszlo Institute of New Paradigm Research (LINPR), 13/5 Paulanergasse, 1040 Vienna, Austria
e-mail: alexander.laszlo@bcsss.org; alexander@thelaszloinstitute.com

K. Huber-Heim
Bertalanffy Cener for the Studies of Systems Science/ Academic Programme Director, University of Applied Sciences BFI, 13/5 Paulanergasse, 1040 Vienna, Austria
e-mail: karin.huber-heim@bcsss.org

S. Blachfellner
Bertalanffy Center for the Study of Systems Science (BCSSS), 13/5 Paulanergasse, 1040 Vienna, Austria
e-mail: stefan.blachfellner@bcsss.org

What we call *sustainability* goes by various names and terms in other languages. In some, such as Spanish, there is a distinction between 'sustainability' as *sostenibilidad*: the ability to support something by propping it up and keeping it from collapsing; and 'sustainability' as *sustentabilidad*: the ability to nurture a pattern of emergence in ways that foster its evolution. In English, we don't make that distinction since we have only one word: sustainability. So some went ahead and added the modifier 'development' after the term in an effort to specify that we wish to indicate strategies that ensure the evolutionary maintenance of an increasingly robust and supportive environment; regenerative strategies that identify opportunities for increasing the dynamic stability and self-sufficiency of an individual, a group, or a society by indicating areas of socio-economic potential to be developed to the advantage of all the stakeholders involved—both those who benefit from the system at present, as well as those who stand to benefit from the system in the future. The fact that these times represent an unprecedented challenge to our economy, our way of thinking, and our way of life as a species on this planet is the source of both great despair and great hope. There can be no doubt we live in VUCA times — characterized by events and situations that are Volatile, Uncertain, Complex, and Ambiguous. In our daily experience, this easily translates to RUPT experiences — when we sense that everything is too Rapid, Unpredictable, Paradoxical, and Tangled. These acronyms have become commonplace in contemporary writings on change management and change leadership, the former more frequently in scientific and analytical studies and the latter more in social and psychological reports. These new frames of systemic conceptualization point to how easy it has become to feel overwhelmed, trapped, and too small to cope with the contemporary dynamics of change. Especially when the information we have at our disposal re-emphasizes its VUCA nature. The combined threat posed by the global Covid19-pandemic, the looming economic crisis, resource scarcity, the underlying climate crisis, the threat to biodiversity, and even the possibility of human extinction may prove to be the biggest and most extensive test of our capacity — both individually and collectively — to rise to the challenge of our times and respond with evolutionary smarts.

In collaboration with an international network, we at the Bertalanffy Center engage in action research to enable these advantages with and for all stakeholders with awareness to the evolutionary patterns and structures that arise from the interdependence of guiding regulations, multi-level governance and empowering metrics and the system dynamics of embodied inter-subjectivity which determines the purpose of our individual and collective behaviour and the emergence of enlivening narratives, guided by collective worldviews.

18.1   A History of Multi-level Governance: The Emergence of SDGs as Guiding Self-regulations

When the Millennium Development Goals (MDGs) were issued in 2000, a period of 15 years for halving extreme poverty rates, halting the spread of HIV/AIDS and providing universal primary education in developing countries seemed ambitious, but doable. They were agreed to by all the world's countries and all the world's leading development institutions in a multi-national, multi-level governance effort, to meet the needs of the world's poorest.

By 2015 the world had changed in many ways: the target of reducing extreme poverty rates by half had been met already five years ahead of the 2015 deadline! Nevertheless, extreme poverty in certain areas still exists—nearly 10% of the world's population live from $1.90 a day and 12.9% in 2014 remained undernourished. Primary school enrolment figures could be raised impressively, but the goal of achieving universal primary education had been missed. The fight against diseases showed mixed results: while new HIV/AIDS infections decreased, almost half the world's population is at risk of malaria. The fact that humanity is setting global development goals, and making progress on reaching them, is evidence of a new era in the collective self-determination of our species. These approaches are emerging in response to the shifting set of challenges facing humanity today. There are five mega-trends that we, as a species, are learning to cope with and respond to:

- Globalization of markets—business is increasingly moving to 24/7/365 non-stop modalities of production and service availability
- Globalization of technologies—information processing and communications technologies permit, foster, and encourage the globalization of markets genetics, nano-tecnology, robotics, Smart Data, IoT, deep AI, VR, AR, AE[1] → disruptive individually; explosive when combined
- Evironmental pressures—increasing interdependencies between human and natural systems with threshold limit implications given the finite carrying capacity of local and global biomes
- Geo-political and socio-economic challenges—a fundamentally new reality with regard to the potential for systemic crises as well as for opportunities to transcend them
- Health and wellbeing—Individual and collective responses to global pandemics and the necessity for greater reliance on technology mediated interactions

The particular pressures exerted on humanity by the challenge of coping with a global pandemic has resulted in the need for an entirely new social transaction system. Clearly, no one person or team can create the needed pathways to viable futures in isolation—we are all in this together. Official development assistance from wealthy countries to developing countries increased by 66% reaching $135.2 billion—but since it was not designed as global partnerships for development it did not lead to

---

[1] IoT = Internet of Things; AI = Artificial Intelligence; VR = Virtual Reality; AR = Augmented Reality; AE = Artificial Empathy. Each of these represent distinct technological advances.

widespread improvement in people's living conditions, where needed the most (The World Bank, 2019). Important improvements had been achieved, as exemplified in the data excerpts above, yet not enough to make a significant difference. Further issues had added complexity, uncertainty, and urgency on many different levels calling for actions. A new set of goals was to be built on the Millennium Development Goals to complete what these did not achieve.

Based on the remaining tasks and due to the pressure that climate change induced natural disasters, and eco-systems decline have put on populations in all parts of the world, an enhanced systemic approach to change has been developed. To guide all existing interests into the same direction, the 193 member states of the United Nations started a multi-stakeholder process that lasted three years. Upon deliberations of the United Nations Conference on Sustainable Development in Rio de Janeiro, Brazil, in June 2012, and its outcome document "The Future We Want", the UN High-level Political Forum on Sustainable Development was established (United Nations, 2019). In 2013, the UN General Assembly set up a 30-member Open Working Group to develop a proposal on subsequent goals, the Sustainable Development Goals (SDGs). The annual Forum on Sustainable Development serves as the central UN platform for the follow-up and review of the SDGs, where member states must report their progress. As a result, the 2030 Agenda for Sustainable Development with 17 SDGs at its core was adopted in the general assembly meeting at the UN Sustainable Development Summit in New York in September 2015. It was considered as a landmark for multilateralism and international policy shaping. *Transforming our world: the 2030 Agenda for Sustainable Development* was adopted the same year as the *Paris Agreement on Climate Change* (December 2015) and refers to it in SDG 14.

All member states agreed and committed themselves to achieve the 17 Global Goals for Sustainable Development at national, regional, and international level by 2030. Addressing the multiple challenges humanity is facing to achieve well-being, improve health, education and gender equity, economic prosperity, and environmental protection for all, they provide a holistic and multidimensional view on development rather than a restricted set of dimensions and targets (Pradhan et al., 2017), an approach which truly can be called systemic. While there has been much discussion about the spread of false or misleading information via media in recent years, the rise of digital technologies and the concomitant pressures of new behavioral norms driven by a global pandemic, knowledge access has also migrated from specialized, localized knowledge "hot spots" to the Internet. The old hot spots were physical brick-and-mortar libraries, schools and universities. Not only do these hot spots now exist in virtual form online, but structured learning environments that deliver access to them make knowledge acquisition an easy-access and on-demand affair.

18.2   From Self-regulation to an Empowering SDG Metrics

To reach the SDGs, a global plan of action for people, planet, and prosperity has been developed. Additionally, each of the 17 goals is supplemented by a set of targets to demonstrate the scale and ambition of this new universal agenda and to balance the four dimensions of sustainable development: the economic, social, cultural, and environmental. The interlinkages and the integrated nature of the goals and targets are of crucial importance in ensuring that the purpose of the new agenda is realised. As all 17 goals are interdependent, reaching the targets will sometimes lead to synergies as well as to trade-offs (Pradhan et al., 2017) and thus cause a massive institutional challenge at both national and international levels following Ashby´s law of requisite variety (1958). This law states that a system needs to increase its variety of responses to the number of challenges that its environment produces in order for it to be able to deal successfully with the diversity in its environment. In 2016, the 169 targets supporting the Goals were provided with a proposed list of 230 SDG indicators developed by the Inter-Agency and Expert Group on SDG Indicators (IAEG-SDGs, 2016) as a practical starting point for action.

Taking, for example, certain actions related to SDG 6, 7, 11, 12 and 15 will generate synergies and co-benefits for other SDGs. Investments in wastewater treatment with energy co-production may simultaneously contribute to increasing water (SDG 6) and energy (SDG 7) security, public health (SDG 3) and contribute toward more sustainable cities (SDG 11) (IIASA, 2018). Actors and decision makers should be aware of these affects when developing and designing measures and strategies. The greatest risk we face to reach the goals is delaying urgent decisions and actions, the greatest barriers are competitiveness and acting in silos. Some member states govern their public policy sectors, such as health, energy, agriculture, and education, through sectoral ministries and agencies, while others don't—leading to a lack of joint agendas and coordination often resulting in inefficient or even contradictory policy actions within and among states. Target 17.14 can therefore serve as a reflection of the aspirations that already exist at the national level to work across policy sectors. This will also entail a political exercise, as political, institutional and cognitive limitations to how large complex problems can be addressed in policy making (Nilsson, 2016). The currently ongoing national responses to the pandemic may not serve as a blueprint for collective action to tackle global warming and biodiversity loss, but some of the multi-lateral activities already provide us with some hope for the necessary change.

According to the 2019 report of *the Bertelsmann Stiftung* and the Sustainable Development Solutions Network, there are mainly 3–4 SDGs in which all countries are at risk stagnating or experiencing a deterioration: 12 (Sustainable Consumption & Production), 13 (Climate Action), 14 (Life below Water), and 15 (Life on Land). Thus, no country on Earth is on track when it comes to achieving the full range of the SDGs. Even the countries that are generally at the top of most development rankings still need to invest a lot of effort (Sachs et al., 2019). In regard of the current political situation in Europe and the polarisation trend in international politics, the authors suggest also to bring SDG 10 into the focus, as inequalities within or among states can prove to be an enormous barrier for positive transformation and collaboration. Countries and regions, governments, the private sector and civil society are still called upon to implement and bring this plan to life through collaborative global multi-actor partnerships to mobilise and share knowledge, expertise, capacity building, technology, and financial resources, thereby making SDG 17 the key-goal to achieve all of them. Especially as the most debated issue of growth needs to be addressed together and is different for industrialized countries than for developing and emerging countries. While the former need to invest in regenerative systems for production and sustainable consumption, the latter will need to unlock their potential in the most sustainable and regenerative way. Collaborative partnerships we can pave the way for shortcuts to clean and sustainable lifestyles for millions in emerging countries, without detouring to environmentally and socially damaging processes that industrial states were going through to progress. Likewise, industrialized countries can learn from the possibly frugal innovations of emerging countries how to anchor awareness of sustainable living and economic practices in society, how to foster world citizenship carried by the spirit of global solidarity, as well as appreciation of cultural diversity and the contribution of culture to sustainable development. The imperative is acting together for 2030, with the participation of all countries, all stakeholders, and all peoples. The Covid19 pandemic not only painfully highlighted the ways in which we are globally interconnected and how rapidly events and phenomena on one side of the world can reach and affect the rest but also that we cannot solve global problems through national strategies. Only multilateral coordination and collaboration can bring solutions to global issues we are facing.

In the envisioned collaborative efforts, we need to be aware of the worldviews and narratives that nourish our individual and collective behaviour or human becoming as unconscious and conscious conditions, constraints, and opportunities from a systems point of view. This entails taking the dynamics of embodied subjectivity and intersubjectivity into account given that they are embedded in the enabling structures, sustainability-oriented innovations, multi-level governance, guiding regulations, and empowering metrics that originate from and further cultivate our worldviews.

18.3 The Case for an Enlivening Narrative to Enable Our Co-Evolutionary Pathways

In essence, what we are after are ways of *humaning better*: how can we, individually and as a species, act in dynamic harmony with all of life and the life support systems of Earth? The challenge of addressing this question of how to human better has become both profound and urgent. The practices, dispositions, and values that favor the emergence of an authentic expression of our full potential to human are varied and multiple—and often ancient. The underlying dimensionality of humaning that holds greatest potential for actionable frameworks that address the SDGs as considered in the Kyoto Manifesto II lies in our potential to harness the power of collective intelligence. As we engage in the process of ushering in the conditions for the emergence of a truly thrivable planet—listening into the systemic nurturance spaces and seeking to identify the systemic leverage points for the emergence of a *glocal* eco-civilization— it will be increasingly important for our species to continue to explore ways of fitting our individual melodies together to create sustaining and enduring harmonies with the broader symphony of life on Earth. This is more than just a nice metaphor: it is the essence of *syntony*. As an organizing force in societal evolution, syntony involves an embodiment and manifestation of conscious evolution: when conscious intention aligns with evolutionary purpose, we can foster and design evolutionarily consonant pathways of human development in partnership with Earth. This goes way beyond merely sustainable development strategies. Indeed, it is the essence of regenerative, thrivable development.

As part of this action inquiry, a fundamental task for the agents of systemic change of today, for tomorrow, is the creation and promotion of relational intelligence applied to systemic innovation. If connective intelligence is the capacity to identify and connect with individuals and resources relevant to humaning for thrivability, and collective intelligence is the ability to foster synergetic initiatives based on such connective intelligence, then relational intelligence is the sense-*ability* required to harness collective intelligence for the greater good. Such evolutionary competence is at the heart of our emerging collective expression of life as Earth. Authoring this narrative involves a collective act of re-*membering* and re-*storying* our interbeing. "[…] There are other stories of self, however. We could see ourselves, as many spiritual traditions do, not as separate beings but as "interbeings," not just interdependent but interexistent" (Eisenstein, 2014). This is the celebration of our deepest sense of being and belonging—of coming home and being home. The emerging narratives of systemic sustainability, of evolutionary syntony, of *glocal thrivability* all draw upon this wellspring of understanding (Wheeler, 2006). Re-membering our community— not as human beings with myopic self-centered interests, but as human becomings who are consciously evolving members of an interdependent web of life—is fast becoming an evolutionary imperative, extending and fostering the imperative of acting together for 2030.

In the collection of essays that comprise the book *Beyond Fear and Rage* (Laszlo, 2017), the need for such hope is recognized. Hope derives from the knowledge that we are all part of patterns that emerge and evolve. Hope lies in the process, in the joy of being a part of a consonant, coherent, connected meta-narrative of life on/in/with Earth. It also derives from the knowledge that we can and always do, whether wittingly or not, affect the harmonics of emergence. So, the question becomes, how do we choose to join, and what patterns of consonance do we help give rise to?

Reclamation, resilience, and regeneration are critically important orientations for our times, but it is through transformation, transmutation, and transcendence that we will emerge the new realities that will takes us out of and beyond these times. Doing so will require diligence, integrity, and commitment. Even if we are not aware of them, with diligence, integrity, and commitment, they will manifest—just without efforting. It is a consonant alignment of being, a state of syntony, and it is often non-conscious. But we also can create a process of syntony, if we care enough to learn how and when to be empathetic for "all of us" (people, beings, things), and if we stop separating things into atomistic, individualistic compartments. In short, it means reaffirming the sacredness of life—of life as a dynamic process to be maintained and furthered, and not just as a state of being. Humaning affirms our true nature is as Human Becomings, not merely as Human Beings. In his book on *Birth Without Violence,* Frederick Leboyer (1975) evokes the attitude that the sacredness of greeting a new life invites: "Only a little patience and humility. A little silence. Unobtrusive but real attention. Awareness of the newcomer as a person. Unselfconsciousness." And if that is how to engage with a new life coming into this world, then it must also be appropriate for how to engage with all things sacred. When all things are considered sacred—all the time—it evokes an entire worldview.

Learning how to listen, that is the first step toward syntony. In the spirit of the Kyoto Manifesto II, it is what we are called to do in fulfillment of our higher potential, both individually and collectively. Erich Jantsch (1975) suggests that "[…] we are in the process of learning to take seriously those responses which are no longer innate but emerge from tuning in to general evolutionary forces. Syntony is on the verge of becoming more conscious." The act of listening into what Stuart Kauffman (2003) has called the adjacent possible, of curating that which appears as though it were almost seeking to emerge, this is the act of intuiting, imagining, and co-creating a narrative of syntonious thrivability. It is what was so deliciously captured by Arundhati Roy's (2003) evocative assertion: "Another world is not only possible, she is on her way. On a quiet day, I can hear her breathing." Cultivating this sense-*ability*—and the corresponding response-*ability* that it calls for—is part of the new set of competencies needed for the type of thrivable human presence on Earth at the heart of the Kyoto Manifesto II, to human better. It is both the simplest and most natural thing with many ways in the world, and at the same time requires focus, attention, and above all, practice of awareness. If we learn to ease that part of your consciousness that keeps up the constant chatter in our head, commenting on and judging everything, we start to make ourselves more available to the information flows of syntony, for we are never truly cut off from them. *Quieting the mind*, then *releasing into the moment*, without the need to "do anything" with it, just being fully present, and then *allowing our perceptions to flow* with whatever arises in our field of awareness, this is the practice. These three simple steps may take a lifetime to cultivate. The result is greater flow with what's going on in your life, greater coherence with yourself, with others, with nature, with your ancestors and those who will come after you, and even with other times and places of the cosmos. David Price (2014) writes about the notion of engaging in a *daologue with Earth*, which evokes this exploration of and engagement with the way in which conversation, play, dance, and all aspects of life-as-art connect us to the quintessence of humaning as an expression of the cosmos, itself.

The quality and character of this story of our individual and collective being and becoming, therefore, depends on the way in which we author our life and cultivate our full potential to human throughout the five Syntony Spheres and their respective practices:

1. In the first syntony sphere—*humaning with oneself*; personal or internal syntony—the practice involves centering, quieting the mind, listening with every cell of our being. These practices cultivate intuition, empathy, compassion, insight that matches outsight, and a willingness to explore and follow our deepest calling.

2. In the second syntony sphere—*humaning with others*; community or interpersonal syntony—the practice involves deep dialogue and collaboration. Coming together to learn with and from each other and to engage in coordinated action with considerateness, openness, and joy in order to enable collective wisdom.

3. In the third syntony sphere—*humaning with nature*; ecosystemic or transspecies syntony—the practice involves communing; listening to the messages of all beings (whether they be waterfalls, animals, mountains or galaxies) and acknowledging our interdependence and ultimate unity.

4. In the fourth syntony sphere—*humaning with ancestors and future generations*; evolutionary or integral syntony—the practice involves listening to the voices of those who have come long before us and prepared the ground for our own being in the here and now. Simultaneously, it involves sensing into future generations and what kind of history would best serve them for us to create in the here and now. These practices cultivate our ability to flow with the process of being and becoming that gives direction, dimension, and meaning to our life.

5. In the fifth syntony sphere—*humaning with the deep dimension of the cosmos*; pan-cosmic or holistic syntony—the practice involves learning to read the patterns of change of which we are a part; learning to hear the rhythms of life that emanate from the deepest dimension of the cosmos, and becoming familiar with the improvisational jam session that nature has been playing since time immemorial. These practices cultivate our ability to play our own piece; to sing and dance our own path into existence in harmony with the grand patterns of cosmic creation, and to participate in the ongoing flourishing of life.

Full syntony occurs when all five Syntony Spheres become harmonically aligned in daily practice, resulting in an integral engagement with the syntony-carrying information flows that continually manifest the universe. In order to use syntony to human better, we have to learn certain skills, to develop and practice certain competencies, and to manifest a willingness to think and act interactively. The notion of "will"—of active intention and passionate purpose—is crucial here. In fact, it is what makes the difference between merely seeking harmony and consciously curating a constantly emerging dynamic of syntony. When we approach the issues of humaning from the standpoint—or rather, the flowpoint—of syntony, the aim is not for either "the best way" or "the right way," and not even for "the most convenient or gratifying way," but rather for the ways (any of many) that will lead to the greatest potential for conviviality while assuring the continual maintenance of an increasingly robust and supportive environment. When we really open ourselves to the deeper flow of syntony-informed humaning, we realize that there is no stage in an evolutionary process that does not take every previous stage into account. Biologists have expressed this with the dictum "ontogeny recapitulates phylogeny." Even seemingly drastic changes—the evolutionary leaps that are described in Gould and Eldridge's theory of punctuated equilibrium (1972), for instance—can be seen to "make sense" when viewed as part of a broader continuum of change. But they only make sense in hindsight: evolutionary change is not predictable, and yet it is coherent and consistent with all with which it is interconnected—in terms of both phenomena and processes. This is the deeper pattern of syntony.

What would it be like if we were to "play by rule of syntony" as we sought to address the Sustainable Development Goals in the framework of circular economies as put forth by the Kyoto Manifesto II? The virtuous cycle of interdependence would call us to "see" "hear" "sense" (Laszlo, 2015) the changes that are happening in the world around us, as well as to pay attention to the ways in which the individuals and groups with which we interact perceive these changes. We would need to cultivate our evolutionary vision for change in our world—and we would need to be able to communicate our sense-*abilities* more interactively, including all those aspects of life and living that involve a sense of joy, love, awe, the sacred and the celebratory experiences of life. If we can realize these universal and transformational ambitions across the full extent of the Agenda for 2030, the lives of all stand to be profoundly improved and our world will be transformed for the better. We are the generation that can create the future we will live in—so let us start today!

References

Ashby, W. R. (1958). Requisite variety and its implications for the control of complex systems. *Cybernetica, 1*(2), 83–99.

Eisenstein, C. (2014). Qualitative dimensions of collective intelligence: Subjectivity, consciousness, and soul. *Spanda Journal, Collective Intelligence, V*(2), 65–69.

Eldridge, N., & Gould S. J. (1972). Punctuated equilibria: An alternative to phylogenetic gradualism. In: Schopf (Ed.), *Models in paleobiology*. San Francisco: Freeman, Cooper.

IAEG-SDGs. (2016). *Report of the inter-agency and expert group on sustainable development goal indicators*. Final list of proposed Sustainable Development Goal indicators. https://sustainabledevelopment.un.org/content/documents/11803Official-List-of-Proposed-SDG-Indicators.pdf. Accessed 5th July 2019.

IIASA - International Institute for Applied Systems Analysis. (2018). *Transformations to achieve the sustainable development goals*. Report prepared by the World in 2050 initiative. Retrieved from http://pure.iiasa.ac.at/id/eprint/15347/1/TWI2050_Report081118-web-new.pdf. Accessed 13th December 2019.

Jantsch, E. (1975). *Design for evolution: Self-organization and planning in the life of human systems*. George Braziller.

Kauffman, S. A. (2003). *The adjacent possible: A talk with stuart A. Kauffman"* November 9. Edge Foundation. https://www.edge.org/conversation/stuart_a_kauffman-the-adjacent-possible. Accessed 13th December 2019.

Laszlo, A. (2015). Living systems, seeing systems, being systems: Learning to be the systems we wish to see in the world. In: Helene Finidori (ed.), *Spanda Journal, Special Issue on Systemic Change, VI*, 1, pp. 165–173.

Laszlo, A. (2017). Ripples from the Deep End: Tuning the harmonics of cosmic coherence. In E. Laszlo (Ed.), *Beyond Fear and Rage: A manifesto by the authors of What is Reality?* The New Map of Cosmos and Consciousness with comments from The Laszlo Institute of New Paradigm Research. London: Waterfront Press.

Leboyer, F. (1975). *Birth without violence.* New York: Alfred A. Knopf, 1978 trans.

Nilsson, M. (2016). Understanding and mapping important interactions among SDGs. Background paper for Expert meeting in preparation for HLPF 2017. Readying institutions and policies for integrated approaches to implementation of the 2030 Agenda Vienna, 14to 16 December 2016. https://sustainabledevelopment.un.org/content/documents/12067Understanding%20and%20mapping%20important%20interactions%20among%20SDGs.pdf. Accessed 5th July 2019.

Pradhan, P., Costa, L., Rybski, D., Lucht, W., Kropp, J. P., (2017). A Systematic Study of Sustainable Development Goal (SDG) Interactions. In *Earths Future*, Vol. 5, No. 11, pp. 1169–1179.

Price, D. (2014). "Daologue" in Open to Persuasion… open reasoning in a complex world. https://opentopersuasion.com/2014/05/22/daologue. Accessed 29th May 2015.

Roy, A. (2003). *War talk.* South End Press.

Sachs, J., Schmidt-Traub, G., Kroll, C., Lafortune, G., & Fuller, G. (2019). *Sustainable Development Report 2019.* New York: Bertelsmann Stiftung and Sustainable Development Solutions Network (SDSN). https://s3.amazonaws.com/sustainabledevelopment.report/2019/2019_sustainable_development_report.pdf. Accessed 13th December 2019.

The World Bank. (2019). *World Bank Open Data. Free and open access to global development data.* https://data.worldbank.org/. Accessed 5th July 2019.

United Nations. (2019). *Sustainable development goals knowledge platform.* https://sustainabledevelopment.un.org/sdgs. Accessed 5th July 2019.

Wheeler, W. (2006). *The whole creature: Complexity, Biosemiotics and the evolution of culture.* Lawrence And Wishart Ltd.

Alexander Laszlo President of the Bertalanffy Center for the Study of Systems Science, Director of Development at the Laszlo Institute of New Paradigm Research, 57th President of the International Society for the Systems Sciences, is known for his work on systems theories and "education ecosystems" and his outstanding contributions in the fields of leadership, systemic innovation, and sustainability. Laszlo is on the Editorial Boards of *Systems Research & Behavioral Science*; *World Futures: The Journal of New Paradigm Research*; *Kybernetes: The International Journal of Cybernetics*; *Systems and Management Sciences*; *Markets and Business Systems*; and *Managing Global Transitions: International Research Journal* and is author of over one hundred journal, book, and encyclopedia publications.

Karin Huber-Heim research group lead at Bertalanffy Center for the Study of Systems Science is focusing on Circular Economy Systems and Behaviour Change. As Academic Programme Director and Associate Professor at several Universities of Applied Sciences she has a strong focus on education and promotes the SDGs in curricula, research and teaching. Karin has been a member of the board at the Global Compact Network Austria and has an international reputation in advising organisations in the strategic integration of the SDGs for sustainability and innovation.

Stefan Blachfellner Managing Director of the Bertalanffy Center for the Study of Systems Science in Vienna, Austria, Conference Manager for the European Meetings on Cybernetics and Systems Research, Chair of the Special Integration Group on Socio-Ecological Systems and Design and former Vice President of the International Society for the Systems Sciences, General Secretary of the International Federation for Systems Research, author, guest editor and reviewer for several international peer-reviewed journals and reputable publishers, former Special Adviser to the European Commissioner for Transport, is focusing on the development of a General Systems Transdiscipline, Systems Design, Systemic Innovation and Impact Assessments to improve methods for addressing complex challenges towards the so called Next Economy.

Part IV

Conclusion: From Our Shattered Society to a New Economics

Chapter 19
Where Did Humanity Go?

Stephen Hill, Tadashi Yagi, and Stomu Yamash'ta

Abstract As Section 4, this Chapter and Chap. 20 draw the evidence and arguments of the Book together to show the way forward to a Humanity-centered New Economics for The Future. As this chapter demonstrates in high relief, what we must deal with is the *systemic* destructiveness to both our Humanity and our Planet that has resulted from Self-Interest-Based Economics over more than two centuries of industrialization. At heart is the question, "Where Did Our Humanity Go?" Particular attention is paid also to how the *new* context for global society—the COVID Pandemic—changes things, both now and for the future. We stand on a precipice looking down at a very uncertain future. The LINK from this chapter into the final Chap. 20 is the final question, "What can save us?".

S. Hill (✉)
Faculty of Arts, Social Sciences and Humanities, University of Wollongong, Humanities and the Arts Northfields Ave, Wollongong, NSW 2522, Australia
e-mail: sthill@uow.edu.au

T. Yagi
Faculty of Economics, Doshisha University, Karasuma Higashiiru, Kamigyo, Kyoto, Japan
e-mail: tyagi@mail.doshisha.ac.jp

S. Yamash'ta
Artist, Tokiwashimodacho 20-511, Kyoto 616-8228, Japan

© Springer Nature Singapore Pte Ltd. 2022
S. Hill et al. (eds.), *The Kyoto Post-COVID Manifesto For Global Economics*,
Creative Economy, https://doi.org/10.1007/978-981-16-8566-8_19

19.1 Guiding Thoughts

19.1.1 A Child Who Could See

Fifteen year old Climate Change Protestor, Greta Thunberg, could see it in 2018 when she sat down alone in a personal *strike* outside the Swedish Parliament. Sweden was not honouring its Climate responsibilities and the world had to reach zero carbon emissions by 2050, the time she will be 47 years old, or she and her entire cohort of fellow teenagers, may not *have* a future of any worth beyond this.

Greta's tiny, lone voice immediately appealed to hundreds of thousands of the young, and via social media, spread to millions. The world's top authorities noticed.

Within just four months Greta was invited to speak to her first International Conference—on Climate Change, a United Nations Conference in Poland:

"Adults, Decision-Makers – WAKE UP!" "You say you love your children above all else and yet you are stealing their future in front of their very eyes" (Davies, 2019).

And then, a month later, invited to the World Economic Forum in Davos, Greta Thunberg firmly told the world's economic leaders, to surprised but enthusiastic applause, that the Climate Change crisis was a product of their own rampant self-interest, in particular as they may well have come to talk about Climate Change by heavily polluting Private Jet:

"Some people, some companies, some decision-makers in particular, have known exactly what priceless values they have been sacrificing to continue making unimaginable amounts of money. And I think many of you here today belong to that group of people" (Davies, 2019).

Since 2018, Greta Thunberg has been a powerful voice of attention to Climate Change and its source in self-interest. She spoke however when the world was just ready to hear.

19.1.2 You Can't Avoid Seeing It Now: We Have Changed Our World!

For Climate Change penetrates more deeply into our consciousness by the day.

We see it in unusual events which are 'interesting' until we recognise what they imply.

For example, it rained in Greenland on Saturday 14th August this year, 2021.

What was significant is it rained – for the first time ever, it appears - at 3,000 m, the highest point on Greenland's 1.7 million square km × 3.2 km thick Ice Sheet.

Warming accompanying the rain caused melting over more than 50% of the Ice Sheet surface NOW. Over the last few years to now, 350 million tons of Greenland's ice melts each year. If, at three times the size of France, it all melted, the world's oceans would rise by 7 m (Fountain, 2021; NDTV, 2021).

The unprecedented temperature level at the highest point in Greenland's massive ice sheets is not isolated but sweeping across the whole Arctic: the temperature at the North Pole on Thursday 29th July 2021—when we were starting to finalise this Chapter—was 24 °C (75° Fahrenheit) (North Pole Weather Forecast, 2021).

What we are now seeing is unprecedented temperatures world wide. Indeed, the year 2020 was *the hottest year on record*, with average global temperatures higher by just over one degree Celsius compared to the 1880s. But, there, at the top of the world, the global temperature rise is multiplied—rising three times faster than the rest of the world. So we are already losing 13% of the Arctic Ice Cap *every* decade, that is an area lost since 1979 that is three times the size of Texas.

With the ice melting, the oceans are rising—by just 20 cm with Global Warming since the late 1880s, but, the situation is changing. The projected further rise by the end of the century, 2100, is between another 30 cm to 1 m by current trends, but if the Arctic and Antarctic Ice Sheets accelerate in their rate of melting—as is happening—in a worst case scenario, the world's oceans could rise by up to 2 m by 2100 and 5 m by 2150 (IPCC, 2021; Sleezak & Timms, 2021).[1]

The number of people affected is astronomical. As but one indicator, there are *presently* 410 million people living below 2 m above the ocean, all of whom must relocate and find new sources of food and sustenance in a world wherever they go which is already crowded and resource poor (Bamber et al., 2019; Storer, 2021; Wanless, 2021).

Perhaps many turn their attention away from what is happening in the Arctic, and from a *possible* future some decades away … 'it's a long way away and does not seem to affect us now'. But we *cannot* turn away from another direct product of rising global temperatures, and that is they have fueled uncontrollable bushfires from late 2019 to now (2021) in Australia, Indonesia, Siberia, Amazonia, California, Canada and even extending to the Greek Islands (Cribb, 2019).

All of these phenomena are now universally acknowledged in science, as a product of human industrial activity, in particular, carbon dioxide emissions feeding the blanketing Greenhouse Effect over our planet.

A clarion call for change was released to the world in early August 2021—based on wide-ranging and impeccable science, approved by 200 Member States of the United Nations—the State-of-the-Science Report from the United Nations Intergovernmental Panel on Climate Change (IPCC) developed as platform for the UN Climate Change Conference in November 2021. Even worse than previously expected, by the *current* trajectory, the Earth may have warmed by 1.5 °C by 2030, just over eight years from now … and, even with *current* National Carbon Dioxide Pledges, the Earth may possibly have warmed by 3.0 °C by the end of the Century.

Antony Guterres, Secretary General of the United Nations calls the evidence "a Code Red for Humanity (IPCC, 2021; Sleezak & Timms, 2021).

Meanwhile, we tend to forget how *inter*-connected we are with our natural world. We humans have an enormous though often unintended impact on other species around us but because of the complexity of our impact, we most frequently, don't even realise it. As Stephen Hill noted in Chap. 1 of this Book however, *One million species are currently threatened with extinction.* 75% of global food crops that depend on animal pollination are threatened—the annual value of which, with pollinator loss, is between $235 billion and $577 billion (UN, 2019).

19.2 The Grammar of Destruction'—Self-interest Focused Global Economics

19.2.1 Today's 'Normal'

Again, back to Greta Thunberg. She rubbed the faces of the world's economic elite in what is the basic message of this Book when she stated … "what priceless values *they* have been sacrificing to continue making unimaginable amounts of money". As she went on to say, 'they' means 'you' in particular as world economic leaders.

Even Adam Smith could see the problem way back at the start of 'free market' industrialization, as several authors in the present book have observed. In his "Wealth of Nations" book published in 1776, Smith observed that, paradoxically, an "invisible hand *harmonized* resource allocation through trade by *selfish* economic agents". However, well before this, as expressed in his "Theory of Moral Sentiments" published in 1757—Smith emphasized a counter-concern he had … right to the time he died—the need for 'suppressing selfish behavior' and developing 'empathy' and 'sympathy' if a peaceful state of the market was to be maintained (Smith, 1999, 2018).

Adam Smith rightly observed the beginning of values underlying economic action which ultimately set the basic grammar of today's Global Economic enterprise: *self-interest".* Perhaps the result of free-market actions by self-focused individuals *appeared* as *harmony,* but it moved into the hands of fewer and fewer of those whose self-interest was most successful in beating out the opposition. Wealth and control inevitably became centralized whilst the consequence for those left out has been massively divisive inequality ending for so many in desperate poverty.

Not to put too fine a point on it, this same dynamic that Adam Smith could see over 260 years ago, now threatens humanity's very survival beyond the next 100 years … and perhaps even sooner. For unbridled greed to pillage Earth's resources, carelessly turn them into sellable consumer products without attention to what the production system is doing to the planet …. leaves us in precisely the perilous position that Greta Thunberg has exposed. Meanwhile, these same controllers' prioritization of profit for self, may well lead them to *hide* the danger from the public that they are directly creating by their self-interested actions. Exxon Mobil is a case in point.

Brought to trial initially 2018 by the City of New York whose representatives were seeking damages for climate change injuries, the case continues through a Massachusetts Lawsuit (2021) alleging Climate Change deceit. What has been revealed already is that Exxon fought strongly to prevent the United States signing the Kyoto Protocol limiting carbon emissions and since the Kyoto Protocol was signed has donated more than $20 million to organizations supporting Climate Change denial. More culpably, Exxon has been conducting research since 1957 that revealed to the corporation exactly what they were doing to the planet for nearly 50 years, but ignoring it, they then sought to deceive humanity while ramping up carbon output – *for self-interested financial gain* (Stempel, 2021; Farmer & Cook, 2013).

We have spoken throughout this whole Book about the power of the self-interest *assumption* in producing highly centralized control of the world economy and wealth, which in turn pays off in massive inequality ... and 'whitewashing' of the truth So, we do not need to provide further detail here. Except ....

Except ... played out in high relief before the world's eyes NOW is a quite extraordinary caricature of the self-focused phenomenon we are talking about, a useful reminder of the depth of world problem we must deal with.

Stephen Hill talks in Chap. 1 of this Book about the 2021 Commercial Space Race between the three most wealthy men in the world, Jeff Bezos, Richard Branson and Elon Musk (Hill, 2021a). It is worth singling out Jeff Bezos as his goals, actions, resources and values place the present dilemma of the world into high relief.

First, Jeff Bezos, the richest man on Earth, with personal worth estimated at $179 billion, made it into Space in his 'New Shepard' Rocket Ship on Tuesday 20th July, nine days after Richard Branson's lower orbit but successful leading flight which we wrote about in Chap. 1. Bezos, like Branson, was inaugurating a multi-multi-billion dollar tourist industry for the mega rich.[2]

Second, Bezos's flight links to the COVID-19 Pandemic for his financial resources to power his Space flight were complemented by, for example, $92 billion made directly because of the COVID-19 Pandemic—from 18th March to 20th August 2020 (Dolan et al., 2020).

Third, meanwhile, whilst 8.6% of the world's people barely survive on less than $1.90 per day, Jeff Bezos makes $8.9 million *per hour*. His employees, such as Dock Workers, make $15.00 per hour, or $(US)20,000 per year. He thanked them along with all Amazon employees, for the funding for his trip into space. Their productivity pays while Bezos makes a *half million times more per hour than these $15 per hour Amazon employees* whose labour was funding his extra-terrestrial play (Hoffower, 2019).

There could be no better signal of the massive inequality which follows from this self-focused world order where, below where Bezos's space rocket played, 689 million people live in *extreme poverty* with incomes less than $1.90 per day, a population number which is likely to rise by an additional 150 million people by the end of 2021 due to the impact of the COVID-19 Pandemic (World Vision, 2021).

Fourth, Bezos created a "Climate Pledge Fund in 2019, now enrolling 53 companies (including Amazon) which have pledged to reach zero carbon emissions by 2040, 10 years *before* the Paris Agreement between the world's nations. But, this Pledge must be measured against both the massive impact of a Space Travel based Tourist Industry for the mega-rich, and what Bezos declared just after he returned to Earth:

We need to take all heavy industry, all polluting industry and move it into space, and keep Earth as this beautiful gem of a planet it is (Rincon, 2021).

The problem is that Bezos, and also Musk, are close to being quite serious about pushing our pollution and production problems into Space—when by others' calculations, by 2050, we could need the equivalent of three Earth Planets' worth of resources just to produce what we need and get rid of the rubbish (Pond & Butler, 2021). Kate Crawford, critic of the misuse of artificial intelligence, after noting that AI Corporations are now the world's largest consumers of electricity—for Cloud Computer Data and Web Services, and so on, observes,

"These are the billionaires who made their fortunes from AI and they're spending all that money trying to leave the planet. It's not, 'How do we address the problem?', it's 'How the hell do we get out of here?'" (Wood, 2021).

Fifth, Amazon staff handling stock in their so-called "Fulfilment Centres" (or stock warehouses) are already monitored by surveillance systems which automatically record their "picking rate", or the rate at which they gather products to meet orders—so AI adds pressure to physically perform. Not surprisingly, as a result, the workers have been suffering Musculo-Skeletal Disorders (MSDs) from their regime of lifting and carrying while under constant surveillance, so, as researcher Kate Crawford observed, multiple workers will have knee braces, elbow bandages or wrist guards, and at intervals there are vending machines stocked with over-the-counter painkillers for anyone who needs them.

In his final Annual Letter on 15th April 2021 to Shareholders (before passing on his CEO responsibilities to Andy Jassy later in the year), Bezos announced that in 2020 he had launched his *WorkingWell* program—initially for 859,000 employees at 350 sites across North America and Europe. The program targets body mechanics, pro-active wellness and safety plus new automated staffing schedules that use sophisticated algorithms to rotate employees among jobs that use different muscle–tendon groups to decrease repetitive motion and help protect employees from MSD risks." (Bezos, 2021).

After visiting US Amazon Fulfillment Centers, and seeing the new WorkingWell algorithmic system in operation, AI observer, Kate Crawford, concluded,

"They're resisting unionization every step of the way and using rampant surveillance technology to try to produce the most efficient mechanism to extract value from human bodies down to the level of muscles and ligaments" (Wood, 2021; Crawford, 2021).

What we therefore see with Jeff Bezos is product at the extreme end of a self-interest based system which with the tourist rocket business is targeting and supporting the richest people on earth who then relax by flying at great cost over the many millions of the poorest who gain *nothing* from the enterprise except depletion of more of their scarce resources. The business is drawing its capital directly from the misery of the COVID-19 Pandemic and workers who earn a miniscule fraction of their CEO's hourly income, yet it is dressed in the counterfeit clothing of a bene-factor—establishing the 'Climate Pledge Fund' and 'WorkingWell' programs, the first of which will contribute a tiny tiny drop into the bucket of action needed to fend off further Climate Change—but meanwhile offers excellent PR for Amazon, the second, which treats peoples' *muscles* as the employed resource—extracting value from human bodies as if they, the people, are algorithm-controlled robots. And stretched across the whole is the most extraordinary fantasy … we can solve the most basic of industrial production and waste problems delivered by this same self-interest based enterprise by simply tossing them off the Earth into Outer Space.

> It is sad to think that Jeff Bezos, perhaps with self-assured good will, is looking at his world through the glass of *artificial* intelligence framed by *self-interest* and has lost the ability to *see*. Humans are reduced to muscles and tendons, humanity is an algorithm, and human connectedness and care is preserved by throwing all problems into outer space.

Jeff Bezos is not alone. His concern for impact on our planet through founding his 'Climate Hedge Fund' as a 'moral' or 'pro-social' action, is, as Tadashi Yagi—along with Stomu Yamash'ta—describe in Chap. 3, *strategically* motivated—to draw in the more sensitive customers (even though meantime he is now wedded to his prime new love, circling the earth with the mega-mega rich in climate-challenging space ships). As opposed to genuinely altruistic pro-social behavior where customers and consumers can have long-term faith in the company, the Sustainable Development Goal (SDG) initiative in a *strategically* motivated pro-social company is likely to be at severe risk if it makes profits start to fall.

Perhaps more significantly what we see in the nihilistic excitement of Bezos's face is the complexion of what humanity of the post 2020s world has become. Toshiaki Maruyama captures this well in Chap. 7 of our present book. I quote:

> "Looking back on humankind's past journey, we can see that humans were one with the Earth before the beginning of agriculture, in the time when they lived as hunter-gatherers. Agriculture, however, gave birth to civilizations that exploited the Earth. Industrialized societies that arose later then focused their goals on developing industries for the future while depending on underground energy sources, thus turning into civilizations that gradually depleted the Earth. Furthermore, today's information industry society (i.e., the IT era), which grew from even more developed technical revolution, has made us into a civilization that is completely detached from the Earth.
>
> We are already in the midst of a 'hyper-IT' civilization. Young people today grow up in an internet environment from the time of their earliest recollections, and they are able to operate all kinds of machines at will. They are, however, also drowning in their world of virtual spaces and sounds."

The agrarian society base of Japan, the Jomon Civilization—which developed 15,000 years ago and forms the original platform of long-term Japanese culture, lasted 10,000 years. In the *250 years* or so since we discovered the power to be gained by dredging our planet for energy and resources for self-interested gain, we are in serious trouble. In one fortieth the time! We are on a path to destroying the planet which sustains us, and have enshrouded the resource which could get us out of here, our humanity, in arrogant artificiality.

So, in what is happening right now, October 2021, as we complete this Book, we see … in high relief … the message of our Book. To seriously address the BIG issues like Climate Change, ecological destruction, highly centralized control and massive inequality …. treating our humanity as pawns to be shuffled and *used* …..

we must learn to *see* behind the screen of artificiality and self-interest—address the root cause … the underlying assumptions or 'grammar' within which our global economic world is set. Played out, as Stephen Hill explains in Chap. 1, down to the blindness to 'community' in most modern urban design, in an obsolescence oriented consumer world by which we relate to each other by 'emojis' of life which come to stand *for* our humanity … we have come to live in a *shattered world*.

19.2.2 System Complexity—A New Disguise

Finally, progress into today's global economic world has produced another 'blanket' which hides 'self-interest within the sheer complexity of today's global economic and social *systems* which have now grown globally to connect people, production, animals, plants and resources in what come to appear as unstoppable, even independent, controllers of all humanity's decision and action.

Whilst Liu et al. (2015) identify potential benefits, Len Fisher, in demonstrating the unexpected breadth of reach of complex systems in Chap. 8, provides an excellent example of how the complexity can even bring you back to your starting point:

> Deforestation in Brazil due to soybean production provides food for people and livestock in China. Food trade between Brazil and China also contributes to changes in the global food market, which affects other areas around the world, including the Caribbean and Africa, that also engage in trade with China and Brazil. Dust particles from the Sahara Desert in Africa—aggravated by agricultural practices—travel via the air to the Caribbean, where they contribute to the decline in coral reefs and soil fertility and increase asthma rates. These in turn affect China and Brazil, which have both invested heavily in Caribbean tourism, infrastructure, and transportation. Nutrient-rich dust from Africa also reaches Brazil, where it improves forest productivity.

With, as Len Fisher goes on to explain, with such complex *inter*-connections—even across the whole world and natural environment, economic *systems* may seem to be beyond human agency—an inaccessible 'grammar' framing economic action and interest, but, also with a life of their own. They can suddenly collapse from what appear as small disturbances in one part of the system impacting on immediate then distant connections (as in the previous example, with food trade between Brazil and China affecting tourism in the Carribean)—ultimately smashing through the whole set of connections. Or alternatively, an unsustainable 'contagion' may spread across the whole system, in particular, from greed at each node of human participation—as did happen with the 2008 collapse of the world stock market when Lehman Brothers went bankrupt. This was a direct result of the contagion of immoral behavior of lenders who offered mortgage-backed securities without checking lender ability to repay—offering high risk but lucrative profits … until the housing market boom ended, financial derivatives of the artificial market became worthless, Lehman Brothers collapsed, and brought the world stock market *system* down with them.

The 'system' product therefore *can* destroy the self-interest advantage of all—even though, at heart, these *systems* are set in the molding wax of self and self-interest at each point where human decisions connect, ie: the 'system' based on self-interest can even deny all participants individual self-interest benefit.

Meanwhile, however, Modern System Complexity, and the image of apparent 'independence' even from individual self-interest, acts as a 'blanket' which *hides*— as seemingly '*natural* processes'—the self-serving dynamic and values which lie underneath—and, which, themselves, may even fail when aggregated. This is the same dynamic which has created centralization of control over the whole economic system—by concentration of control of major system elements (eg: corporations) by those with greater economic clout, leading to massive inequality more generally. Ultimately, with self rather than wider interest at the core of decisions in the complex systems now populating our corporate world, these 'systems' have taken us and our planet to the very edge of physical extinction.

> At heart is the ideology that self-interest is good and the only way a Global Economic System can operate effectively.

The play of self-interest within economics has, however, left us now perched on a precipice from which these same values intrinsically *cannot* guide us down safely. Oxford Philosopher, Toby Ord, reinforces the fragility of this 'precipice' even using the same metaphor which we, independently, found useful:

> We live during the most important era of human history. Major risks to our entire future are a new problem and our thinking has not caught up (Ord, 2020: Introduction).

We have lost our humanity or hidden it behind screens of self-interest. And it is only by re-asserting this humanity over the self that the problems which Greta Thunberg highlights, the risks such as nuclear annihilation that Toby Ord talks about … the problems which our Book exposes, can be fixed.

19.2.3 Suddenly—The Tiniest of Things Turned the World on its Head: The COVID-19 Pandemic

Having worked through these issues for some time—including a final International Symposium in Kyoto in June 2019, we felt we had some useful ideas on what to do about helping this transformation along.

BUT, *then*, a totally unexpected, dark and distracting shadow was cast across the whole world—over this same time period as Greta Thunberg's voice was starting to be heard and responded to … after 2018.

> The COVID-19 Pandemic suddenly launched into the world at end-2019 from Wuhan, China, either as a single cross-species mutation from bat to human, or, as seems increasingly credible, as a virus escaping inadequately hygienic laboratory experiment … and suddenly … unexpectedly, the *entire world of humanity* was overwhelmed.
>
> Now, at the time we are writing this Book, over 4.5 million people world-wide have died from COVID infection, most countries are in economic and social chaos or lock-down, international connectedness remains tethered to the empty wharves of cruise ships unable to travel and airlines barred from landing … and the world economy is in tatters.

When we completed and published our earlier Book, "The Kyoto Manifesto for Global Economics—the Platform of Community, Humanity and Spirituality", Climate Change was already firmly on the world agenda and ours, but the idea of a world-changing Pandemic such as COVID-19, could not even be imagined. That was why, as we said in the Introduction of this Book, we *stopped* in early 2020 in finalizing this Book, our Sequel to the 'Kyoto Manifesto', to watch this new world unfold, and to gain some idea of its impact on global economics and society.

Well, by now, we have a reasonably informed view of what COVID-19 is doing to the world. It's not a pretty sight.

The ubiquity of COVID-19's impact over just about everything unfolded from an initial localized and apparently minor infection problem to what became a world-wide COVID-19 Pandemic in just a few months. In the process it increasingly shattered the securities and norms of our *outside world*, but at the same time, also our *inside mental world* as Masatoshi and Tomoko Murase point out in their Chap. 12 of our present Book the greater burden of depression symptoms, for example, was *three times higher* in the U.S during the COVID Pandemic than before, and growing (Ettman et al., 2020). For the Pandemic's impact is not only physical and 'external'— causing immensely easy infection resulting in serious illness and frequent death, but also 'internal' or mental. With its geometric infection rates and therefore ubiquitous presence, far-reaching preventative social strategies have been introduced almost universally to limit inter-personal contact and infection. Cutting people off from each other and closing down many lines of employment and working with others, has enormous consequences for our society …. effectively, these actions are pulling apart our *humanity* whilst at the same time removing many supports for economic safety and resilience.

As a consequence, COVID has produced secondary products which are potent factors in mental illness—lower social and economic resources and exposure to continuous stress and uncertainty not just for oneself, but for one's relationships to loved ones who, because of imposed infection controls, one may not even be able to access to care and share. Being alone, not by choice, but compulsion … being cut off from our *humanity* … can have a terrible consequence, in particular, as a seedbed for growing anxiety, depression … desperation … and inability to *do* anything constructive.

COVID-19—particularly in the context of the massive self-based distortions of our economic, social and now environmental worlds which we have already talked about in these Conclusions—has left global 2020s society shattered more comprehensively, and *connectedly* than perhaps ever before. Not only is COVID stalking close by, but if the people are, for example, in the Eastern United States where Hurricane Ida hit with unprecedented force at the start of Spring 2021 (fed by the warmer waters now off the East Coast), or in the Western States escaping unprecedented bushfires (nurtured by hotter climate)…. what is also stalking increasingly close by, with ever greater destructive power, is Climate Change. And where did this come from? Self-focused global economic enterprise which is yet to look outside its mansions of greed to connectedness with and care for the wider world and its people.

The COVID Pandemic will continue to be an imminent horror—standing right in front of us, on all sides, whilst at the same time stalking up closely behind us with hidden but potentially deadly force. Vaccination for years to come will almost certainly remain unavailable to the very poor largely because of their place at the bottom of the global economic equity ladder. In 2021, new mutations beyond the very lethal Delta strain have already been emerging—in this case in South Africa, and spreading:

On August 14th 2021 – as we were writing this book, a new COVID variant, 'C.1.2' was reported scientifically (though not yet peer-reviewed) having been found originally in South Africa in May 2021 - and later in England, China, the Democratic Republic of the Congo, Mauritius, New Zealand, Portugal and Switzerland. It appeared to be mutating twice as fast as all previous variants, was more mutated away from the original Wuhan virus than any other variant as well as being more infectious and more able to evade vaccines (Scheepers, Bhiman et al., 2021). As of 24th August 2021, the World Health Organisation (WHO) was currently investigating *eight* COVID mutations of *concern* or *interest* including the 'C.1.2' strain (Joffre, 2021).Then, as we were finalising this book, the highly mutated OMICRON virus emerged from South Africa in late November, 2021, massively infectious though apparently less serious in effect than the previous COVID Delta mutation.

New and potentially increasingly dangerous mutations are very likely to continue whilst large populations, such as in developing countries, remain unvaccinated. The length of efficacy of any vaccines now and in the future will therefore continue to remain in need of constant review, as will world attention to providing significant vaccine support for the very poor.

The demonstrated aggressiveness of COVID mutation almost certainly requiring at least annual booster vaccinations, may, long term, even require innovative physical architectures and new norms of social interaction for a world which no longer *can* be fully protected. Eventually, the world economy will recover, though almost certainly it will be shaped differently, for example, with shorter supply lines less subject to international disruption, and the organization of work much more decentralized— back into the home of the workers, joined by electronic media and the demands of performance algorithms—so, also probably intrusively monitored via increasingly sophisticated artificial intelligence.

Human society *will* need to make a long-term adjustment to what *will* be a new dimension of our human existence. We confront this challenging new environment however, whilst meanwhile standing very precariously on a dangerous precipice of physical and social danger which is product of the self-centred global economic system which has come to enframe our lives and opportunity.

Surprisingly, COVID-19 *may* end up having a longer term *positive* impact—even on the underlying self-interest dynamics which underscore and strongly distort wider social and economic life.

As Stephen Hill points out in Chap. 4 of this Book, the Chinese word for "crisis", "weiji" may, in the way it has been brought into the English language domain, offer hope. For, according to the two meanings embedded in 'weiji', 'crisis' represents both 'danger' and 'opportunity'. Everything has been thrown up into the air, and, as even quite senior economists are now proposing, perhaps the shape of the global economy of the future may itself come down in a more humanistic form.[3]

19.2.4   We Stand on a Precipice Looking Down at a Very Uncertain Future: What Can Save Us?

So, this, our Sequel to the original Kyoto Manifesto, is shaped to handle a totally unexpected world-revolutionizing phenomenon, the COVID-19 Pandemic. But, perhaps unexpectedly, this crisis, whilst 'shattering' our everyday world and causing massive pain and distress, may also have opened a door for positive change out of our currently repressive self-based economic system that is threatening us with even more dangerous consequences—in particular, Climate Change and environmental destruction, but also the stress of centralized and global vested interest and massive inequality.

It has been the objective of our present Book to highlight these threats, but then to show where our collective strength lies to do something about them. This is our *Humanity!*

The final Chapter—which now follows, sums up what we have brought together to understand this humanity and how we can empower ourselves and broader society to grasp this strength and build a future guided by a New Economics based on sharing, caring, compassion, …. our humanity rather than self-interest—for institutionalized self-interest is what got us onto this dangerous precipice in the first place.

Notes

1. See also the comment by Professor Baylor Fox-Kemper on 9th August 2021, immediately after the IPCC Scientific Report was released. Fox-Kemper was a member of the investigation team and speaking for the IPCC:

    > "My role in the IPCC is a chapter that was focused on sea level rise, as well as changes in the ocean and frozen parts of the earth. And sea level rise is one of the most important, slow-moving processes, or slow-moving impacts of climate change. And so, as we get toward the end of this century, if we have low emissions, we expect to see something like one to two feet of sea level rise and something higher like two to three feet under high emissions. But in fact, if certain changes in Antarctica occur, we could see as much as six feet—or it's really as much as six feet can't be ruled out as a possibility." (Posted August 9, 2021) - Baylor Fox-Kemper, Ph.D. Professor of earth, environmental, and planetary Sciences, Brown University) (SciLine/AAAS, 2021).

2. The first fully tourist Space Flight flew just eight weeks later—on Thursday 16th September 2021 under Elon Musk's SpaceX 'Crew Dragon' banner. A somewhat expensive Pleasure Cruise at the cost of $(US)199.3 million for the billionaire, Jared Isaacman, footing the bill for 3 days in space for himself and three other tourists, it circled the Earth from 160 km higher than the International Space Station (Euronews, 2021).

3. For example, Dame Polly Courtice, Director of the Cambridge Institute for Sustainable Leadership, Oxford Economists Paul Collier and John Kay, the recently retired Governor of the Bank of England Mark Carney—now UN Secretary General's Special Envoy for Climate Science … and others. See Stephen Hill's Chap. 4 in this Book.

References

Bamber, J. L., Oppenheimer, M., Kopp, R. E., Aspinall, W. P., & Cooke, R. M. (2019). Ice-sheet contribution to future sea-level rise from structured judgment. *Proceedings of the National Academy Science, USA, 116*(23), 11195–11200. pubmed.ncbi.nim.nih.gov.

Bezos, J. (2021, April 15). 2020 Letter to Shareholders. https://www.aboutamazon.com/news/company-news.

Crawford, K. (2021). *Atlas of AI: Power, politics and the planetary cost of artificial intelligence.* Yale University Press.

Cribb, J. (2019, November 30). Countries from Siberia to Australia are burning: The age of fire is the blackest warning yet. *The Guardian.*

Davies, P. (2019, June 2). 29 of Greta Thunberg's Best Quotes. *Curious Earth.*

Dolan, K. A., with Peterson-Withorn, C., & Wang, J. (Eds.). (2020). The Definitive Ranking of the Wealthiest Americans in 2020–The Forbes 400. https://www.forbes.com/forbes-400.

Ettman, C. K., et al. (2020). Prevalence of depression symptoms in US adults before and during the COVID-19 pandemic. *JAMA Network Open, 3*(9), e2019686. https://doi.org/10.1001/jamanetworkopen.2020.19686

Euronews. (2021, September 16). SpaceX launches 4 amateur astronauts space in giant leap for space tourism. Euronews.next. *Euronews & AP, 12*(23).

Farmer, T. G., & Cook, J. (2013). *Climate change science: A modern synthesis, Volume 1: The physical climate* (p. 461). Springer Science and Business Media.

Fountain, H. (2021, August 20). It rained at the summit of Greenland. That's never happened before. *The New York Times.* https://www.nytimes.com.

Hoffower, H. (2019, January 9). We did the math to calculate how much money Jeff Bezos makes in a year, month, week, day, hour, minute, and second. *Insider.* https://www.businessinsider.com.

IPCC. (2021, August 9). *Climate change 2021. The physical science basis* ("Contribution of Working Groups to the Sixth Assessment Report of the Intergovernmental Panel on Climate Change"), Sixth Assessment Report (approved on August 6th by 195 Member States of the IPCC.

Joffre, T. (2021, August 29). New COVID variant detected in South Africa, most mutated variant so far. *The Jerusalem Post* (14.47).

Liu, J., et al. (2015). Systems integration for global sustainability. *Science, 347*, 1258832. https://doi.org/10.1126/science.1258832.

NDTV. (2021, August 14). *Rain on Greenland ice sheet, possibly a first, signals climate risk.* (quoting Martin Stendel, a researcher of the Danish Meteorological Institute), *Agence France-Presse.* Science. https://www.ndtv.com/science/rain.

North Pole Weather Forecast. (2021, July 29). https://www.weather-forecast.com/forecasts/latest.

Ord, T. (2020, March). *The precipice: Existential risk and the future of humanity.* Bloomsbury Publishing.

Pond, S., & Butler, P. (2021). Towards a waste-free future. *IMPACT, 21*(1), 6–9.

Rincon, P. (2021, July 20). Jeff Bezos launches to space aboard New Shepard rocket ship. *BBC News*, (Science Editor).

Scheepers, C., Bhiman, J., et al. (31 others) (2021, August 24). The continuous evolution of SARS–Cov-2 in South Africa: A new lineage with rapid accumulation of mutations of concern and global detection. *MedXiv* (Pre-paid Server for Health Science). Posted. https://doi.org/10.1101/2021.08.20.21262342.

SciLine/AAAS. (2021, August 9). Quotes from experts. New IPCC Report: Quotes from authors.

Sleezak, M., & Timms, P. (2021, August 10). The IPCC has released the most comprehensive climate change report ever. Here's what you need to know. *ABC News.*

Smith, A. (2018). *Theory of moral sentiments* (originally published, 1759). Eastford, USA.

Smith, A. (1999). *Wealth of nations:* (originally published, 1776), Penguin Books (Book 4, Chapter 2, para 9 in original).

Stempel, J. (2021, June). Exxon must face Massachusetts lawsuit alleging climate change deceit. Reuters–Business.

Storer, R. (2021, June 30). Up to 410 million people at risk from sea level rise–study. *The Guardian*.

UN. (2019, May 6). Sustainable Development Goals. UN Report: Nature's Dangerous Decline 'Unprecedented'; Special Extinction Rates 'Accelerating', Intergovernmental Science, Policy Platform on Biodiversity and Ecosystem Services (IPBES). 7th Series Plenary, 29th April to 4th May: Announcement, Paris. un.org.

Wanless, H. R. (2021, April 13). Sea levels are going to rise by at least 20 ft. We can do something about it. *The Guardian*. https://www.theguardian.com/commentisfree/apr.

Wood, S. (2021, August 21). "Facetime–Artificial intelligence is one of the most profound innovations of our time. And according to Manhattan-based Australian expert, Kate Crawford, we're sleepwalking our way through its inherent risks. *The Sydney Morning Herald, Good Weekend*, pp. 6–9.

World Vision. (2021). Global poverty: Facts ….. https://www.worldvision.org/global.

Chapter 20
Discovering Our Humanity—Economics of the Future

Stephen Hill, Tadashi Yagi, and Stomu Yamash'ta

Abstract The core argument of this chapter is that transformation cannot lie in just re-organizing or constraining the self-focused jigsaw puzzle of current Global Economics. Instead, it lies where our human strength lies—in change based on the power of our *Humanity*. To ensure the Book's validity of conclusions, particular attention is paid in this chapter to understanding Humanity—from historic, philosophic and existential perspectives. This power resides where the people are—where intersubjective relations and cultural meaning are at home—in local community. The power is like that of an earthworm in a garden—here providing nutrition for the 'garden' of human connectedness, creativity and enterprise. Power of positive transformation comes from below. It *cannot* come from above, from the 'rulers' with intrinsic investment in the present self-based economic system. Eight Principles for a Humanity and Local Community centered Economics are presented, including the importance of Circular Economy and Circular Triangle thinking, and the 'Global Localism' concept which connects the local with *global* change. Particular attention is paid to the role of Universal Basic Income and to building a successful Humanity-based Economics and Society within a longer-term COVID-influenced future. Indeed, solutions for handling COVID long-term mirror and strengthen those of the New Economics this book is developing and presenting.

S. Hill (✉)
Faculty of Arts, Social Sciences and Humanities, University of Wollongong, Northfields Ave, Wollongong, NSW 2522, Australia
e-mail: sthill@uow.edu.au

T. Yagi
Faculty of Economics, Doshisha University, Karasuma Higashiiru, Kamigyo, Kyoto 602-8580, Japan

S. Yamash'ta
Artist, Tokiwashimodacho 20-511, Kyoto 616-8228, Japan

© Springer Nature Singapore Pte Ltd. 2022
S. Hill et al. (eds.), *The Kyoto Post-COVID Manifesto For Global Economics*, Creative Economy, https://doi.org/10.1007/978-981-16-8566-8_20

20.1 Discovering Our Humanity

So, back to the 'precipice' on which we were poised before COVID came along as well.

Transformation cannot lie in just re-organizing or constraining the self-focused jigsaw puzzle of current global economics. Instead it lies where our human strength resides—in change at the level Len Fisher describes in Chap. 9, from social entrepreneur, Hilary Cottam, as the "Earthworm" strategy of governance, that is, as a 'gardener who tends to the wellbeing of all of the organisms in the ecosystem', the idea of the earthworm buried deep down emphasises "the need to radically redistribute power to the lowest levels". The idea of the earthworm takes us further however. For power at the lowest levels means nothing unless the environment the people are in is providing their nutrition for understanding and action—the product of an earthworm within the soil. Power to change lies with the subjective power of *people* in communities within a nutritive change environment—*not* at the top of a power hierarchy.

The nutrition is the depth of our humanity and we have spent quite a lot of time in this Book exploring what our humanity *is* and therefore where its power to create transformation lies. Not only that. As Len Fisher further points out in his Chap. 9 in this Book, "… the more diverse a society, the higher its potentiality for change from below". So, the earthworm concept beds in well within the complexity of contemporary society.

As authors of the present Book it was important to seek to understand *Humanity* at some depth. So, we went exploring.

20.1.1 Contributions from Long-Standing Tradition

We were assisted by 'Taiji' Master Xing Qi Lin who came to Kyoto in 2019 to share with us Taiji philosophy (and associated martial arts) which developed over thousands of years of Chinese civilization—as a holistic philosophy, the core foundation of which is "He", 'harmonization' and balance within the all-encompassing sphere of Taiji, heaven, earth and man—which are constantly emerging and transforming.

> It follows within Taiji philosophy that we are intrinsically part of this constantly emerging and harmonizing universe, indeed we rely on our environment to survive – but to *thrive* we need to also be in *harmony* – with our environment, and in mutual respect for all human and living things. In this way we sustain and nourish each other – even as the world changes around us. As we embrace not only ourselves but also others, tolerance, understanding and kindness result. By being compassionate and moral, the heart opens up, bringing happiness and contentment.
>
> Ego or 'Self' gets in the way: "one must aspire to achieve a state of not being controlled and driven by desires, selfishness, and sensory fulfilment," and, as Master Xing Qi Lin goes on to say in Chap. 13, "people today are generally too egocentric, only focusing on the self."

The reader of this book, 'The Kyoto Post-COVID Manifesto' will find the core message of this very brief summary of the vast depth of Taiji Philosophy sounding rather familiar. Not surprising. It is our core message. We have been asserting very much the same principles—to replace the *rule* by our current Global Economic Dynamic which is the exact opposite—fundamentally based on the *self* and self-interest, denying care and compassion for the sake of greed, creating world-wide inequality and distress!

So, when *we* promote *humanity* as the new platform for our future—built into the New Economy, we are not suggesting the 'latest' 'buzz-craze' from an enthusiastic promoter's latest action list, or a 'cool idea' from hippies descending from their hallucinogenic fogs of contemplation ..... The philosophy has been around for thousands of years ... and it works. Master Qi demonstrates the practicality *now* of Taiji philosophy through reporting a series of case studies of practical application in business, education and the community.

20.1.2 Looking at Humanity Through the Eyes of Contemporary Transdisciplinary Study

We explored 'Humanity' as platform a great deal further in the present however.

Masatoshi and Tomoko Murase have contributed three linked and creative Chapters on "The Self-Non-Self Circulation Principle of 'Living' Wholeness"— Chaps. 10, 11 and 12. Their approach to understanding our Humanity moves us on from historically formed spiritual tradition brought to our attention by Master Xing Qi Lin, and into an innovative holistic interactive model of understanding and analysis of *Life* itself, which includes contemporary science but is not limited by it. *LIFE* cannot be studied just from outside.

As the authors argue, at heart of 'Life' is constant interaction, negation, emergence and affirmation of Living Nature as an evolving interaction between Self (the Endo System, or the Mental World) and Non-Self (the Exo System or Multi-faceted External Environment or World). Life as process and as experience is a Hermeneutic Circle—never static but in constant motion, macro and micro being mirrors to each other.

Thus 'Life' and therefore our Humanity intrinsically cannot be studied or understood by scientific reductionist thinking of itself, but must be approached through *trans*-disciplinary interrogation which at the same time needs also to involve exploration of practical experience, and recognition of the reproducibility of the 'whole' at all levels in the 'parts'- and vice-versa—as in fractals, whilst the properties of any one particle .... or, element in Living Nature ... are determined by all the other particles. Life therefore cannot be seen in any other way than as holistic and transient.

Furthermore, *Time* is included. The future and the present are intimately connected as mental anticipation can pull the future into the present, whilst 'hope' in the present can shape and re-shape the future. The Murases' therefore complete their theoretical framework by expressing the sequence of dynamic interactions between the Self and Non-Self within their Self-Non-Self Circulation Theory as five successive processes, which, as represented by the first characters in each name is the "NECTE Principle":

(1)   Negation → (2) Expansion → (3) Convergence → (4) Transference → (5) Emergence

They then cast NECTE into both a horizontal and vertical bidirectional relationship, with the Yin-Yang emergence/negation philosophy represented in both a *present* and a *time-related* drawing of the Yin-Yang symbols, the NECTE philosophy operating in both directions simultaneously.

With this theoretical base in place, the authors turn their attention to the problem of Our Age, reflected in the sub-title of our shared Book ... we confront a "Shattered Society ". In the authors' terms, the *coherence* of the Circles of Life are 'shattered'—through all the forces highlighted throughout this Book and in these Conclusions—self-focused economic and social distortion, consequent fast developing environment threat to our Planet and Life itself ... and the tensions of living also within the prison of fear and deprivation surrounding us from the global COVID Pandemic. Complex but interlinked *Chaos* emerges as *Order* recedes—in a process that mirrors the emergent and negating transformations of Yin and Yang in Eastern Philosophy.

The authors go on to show the applicability of their Life Theory at a general and a specific level.

At a general level, the historic shaping of Human Nature and classic Evolution Theory are explained through the new filters of NECTE Theory, as are Learning and Unlearning. Development relationships between the Local and the Global are also explored as is the potential for formation of a novel mental system within the individual person through co-evolution of a new relationship between external and internal worlds, drawing the external world within their self, and through mental anticipation, drawing the future into the present and acting to make change happen.

At a specific level, Tomoko Murase (along with Masatoshi) applies their Self-Non-Self Theory of Life to her professional nursing treatment of mental illness (Chap. 12) where both 'Self' (internal) and 'Non-Self (external) Therapies are applied to heal patient *depression*, bringing Life back from its 'shattered world' context.

20.1.3 An Existential and Polyphonic Perspective on Our Shared Humanity

The Self-Non-Self Theory of Life—with its holistic base and transdisciplinary method, aligns directly with the 'Starting Points for Transformation' which we outlined in the Introduction to this Book. We observed the need to extend our concept of knowledge to *trans disciplinarity*, ie: across different 'domains' or 'territories' "such as 'objective', 'subjective', spiritual, cultural, eastern philosophy western science, economic, political—each with its own internal validity criteria" … "the knowledge needs to relate to 'the whole person' in relation to their 'whole environment'".

The interplay between emergence and destruction, between self and non-self, between now and the future—continuous resolutions of difference—which Masatoshi and Tomoko Murase theorise and test, brings us directly to the most central organizing principle of this Book, the concept of "Polyphony". Drawn from its use in music, both our previous Book, "The Kyoto Manifesto for Global Economics", and this one, follow its meaning, finding harmony and symphony in difference, what we regard as a basic principle for developing a New Economics based on our Humanity, and strengthening the essence of Humanity itself—in mutual care, sharing and trust.

Further, on Polyphony, our strategy through this whole Book has been to bring two or more separate themes (domains) together into an overall harmony no matter their difference. But then the tests of validity matter. Each input needs to be judged by its own established validity criteria, mainstream science by evidence-based peer-review, and subjective experience by 'feeling,' for example. However, as we state in the Introduction of this book, the final overall 'symphony which results is *not* to be judged by any one of the constitutive domain criteria of validity, but by its overall contribution to human empowerment, mutual understanding and mutual harmony—support for human values of sharing, care and trust rather than self-interest. In addition, the *whole*—seen here as a symphony created from separate contrasting themes (or 'domains') brought together, can also be seen in Len Fisher's terms in Chap. 8 as "a complex adaptive system" where the *whole* is MUCH greater than the sum of its parts.

Tadashi Yagi takes us further—along with Stomu Yamash'ta—in their Chap. 3. They note that one of the special roles of the Arts is to break through the limitations of "taboos" or "norms" in society. "Norms are required to stabilize the society. On the other hand, norms reflect the preferences of the majority, whilst the preferences of the minority are suppressed." Artistic performance on the other hand, allows a minority view or expression to be legitimately expressed and heard, potentially encouraging sympathy with the minority, creation of new value and harmonization of different people. _Co_-creation across difference can then be a powerful tool for drawing the marginalised into _harmony_ with wider society. An example is the Hana Art Centre in the Nara Prefecture of Japan which promotes co-creation between artists and persons with disabilities—not as an 'altruistic gift' but _inclusively_—to draw out the very different skills that may be associated with disability, for example, the sense of touch of a blind visual artist.

Similarly in business collaboration, co-creation across difference can be a powerful tool for harmony rather than self-focused conflict, and diversification may be source of both cooperative innovation as well as resilience against market shocks.

Again, co-creation across difference is a power of _polyphony,_ which, as Toshiaki Maruyama reminds us in his Chap. 7, requires listening when _establishing_ polyphonic connection.:

> … polyphony could only be achieved by carefully listening to the sound (i.e., voice) of the other. If one insists on emphasizing one's part alone, the harmony of the whole would not be achieved.[1]

We talked about 'listening' in our previous Book, "The Kyoto Manifesto for Global Economics" (Hill, 2018a, b) —coming to the same conclusion as Toshiaki Maruyama, ie: listening is about accepting others and their feelings as at least able to align with our own rather than imposing our 'self'. Sharing our human world with the other, explained by Masatoshi and Tomoko Murase in their Chap. 10, means the same thing, but as an affirmation of Living Nature through an evolving interaction between Self (the Endo System, or the Mental) and Non-Self (the Exo System. or the External Environment or World).).

So, in this, our current Book, we explore down to some existential depth in seeking to understand "humanity". We observe its fundamental properties of transience, emergence and negation—and inner-outer connected, 'becoming'—_Life_— "the self as a narrative unity" (Hill, 2018a, p. 301). Looking at humans in relation to each other, we have seen, as with the thousands of years old Taiji culture, the critical importance of 'harmonization' and balance within the all-encompassing sphere of heaven, earth and man—which are constantly emerging and transforming—thus the need to escape being taken hostage by self-interest, in particular, in achieving harmonization over time. Masatoshi and Tomoko Murase, in their Chap. 10 then build _time_ into their Yin-Yang emergence/negation philosophy represented in both a _present_ and a _time-related_ drawing of the Yin-Yang symbols, their NECTE philosophy operating in both directions simultaneously. Oxford philosopher, Toby Ord reinforces this importance we observe for _time_ in understanding _humanity,_ pointing to the importance of seeing humanity over "deep time", for, as he observes,

> This perspective allows us to see how our own time fits into the greater story, and how much is at stake. It changes the way we see the world and our role in it, shifting our attention from things that affect the fleeting present, to those that could make fundamental alterations to the shape of the long-term future. (Ord, 2010, p. 54)

Furthermore, if only we look away from just ourselves, we can experience the co-creating power of cultural frameworks of meaning to form polyphonic relationships which potentially hold *difference* between people and groups together within a relationship of harmony … and we have been led into the *systems* which humanity has created to handle organization of collective action—along with the intrinsic weakness of increasingly complex systems where the *self* displaces sharing as the basic organizing principle … and, step by step, we approach humanity's essence, Human Connectedness! We are fundamentally *social* animals in continual interaction with many environments of nurture and meaning.[2]

Our deeper explorations therefore return us full circle to where we started in this Book, and we quote from our Introduction:

> "The fundamental tenet of this book is that our power to 'heal' our currently 'shattered' society lies in the depth of our humanity – that is, in our shared human spirit, or spirituality. What is sacred or of imperishable supreme value is *what we can be* as a human race – *empowered* fulfilled individuals, living in harmony, deeply *sharing* and *caring* for each other across our separate cultural and life worlds."

Our return journey to early in this Book really is 'full circle' for we see the depth of our humanity is expressed as a "*Circle* of Wholeness" in relation to others within our shared social world and life. As Stephen Hill observes in his Chap. 2:

> "The 'Circle of Wholeness' represents the full power of our existential being as social human persons – inclusivity of our full sharing and care for others, of guidance from the many domains of human knowledge connecting in overall harmony, with caring and knowledge held into relationship by the 'circle's' central point, integrity and trust.
>
> To 'embrace and assert' the Circle of Wholeness for a Harmonious Humanity-based World Order therefore requires us to do three things.
>
> > First, we must *listen* to the silence otherwise occluded by the noise of the self in economic globalization.
> >
> > Second, we need then to drill down to the most basic values of our humanity – mutual care, mindfulness, compassion, and, truth.
> >
> > Third, having found these values, we must act within their rule in *every action*, starting *in my street*, that is, 'my immediate inter-subjective community or organization – with a clear litmus test, ie: 'does my action strengthen or weaken my own and wider 'community' and values of sharing and mutual care.
>
> Embracing the Circle of Wholeness also requires paying new attention to the knowledge base we live by – which needs to be one of truth across all worlds – subjective, objective, cultural, spiritual … across all Domains of Knowledge surrounding and guiding our life actions. Here, the music-based metaphor of 'polyphony' provides cohesion – drawing the different Domain 'themes' into a 'harmonic whole'.
>
> At the center of the Circle is our humanity's truth - action, not for a deal but as a gift anchored in honesty and integrity – the basis of trust."

20.2 Building a New Economics Based on Our Humanity

20.2.1 The Power of the Local

Following these explorations, *our goal* in building a New Economics, instead of a *self*-driven economy and society, has to be to build the fundamentals of our Humanity into *all* relationships, including economic—trust into agreements; community, sharing and care into living and relations with others—including economic; and nurture into the way we use our environment 'economically' for production and life. Additionally, we must remember, there are many cultural 'houses' within Humanity's overall domain. Our task is to be *inclusive*—build the essential feature of *harmony* through polyphony and co-creation across difference—applied to our shared economic participation and values.

> With truth, integrity and trust-*worthiness* at the center, with understanding that our existential 'Life' and its world are in constant interaction and evolution, fundamentally transient but in constant 'becoming' we reach 'The Circle of Wholeness'

The 'local' focus of The Circle of Wholeness leads us back to the Earthworm concept that Len Fisher brought to our attention earlier. Building from our human roots means building from our inter-subjective relations with others down at the *local* or *community* level, *not* giving orders from the top of a bureaucratic pile, *not* building large impersonal organizational structures where one's work neighbors are strangers within an abstract organizational 'plan'.

With focus on the local and inter-subjective, the idea of *Amoeba Management* is attractive—as identified in successful long-running Japanese organizations guided by the Inamori Philosophy that Tadashi Yagi and Stomu Yamash'ta bring to our attention in their Chap. 3.

> A key condition of the 'pro-social' behavior which characterizes Amoeba-based organizations is *normative* values and understanding across the *whole* organization into which each amoeba unit fits, and which therefore are applied by each amoeba unit – as participants within, and contributors to, this common philosophy. By Inamori design, these are not just any values, but altruistic norms fostering wider societal benefit of their work for which all (Amoeba) organization members can be proud ... *and* which foster *trust* in the organization from stake-holders and wider society.
>
> This positive normative environment has to be built, not assumed, and that requires company investment in human capital, education, sharing, and leadership by *being* the values which are espoused. Applying the principle of polyphony, differences in optimal strategy can be debated and even maintained, *but* the overall altruistic principles are the frame of harmony.

As Tadashi Yagi and Stomu Yamash'ta go on to explain, this form of organization intrinsically relates to its societal environment and is constantly interacting—as with the principles the Murases bring forward. A key result, beneficial to both company and its wider society, is the absorption *into* the organization of an understanding of wider society and its needs, therefore an essential platform for *innovation* in products and services. Furthermore, the close relationship to the wider local community can be the basis of *co-creation* of social value by company and community together, as with the case study presented of the Toho Leo Company which cooperatively designs communities and cities by 'greening' their environments.

Len Fisher then makes a very useful proposal to strengthen the community's role in building a collective enterprise-community pro-social culture. Drawing on Senatore's philosophical thoughts (Senatore, 2019), Len Fisher's proposal in Chap. 10 is to create a market for moral, organizational and cultural values—involving exchange of documents between individuals, companies and local communities listing benefits experienced from applying pro-social moral, organizational or cultural values; developing quantitative and verifiable indicators (eg: company reduction of CO_2 emissions, or individual contributions to social justice or environmental improvement; and rewarding positive actions). The ideas of this being a 'market' would dissolve as cooperation and mutual benefit develop.

A central feature of Stephen Hill's early chapters is also a focus on where the people are, where their *inter-subjective community*, their *humanity* is expressed—at the *local* level. This is where we construct meaning, our 'design for living'—in subjective relations with others, in socially producing together, in direct sharing … in our *local* world (Hill, 2018a, p. 302; Hill, 2018b, 1995) 'Local'—where people create meaning … and change it—is where the 'Earthworm' lies, where transformative change begins. Stephen Hill also draws in the principle promoted by Chief Economist of the Australia Institute, Richard Denniss, for Government *stimulus* funding to support enterprise at the local level. Dennis demonstrates that recent multi-billion dollar funding support to create value to release COVID stress for 'the big end of town'—with the intention of fostering Australian employment generation and technology development—had been wasted. Cutting tax rates for large corporations, $A90 billion line of credit to privately owned banks but not focusing on the local, ended up with little enterprise or employment stimulus, whilst international outflows and higher executive remuneration were enhanced. Instead, Denniss argues for the 'Three Ls': "Local, Labor and Long-Term", mirroring our own argument—community connectedness in enterprise plus, or course, attention to sustainable and environmentally sustainable production (Denniss, 2020a, b).

Furthermore, 'local' enterprise can readily stimulate value development more broadly, indeed, globally—if we apply the "Global-Localism" principle that Stephen Hill develops throughout the book. On the one hand this is like the 'fractal' relationships in Humanity-Life that the Murases discuss, that is, at a micro and macro level the principles and actions are mirrored in each other. But more importantly, the Global-Localism connection principle implies a strategic path for action. The local, the innovative community, absorbs, adopts and tests the idea and identifies what works; by training key leaders and groups from other 'local' communities the idea can be applied elsewhere and spread, a practice that is then complemented by building and maintaining inter-community networks.

This is not just theory. Stephen Hill was privileged to lead such a program over a period of about eight years to its full independence – with excellent and committed staff, when Director of UNESCO programs in Jakarta, Indonesia (and elsewhere) - in the originally low-income polluted urban village of Banjarsari, Jakarta. Fundamental was commitment of the people, whilst some guidance and resources from outside provided the stimulus for them knowing, or *discovering* what to do. Eventually the community turned the village into a fully 'greened', almost forest-like, environment, built related small businesses and both traditional and aliphatic medical practices – with Banjarsari eventually being declared Official Jakarta Urban Ecotourism Site by the city's Governor. What mattered was that the people saw they could produce something useful together, listened to their community and even to their parents and grandparents, ie: the past, while children, youth, and the local very poor scavengers, were fully included and became innovators too. The idea spread broadly as a result. By 2005 when Stephen Hill retired, Banjarsari was attracting 210 official visitors per year – some even from overseas, the Indonesian Navy was introducing similar initiatives in villages associated with Naval Bases, and the Indonesian Boy Scouts Movement (with membership of one million) was conducting outreach to other communities. [3] (Hill, 2018b, p. 325).

The reader should be reminded that Stephen Hill's early chapters also demonstrate that the 'local' as the world economy moves into the 2020s and beyond, is increasingly where the source of wider economic *value* is located—*if* supportive action is taken to build a *nutritive* (including *knowledge*) environment (back to the 'Earthworm Concept') both for community sharing and empowerment, and, for creative enterprise. His Chap. 5 demonstrates that this strategy can work even in developing countries—if the 'nutrition' is supplied.

In addition, wider network theory can also support local-focused practice. Len Fisher's analysis in Chap. 8 of this book of 'Small World Networks' within 'Complex Adaptive Systems' offers real possibilities—where 'long-range' links can be built strategically across the network *between local communities or 'clusters'*.

By current systems theory and practice remote connection is seen as possible across *clustered homogeneous* (similar culture) nodes, and this can well apply where new local communities wish to link and follow the original community 'node' culture – as with the previous Banjarsari case. Here, similar practice or cultural values are shared and developed collaboratively towards mutual advantage.

However, the image of Small World Networks suggests how we might handle *heterogeneous* connectedness (eg: different cultural contexts) rather than (more normal) *clustered* (similar culture) connectedness' by establishing just a few "long-range" links between distant cultural approaches. An important technique in building the heterogeneous linkage into the wider 'complex adaptive system' is '*the power of the gift*', ie: contributing consistently to the 'other' node (or cluster) having '*listened*' and '*responded*' in the other's terms – without necessarily expecting reward, thus building '*trust*' across distance and difference.

As in this 'systems' case, we keep coming back to the same fundamental principles:

Basic to all 'Humanity' building action we propose – in particular in forging harmony out of difference as in Polyphony – is *Trust, the Power of the Gift, and Listening!* Values of *Care. Values of our Humanity!* Focus where Humanity's direct intersubjective relationships are built and lived – *at the Local Level.*

So, we have a basic design concept for the platform we need in order to rebuild the dynamic of economic exchange, influence and behaviour ... based on our Humanity rather than Systematic Self-Interest.

BUT, the concept that Len Fisher draws to our attention, "Complex Adaptive Network *Systems"* also reminds us of a critical *context* for humanity we must *never* forget. For, not only in our relations to each other, but also in our relations to the physical world we live in and depend upon, we are *inhabiting* the complex adaptive system of *nature.* Indeed, it was our playing around with, or accidently impacting on, one absolutely *tiny* element of nature, the COVID virus, that has so suddenly exposed global society to the 'shattering' impact of enormous disturbance, illness … and widespread death!

In no way does this wider relationship of humanity to nature threaten the essential need for a humanity-based economics and social world as our future. However, nature's *context* for human action and response—*as participants in this wider complex adaptive system*—must *never* be forgotten.

20.2.2 Addressing Environment Destruction—Bringing the Circle of Wholeness into Business as the 'Circular Economy' and 'Circular Triangle'

Furthermore, it is long-term abuse of our relationship to nature's context which has led to the *global threat to our very existence* which is very much in the forefront of international attention right now.

As Chap. 19 made very clear, we have run out of time. Climate Change and Global Environmental Damage is upon us NOW! The consequence is already emerging global environmental … and social … catastrophe. The Secretary General of the United Nations, reported in Chap. 19, warned the world in August 2021 the evidence is irrefutable … this is a "Code Red for Humanity".

Immediately, a prime obligation is placed on the major cause - business-based industrial production. *now.*

As Ladeja Kosir in Chap. 14 demonstrates and the other Chapters in Sect. 20.3 of this Book elaborate, the design of industrialism for the last 250 years, has involved a *linear* design of production. Capitalizing on resources from the production environment to process into products to be sold for profit, this is a "Take $\rightarrow$; Make $\rightarrow$; Dispose" model which intrinsically creates *waste* at the end of production, and throws off waste gases and pollutants along the way. The *linear* waste-rich production design was further empowered by a social invention at the dawn of the 20th Century, the discovery of the *social* power of obsolescence. At that time this marketing triumph fueled the linear economic model's power to create wealth even further. For invention now started to be turned to 'newness', to *conspicuous consumption,* where you could *show* off your worth publicly by having the 'latest' model of whatever products you purchased. The previous year's model got tossed onto the Council Dump, quality of products was minimized to save cost ….. and, "Waste was Good!

What matters now though is that over the last decade or so, Business Leaders have started to wake up.

Values of Care are at the core of the actions now being taken and spreading across the world in what has come to be called 'The Circular Economy' Movement—action which turns the "Circle of Wholeness" we talk about into new normative business practice.

As authors in Sect. 3 demonstrated, the Circular Economy confronts the design of industrialism for the last 250 years—the *linear* concept of production—with not just an adjustment but a *New Narrative* which sees waste as an intrinsic part of production, to be recycled back into the production system, not just thrown away or left to leak into the atmosphere or groundwater.

Historically, the first level of strategy to deal with the problem of too much waste from the linear system—when its impact was finally recognized at the end of the 1960s, quite sensibly focused on the waste itself and tried to minimize it. But this strategy was addressing only one part of the problem. The genius of The Circular Economy Movement is that it looks at production from a greater height and redefines the problem as to do with how we produce, not on waste as such, recognizing that waste and pollution are not accidents, but the consequences of decisions made at the design stage, where 80 per cent of environmental impacts are determined. So, by Circular Economy Principles, waste at all stages of production is cycled back into the production system and anything left over is designed to be an input for another production system.

Consequently, as Janez Potocnik goes on to emphasize in his Chap. 16, our new economic model, hence the Circular Economy, cannot afford to just be making adjustments without changing the underlying system of economic relations and dynamics—for the *system* is creating the problem in the first place and will continue to do so unless challenged and transformed to be consistent with Sustainable Development Goals (SDGs). For example, not focusing on quantity—as in selling light bulbs for maximum quantity and therefore profit, but on purpose—as in supplying light by sustainable means.

As Potoknik further demonstrates, the 'system' is not just that of commercial production. Responsibility for the new paradigm of production does not rest just on the shoulders of industrialists alone. *All* stakeholders in the lifecycle of a product need to take responsibility for its environmental, economic, health, and safety impact. Good governance of the society as a whole is particularly required in relation to *all* of the production process—from legislating about waste, to legislating about products and services or–both backed by supportive stimulus funding. To quote Potoknik's observation about *transition* to a more sustainable economy and society:

> "Good management of the transition depends on good governance. System change we are witnessing requests mobilization of all the society. It requests clear political and private sector leadership, it requests broad understanding and ownership of the transition, it requests more cooperation and coordination on all the levels, including global, it requests major innovation efforts and the power of creation and it requests an agreement and a clear inter-generational agreement, a contract for the future we want and need."

In keeping with this Book's emphasis on co-creation across difference—polyphony—Einer Kleppe Holthe then demonstrates in his Chap. 15 the power of cross-cultural lessons and sees enormous value in crossing cultures and combining

Eastern long-term and nature-oriented philosophy with Western economic methodology of the modern market—making *sustainability over time* the core market ideology and driver—a necessary *replacement* of competitive action and belief, very much in keeping with the main non-self dynamic of economics which our shared 'Kyoto Post-COVID Manifesto' has developed.

In the following Chap. 17, Petra Kuenkel and Elisabeth Kuhn take us further down this humanity path with their "aliveness principle" for which they see six "transformative enablers" bring this principle to life—pathways to a new civilization in human and ecological balance—invigorating human capability to collectively shape their futures, collaborate meaningfully, thrive on diversity, venture into the unknown and more. As with *fractals*, these aliveness principles apply at *all* levels, and are *not* based on the self but on *shared* enterprise.

Then, to complete the Circular Economy story, drawing the model ever closer to our shared *humanity* base Alexander Laszlo, Karin Huber-Heim and Stefan Blach-fellner look, in their Chap. 18, towards the aftermath of the COVID-19 Pandemic, and the lessons we have or can learn from being confronted by this enormously challenging experience. They point to a new norm for collective wellbeing and regeneration which they see is emerging in action, driven by the Global COVID-19 Pandemic—when resourced by collective intelligence—of "thrivability." The dynamic of circularity and inclusion of living systems in all our relationships are included—creating the underlying evolutionary dynamics of change.

> Most deeply, the achievement of not only sustainable development strategies but the essence of regenerative, "thrivable" development is, according to the authors, the embodiment and manifestation of conscious evolution – when conscious intention aligns with evolutionary purpose and individual 'melodies' together create sustaining and enduring harmonies with the broader symphony of life on earth … a process of "syntony", or, "the state of being normally responsive to and in harmony with the environment". (Merriam-Webster, 2021)
>
> This process and goal aligns in philosophy with that of Masatoshi and Tomoko Murase in Chaps. 10, 11 and 12 —discussed earlier in this Chapter, and with particular significance, directly with the overall metaphor of this book, 'The Kyoto Post-COVID Manifesto' and our central concept for drawing together different, even potentially conflicting, 'domains' of knowledge into an overall *polyphonic* symphony or resolution. Laszlo and colleagues therefore draw the Circular Economy initiative quite directly into the overall theme of our Book. Indeed, they identify, as does the Book more generally, the first step towards 'syntony', as "learning how to listen".

20.2.3 Humanity—The New Platform for Future Global Economics

The Circular Economy Movement is both timely and appropriate as a concrete response to our current Climate Change Crisis—starting where it matters, that is, in reforming industrial production which is the prime cause of both Climate Change and wider alienation from, thence destruction of, the Ecosystem on which we all depend, 'Nature's' context.

A more comprehensive application of the Circular Economy Movement has been developed to target the broader more interdependent context of today's business systems—where system complexity and threat of unexpected disruption require a new consciousness in order to prepare and respond.[4] Presented by Ladeja Kosir in Chap. 14, this new concept is "The Circular Triangle"—comprising three interacting domains of action: the Circular Economy (from linear to circular business models, as we have just been discussing); Circular Change (comprehensive policies to support the transition—including wider engagement as of society, and government legislation across all aspects of producing and use, again as discussed in the last Section), and Circular Culture (reflection on values and a new narrative).

With the Circular Economy and Circular Triangle initiatives we are now seeing in practice core elements of our 'Circle of Wholeness' Platform for transforming Global Economics to provide an environmentally and socially viable future beyond this century.

There is, however, a long way further to go. The challenge that has to be met is to penetrate beyond even the highly important practices of the Circular Economy and Triangle Movements to the underlying 'grammar' or 'framework of self-focused assumptions' of our current global economic system as a whole. Then, we come back to *Where the Strength of Humanity Lies*—in *people and their caring, sharing immediate world*—the local intersubjective community. It is from here that we build our new economy.

So, to draw our Conclusions towards completion, we will extract the most basic Principles we have arrived at in this Book.

(1) *Principle 1*: Accept and Promote generally that *all* fundamental Principles of Economic Action for the Future are to be grounded in the basic principles of our Humanity, ie: Sharing, the Power of the Gift in Building Trust, Listening… and, as in Polyphony, targeting collective Harmony across Difference. Build the new dynamic of economics from understanding the culture of business and consumers from inter-subjective depth, not algorithmic assumption.

(2) *Principle 2*: Maintain and promote consciousness of human impact on our surrounding and sustaining ecosystem; increasingly build action, as with the Circular Economy Movement, to minimize the negative impact of humanity within the complex adaptive system of nature.

(3) *Principle 3*: Focus on the Local as Source of Enterprise, Collective Action and Sustainability-oriented Economic Value—use the 3 L Principles—"local, labour, long-term".

(4) *Principle 4*: Provide a "Nutritive" Environment at Local Level—the "Earthworm" concept—of necessary knowledge, education, community and enterprise empowerment; turn government legislative, funding and institutional *stimulus* support towards decentralization and the 'local' rather than providing tax, stimulus and other primary support for 'big business' at the direct expense of the 'local'; encourage empowerment to collaborate; free up people (eg: by time, opportunity and incentive) to create and innovate.

(5) *Principle 5*: "Global Localism"—Build action and test at Local Level focusing on the power of Community relations and cohesion, in parallel building linkages and educative support for reproducing similar community-enterprise based initiatives in other communities; empower local business entities to maintain and strengthen their identity *in* their local environment as their platform for contributing to global cooperation, and systemic change. Here principles of 'Small World System' approaches to both 'homogenous' and 'differentiated' clusters at other 'nodes' can be applied with attention to Principle 1 dynamics, ie: 'gift' of acceptance, listening, and building trust—build understanding via these system relations with other business and community cultures to enrich local knowledge and outreach.

(6) *Principle 6*: Refashion enterprise organization towards 'Amoeba' organization principles wherever possible, ie: maintaining small-group focus of responsibility, but in parallel across the whole wider organization, through education and moral support, build strong pro-social norms as the interactive frame for the action of all sub-organization 'Amoebas'. Such pro-social norms need to be inclusive of the 'three party' principle, ie: all decisions to be assessed against their contribution to not only corporate profit but also client and wider social (humanity and environmental) welfare. Build relations with and consciousness of the community into the business organization to encourage wider support and trust plus intelligence and stimulus for innovation.

(7) *Principle 7*: Capitalize on and develop the practice of working from home which has already developed significantly under Lockdown requirements of response to the COVID Pandemic. However, ensure face-to-face relationships continue for a proportion of the week in order to maintain inter-subjective communication and knowledge within teams, and, as an innovation, build the employees' development of wider community relations and support into job prescriptions—along with work practices of sharing local community knowledge, understanding and company empowerment, ie: use the practice for both knowledge for the business (a base for possible innovation) as well as trust from the community.

(8) *Principle 8*: Build Wider Community Consciousness to popularize and *normalize* the New Economy Humanistic Values and Frame of Reference: Promote programs, contests, exhibitions, public debates, TV shows—to popularize the core *new* humanity-based principles, related promotions and slogans in order to raise general public consciousness of the *sharing* base for new economics. In particular, get young people and schools engaged. Build community-centred moral collaboration with business to ensure a holistic community-enterprise pro-social relationship.

With these Principles as guide, we move on to perhaps the most far reaching and seemingly radical innovation of all, *Universal Basic Income* or UBI. We have developed the *essential* applicability, practicality and value of this concept in the Chaps. 4 and 5 by Stephen Hill, Chap. 6 by Tadashi Yagi—also in Chap. 3 with Stomu Yamash'ta, and by Toshiaki Maruyama in his Chap. 7. UBI allows focus of creating value to lie where the strength of humanity lies—in *people and their caring, sharing immediate world*—the local intersubjective community. It is from here that we build our new economy through a Universal Basic Income for all as platform which, critically, in parallel, *must,* (repeat … *must*) be backed, as in Principle 4 above, by building a nurturing environment of community support, education, creativity and enterprise opportunity. A further major alignment of economic practice with humanity is that UBI can include *all*, thus be a major contributor to healing inequality, but, as evidence shows now, if cast into a nutritive social and enterprise environment, UBI also offers enormous potential as the source of economic value from the 2020s on. Not only that, but early indications, as presented in Stephen Hill's Chap. 5, suggest that UBI—with more modest financial outlay but the same attention to creating a nutritive environment—can also work in developing countries as well as the more financially well-endowed nations of our shared (human) world.

20.2.4   Handling a COVID-19 Future

To conclude our general discussion about the future, we have no alternative but to look COVID-19 directly in the face and measure its consequence against our Kyoto Manifesto Principles.

Completely out of vision just two years ago, we now realise that our future may well be tarnished permanently by COVID-19—with development of new even more deadly virus strains, possible sudden unexpected outbreaks that need to be contained, and sudden demands for re-organization of work, economic and social relations in order to cope.

Preparation of adequate medical facilities and prioritized research on the virus and its prevention are clear and continuing public policy priorities, as are increasingly effective vaccination campaigns.

But these can only be stop-gap measures. *We have to learn to live with the virus!*

We may well need to get used to a *new normal* that sets into *continuing* practice what we are doing now as 'temporary' measures – including, for example, lockdowns, travel and transport restrictions, social distance caution – with strong restrictions on gathering together in numbers, particularly where crowds are sourced widely.

But that has to be short term else the economic, social and cultural fabric and vitality of all society starts to erode dangerously.

Reflecting a little further, we are basically dealing with *one dimension*—the tyranny of distance … either when close and infection is a risk, or too far, and travel or longer supply lines are problematic. And guess what! The Guiding Principles of this Kyoto Manifesto, just presented, offer the solution. Focus economic enterprise, social relations of production, access to food, energy and water, to necessary lifestyle amenities—back to *local level*. However, *design* the local comprehensively in order to do the job—including with developed access to global linkages identified under our Global Localism Principle 4.

China saw this possibility very early and offer us a model for possible wider application.

> Quite early in 2020 China initiated an international design contest – for a COVID-ready city. The Barcelona-based company Guallart Architects was announced as winners in August 2020.
>
> The city community – being built at Xiong'an, 130km southwest of Beijing, is based on wooden apartment blocks – with large balconies, drone-friendly rooftop terraces– also designed to serve as small farms. Energy is being supplied locally from renewable sources, ample space to work from home is built into the apartments – which *share* 3-D printers. Residents are able to produce resources locally, have all amenities, but also communicate and work within wider office complexes (eg: with drones providing material linkage.) (Chandran, 2020)

Designing the local into the future therefore not only presents a way forward for a New Economics based on humanistic rather than self-interest values, it also offers a way of handling an endemic COVID-19 future as well, whilst building the framework for a 'nutritive' environment of support for enterprise—in the hands of *every* member of the community, along with empowerment focused very directly at community level—in keeping with our Kyoto Manifesto Principle 3. The concept of a Universal Basic Income (UBI) then applies with particular relevance within a COVID-prepared community-based social design for the future such as in the Xiaong'an model.

This alignment is strengthened even further when we then also reflect on the core values of the Kyoto Manifesto—expressed in Principle 1: the basic principles of our Humanity, ie: Sharing, the Power of the Gift in Building Trust, Listening… and, as in Polyphony, targeting Collective Harmony across Difference ….. all to do with *care* for others.

Many faces of peoples' response to the COVID-19 Pandemic now reflect *care*—in line with these humanity-sharing values. Whilst vaccination has a proven impact on recipients being less vulnerable to infection or to severe consequences of COVID-19, it also has a wider and very serious function of protecting those around us—as do Lockdowns and the sacrifice involved in loss of sharing with one's own wider family or friends, even of personally earning income—for the good of all.

We need to remain aware, however that *isolation* in particular, *separation* from our *social* selves, potentially can have very real personal costs, in particular for some who cannot handle the absence of others within their lives:

> From US Census Data, December 2020, 42% of respondents reported symptoms of anxiety and depression compared to 11% in response to the Census one year earlier before COVID-19 impacted. Other information suggests similar response world-wide. Young people consistently appear as more vulnerable to increased psychological distress – most probably because their need for social interaction is stronger. (Abbott, 2021)

In both cases—vaccination and voluntary isolation even with distress—we see care for others. We do, however, need to strengthen support for those suffering mental stress from forced isolation from others—perhaps best by building community awareness and virtual contact.

As we do see with the COVID-19 Pandemic, response to crisis generally, when suffered at local community level, *most commonly* tends to draw communities together to care for each other—shown world-wide in response to current bush-fires or hurricanes, stimulated particularly by Climate Change as is now increasingly becoming our future.

So, in facing our future—now inhabited by COVID-19 as a new factor in our human environment, we already find a humanitarian response—and this humanity in relation to others is fundamentally strengthened in a local more intimate community context.

We do need to add however that in the case of COVID-19, our humanity must, even for our own personal sakes, extend with global reach and not stop at the edge of our own direct community.

> Selfishness at this apparently remote level intrinsically *cannot* work. At present, poorer countries do not have nearly adequate access to vaccine supplies – and it there that new strains of the virus are most likely to develop to affect *everybody*.
>
> > The more toxic Delta Strain of COVID-19 originated out of India at the end of 2020; the more infectious C.1.2 virus, then, particularly, the OMICRON virus originated in South Africa during 2021, as reported earlier. Most developed countries *now* are already moving on to use vaccine supplies for 'booster' shots of their populations whilst, in contrast, as at September 8th 2021, the Democratic Republic of the Congo had been able to provide initial vaccination to only 2.9% of its people. (Reuters, 2021)

So this, our "Kyoto Post-COVID Manifesto for Global Economics" admits COVID-19 directly into our Manifesto for the same Principles apply as in our wider thesis of a New Economics which replaces self and self-interest as dynamic with the power of our Humanity. As with the Manifesto as a whole, focus of action is at the local community level where our culture—of care—is formed and sustained. But our shared Humanity means that own local community is also embedded world wide in other communities where our care can make a difference.

Even so, it is imperative to maintain a note of caution. The effect of the COVID-19 Pandemic has been, in particular, to 'shatter' global society in so many ways, throwing so much of what we previously took for granted into the air. We need to watch, in particular, the many ways, both positive and negative, that our COVID-shattered world comes down. Watch, even to verify assurances and 'facts' offered to us under COVID duress from governments and experts. We need to *listen* to the people, their experience, and their new dreams. So, whilst we propose a 'local' way forward, we also say …. *Be conscious!*

20.3 From a Shattered World to a Culture of Care

Rather like Greta Thunberg, with whom we commenced these two Chapters of Conclusions, we are calling for our society, and in particular, those charged with responsibility, *TO WAKE UP!*

We are standing on a precipice, looking down at the fragile future we have created, perhaps unwittingly, as we did not notice the danger. We, and particularly those in control, also did not notice for way too long the increasingly massive distortions in both our physical and social worlds which resulted from dealing with them through self-interest based economics. Added to blindness was purposive hiding by vested interests of the sour fruit of the self-focused economic tree under a blanket of distraction or misinformation.

Greta Thunberg saw the enormous consequence in the most pressing result, Climate Change. Millions woke up, and governments and the people were kicked into more committed action.

We are different in our call to 'Wake Up' to Greta Thunberg though.

Critically important as redressing Climate Change is, this is a *product* of the deeper *underlying* self-based economic dynamic which we have sought to expose and explain throughout this Book. Longer term, those underlying values into which Climate Change negligence are embedded *must* be changed, or we will be back where we started.

Our focus, our 'Wake Up' call, is therefore on action to change this underlying dynamic, this 'grammar' which sets the frame for economic exchange, our daily lives and our impact on nature. Aligned with Greta's cry is urgency. This self-focused dynamic must be addressed as priority in order to save humanity falling from its current fragile precipice into even more danger in the future. Principles for change are also those which, in parallel, provide a way of responding to the likely ongoing impact of COVID-19.

In the course of these Conclusions we have sought to highlight key conscious managerial and social strategies needed to save us falling off the Precipice of the 2020s Self-focused Economic and Social Present—including as practical example, the Circular Economy and Triangle Business-focused Movements. At the heart of our strategies,

Empowerment for taking command of our future

and our economic base for making things happen differently

lies in the strength which was always there—

Our Humanity!

To conclude, it is important to highlight the nutritive cultural context needed to allow these strategies to take root and to grow—dug in deeply within local community—where meaning and sharing are born and sustained … but then expanded across the wider world of *other* local communities, in a process Stephen Hill has termed 'Global Localism'.

At heart is the value of a culture of care for others …. kindness. This is to be found within our subjective experience where we have direct and full relationships with others, not in Social Media no matter how deeply it may increasingly penetrate into subjective life.

You can have but a 'ghost' of communications via Social Media – where algorithms designed by others to make money are in control, Tik Tok is a path to indulgence, and Face Book friends are counted and 'possessed' rather than loved, ultimately to make a profit for the Social Media owners.

Kindness is then the currency of daily life.

Leo Tolstoy, famous and perceptive 19th Century Russian Novelist, could see the importance of a culture of kindness as far back as the turn of the very early 20th Century. In his last words in a diary entry just before he died in 1910, Tolstoy observed,

> The kinder and more thoughtful a person is, the more kindness he can find in other people. Kindness enriches our life; with kindness mysterious things become clear, difficult things become easy, and dull things become cheerful. (Tolstoy, 2021)

Social Scientist and Author Hugh Mackay has brought 'kindness' up to date. He argues that the trauma and response to the COVID Pandemic, in particular, are stimulating a "Kindness Revolution". But he goes further to talk of the future in terms which directly align with those of our own book:

> "If we dare to dream of a more loving country – kinder, more compassionate, more cooperative" … "more inclusive" … "more harmonious" … "there's only one way to start turning the dream into reality: each of us must live *as if* this is already that country. If enough of us live like that – and, in turn, demand that our elected representatives embrace those same values and aspirations – change will come. Revolutions never start at the top." (Mackay, 2021, p. 245)

Our "World" is then no longer "Shattered" but connected and caring. Our Strategies within the "Post-COVID Manifesto for Global Economics" are planted in a nutritive seedbed for the flowering of humanity-centered transformation … and, we can thrive within an increasingly broad culture of trust and cooperation rather than divisive self-interest and greed.

Notes

1. Toshiaki Maruyama's observation on the importance of *listening* within the play of polyphonic music was drawn from fellow Editor of this Book, Stomu Yamashta. Stomu was producing a ceremony, "ON ZEN Hoyo", an annual event to bring Zen Buddhist and Shinto cultures together in a memorial service for sound in the Daitojuki Temple in Kyoto each June. This service has been directly associated with the Annual International Symposia we have developed to draw international scholarship into the creation of our Kyoto Manifesto Books.

   > In 2018, the year we published the original Kyoto Manifesto, Stomu had brought in a four-person Gregorian Chant choir from France to participate. During rehearsals however the Gregorian Choir complained that they could not sing in the Temple. The reason was that each choir member would sing by 'layering' each individual part over the other voices that they could hear echoing around them …. A *practice* of 'polyphony'. The problem was that the Gregorian singers normally perform in European churches which are made of stone and reflect sound well, but with temples in Japan, their wooden construction makes it difficult for sounds to reverberate, thus causing challenges for the layering of voices. The choir's problem was eventually solved before the public performance by using microphones and speakers.

2. The distinction between 'self' focused action and cultural meaning, and a humanity-sharing action and culture, brings us to a way of seeing *'globalization'*—where these two cultural forces are demonstrably present—and likely to be in opposition. More powerful and unscrupulous nation states, international business organizations and those seeking access or protection of personal wealth are prime examples of 'self-focused' action and meaning. Their impact on the life domain of the disadvantaged is potentially likely to enhance greater inequality and suffering globally. However, when we explore how globalization brings together cultures which can be very different from each other, yet, as with a 'polyphonic' relationship, find harmony across difference, we find the alternate 'sharing' power of globalization.

Toby Ord, who we quoted just now about the need to explore 'deep time', further observes that, depending on the question, we, as observers, may choose to focus across a range of "groups as agents"—increasingly large aggregations of people, beyond individuals, to "teams, companies or nations" thence, as we would describe, 'globalization collectives' … then ultimately to *humanity* as a whole. Toby Ord goes on to emphasize that focus on "humanity as a whole is increasingly useful and important" (Ord, 2020 , pp. 54–55).

Our focus in The Kyoto Post-COVID Manifesto is on humanity. Whilst there are then 'globalization' sub-questions concerning power, exploitation, cohesion and cultural relations across formally created boundaries, these can best be dealt with once we have a clear vision at the higher 'humanity' level of aggregation. Therefore, *our* problematique is not to do with globalization at this stage.

3. The new atmosphere of Banjarsari Village (as at 2005 when he retired) is captured in Stephen Hill's description in our original Kyoto Manifesto for Global Economics:

> "The village is now 'green', quite literally a garden paradise in what was a low income polluted urban village" … "The ambience of the village now includes roadside restaurants, tiny convenience stores, travelling musicians, and pushcart VCD sellers. The streets are made of paving stone rather than asphalt or cement—adding a park-like atmosphere as well as serving the practical purpose of allowing rainwater to penetrate through the cracks thus reducing the risk of flooding during the torrential rain season…."houses a central paper recycling facility primarily where youth are engaged (eg: making and selling origame), a village medicinal garden, a community hall—concentration points for village activity… several small businesses marketing traditional medicinal and herbal products..the older women have established a traditional medical based practice to provide free medical treatment for the very poor and scavangers associated with the community ……" (Hill, 2018b, p. 325).

4. System complexity and response was discussed at some depth earlier in Chaps. 8 and 9 by Fisher.

References

Abbott, A. (2021). COVID's mental health toll: How scientists are tracking a surge in depression. *Nature*, News. www.nature.com

Chandran, R. (2020). This self-sufficient Chinese city is being built with future pandemics in mind. World Economic Forum. https://www.w.e.forum.org>agenda>2020/09>chinese

Denniss, R. (2020a). 'After the crisis' - Conversation with Jim Chalmers, Shadow Treasurer, Australia. Australia Institute Webinar

Denniss, R. (2020b). Weal of Fortune–rebuilding the economy means government investment, but not all public spending is equal. *The Monthly*

Hill, S. (1995).The formation of identity as scientist. *Science Studies, 8*(1), 53–72; republished from the original 1979 article by invitation and with review editorial by John Ziman

Hill, S. (2010). Ways of seeing – science and technology within their cultural setting, Invited Chapter in A. Jain (Ed.), *Science and the public,* Section: "Science in society", pp. 252–280. New Delhi: Sage. Volume in Series: "Civilization, philosophy, science and culture", (Series Editor: Prof. P. Chatapadhyaya)

Hill, S. (2018a). Sacred silence– the stillness of listening to humanity. Yamash'ta et al., 2018, Chapter 17, pp. 285–308

Hill, S. (2018b). Community: Platform for sustainable change. Yamash'ta et al., (2018), Chapter 18, pp. 309–327

Mackay, H. (2021). The kindness revolution–how we can restore hope, rebuild trust and inspire optimism. Australia: Allen & Unwin

Merriam-Webster. (2021). Definition of syntony. https://www.merriam-webster.com

Ord, T. (2020). The precipice: Existential risk and the future of humanity. Bloomsbury Publishing

Reuters (2021). Republic of the Congo: The latest coronavirus counts, charts and maps. Reuters COVID-19 TRACKER- Republic of the Congo. https://graphics.reuters.com>republ...)

Senatore, M. (2019). Should we create a market for values?, *The Philosophic Salon*, https://thephilosophicsalon.com/should-we-create-a-market-for-values.

Tolstoy, L. (2021). AZ Quotes.com, Wind and Fly LTD, 2021. https://www.azquotes.com/quote/854173. Accessed 16 September 2021

Wood, S. (2021). Facetime – Artificial intelligence is one of the most profound innovations of our time. And according to Manhattan-based Australian expert, Kate Crawford, we're sleepwalking our way through its inherent risks. *The Sydney Morning Herald, Good Weekend*, pp. 6–9

Yamash'ta, S., Yagi, T., & Hill S. (Eds.) (2018). The Kyoto Manifesto for Global Economics—The Platform of Community, Humanity and Spirituality, Springer.